THE POSTWAR RESIDENTIAL
MORTGAGE MARKET

NATIONAL BUREAU OF ECONOMIC RESEARCH

Studies in Capital Formation and Financing

1. Capital Formation in Residential Real Estate: Trends and Prospects
   Leo Grebler, David M. Blank, and Louis Winnick
2. Capital in Agriculture: Its Formation and Financing since 1870
   Alvin S. Tostlebe
3. Financial Intermediaries in the American Economy since 1900
   Raymond W. Goldsmith
4. Capital in Transportation, Communications, and Public Utilities: Its Formation and Financing
   Melville J. Ulmer
5. Postwar Market for State and Local Government Securities
   Roland I. Robinson
6. Capital in Manufacturing and Mining: Its Formation and Financing
   Daniel Creamer, Sergei P. Dobrovolsky, and Israel Borenstein
7. Trends in Government Financing
   Morris A. Copeland
8. The Postwar Residential Mortgage Market
   Saul B. Klaman

The Postwar Residential Mortgage Market

BY

SAUL B. KLAMAN

A STUDY BY THE
NATIONAL BUREAU OF ECONOMIC RESEARCH

PUBLISHED BY
PRINCETON UNIVERSITY PRESS, PRINCETON
1961

HG
5095
K63

This report is one of a series emerging from an investigation of postwar capital market developments in the United States aided by a grant to the National Bureau from the Life Insurance Association of America. Publication of this study was aided by a special grant from the Research and Educational Trust Fund of the Mortgage Bankers Association of America. The Life Insurance Association and the Mortgage Bankers Association are not, however, responsible for any of the statements made or views expressed in the report.

RELATION OF THE DIRECTORS TO THE WORK AND PUBLICATIONS
OF THE NATIONAL BUREAU OF ECONOMIC RESEARCH

1. The object of the National Bureau of Economic Research is to ascertain and to present to the public important economic facts and their interpretation in a scientific and impartial manner. The Board of Directors is charged with the responsibility of ensuring that the work of the National Bureau is carried on in strict conformity with this object.

2. To this end the Board of Directors shall appoint one or more Directors of Research.

3. The Director or Directors of Research shall submit to the members of the Board, or to its Executive Committee, for their formal adoption, all specific proposals concerning researches to be instituted.

4. No report shall be published until the Director or Directors of Research shall have submitted to the Board a summary drawing attention to the character of the data and their utilization in the report, the nature and treatment of the problems involved, the main conclusions, and such other information as in their opinion would serve to determine the suitability of the report for publication in accordance with the principles of the National Bureau.

5. A copy of any manuscript proposed for publication shall also be submitted to each member of the Board. For each manuscript to be so submitted a special committee shall be appointed by the President, or at his designation by the Executive Director, consisting of three Directors selected as nearly as may be one from each general division of the Board. The names of the special manuscript committee shall be stated to each Director when the summary and report described in paragraph (4) are sent to him. It shall be the duty of each member of the committee to read the manuscript. If each member of the special committee signifies his approval within thirty days, the manuscript may be published. If each member of the special committee has not signified his approval within thirty days of the transmittal of the report and manuscript, the Director of Research shall then notify each member of the Board, requesting approval or disapproval of publication, and thirty additional days shall be granted for this purpose. The manuscript shall then not be published unless at least a majority of the entire Board and a two-thirds majority of those members of the Board who shall have voted on the proposal within the time fixed for the receipt of votes on the publication proposed shall have approved.

6. No manuscript may be published, though approved by each member of the special committee, until forty-five days have elapsed from the transmittal of the summary and report. The interval is allowed for the receipt of any memorandum of dissent or reservation, together with a brief statement of his reasons, that any member may wish to express; and such memorandum of dissent or reservation shall be published with the manuscript if he so desires. Publication does not, however, imply that each member of the Board has read the manuscript, or that either members of the Board in general, or of the special committee, have passed upon its validity in every detail.

7. A copy of this resolution shall, unless otherwise determined by the Board, be printed in each copy of every National Bureau book.

(*Resolution adopted October 25, 1926 and revised February 6, 1933 and February 24, 1941*)

CONTENTS

FOREWORD BY RAYMOND W. GOLDSMITH   *xxi*

PREFACE   *xxvii*

1. PLAN OF THE BOOK AND SUMMARY OF FINDINGS

Plan of the Book   3

Summary of Findings   5

    Postwar Changes in the Structure of Mortgage Debt   5

    Pattern of Mortgage Flows and Underlying Influences   7

    Pattern of Mortgage Interest Rates   12

    Institutional Framework of Mortgage Markets   15

2. SURVEY OF POSTWAR CHANGES IN MORTGAGE DEBT STRUCTURE AND IN MORTGAGE FLOWS

Long-Term Position of Mortgage Debt in the Economy   25

Mortgage Debt before and after Two World Wars   30

Structure of Mortgage Debt at Beginning of Post-World War II Decade   30

Net Flow of Mortgage Funds in Postwar Decade   39

Structure of Mortgage Debt at End of Postwar Decade   45

3. ELEMENTS IN THE CHANGING POSTWAR MORTGAGE MARKET

Expansionary Influences at Work, 1946–1950   49

    Demand for Mortgage Credit   50

    Liquidity of Financial Institutions   50

    Federal Mortgage Programs and Policies   52

Mortgage Markets in a Changing Setting, 1951–1956   55

    Mortgage Markets under Restraint, 1951–1953   56

    Resumption of Expansionary Forces, 1953–1956   66

    Mortgage Markets Once Again under Restraint, 1955–1956   69

4. POSTWAR PATTERN OF MORTGAGE INTEREST RATES

Course of Conventional Mortgage Interest Rates   74

    Amplitude of Conventional Mortgage Interest Rate Movements   75

    Lag in Mortgage Interest Changes   78

    Comparison of Interest Rates on Home and Income Property Loans   80

Longer-Term Movements in Conventional Mortgage
Interest Rates   82
FHA and VA Mortgage Interest Rates and Prices   83
Discounts and Premiums   85
Yield Differentials between FHA, VA, and Conventional
Mortgages   90
Geographic Variation in Mortgage Yields   95

5. FLOW OF FUNDS INTO MORTGAGE MARKETS
Net Flow of Mortgage Funds Under Expansionary Influences,
1946–1950   99
Mortgage Flows Relative to Other Capital Market
Flows   100
Flows into Various Mortgage Market Sectors   107
Home Mortgage Flows, by Type of Mortgage and Financial
Institution   110
Net Flow of Mortgage Funds in a Changing Capital Market
Framework, 1951–1956   120
Mortgage Flows Relative to Other Capital Market
Flows   121
Flows into Various Mortgage Market Sectors   123
Home Mortgage Flows, by Type of Mortgage and Financial
Institution   125

6. MORTGAGE LENDING POLICIES OF FINANCIAL INTERMEDIARIES
Beginnings of Mortgage Lending   135
Financial Intermediaries and Mortgage Markets   136
Life Insurance Companies   137
Factors in Mortgage Investment Decisions   138
Mortgage Lending Policies and Practices   141
Mutual Savings Banks   147
Factors in Mortgage Investment Decisions   148
Mortgage Lending Policies and Practices   149
Savings and Loan Associations   156
Background and Development   156
Mortgage Lending Policies and Practices   158
Commercial Banks   165
Significance of Real Estate Loans   165
Mortgage Lending Policies and Practices   166
Other Financial Institutions in the Mortgage Market   172

7. MORTGAGE MARKET TECHNIQUES AND CHARACTERISTICS

Time Lags in Mortgage Lending 175
Relationship between Construction, Interim, and Permanent
    Mortgage Financing 176
Mortgage Commitment Techniques 178
Interim Financing Developments 182
    Variations in Technique 182
    Data on Interim Financing 190
Primary and Secondary Mortgage Market Characteristics
    and Relationships 195
    Concepts and Definitions 196
    Statistics on Secondary Market Activity 200
    Marketing Organization, Costs, and Prices 213
    The Federal National Mortgage Association 217
Junior Mortgage Financing 227
    Size of the Market 227
    Nature and Purpose of Junior Mortgage Financing 230
    Market Participants 232
    Market Organization and Techniques 233
    Prices and Terms of Junior Mortgages 235

8. THE POSTWAR RISE OF MORTGAGE COMPANIES

Nature and Characteristics of Mortgage Companies 239
    Regulation of Activities 243
    Sources of Income 244
    Relationship to Investors and Borrowers 245
    Age, Growth, and Geographic Distribution 248
Mortgage Operations 255
    Mortgage and Construction Loans 256
    Types of Mortgage Loans 258
    Principal Purchasers of Mortgage Company Loans 260
    Loan Closings and Investor Commitments 262
Financial Structure 264
    Asset-Size Distribution 264
    Uses and Sources of Funds 266
Short-Term Movements in Uses and Sources of Funds,
    1953–1955 274
Concluding Comments 278

CONTENTS

APPENDIX

Supplementary Tables to Text Charts   283

EXHIBIT

Facsimile of Questionnaire on Mortgage Market Activity of
Savings and Loan Associations   291

SUBJECT INDEX   295

AUTHOR INDEX   300

TABLES

1. Real Estate Wealth and Mortgage Debt, Selected Years, 1900–1956   28

2. Nonfarm Mortgage Loans and Total Assets Held by Main Types of Financial Institutions, Selected Years, 1900–1956   29

3. Structure of Mortgage Debt and Net Mortgage Flows, by Type of Property Mortgaged, 1945–1956   32

4. Structure of Residential Mortgage Debt and Net Residential Mortgage Flows, 1945–1956   33

5. Structure of Mortgage Debt and Net Mortgage Flows, by Type of Holder, 1945–1956   35

6. Percentage Distribution: Ownership of Mortgage Debt, by Type of Property and Mortgage, 1945–1956   36

7. Percentage Distribution: Composition of Mortgage Portfolios of Main Types of Financial Institutions, 1945–1956   37

8. Structure of Mortgage Debt and Net Mortgage Flows, by Type of Borrower, 1945–1956   39

9. Percentage Distribution: Net Flow of Mortgage Funds from Lenders, by Type of Property and Mortgage, 1945–1956   43

10. Net Sale of Federal Government Securities and Net Acquisition of Mortgages by Four Main Types of Financial Institutions, 1946–1956   51

11. Terms of Mortgage Lending Under Regulation X   59

12. Turning Points in Interest Rates and Yields on Capital Market Securities   79

13. Regional Prices for VA-Guaranteed Mortgages, by FNMA Agency Area, January and June, 1953–1956   97

14. Mortgage Loans Acquired by New York State Mutual Savings Banks Within the State and Out-of-State, 1946–1955   151

15. Mortgage Loans Held by Mutual Savings Banks Within Their States and Out-of-State, Selected Dates, 1954 and 1955   152

16. Savings and Loan Association Loans for Construction of Homes, by Size of Mortgage Portfolio, Fifty-five Reporting Associations, 1955   160

17. Proportion of Savings and Loan Association Home Construction Loans Made to Builders, by Size of Mortgage Portfolio, Fifty-five Reporting Associations, 1955   161

18. Relationship between Proportion of Savings and Loan Association Loans Made to Builders and Proportion of Their

Loans Made for Home Construction, Fifty-five Reporting
Associations, 1955   161

19. Percentage of Savings and Loan Association Loans to Builders Resulting in Permanent Mortgage Loans, Fifty-five Reporting Associations, 1955   162

20. Outstanding Interim Financing Credits Extended by Commercial Banks to Mortgage Lenders, by Type of Borrower and Type of Loan, Selected Periods, 1950–1956   192

21. Percentage Distribution of Outstanding Interim Financing Credits Extended by Commercial Banks to Mortgage Lenders, by Type of Borrower and Type of Loan, Selected Periods, 1954–1956   194

22. First Mortgages Originated and Purchased on Owner-Occupied Properties, by Type of Holder, 1950   201

23. First Mortgages Originated and Purchased on Rental Properties, by Type of Holder, 1950   202

24. Primary and Secondary Market Activity of Main Types of Financial Institutions in FHA-Insured Home Mortgages, 1947–1956   204

25. Purchases and Sales of FHA-Insured Home Mortgages as Per Cent of Total Transfer Activity, by Type of Institution, 1945–1956   205

26. Mortgage Loans Purchased by Life Insurance Companies, 1946–1955   209

27. Primary and Secondary Mortgage Market Activity of Savings and Loan Associations, 1952–1955   210

28. Percentage Distribution of Amounts of Mortgage Purchases and Sales by Savings and Loan Associations, 1953–1955   212

29. Percentage Distribution of Sellers of Mortgages to FNMA, 1949–1956   224

30. Number of Purchasers and Amount of Purchases of Mortgages from FNMA, and Percentage Distribution of Each, August 1949–June 1955   225

31. Geographic Distribution of FNMA Mortgage Purchases, 1954, and Sales, 1949–1955   226

32. First and Junior Mortgages on Residential Properties, 1950 and 1956   228

33. First and Junior Mortgages on Owner-Occupied One-Family Unit Properties, 1950 and 1956   229

34. Mortgage Companies Classified by Asset Size in 1946 and 1954   251

35. Distribution of Mortgage Loans Sold by Selected Mortgage Companies to Institutional and Other Investors, 1953–1955   261

36. Distribution of Mortgage Companies and Assets, by Asset-Size Class in Selected Years, 1946–1954   264

37. Combined Balance Sheet of Mortgage Companies, 1945–1955   268

38. Percentage Distribution: Combined Balance Sheet of Mortgage Companies, 1945–1955   269

39. Percentage Distribution: Combined Quarterly Balance Sheet of Sixty-six Selected Mortgage Companies, December 31, 1952 through 1955   275

40. Percentage Changes in Mortgage Inventory of Mortgage Companies and One- to Four-Family Mortgage Debt Outstanding, 1953–1955   278

APPENDIX TABLES

A–1. VA and FHA Gross Mortgage Flows, and Yield Differentials Between Contract Interest Rates on VA and FHA Mortgages and Yields on New Issues of Aaa Corporate Bonds, Quarterly, 1951–1958   283

A–2. Ratios of Nonfarm Mortgage Debt to Gross National Product and to Total and Private Debt, 1900–1956   284

A–3. Relative Position of Nonfarm and Farm Mortgage Debt in the United States Economy Before and After Two World Wars   284

A–4. Comparison of Interest Rates and Yield on Mortgages and Other Capital Market Securities, Quarterly Averages, 1946–1956   285

A–5. Comparison of Average Interest Rates on Conventional Mortgage Loans Closed on Homes and Income Properties, Quarterly, 1951–1956   286

A–6. Comparison of Average Interest Rates on Conventional Mortgage Loans Closed on Homes and Income Properties, Annually, 1920–1956   287

A–7. Comparison of Calculated Yields on FHA and VA Home Loans and Contract Interest Rates on Conventional Home Loans, Quarterly, 1953–1956   288

A–8. Comparison of Net Mortgage Flows and Other Net Capital Market Flows, 1946–1956   288

A–9. Percentage Ratios of Net Mortgage Flows to Total Net Capital Market Flows Through Main Financial Institutions, 1946–1956   289

A–10. Gross Mortgage Credit Extended to Finance House Purchases, and Number of Houses Purchased, 1950–1956   289

A–11. Typical Disbursement of Mortgage Funds Following Date of Commitment   290

CHARTS

1. Comparison of FHA and VA Gross Mortgage Flows, with Differentials between Contract Interest Rates on FHA and VA Mortgages and Yields on New Aaa Corporate Bond Issues, Quarterly, 1951–1958   14

2. Ratios of Nonfarm Mortgage Debt to GNP and Total and Private Debt, 1900–1956   27

3. Mortgage Debt in the United States Economy—Before and After Two World Wars   31

4. Net Flow of Funds into Main Capital and Money Market Sectors, 1946–1956   40

5. Net Flow of Mortgage Funds, 1946–1956   41

6. Comparison of the Structure of Postwar Mortgage Debt, December 31, 1945, and December 31, 1956   46

7. Interest Rates and Yields on Mortgage Loans and Other Capital Market Securities, Quarterly, 1946–1956   76

8. Conventional Mortgage Interest Rates on Home and Income Property Loans Closed, Quarterly, 1951–1956   81

9. Conventional Mortgage Interest Rates on Home and Income Property Loans, 1920–1956   83

10. Average Prices of FHA and VA Four and One-Half Per Cent Mortgages, Monthly, 1953–1956   91

11. Comparison of Average Yields on VA-Guaranteed Mortgages, FHA-Insured Home Mortgages, and Average Contract Interest Rates on Conventional Home Mortgages, Quarterly, 1953–1956   92

12. Net Flow of Funds into Capital Markets, 1946–1956   101

13. Ratios of Net Mortgage Flow to Total Net Capital Market Flow Through Main Types of Financial Institutions, 1946–1956   102

14. Net Flow of Mortgage Funds from Main Types of Financial Institutions, 1946–1956   103

15. Net Flow of Mortgage Funds from Broad Lender Groups, 1946–1956   108

16. Net Flow of Mortgage Funds for Loans on Main Classes of Property, 1946–1956   109

17. Net Flow of Home Mortgage Funds, by Type of Mortgage, 1946–1956   112

xix

18. Gross Flow of Federally Underwritten Mortgage Loans, 1946–1956   113

19. Net Flow of VA-Guaranteed Mortgage Funds from Main Types of Financial Institutions, 1946–1956   117

20. Net Flow of FHA-Insured Home Mortgage Funds from Main Types of Financial Institutions, 1946–1956   118

21. Net Flow of Conventional Home Mortgage Funds from Main Types of Financial Institutions, 1946–1956   119

22. Gross Mortgage Credit Extended to Finance House Purchases, 1950–1956   127

23. Mortgage Portfolio Composition of Life Insurance Companies, 1945–1956   142

24. Percentage Distribution: Typical Life Insurance Company Disbursement of Mortgage Funds Following Month of Commitment   146

25. Mortgage Portfolio Composition of Mutual Savings Banks, End of Year, 1945–1956   154

26. Mortgage Portfolio Composition of Savings and Loan Associations, End of Year, 1945–1956   164

27. Mortgage Portfolio Composition of Commercial Banks, End of Year, 1945–1956   171

28. Mortgage Purchases of FNMA Under Reorganized Secondary Market Program, November 1, 1954–1956   223

29. Asset Growth of Mortgage Companies, by 1954 Asset-Size Class, 1945–1955   250

30. Mortgage versus Construction Loans Held and Closed by Mortgage Companies, 1953–1955   257

31. Types of Mortgage Loans Held and Closed by Mortgage Companies, 1953–1955   259

32. Lorenz Curves of Assets of Mortgage Companies, 1946, 1950, and 1954   265

33. Total Assets, Mortgage Loans, and Notes Payable of Mortgage Companies, 1945–1955   267

34. Relationships Among Mortgage Loans, Notes Payable, and Total Assets of Mortgage Companies, 1945–1955   270

35. Main Assets and Liabilities of Mortgage Companies, 1946, 1950, and 1955   272

36. Total Assets, Mortgage Loans, and Notes Payable of Sixty-six Companies, Quarterly, December 31, 1952 through 1955   275

FOREWORD

IN OUR admiration for technological achievements—giant dams, steel mills, and cyclotrons—we may fail to recognize that residential real estate, though changing but slowly in form and efficiency, has been and is still the largest single component of national wealth, in the postwar decade as well as throughout the nineteenth century and in the United States as well as in foreign countries. At the present time, residential structures account for almost one-third of the total value of all reproducible tangible wealth in this country, and residential real estate (including land) represents practically as high a fraction of total national wealth.[1] Similarly, expenditures on residential structures are the largest single component of capital formation, gross or net. During the 1950's, these expenditures accounted, on the average, for one-fifth to one-fourth of national and for one-fourth to one-third of private capital formation. Residential real estate is also the most important single investment nonfarm consumers own, representing about one-fourth of their total assets. Since the proportion of borrowing to owners' equity investment is higher for residential real estate than for most other forms of capital formation (excluding consumer durables), the extension of residential mortgage credit and the increase in the residential mortgage debt constitute a large proportion of total debt financing and a still larger proportion of external long-term financing. In the decade ending in 1955, the volume of residential mortgage debt outstanding increased by almost $80 billion. This is considerably more than the increase in most other forms of financial assets (disregarding pure valuation changes). The volume of corporate bonds outstanding and of consumer credit, for instance, each increased by only slightly more than $40 billion during the same decade. The debt of state and local governments rose by only $30 billion and total net sales of corporate stock aggregated less than $20 billion, while the volume of federal government debt available to the public remained virtually unchanged. The growth in residential mortgage debt also exceeded the increase in financial assets, such as the premium reserves of life insurance companies ($36 billion), or the time deposits with commercial banks ($20 billion) and mutual savings banks ($10 billion), and share accounts with saving and loan associations ($25 billion).

[1] The figures used in this Foreword, for illustration purposes only, have been rounded. Sources are not specifically cited, nor is attention drawn to the usually well-known limitations of the estimates.

Even if residential mortgage loans did not constitute so large a proportion of the entire capital market, the development and operation of the residential mortgage market during the postwar period would still be of great interest within the framework of a general analysis of the American capital market. For in the market for residential mortgages we can observe, through the detailed discussion of its quantitative and qualitative aspects provided in Saul Klaman's book, several of the basic features and trends that have characterized the American capital market in the postwar period. We can observe them possibly with more clarity, and certainly on the basis of more adequate statistical data and qualitative first-hand information, than in almost any other segment of the American capital market.

The first of the basic tendencies exemplified by developments in the residential mortgage market during the postwar period is its institutionalization. At the end of 1956 nearly 90 per cent of all outstanding residential mortgages were held by financial institutions, 83 per cent of them by the four types of institutions which dominate the market—saving and loan associations, mutual savings banks, commercial banks, and life insurance companies. Financial institutions also absorbed over 90 per cent of the net increase in residential mortgage debt during the postwar period.

The second characteristic which the market for residential mortgages shares with many other segments of the capital market is the delayed fruition during the postwar period of a crop from seeds planted in the mid-thirties—the large-scale adoption of government guaranteed mortgages. This process involved the use of legal and technical forms and of facilitating government agencies which were created as part of the far-reaching reconstruction of American finance under the New Deal—a development that is still often underrated in its long-term significance, possibly because many of the present-day users of these new instruments and organizations would like to forget their origin.

The standardization of mortgage contract terms, with its limitations on length of life, interest rate, and loan-to-value ratios, and the introduction of regular amortization may well be regarded as a separate third characteristic of the postwar market for residential mortgages, even though it is but the outstanding example of the rise to predominance of techniques that were actually introduced during the 1930's. It is only since guaranteed mortgages became standardized and almost fungible instruments that a true secondary market in residential mortgages could develop, a market comparable in essence to that existing for government and corporate securities, even though during the postwar decade it was still limited to a wholesale market among financial institutions.

The market for residential mortgages, fourthly, has provided some very interesting examples of financial innovation, the mechanism of challenge and response operating more clearly here than in most other segments of the capital market. The first of these innovations is the rise of the technique of forward commitments, primarily between large lenders such as the insurance companies and large-scale builders of single-family homes and apartment houses. This technique, described in detail in Chapter 7 of Klaman's book, has had far-reaching influence, not only on the timing of residential building and on the portfolio management of financial institutions (to say nothing of its effect on the interpretation of current mortgage statistics), but also on the behavior of the capital market and beyond that on the timing and width of the business cycle. A second innovation is the development of a new type of financial institution, the mortgage company, which acts as an agent of large-scale institutional investors and is closely tied in its growth and operations to the market in guaranteed home mortgages. This innovation is summarized in Chapter 8, a condensation of the fuller description in his *Postwar Rise of Mortgage Companies*.

This is not the first time that the National Bureau of Economic Research has turned its attention to the market for residential real estate. One of its first publications dealing with it, Wickens' *Residential Real Estate* of 1941, may well be regarded as one of the starting points of serious detailed statistical study in the field. The six volumes reporting the Studies in Urban Mortgage Financing, mostly published from 1950 to 1952, and *Capital Formation in Residential Real Estate*, by Grebler, Blank, and Winnick, published in 1956, represented later substantial contributions to our knowledge of that market. They deal, however, primarily with developments before or immediately after World War II. Klaman's book, in keeping with the program of the Postwar Capital Market Study, concentrates on the financial side of the market for residential real estate, and within that field is limited to the use of credit in financing the construction and sale of dwellings, and deals only peripherally with owners' equity investment and with changes in it that represent realized or unrealized capital gains.

Klaman's study reported here and in two papers previously published by the National Bureau, apart from providing the first reasonably complete, statistically founded study of the market for residential mortgages during the postwar period, makes several contributions to the analysis of this segment of the capital market. It provides the most consistent and detailed analysis of mortgage holdings and flows and—very important for cyclical analysis—puts them on a quarterly basis. It originates a series of interest rates on conventional mortgages which, we hope, will be continued and improved by some of the organizations with practical or research interests in the field. It supplies a detailed description and analysis of institutional arrangements and market techniques and a discussion of the economic problems they raise. It presents for the first time a comprehensive discussion of the mortgage portfolio policies of the main types of financial institutions. Finally, it provides a substantial body of new material on the growth and operation of mortgage companies.

Much, however, still remains to be done before a complete analysis of past and current developments in the residential mortgage market will be possible, and Klaman is careful to point out, particularly in the preface, the gaps in our information and the deficiencies of the material he has been dealing with, most of them entirely beyond remedy in this study.

Even in the narrow field of straightforward statistical information on flows and holdings of residential mortgages the gaps in our knowledge are still wide and serious. We are still unable to present an adequate picture of mortgage flows on a gross rather than a net basis, as we are unable to separate for each of the involved major groups of lenders and borrowers new mortgage loans made, contractual and other repayments. We cannot as yet separate, on either a gross or a net basis, mortgage flows for new and old structures or owner-occupied and rented properties. We also have very little information on current terms of lending. More-over, virtually all of our market information on mortgage lenders is limited to the administration of and transactions in residential mortgages by financial institutions. To be sure, there is every indication that financial institutions now account for at least four-fifths of all residential mortgages, but the remaining fifth is still large enough compared to many other segments of the capital market to merit more than to be clouded in almost complete statistical obscurity.

Turning to broader aspects of the market for residential mortgages, we know as yet very little about the demand for mortgage loans. Klaman's book, as virtually all the literature in the field, concentrates on the supply side, partly because, as he suggests, it has been supply rather than demand that has determined volume and price in the postwar residential mortgage market. As a result, our knowledge is scant about consumers' decisions to buy or rent housing facilities; about the selection of types of shelter; and—what is more pertinent—the way in which the acquisition of a home, the provision of the initial equity, and the later servicing and repayment of the mortgage loan fit into the consumer's over-all financial picture.

Finally, we are not yet able to integrate what we have learned about the residential mortgage market into the picture of the whole American capital market. This deficiency, which is felt particularly when we try to explain the level and movements of residential mortgage interest rates and the differentials between them and other yield rates, is due, of course, less to deficiencies in our statistics of the residential mortgage market and their analysis than to the still greater gaps in our information and analysis in several other important sectors of the capital market. Outstanding among them is the market for nonresidential nonfarm mortgages. In view of the size and importance of that market the degree of our lack of relevant statistics and the almost complete absence of analysis of what happens in that market is truly astonishing. Not the least to be gained from reading a description and analysis of the market for residential mortgages, which Klaman's book provides, is the realization of how great is the need for a similar study of the market for nonresidential nonfarm mortgages.

RAYMOND W. GOLDSMITH
*Director, Postwar Capital
Market Study*

PREFACE

WHEN this study was undertaken in 1956 it was clear that it would have to deal selectively with the broad and complex subject of postwar real estate finance. Several earlier studies of the National Bureau of Economic Research had already dealt with various aspects of real estate markets,[1] and also the time available for the study was limited essentially to one year.

The selection of areas for investigation was guided, of course, by what had been developed in earlier studies. Attention was centered on fields either previously neglected or for which new or later information had become available. The economic and statistical framework in which the study was cast as part of the National Bureau's Postwar Capital Market Study, moreover, was fundamental in determining its nature and organization. As such, this study is oriented economically towards capital market analysis and statistically towards flow-of-funds accounts. Therefore, it differs basically in subject matter and orientation from earlier National Bureau studies of real estate finance.

It differs in yet another important respect. Compared with the earlier investigations of basic long-run developments over several decades, this study is concerned with the recent relatively short period of postwar economic history from 1945 to 1956. The concern with short-run market changes and their causes results in an analytical approach fundamentally different from that associated with longer-run trend analysis.

Within the basic guideposts established for the selection of subject matter and organization of the study, a wide choice still remained. The final form and content of the report reflects in part personal preferences and interests of the author, and in part the relative feasibility of developing new information about previously uncharted areas. Each of these elements acted to limit the full realization of the other. As a result, several important subdivisions of real estate finance—both statistical

---

[1] Published by the National Bureau of Economic Research: David L. Wickens, *Residential Real Estate: Its Economic Position as Shown by Values, Rents, Family Incomes, Financing, and Construction, Together with Estimates for All Real Estate* (1941); Raymond J. Saulnier, *Urban Mortgage Lending by Life Insurance Companies* (1950); Miles L. Colean, *The Impact of Government on Real Estate Finance in the United States* (1950); Ernest M. Fisher, *Urban Real Estate Markets: Characteristics and Financing* (1951); and Carl F. Behrens, *Commercial Bank Activities in Urban Mortgage Financing;* also Edward E. Edwards, "Urban Real Estate Financing by Savings and Loan Associations" (1950, unpublished). Published by Princeton University Press for the National Bureau: J. E. Morton, *Urban Mortgage Lending: Comparative Markets and Experience* (1956); Leo Grebler, David M. Blank, and Louis Winnick, *Capital Formation in Residential Real Estate: Trends and Prospects* (1956); and Raymond J. Saulnier, Harold G. Halcrow, and Neil H. Jacoby, *Federal Lending and Loan Insurance* (1958).

and economic—remain yet to be explored. Among these subjects are nonresidential finance, gross mortgage flows, terms of mortgage lending, mortgage borrower analysis, and real estate market transactions. Some were ruled out early in the study, others were discarded only after strong efforts were made to develop new information.

Among these subjects, perhaps the one developed furthest, yet not far enough to yield well-rounded results for inclusion here, was that on gross mortgage flows. Considerable progress was made in achieving a framework for gross mortgage flow analysis, by main types of lender and type of mortgage. The work done indicates the feasibility of maintaining—on an annual basis at least—detailed gross mortgage flow accounts for life insurance companies, mutual savings banks, and savings and loan associations. Only for commercial banks, among the main types of financial institutions, are basic data inadequate to support estimates of gross mortgage lending. For other less important mortgage lenders, not only are estimates of gross mortgage flows impracticable at present, but also data on net flows are inadequate.[2] Notwithstanding the many shortcomings in the data, it is unfortunate that circumstances prevented the completion of even a truncated framework for gross mortgage flow analysis. It is to be hoped that the preliminary unpublished data developed in this study will be amplified by others and incorporated into a useful set of accounts.

The advantage of gross over net financial flows for analysis of market developments is clear. By distinguishing between credit extension and repayment, gross figures permit a more complete analysis and understanding of the response of various market participants to shifting forces at work in capital markets. Moreover, breaking down mortgage debt repayment between contractual obligations and prepayments provides further insight into the nature of real estate market activity. Limiting analysis to net changes in outstanding indebtedness, on the other hand, obscures the distinction between incurrence of debt and its repayment, and between types of debt repayment. Changes in the net flows of mortgage funds from various types of financial institutions reflect not only shifts in response to relative yields and other factors, but also differences in rates of repayment between time periods and types of institutions.

Another basic statistical gap hampering analysis of mortgage markets relates to the inadequacy of comprehensive series on mortgage lending terms—loan-to-value ratios, amortization provisions, maturities, downpayments, and interest rates. A serious attempt was made in the present

---

[2] See Saul B. Klaman, *The Volume of Mortgage Debt in the Postwar Decade*, Technical Paper 13, New York, National Bureau of Economic Research, 1958.

study to develop current information on this subject, so that the National Bureau's series carried through 1947 could be extended. It proved feasible, however, to obtain data only on conventional mortgage interest rates, and these were not as comprehensive as desired. For a fuller understanding of shifts in mortgage flows and of movements in mortgage interest rates, it is essential that current reporting of data on contract mortgage terms be developed.

Nonresidential real estate finance was recognized in the preliminary phases of investigation as too vast a subject to treat adequately within the framework adopted. The over-all statistics on nonresidential mortgage flows are presented in Chapter 2, but thereafter the report is devoted principally to residential mortgage markets. Postwar institutional lending policies and general market techniques have been significantly different in nonresidential from those in residential transactions. Financing of non-residential building and transfers by other means than mortgages has become increasingly important in recent years. Equity financing, sale-leaseback arrangements, and directly placed bond issues, among other financing techniques, have for one reason or another been better suited than mortgage financing to some transactions. Thus, the decision to concentrate in this study upon the residential sector resulted partly from its orientation towards real estate mortgages rather than real estate finance generally, and partly from the fact that the bulk of postwar mortgage flows has been associated with residential transactions. In addition, the development of the relevant information on nonresidential market developments was beyond the scope of the work as planned.

A broad aspect of mortgage market analysis given only minor con-sideration in this monograph concerns the mortgage borrower or demand side of the market. Demand factors are, of course, basic to developments in any market, and in the summary appraisal of major elements influencing the postwar mortgage market those factors have been taken into account. Summary data on mortgage debt by type of borrower are also presented. But in the more detailed appraisal of shifts in mortgage flows and of institutional aspects of mortgage markets, the analysis deals largely with the supply side of the equation. This course was taken mainly because the supply of mortgage funds—its availability and terms—has been a much greater factor than the demand for mortgage funds in influencing postwar changes in the residential mortgage market. More-over, information bearing on mortgage demand, including borrower characteristics, is fairly limited compared with data on mortgage supply.

This is not to suggest that analysis of the demand side of mortgage markets is unimportant. On the contrary, in view of the paucity of data and of analysis in this area—compared to other sectors of the capital market, for example—it would seem eminently worthwhile for students of real estate finance to devote more attention to it. There is outstanding need for improvement of knowledge and for appraisal of the economic position of mortgage borrowers, and measuring the forces underlying demands for mortgage funds in both residential and nonresidential markets.

In the investigation reported here, I have incurred debts to many individuals and organizations. My indebtedness to some has already been recorded in two previous reports published by the National Bureau.[3] I am happy to acknowledge here the assistance and guidance of others. The staff reading committee, Leo Grebler, Richard Selden, and Raymond W. Goldsmith, carefully reviewed the preliminary manuscript and their suggestions and comments were the basis for improvement and revision of the final draft. Wallace J. Campbell, Harold G. Halcrow, and Gabriel Hauge, all of the National Bureau's Board of Directors, rendered helpful criticism. The influence of Raymond Goldsmith, as director of the Postwar Capital Market Study, upon the report throughout its development and his constant support and interest are gratefully acknowledged.

Grateful acknowledgment is also made to the Advisory Committee on the Postwar Capital Market Study, which assisted in drafting plans for this investigation. Members were: W. A. Clarke, George T. Conklin, Jr., W. Braddock Hickman, Norris O. Johnson, Arnold R. LaForce, Aubrey G. Lanston, Robert P. Mayo, Roger F. Murray, James J. O'Leary, Winfield W. Riefler, Robert V. Roosa, R. J. Saulnier, William H. Steiner, Donald B. Woodward, and Eugene C. Zorn, Jr.

I am indebted to many individuals for sharing with me their time and knowledge, through interview and correspondence, in my search for factual and interpretive information about institutional arrangements, market techniques, and lender policies in the postwar residential mortgage market. Among them are George Bliss, R. Manning Brown, Jr., Norman Carpenter, Thomas P. Coogan, George Conklin, Harry Held, John Jewett, William Keesler, Robert M. Morgan, Raymond T. O'Keefe, John Traynor, King Upton, and William Yoars.

James J. O'Leary, besides paving the way for interviews with officers of several financial institutions, provided valued counsel and encouragement throughout the study. The painstaking job of editing done by Margaret

[3] *Ibid.*, and *The Postwar Rise of Mortgage Companies*, Occasional Paper 60, New York, NBER, 1959.

T. Edgar has greatly improved the readability of the book. The charts were drawn by H. Irving Forman, who did his usual peerless job.

I would not have been able to conduct this investigation without the generosity of the Board of Governors of the Federal Reserve System and of Ralph A. Young, now Advisor to the Board, in permitting me a year's leave of absence from my post as staff economist. To them I am deeply grateful.

These acknowledgments would be incomplete without recognition of the contribution of my former colleagues in the Federal Reserve System who were a constant source of intellectual stimulation and challenge through twelve years of association. In this regard I am especially indebted to Ramsay Wood and Frank Garfield, who instilled in me—not without pain—a respect for high standards, which I hope they will find reflected in this monograph.

It remains only to absolve all who have provided generous assistance from any responsibility for the analyses and conclusions of this study and from the inadequacies which undoubtedly remain. Moreover, the views that I have presented do not necessarily reflect those of the Federal Reserve Board, with which I was associated during most of the study, nor the National Association of Mutual Savings Banks, with which I am now associated.

SAUL B. KLAMAN

THE POSTWAR RESIDENTIAL
MORTGAGE MARKET

CHAPTER 1

Plan of the Book and Summary of Findings

IN BROAD terms this report presents analytical materials to meet the dual objective of describing and appraising (1) the flow of residential mortgage funds in the post-World War II decade and the main underlying influences, and (2) the institutional framework of the residential mortgage market in terms of lender policies and practices, and market techniques and characteristics. To the task of meeting these objectives, the study brings evaluations of a variety of information already available and development of new information, both statistical and qualitative.

Plan of the Book

The report is organized around the relatively simple plan of describing at the outset what happened during the first postwar decade in the area under investigation and then appraising the main factors responsible for changes. Chapter 2 sets the stage by describing the special position of mortgage debt in the economy at the end of the war, the record volume of mortgage flows in the succeeding decade, and the resulting marked changes in that debt structure at the end of the period. In Chapter 3 the broad setting in which changes occurred and the main elements underlying mortgage market expansion and restraint are appraised in a time-sequence oriented analysis. The factors include the position of financial institutions, capital market conditions, monetary and fiscal policies, federal mortgage programs, and demands for mortgage funds. Because the yield relationships among capital market securities are such a basic determinant of the flow-of-funds pattern and because so little is known about the postwar movement of mortgage interest rates, both are singled out for separate exploration in Chapter 4. It is left for Chapter 5 to tie more closely together and in considerable detail the changes in postwar mortgage flows, by type of mortgage and type of lender, and their basic underlying causes. There the attempt is to put together the market structure analysis of Chapter 2 and the time-sequence analysis of Chapter 3.

Chapters 6 and 7 shift the emphasis away from the statistical orientation of mortgage flow analysis to the institutional setting of the market place. The analysis in both chapters is more qualitative than quantitative and is concerned basically with differences in mortgage investment policies and practices of the main types of financial institutions, and with the special organization, techniques, and characteristics that distinguish the mortgage market from other sectors of the capital market. Chapter 7 is directed toward an appraisal of the more interesting new postwar market developments which have sprung up in response to shifting financial conditions, and the basic organizational arrangements of primary and secondary markets including junior mortgage financing. Chapter 8 is a summary of a previously published occasional paper[1] and shows how a new type of financial institution—the modern mortgage company—has developed to meet the needs of new institutional arrangements of the postwar mortgage market.

Within that framework of analysis, the reader will find a considerable body of new quantitative and qualitative information. The statistical orientation towards flow-of-funds accounts is supported by more comprehensive data on net mortgage flows than was previously available, for both time intervals and type of mortgage and lender.[2] Given the well-known limitations of net flows data, the more comprehensive series has facilitated and made more meaningful the analysis of postwar mortgage market developments. The analysis has been aided also by new annual and quarterly series on conventional mortgage interest rates, developed in this study. While not as broadly based as desired, these series illuminate a previously dark area and permit new insights into comparative interest rate movements.

The two chapters on mortgage lending policies and market techniques are founded in large part on evaluation of primary information obtained by direct personal interviews with representatives of a variety of institutions and with individuals associated with the mortgage market. In addition to the broad qualitative information obtained, savings and loan associations supplied some new data through questionnaires that—though subject to qualification—tell us a little more about their lending practices than we knew before. The appraisal of the role of mortgage companies in the postwar residential mortgage market is based entirely on new data developed in this study.

The summary of the study's findings to which we now turn must necessarily be brief. Results will often be reported without supporting evidence or reference to underlying causes. For expanded discussion the reader must rely upon the pertinent chapters which follow. The analysis of "yield differentials and gross mortgage flows," (page 13), is an

[1] Saul B. Klaman, *The Postwar Rise of Mortgage Companies*, Occasional Paper 60, New York, National Bureau of Economic Research, 1959.

[2] Klaman, *The Volume of Mortgage Debt in the Postwar Decade*, Technical Paper 13, New York, NBER, 1958.

exception to the general summary presentations in this chapter. It is discussed more fully than in later chapters because expansion of earlier drafts and development of more recent data could be included here more conveniently.

Summary of Findings

POSTWAR CHANGES IN THE STRUCTURE OF MORTGAGE DEBT

At the war's end, the relative importance of mortgage debt in the nation's economic and financial structure had declined to a point lower than in almost any year as far back as the turn of the century. The absolute level of mortgage debt, as well as its structure, was little different at the end of World War II than at its beginning. From the relatively depressed postwar starting point, mortgage debt more than quadrupled in the subsequent years through 1956, and that unusually rapid growth was accompanied by marked changes in the structure and organization of mortgage markets. Between 1945 and 1956 major shifts occurred in the relative significance of real estate properties securing mortgage debt, in types of mortgages outstanding (conventional and federally underwritten), in the types of market participants, and in the portfolio composition of major lenders.

The net flow of funds into nonfarm mortgage markets, in the 1946–1956 period, was markedly larger than the flow into any other sector of the money or capital markets. It amounted to one-third of the total net flow of funds into all types of debt instruments, and was greater than the combined flow into corporate and state and local government securities. Within mortgage markets, mortgages on one- to four-family houses absorbed three-fourths of the entire net flow of funds. One-half of the home mortgage flow was in conventional mortgages, the other half in federally underwritten. Of the latter type, the largest part was guaranteed by the Veterans Administration. The rate of expansion in VA-guaranteed mortgages was far greater than in other types of mortgage debt, reflecting in part the small volume outstanding at the end of 1945.[3]

The chief sources of postwar mortgage funds have been the four main types of financial institutions—life insurance companies, savings and loan associations, commercial banks, and mutual savings banks—which together supplied five-sixths of the total volume. The first two types of institutions alone accounted for more than half the total net mortgage flow. Among the four, savings and loan associations dominated the market for conventional home mortgages, mutual savings banks the market for multifamily

[3] The VA mortgage guarantee program had been operating only a short time by the end of 1945, having been authorized by the Servicemen's Readjustment Act in June 1944.

mortgages, and life insurance companies and commercial banks the market for nonresidential mortgages. Of the other types of financial institutions separately identified in the statistics given here, only mortgage companies accounted for as much as 1 per cent of the net mortgage supply. Their role is that of mortgage originators and servicers, however, rather than investors, and is unique among mortgage market participants. Nonfinancial institutions, federal agencies, and individuals together were a relatively minor source of total mortgage funds in the postwar decade, but they were individually significant in particular markets. Nonfinancial institutions were a dominant supplier in the farm mortgage market and were an important source of nonfarm nonresidential mortgage funds as well.

By far the largest demands for mortgage funds, among all identifiable economic groups, were from consumers borrowing chiefly to finance the purchase of new and existing houses. Net mortgage borrowing by that group amounted to more than two-thirds of all mortgage funds borrowed in the first postwar decade, and was two and a half times the amount borrowed by all nonfarm businesses—the second largest group. The postwar demand for mortgage funds from farm businesses and from nonprofit organizations was relatively small.

By the end of 1956, following more than a decade of rapid but uneven expansion in mortgage markets, fundamental changes had occurred in the structure of mortgage debt. Two-thirds of the debt was secured by one- to four-family properties compared with one-half at the end of the war. Accompanying that sharp increase, debt secured by each of the other types of property declined substantially in relative importance. Within the home mortgage sector, VA-guaranteed debt increased extraordinarily, from 1 per cent of the total at the end of 1945 to 28 per cent, while Federal Housing Administration insured mortgage debt was shrinking from 22 to 16 per cent, and conventional loans from 77 to 56 per cent of the total.

Ownership of the mortgage debt, already fairly concentrated at the end of the war, was even more so by the end of 1956, with over three-fourths held by the four main types of financial intermediaries, compared with less than three-fifths eleven years earlier. Savings and loan associations increased their participation in mortgage markets relatively more, and savings banks relatively less, than the other types of institutions.

Postwar changes in mortgage markets were reflected also in the changing composition of mortgage portfolios of major lenders. Savings and loan associations, while continuing to concentrate their activities in conventional home mortgages, markedly increased the proportion of their holdings in VA-guaranteed loans. Life insurance companies and savings banks sharply increased their holdings of home mortgage loans. Savings banks expanded their VA loans to one-third of their total mortgage portfolio, a larger proportion than any other type of loan. Commercial banks expanded their home mortgage holdings somewhat less sharply than either of the latter two institutions and, unlike them, continued to maintain the same proportion of their loans in nonresidential mortgages.

As to liability for mortgage debt, after a decade of record borrowing consumers owed three-fifths of the total amount of mortgage debt outstanding in 1956, nearly twice that owed by nonfarm businesses. At the end of the war each of these sectors had owed about the same amount of mortgage debt—a little over two-fifths of the total. Farmers and nonprofit organizations continued to owe relatively small amounts of mortgage debt at the end of 1956.

PATTERN OF MORTGAGE FLOWS AND UNDERLYING INFLUENCES

The summary of broad postwar changes in mortgage debt and flows obscures the wide fluctuations within mortgage market sectors and the varying relationships among them. The swings occurred in response to changes in economic and financial activity and in governmental actions. During the first half of the decade the interplay of those factors brought about almost unrestrained expansion in mortgage markets. There were insistent demands for mortgage credit to finance the increasing volume of new construction and real estate transactions at rising prices. Financial institutions with large holdings of government securities were unusually liquid and were actively seeking new and more profitable investment outlets. The Federal Reserve System's policy of supporting government bond prices at par—and therefore at relatively constant and low yields—permitted institutions to sell such securities readily and without penalty. The federal government, moreover, in its efforts to stimulate production of housing, was aggressively pursuing a policy of liberalizing FHA and VA mortgage programs and expanding the secondary market authority of the Federal National Mortgage Association (FNMA). All these elements contributed to the attractiveness to investors of mortgage yields relative to those of other capital market securities through most of the 1946–1950 period. Federally underwritten mortgages had the added advantage of limited risk.

In that setting the flow of funds into mortgages increased almost without interruption, culminating in 1950 in a record volume not exceeded until four years later. In most years of the first half-decade the mortgage flow was larger than the combined flow into other capital market securities; for the period as a whole it was three-fourths larger than the net issue of corporate securities and three times larger than that of state and municipal securities. All major types of savings institutions—mutual savings banks, life insurance companies, savings and loan associations—invested an increasing proportion of their assets in mortgages from 1946 through 1950.

Commercial banks committed a considerably larger proportion of their investment funds to mortgages in the first three postwar years than in the succeeding two, representing conversion of a heavy share of their extraordinarily large volume of government securities. In 1947 and 1948 the net flow of mortgage funds from commercial banks was larger than from any other type of investor.

Mutual savings banks and life insurance companies were slower than commercial banks to take advantage of favorable investment opportunities. Savings banks were handicapped by legal restrictions limiting mortgage acquisitions generally to their own or adjoining states. Since most savings banks are located in the East where construction and real estate markets were relatively inactive, legally eligible mortgage loans were not plentiful in the immediate postwar years. When state laws were modified to permit acquisition of FHA and VA loans throughout the country, savings banks increased their mortgage lending markedly, absolutely and also in relation to other investments.

The relatively slow pickup of mortgage investments by life insurance companies was due in part to the cautious attitude of some companies remembering the experience of the thirties and in part to problems of market reorganization. It was necessary to re-establish mortgage correspondent or branch office organizations, largely dismantled after many years of reduced mortgage activity during depression and war. As these problems were solved and skepticism towards mortgages faded, life insurance companies devoted a steadily rising share of assets to mortgages. Except for the first two years after the war, when commercial banks took the lead in mortgage lending, the net flow of funds from life insurance companies exceeded the flow from any other type of investor through 1951.

Savings and loan associations liquidated about $1 billion in government securities and placed all their capital investments in mortgages during the 1946–1950 period. Even so, the reduced inflow of savings limited their absolute volume to less than that of commercial banks in the first part of the period, and to less than that of life insurance companies in the latter part.

The total mortgage flow from the four types of financial institutions—comprising the bulk of available mortgage funds in each year of the decade—varied with market conditions from a little over three-fourths to nearly nine-tenths of the total. The low occurred during 1949 following a general rise in bond yields and a slight business recession. As institutional funds were attracted to other markets, support for federally underwritten mortgages was provided by FNMA, whose purchasing authority had been expanded in 1948 to include VA loans and had been generally liberalized by the Housing Act of 1948. This support was not sufficient, however, to prevent a decline in over-all net mortgage flows during 1949—the only year of decline in the first half of the postwar decade. The decrease, reflecting both reduced demand and relatively unfavorable yields, was mainly in the market for one- to four-family mortgage loans, with some drop also in the flow of nonresidential mortgage funds. The 1949 flow of funds into multifamily mortgages, however, increased from earlier very low levels, owing entirely to the stimulation of the FHA Title VI program. Through it, construction and financing of rental housing had become both profitable and riskless.

The marked economic expansion of 1950, accompanied by further liberalization of government mortgage programs and declines in yields on competitive securities, brought forth a sharply increased flow of mortgage funds. Evidence of the renewed attractiveness of mortgages to financial intermediaries was their provision of a larger proportion of the increased net flow of mortgage funds in 1950—87 per cent—than in any other year on record. All types of financial institutions increased their participation in mortgage markets during that unusually active year of business and mortgage activity.

Within home mortgage markets, the composition of mortgage flows fluctuated widely. In the first half-decade, the flow of funds into federally underwritten mortgages exceeded that into conventional; in the latter half, the reverse was true. Within the federally underwritten sector, the movements of VA and FHA mortgage flows often diverged because of the effects of basic differences in federal programs and of lender reactions to them. In general, VA financing has tended to fluctuate more widely and irregularly than that of FHA, and both have been far less stable than conventional financing. The relative stability of conventional mortgage flows has been due largely to the flexibility of conventional interest rates compared with relatively rigid maximum interest rates on federally underwritten loans. During the 1948–1949 rise in bond yields, for example, VA mortgage flows declined rapidly, accounting for nearly all of the drop in home mortgage flows. A sharp rise followed in 1950–1951, accompanying the easing in bond yields and the general economic expansion. FHA mortgage flows showed little change during most of that period, however. The markedly different behavior of the VA and FHA loan programs in those years is explained by differences in contract interest rates, in amounts of loan guarantee and insurance, in mortgage terms, in secondary market support, and in availability of special incentive programs for builders and lenders. The influence of these and other factors is evaluated in Chapters 3 to 5.

Underlying the changing composition of home mortgage flows were shifts in the participation of both private financial institutions and FNMA in the various markets. The main shifts among participants occurred in the market for VA loans. In the market for FHA loans, life insurance companies were the dominant lenders throughout the first half-decade; and in the conventional loan market, savings and loan associations led. In the second half-decade, life insurance companies relinquished their dominance of the FHA market to commercial banks and mutual savings banks. In the VA loan market, savings and loan associations and commercial banks were the leading lenders in the immediate postwar years, as life insurance companies and mutual savings banks delayed entering it, for reasons previously noted. In the 1950–1951 mortgage expansion, however, life insurance companies accounted for almost the entire VA loan growth, having firmly established their correspondent organizations and finding these loans attractive relative to other investments.

The strong support provided for the VA loan market by FNMA, following the expansion of its authority in 1948 to include that sector, is indicated by the fact that the Association provided funds for more than one-third of all VA mortgage flows in 1949, a larger proportion than any private lender. Strong FNMA support continued in 1950 even after many private lenders expanded their participation in VA markets. The Association's role in FHA loan markets, though important, was relatively far less significant than in VA loan markets.

Following the outbreak of war in Korea in mid-1950 and the Federal Reserve-Treasury "accord" in March 1951, there was an abrupt change in the capital market setting. This resulted in marked shifts in the flow of mortgage funds relative to other financial flows and within the various mortgage market sectors. Direct post-Korean federal controls tended to restrain mortgage lending activity for nearly three years. Though not measurable, these restraints probably were not as great as those resulting from restrictive monetary policies, alternative investment opportunities, and reduced liquidity of financial institutions. In any case, direct federal restrictions were removed by mid-1953, and mortgage markets alternately expanded and contracted in response to shifting monetary policies, changes in general capital market demands, and federal legislative and administrative actions. The alternate expansion and contraction in the 1951–1956 period was in marked contrast to the almost uninterrupted expansion of the preceding five years.

Notwithstanding the introduction of important restraining forces, the net flow of mortgage funds in each year of the 1951–1956 period continued to exceed other individual capital market flows by a wide margin. The margin narrowed considerably during the 1951–1953 period of credit restraint, widened thereafter through 1955, and declined again in 1956 as restraining forces once again became dominant. During periods of general contraction the four main types of financial institutions reduced their mortgage market participation relatively more than other lenders did, while in periods of expansion they increased their mortgage activity relatively more than other lenders did.

The greater volatility in the one- to four-family than in other mortgage sectors, clearly revealed in this study, is due entirely to the impact of shifting market forces on the flow of federally underwritten mortgage funds. As in the first half-decade, the fluctuation of the flow of VA funds was considerably greater than that of FHA funds, but more in degree than in direction of change. During the 1951–1953 period of Regulation X and associated federal controls, restrictive monetary policy, rising bond yields, and reduced FNMA authority, the drop in the flow of VA mortgage funds was sharper than in FHA funds. Subsequently, in the changed capital market environment of 1953–1955—mortgage credit restrictions removed, monetary policy eased, bond yields in decline, FHA and VA contract interest rates raised, and FNMA's purchasing authority increased—VA mortgage flows expanded much more sharply than FHA flows. Again, the return to restraint in 1955–1956 had a greater impact on VA markets. All of this suggests that investors find the quality and terms of VA loans less attractive than those of FHA loans; that, in comparison with their reaction to FHA markets, they withdraw from VA markets faster when other investment opportunities are favorable and return with more volume when other opportunities diminish.

Quarterly data developed in this study clearly reveal that changes in mortgage market activity lag behind the events that induce or influence them. The increase in VA lending activity, for example, did not start until mid-1954 following the return of expansionary forces in late 1953.

VA flows continued sharply upward through 1955 after restraining forces had already become dominant; the reaction to restraint was not evident in VA mortgage flows until early 1956. The lag in the upturn of FHA mortgage flows was somewhat longer than in VA flows, and the lag in the downturn was about the same. Quarterly data on conventional mortgage flows must be used more carefully in drawing inferences because of recurring and fluctuating movements that stem principally from seasonal activity of savings and loan associations. Nevertheless, time lags are still evident, with the upturn during 1954 sharper and longer than usual to a third-quarter peak, and the downturn in late 1955 greater than usual to a fourth-quarter low. Earlier, during 1952 and 1953, when federally underwritten mortgage flows were declining, conventional mortgage flows increased, as interest rates were free to rise with those on other capital market securities.

PATTERN OF MORTGAGE INTEREST RATES

Lack of comprehensive data has limited empirical evidence on the course of mortgage interest rates and yields in the postwar decade. The development in this study of quarterly contract interest rate series on conventional home and income property mortgage loans closed by life insurance companies permits us now to draw some general conclusions on the movement of conventional mortgage interest rates. First, the amplitude of home mortgage interest rate movements has been considerably narrower than rate movements of other capital market securities. Second, changes in home mortgage interest rates have consistently lagged by about four quarters behind changes in bond yields. Third, broad movements in mortgage interest rates and bond yields have been in general conformity reflecting the pervasive influence of conditions in financial markets. Fourth, interest rates on conventional mortgages secured by income properties have been generally lower and somewhat more volatile than rates on conventional home mortgages. The summary findings, which tend to confirm those reported in earlier National Bureau studies of the first half of this century, are supported and evaluated in Chapter 4.

As for FHA and VA interest rates, their inflexibility has been an important factor in the volatility of federally underwritten mortgage flows. The technique of market discounts has been only partially effective during periods of credit stringency in adjusting maximum rates on these loans—established by law or regulation—to yields competitive with other capital market securities. The failure of that expedient reflects the legal restrictions and complexities associated with the use of discounts and also strong

Congressional criticism, particularly when discounts are large and increasing. As a result, many financial institutions have become unwilling to lend on federally underwritten mortgages when yields on competitive securities are rising.

Yield Differentials and Gross Mortgage Flows

There is a clear relationship between changing capital market yields and FHA and VA mortgage flows. This relationship is reflected in Chart 1, which compares gross VA and FHA mortgage flows with differentials between yields on new high-grade corporate bond issues and VA and FHA contract interest rates. It is apparent that changes in both VA and FHA gross flows generally lag behind changes in yield differentials, and that VA loans are somewhat more responsive than FHA loans to such changes. The lack of close conformity between gross flows and yield spreads in each year is explained partly by the influence of other factors appraised in Chapter 3 and partly by imperfections in the data.

The influence of yield spreads on gross flows has been particularly evident since mid-1953, which marked the end of selective control of real estate credit through Regulation X and associated regulations. Thereafter, the ebb and flow of VA and FHA mortgage funds followed the diminishing and increasing spreads between federally underwritten contract interest rates and flexible yields on directly competitive new Aaa corporate bond issues. A similar pattern emerges when the comparison is made between government bond yields and FHA and VA interest rates. The sharp rise in yield spreads to a postwar high in 1954 was followed by a rapid rise in VA mortgage flows to a record peak in late 1955. The subsequent almost uninterrupted decline in yield spreads from the end of 1954 through late 1957, as corporate yields advanced sharply, was followed by a precipitous drop in VA flows to a postwar low by mid-1958. The turnaround and marked rise in VA flows thereafter reflected the earlier easing in financial markets and the significant widening in the differential between new bond yields and VA contract rates (Chart 1).

It was the FHA market that responded quickly to yield changes in 1957–1958 as contract interest rates on FHA loans were increased from 5 to $5\frac{1}{4}$ per cent in August 1957. The rate on VA loans, meanwhile, was maintained at $4\frac{1}{2}$ per cent, until the spring of 1958 when it was raised to $4\frac{3}{4}$ per cent. The more attractive rate on FHA loans relative to corporate bonds, evident from Chart 1, was largely responsible for the marked upturn in FHA mortgage flows after mid-1957 while VA flows continued to decline for about a year thereafter. In earlier years, when

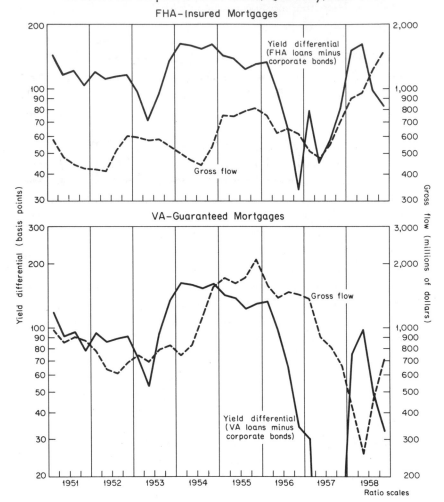

CHART I
Comparison of FHA and VA Gross Mortgage Flows with Differentials between Contract Interest Rates on FHA and VA Mortgages and Yields on New Aaa Corporate Bond Issues, Quarterly, 1951–1958

Data on gross mortgage flow are quarterly averages of monthly figures from the Federal Housing Administration and Veterans Administration. The series on average yields of new corporate bond issues used for comparison with FHA and VA loans is from the First National City Bank of New York; it begins in 1951 and is adjusted to an Aaa basis. This yield series was used because it pertains to securities competitive with FHA and VA loans and because it is more responsive to market change than yield series on outstanding corporate bonds. By the same token, data on gross rather than net mortgage flows were used because they reflect more quickly the response of lenders to changes in financial markets.

A similar comparison with conventional mortgage loans is precluded because of the lack of quarterly data on gross mortgage flows. Comparison of yield differentials with estimated annual conventional mortgage flows reveals much narrower changes than in the FHA and VA loan series, as noted in several places in the text. See Table A-1 below.

FHA and VA contract interest rates were the same, FHA mortgage flows responded more tardily and less sharply than VA flows to changes in yield differentials.[4]

Even when contract interest rates on FHA and VA loans were established at the same level, market prices for FHA loans were consistently higher and yields lower—in part because of the relative differences in quality attributed to each by investors. Interest rates on conventional home loans were generally higher than yields on federally underwritten mortgages throughout the postwar decade (Chapter 4). The spread tended to narrow somewhat when capital markets were tightening in late 1953 and again in late 1955. The amount of spread was due not only to the existence of government guarantees but also to differences in contract terms. The evidence suggests that the market place does not regard VA and FHA loans as riskless assets, but rather applies traditional standards of quality with regard to mortgage terms and underlying properties in judging the values of those investments.

Regional Yield Variations

A fundamental difference between markets where mortgages are issued and traded and markets where other securities are involved is that the former are primarily local and the latter are national. While the interregional flow of mortgage funds has increased sharply since the advent of federal mortgage insurance and guarantee, regional yield variations have persisted. Limited data suggest, for example, that in 1956 yields on VA mortgages available in Philadelphia were about 50 basis points higher than in Los Angeles. That variation was not much smaller than that reported for conventional mortgage yields in 1940. The arbitrage process clearly limits the spread in regional mortgage yields. But it is doubtful that regional yield differentials will soon be eliminated because mortgages are tied to local real estate values; they are inextricably linked to local market developments, to local foreclosure and other real estate laws, and to other peculiarly local economic, social, and political factors. Other more specific reasons for the persistence of mortgage yield differentials by geographic region are suggested in Chapter 4.

INSTITUTIONAL FRAMEWORK OF MORTGAGE MARKETS

Postwar changes in mortgage debt and markets and the influences underlying those changes can be appreciated more easily in the context of the

---

[4] Inclusion of data for 1957 and 1958 in this analysis of yield spreads and mortgage flows is a pre-publication revision, not practicable for the whole study, which covers the years 1945–1956.

institutional framework in which those changes took place. Among important interrelated aspects of the institutional framework of postwar mortgage markets are: fundamental differences in mortgage lending policies and practices of major financial institutions; development of new techniques and characteristics in mortgage market operation; relationships between primary and secondary markets and their changing significance; and characteristics of the market for junior mortgage financing. These subjects are dealt with in Chapters 6 to 8, which are summarized briefly in the remainder of this chapter.

Mortgage Lending Policies and Practices

The major postwar suppliers of mortgage funds differ strikingly in their lending policies and practices. Not only are there basic variations among the types of institutions, but also among individual institutions of the same type. Life insurance companies, for example, are guided in their mortgage operations by a set of factors different from those guiding savings banks or savings and loan associations, but there are also basic operational differences among life insurance companies.

Life insurance companies have a wide degree of investment flexibility and are guided in their choice of investments mainly by yield differentials. Other basic factors influence the volume of their mortgage flows, such as personal biases of investment officers, mortgage correspondent relationships, and the ratio of mortgage loans to assets. Stable and efficient correspondent organizations, which acquire and service mortgages outside the home office states, are regarded as valuable assets. Many life insurance companies—chiefly the larger ones—that have such assets are committed to basic minimum mortgage programs, regardless of changes in mortgage yields. Companies that have established a branch office system to acquire and service mortgages are similarly committed to a minimum mortgage investment program. The degree of expansion beyond what are regarded as irreducible mortgage flows, however, is determined by relative yields in various investment sectors. Upper and lower limits of mortgage expansion and contraction for some companies are adjusted in line with intermediate and longer-range goals of suitable ratios of mortgage loans to total assets. The goals are reviewed periodically and changed as new market circumstances are discerned. The notion of limiting one type of investment to a "desirable" ratio reflects a basic policy of diversification. Other companies, chiefly smaller ones, often disregard the idea of ratios and diversification and vary mortgage flows solely according to changes in relative yield. Smaller companies are also less concerned than larger companies are about correspondent or branch office organizations and hence operate with a greater degree of flexibility in mortgage markets.

Wide variations characterize the residential mortgage lending operations of life insurance companies, but as a group they are better adapted to permanent, long-term financing of large housing projects rather than of single properties. Lending on large-scale income properties is also widespread among life insurance companies. Though closely associated with the construction process, life insurance companies generally do not extend short-term credits directly. This type of lending would be inconsistent with the nature of their business and investment needs.

In their mortgage lending operations, the larger life insurance companies typically operate through the allocation and commitment process. Many plan their operations a year or more ahead, allocating funds to correspondents and committing themselves to accept completed mortgages upon delivery or within a stated time. This type of operation clearly limits flexibility in the short run but eases the problems of keeping large aggregations of funds fully invested over the business cycle. Many large companies are willing to forego the short-run maximization of yields in favor of a long-range program of continuity of operations. The technique, however, gives rise to other basic problems: the uncertain time lags between allocations, commitments, and disbursements of funds; the uncertain rate of attrition in commitments; and the danger of being overcommitted relative to premium and other inflows if market conditions change. Smaller companies that are not so heavily committed to mortgage programs and to the system of fund allocations to correspondents and branch offices probably enjoy flexibility in greater degree than larger companies.

Investment outlets of mutual savings banks are more limited than those of life insurance companies or commercial banks, but less limited than those of savings and loan associations. Savings banks have tended to choose, within the legal list of investments available to them, those bearing the highest yields commensurate with risk. In most of the first postwar decade, that policy resulted in acquisition of available mortgages in the maximum amounts consistent with deposit inflows and statutory requirements. In their mortgage lending programs, savings banks have operated traditionally in local markets as long-term residential mortgage lenders. Since 1950, when most savings bank states amended their statutes to permit investment in out-of-state federally underwritten mortgages, these mutual institutions have become important national mortgage lenders as well. The granting of authority to purchase out-of-state mortgages was probably the most significant single factor influencing the postwar mortgage lending policies of mutual savings banks. But the expanded opportunities brought increased legal and organizational problems. In acquiring out-of-state mortgages, some savings banks patterned their operations after those of life insurance companies (though legal restrictions concerning "foreign corporations" prohibited a true investor-correspondent relationship). As a result, these savings banks have been faced with problems similar to those of life insurance companies with correspondent relationships—problems associated with the long-range commitments process. Partly for this reason other savings banks have preferred in the main to acquire out-of-state mortgages, which have been and are ready for immediate delivery.

Aside from problems of mortgage acquisition techniques, savings banks with an uncertain volume of deposit inflows can hardly plan their mortgage programs so far ahead as life insurance companies with their more predictable premium income. For purposes of internal planning, the banks allocate funds for mortgages on the basis of minimum expected net deposits and mortgage repayments. Programs are under constant review and revision as changes develop in deposit and other cash inflows and in market conditions. A wider degree of short-run program flexibility than most life insurance companies have is afforded by absence of permanent organizational arrangements with mortgage originators and, for many banks, by acquisition of mortgages in the secondary market for immediate delivery.

Compared with other major financial institutions in the mortgage market, savings and loan associations are singularly limited by law and tradition to the specialized role of home mortgage lenders. In home mortgage markets they specialize, also, in providing conventional loans directly to individual borrowers in local markets and thus are less flexible than other financial institutions in adjusting investment programs to changes in capital market conditions. Changes in their mortgage flows, therefore, signify changes in their savings inflows, in their ability to borrow from Federal Home Loan Banks, and in their competitive position among other lenders rather than shifts to and from other investment markets.

While engaged primarily in providing long-term permanent mortgage funds directly to home buyers, the associations have also become important suppliers of short-term construction funds to builders—usually with the intent of acquiring the permanent mortgage loans on completed properties. A significant number of their construction loans, however, has been refinanced as permanent mortgage loans by other lenders, according to information obtained in a survey made for this study (see Chapter 6). Whether or not the original purpose of such construction loans was to obtain the permanent mortgage financing, the ultimate effect has been that of short-term construction financing.

In their permanent mortgage financing activities, savings and loan associations, in addition to dominating the conventional home mortgage market, have supplied a large volume of VA mortgage funds. That volume was about as large over the full postwar decade as the volume supplied by each of the other major financial intermediaries, and in the early years of the decade the associations were the largest source of such mortgage funds. The frequently noted indifference of savings and loan associations to federally underwritten mortgages, therefore, applies only to FHA-insured loans. While there are many individual exceptions, the savings and loan industry as a whole has provided little support to the FHA mortgage insurance program since its inception in 1934—a situation that may change in the years ahead, particularly if the VA guarantee program is allowed to expire.

Among the four major types of financial intermediaries, commercial banks play the most varied role in mortgage markets. Some banks limit their participation to short-term construction loans, others to indirect interim financing credits ("warehousing"), and still others to long-term permanent mortgages. Some commercial banks, of course, provide more than one of these types of financing, while others do not participate at all in real estate financing. In general, the smaller country banks are more actively engaged in permanent mortgage financing and the large city banks in construction and interim financing.

Even among larger banks construction financing is concentrated among the relatively few that have acquired experience in that highly specialized, complex, and lucrative operation. Before extending construction credit, the commercial bank typically requires a firm "take-out" commitment from another financial institution by which it agrees to provide the permanent mortgage financing. In the later part of the postwar decade, the "standby" commitment was often used to back up construction loans when regular take-out commitments were not readily available (see Chapter 7 for discussion of standby commitments).

The most common of the techniques for extending construction loans is that used by most large New York money market banks, which operate through correspondent banks in various parts of the country. The function of a correspondent bank is to place and service the loans, toward which it provides about 10 per cent of the funds, 90 per cent coming from the money market bank. To the large New York bank, the gross return has ranged between 5 and 5½ per cent, but to the correspondent bank the return has been around 10 per cent. That return includes earnings not only on its contribution to the construction loan but also a share of the return on the balance provided by the parent bank.

Interim credits (so-called warehousing) to mortgage lenders have long been extended by commercial banks. This type of financing, used principally by mortgage companies, bridges the gap between the completion of the mortgage loan and its delivery to principal investors. Interim credits enable the companies to carry mortgage inventories far larger than their own resources would permit. Variations and extensions of interim financing in the postwar decade, discussed in Chapter 7, have at times tended to introduce a note of instability into the mortgage market. The volume of interim financing provided by commercial banks increased sharply during the postwar years in response to changes in market conditions and operating techniques, and to demands of mortgage companies, whose operations are vitally dependent upon interim financing.

The story of the growth and change in mortgage company operations during the postwar decade is one of the most interesting and important developments in the institutional setting of mortgage markets. A brief account, more fully presented in *The Postwar Rise of Mortgage Companies* is given in Chapter 8. Mortgage companies originate and service mortgage loans for the accounts of institutional investors, not for their own portfolios, and usually engage in one or more related real estate activities. Relative to their volume of business, mortgage companies have a very small capital investment. Their phenomenal growth is directly connected with the introduction of the federal mortgage underwriting program and its reduction of geographic barriers to mortgage investment. It also stems from decisions by most life insurance companies to acquire out-of-state mortgages through such locally owned independent companies rather than through their own branch offices or subsidiaries.

Characteristics of the structure and operations of mortgage companies in the first postwar decade may be briefly summarized:

1. The unusual growth of mortgage companies is seen in the doubling of their number and tenfold increase in assets from $160 million to $1.8 billion between 1945 and 1955. Further evidence is expansion of mortgage servicing business to about $20 billion by the end of 1955, three times the mid-1951 volume. Their servicing volume covered two-thirds of home mortgages and four-fifths of federally underwritten loans held by life

insurance companies, savings banks, and FNMA (principal purchasers of loans from mortgage companies).

2. The concentration of mortgage company activity in federally underwritten mortgages is shown by data for 1953–1955; 90 per cent of loans closed and 75 to 80 per cent of loans held by surveyed companies were VA-guaranteed and FHA-insured. Of their conventional loans, the bulk were on one- to four-family properties.

3. The financial structure of mortgage companies is relatively simple, their assets consisting largely of mortgage and construction loans and their liabilities of notes payable to banks. The dependence of mortgage companies on commercial banks is indicated by the fact that in most years close to 90 per cent of mortgage inventory was financed through interim commercial bank loans.

4. According to rough estimates postwar mortgage banking has been very profitable—return on net worth amounting to about 15 per cent in 1955, a rate slightly higher than that of sales finance companies and much higher than that of commercial banks.

5. The mortgage banking industry is young. More than one-half of all FHA-approved mortgage companies were incorporated in the postwar decade, and about one-fourth since 1950.

6. In their relationships with borrowers and investors, most mortgage companies closed at least 90 per cent of their loans only after receiving firm commitments from institutional investors.

Market Characteristics and Techniques

The techniques that characterize mortgage market operations have evolved in response to the special needs of the real estate and construction industries, to the changing character of institutional operations, to the effects of monetary and fiscal policies, and to shifts in capital market conditions. One basic characteristic, inherent in the mortgage lending process and in the construction and real estate activity underlying it, is the time lag between commitments to invest and the actual acquisition of mortgages—usually longer and more uncertain than those in other areas of the capital market. One reflection of this characteristic is the substantial lag in mortgage interest rate changes behind those of other capital market securities (Chapter 4). Another is the lag in changes in mortgage flows behind changes in market conditions several months earlier—an observation essential to interpretation of data on mortgage finance.

Fundamental to mortgage market operations is use of the commitment technique in acquiring loans. This technique has become an increasingly important part of the mortgage investment process, as institutional investors have become the major suppliers of mortgage funds. In the basic commitment technique—a promise to provide mortgage credit under specified terms and conditions—modifications have been developed in the postwar decade in response to capital market stringency. The main innovations have been the "forward" and "standby" commitments. The forward commitment—used chiefly by life insurance companies—is an arrangement for disbursing funds within a specified future time, rather than upon the completion of mortgages. It provides a more regularized flow of funds over years of intermittent capital market ease and stringency. The standby commitment comes into wide use only when regular take-out or forward commitments cannot be had. It is given at a price so far below the market price that neither lender nor borrower expects to complete the transaction. Each expects that before the scheduled disbursement of funds regular commitments will become available at current market prices. The standby commitment is important to builders and mortgage originators as an assurance of a source of permanent long-term funds. It is desired by investors mainly because of the fees associated with it.

From the standpoint of market participants and market processes both advantages and disadvantages derive from the standby commitment technique. An advantage to the builder is that he can proceed with construction. An advantage to the originator is that he can maintain or increase his volume of business. An advantage to the investor is that he earns a fee for only a promise to lend. Market processes profit from the technique, in that construction can proceed during periods of temporary credit stringency and that a pool of completed mortgages can be created ready for immediate delivery to investors. Disadvantages of standby commitments to market participants accrue only if anticipated easing of credit conditions fail to develop. Builders may then incur costs for credit substantially higher than planned, and lenders may find their resources taxed by unexpected calls upon them to honor their commitments. From the standpoint of market processes, disadvantages may be instability encouraged by expansion in construction to unsustainable levels and creation of mortgages that cannot be readily absorbed by long-term investors.

Accompanying postwar innovations in commitment techniques was the development of variations in commercial bank interim financing under the broad category of "warehousing." They involved mainly lengthening of loan maturities and adapting old techniques to new types of borrowers.

Like commitment innovations, these variations evolved to overcome temporary shortages of long-term funds and to meet the changing needs of long-term investors. Common to all variations of warehousing is the use of interim bank credit pending the availability of long-term permanent mortgage funds. The collateral for interim loans is usually mortgages, but on occasion interim loans are made in conjunction with construction loans and standby commitments. While throughout the postwar decade mortgage companies have remained the dominant user of warehousing credit, occasional dramatic uses of such credit have been made by life insurance companies that have become temporarily over-committed in mortgages relative to expected cash inflows.

One indication of the significance of interim financing is provided by rough estimates showing that in 1955—the peak year of its use—commercial bank interim credits were associated with the financing of perhaps one-third of all new houses built and purchased that year. If assumed (as evidence allows) to be used only with FHA and VA mortgages, warehousing may have been involved in about one-half the volume of federally underwritten mortgages written on new houses in 1955. Like innovations in commitment techniques, variations and broadened usage of warehousing credits provided by commercial banks may have salutary or harmful effects on market processes, depending on conditions. There is little doubt that the regular short-term interim credit serves a useful purpose in bridging the gap between closing mortgage loans and their sale to investors. The harmful unstabilizing effects arise from excessive use of short-term bank credit in lieu of unavailable long-term funds.

Primary and Secondary Mortgage Markets

The relationship between primary and secondary mortgage markets is unique among capital market sectors. It derives from special institutional arrangements and techniques of mortgage loan origination and investor acquisition. It is upon the clear differentiation of the processes of mortgage origination and ultimate investment that the distinction between primary and secondary mortgage markets is drawn.

Mortgage market participants would regard a secondary market transaction as one in which, for example, a life insurance company acquired a mortgage originated by a mortgage company. Such a definition clearly rests upon the technique of mortgage acquisition and upon the separation of the origination and investment processes between two different types of institutions. Almost all the information available on mortgage originations and purchases is based on this concept. In other financial markets, secondary transactions are generally regarded as market trading in existing securities as distinct from primary transactions in which new debt or equity instruments are created. If the second concept is applied to home mortgage markets, the estimated dollar volume of secondary transactions would probably be no greater than 10 per cent of primary market activity by the end of the first postwar decade. Under the broader concept commonly accepted in mortgage markets, secondary transactions would be relatively much greater.

Under any concept, a secondary market for mortgages scarcely existed before the Federal Housing Administration was established in 1934. Lack of uniformity or standardization in loan contracts, property appraisals, and borrower evaluation limited mortgage transactions to individual local primary markets. Shifting mortgages among investors was difficult and expensive—and risky. The FHA mortgage insurance program endowed federally underwritten mortgages with a degree of quality and uniformity needed to make them broadly shiftable among investors, and reduced geographic barriers to investment. Standardization of mortgage terms and of property and borrower appraisal techniques reduced the need for close lender supervision and for investigation of individual transactions. A secondary mortgage market in federally underwritten mortgages took shape and expanded.

At the same time, changes in primary market transactions were taking place as large-scale production and sale of houses expanded. In many instances, the traditional individual transaction between mortgagor and lender was replaced by mass mortgage transactions between builders and investors on behalf of numerous unknown house buyers and ultimate mortgagors. The individual negotiation process between mortgage borrower and lender, however, remains an important characteristic of primary market transactions.

CHAPTER 2

Survey of Postwar Changes in Mortgage Debt Structure and in Mortgage Flows

THE financing of construction and real estate in the decade following World War II—in heavy demand during the period and at rising costs and prices during most of it—resulted in a rapid growth in mortgage debt and significant changes in the structure and characteristics of mortgage markets. Underlying the quadrupling of mortgage debt in those ten years were marked changes in the importance of mortgage lending institutions, in types of properties securing mortgage indebtedness, in types and terms of mortgage underwriting, and in types of borrowers. A summary comparison of those changes is undertaken in this chapter. Appraisal of basic factors influencing structural changes in the market, and of annual and quarterly net mortgage flows is left in the main for later chapters.

Because the period of the present study begins at the end of a great war and in the midst of the consequent economic and financial dislocations, postwar growth and change in mortgage debt can be seen in perspective only in the context of its long-term changing position in the nation's economy. The following brief discussion sketches the changes in mortgage debt in relation to other economic and financial magnitudes back to the turn of the century, with special consideration given to the decade following World War I.

Long-Term Position of Mortgage Debt in the Economy

At least three fundamental conclusions emerge from the summary appraisal: (1) Mortgage debt as part of the nation's economic and financial structure was relatively less important—or a relatively lesser burden—at the conclusion of World War II than in almost any year back to 1900. (2) Changes in the position of nonfarm mortage debt over the years were markedly different from those in the position of farm mortgage debt. (3) Changes in the relative position of mortgage debt during comparable periods before and after World Wars I and II, while basically similar, differed in important respects. These conclusions are supported statistically, whether mortgage debt is compared with total economic activity, total debt and private debt, real estate wealth, or total assets of financial institutions.

When World War II ended, the level of nonfarm mortgage debt was about the same as at the beginning of the war, though well above the level of earlier years on record except for the late twenties and early thirties. Farm mortgage debt had declined sharply during the war-induced farm prosperity, however, and in 1945 was lower than in any year after the beginning of World War I. Since other economic magnitudes associated with war activity had expanded sharply between 1939 and 1945, nonfarm mortgage debt was a less heavy burden on the economy at the end of World War II—as measured by its relation to GNP (Chart 2)—than in any preceding year from the turn of the century, except for 1918–1919, when the burden was about the same. It was from this low level of mortgage debt relative to GNP, therefore, that the marked postwar increase in mortgage debt began. Although the rise was steep, it did not reach the relative position attained in the prosperous late twenties and remained well below that in the mid-thirties.

In the debt structure of the nation, nonfarm mortgage debt was also relatively much less important at the end of World War II than in preceding years. The sharp relative decline from the peak of the early thirties to an all-time low by 1945 reflected almost entirely the extraordinary expansion in federal debt for government financing of new public activities during the prolonged depression and of nearly four years of total war. Even in the private debt structure, however, nonfarm mortgage debt failed to maintain its prewar position. In the post-World War II decade, the expansion in nonfarm mortgage debt, accompanied by an absolute decline in outstanding federal obligations, carried mortgage debt well above its record low 1945 position in the total debt structure, but not quite to its record high position in the late twenties and early thirties. Postwar nonfarm mortgage debt, moreover, expanded at a considerably faster rate than corporate or other types of private debt did (except consumer credit). As a result, by the end of 1956, nonfarm mortgage debt had attained a new high position in the nation's private debt structure (Chart 2).

Other evidence of the relatively low level within the nation's economic structure to which mortgage debt had fallen by the end of 1945 appears when it is compared with the value of the total stock of real estate. As Table 1 shows, 1945 ratios of nonfarm mortgage debt (total and residential) to capital values had declined to the lowest level since World War I, while comparable ratios for farm mortgage debt had reached an all-time low. These sharp declines reflected limited availability of mortgage credit during World War II and, at the same time, steadily rising capital values. The values of both nonfarm and farm real estate (including land and structures) had been maintained relative to total

CHART 2
Ratios of Nonfarm Mortgage Debt to GNP and Total and Private Debt, 1900–1956

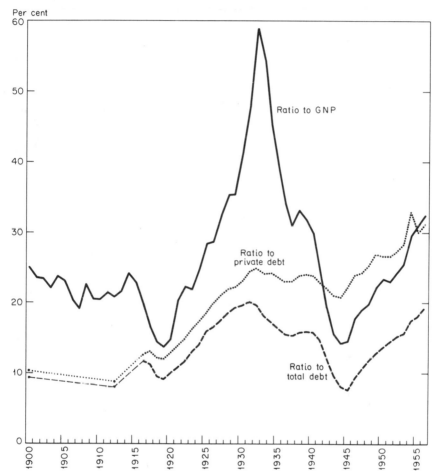

SOURCE: Ratios were calculated from data obtained from following sources: For total and private long term debt, beginning in 1916, Department of Commerce, *Survey of Current Business*, September 1953 and May 1957. For benchmark years prior to 1916, R. W. Goldsmith, *A Study of Saving in the United States*, Vol. III, Table W-9 (hereafter cited as Goldsmith, *A Study of Saving*). For nonfarm mortgage debt, 1945–56, Saul B. Klaman, *The Volume of Mortgage Debt in the Postwar Decade*, Technical Paper 13, New York, NBER, May 1958 (hereafter cited as Klaman, Technical Paper 13); before 1945, Goldsmith, *A Study of Saving*, Vol. I, Table M-3 and M-8. For GNP, 1929–1956, *Survey of Current Business*, July 1957; before 1929, Goldsmith, *A Study of Saving*, Vol. III, Table N-1. See also Table A-2 below.

TABLE 1

Real Estate Wealth and Mortgage Debt, Selected Years, 1900–1956
(amounts in billions of dollars)

End of Year	Real Estate Wealth Nonfarm			Mortgage Debt Nonfarm			Debt–Wealth Ratios, Nonfarm to:		
	Total	Resi-dential	Farm	Total	Resi-dential	Farm	Total	Resi-dential	Farm
	(1)	(2)	(3)	(4)	(5)	(6)	(7)	(8)	(9)
1900	39.1	20.1	17.8	4.4	3.0	2.3	11.3	14.9	12.9
1914	68.7	34.5	38.6	8.7	5.8	5.0	12.7	16.8	13.0
1918	118.7	59.9	57.5	11.1	7.4	7.1	9.3	12.4	12.3
1925	168.7	92.2	49.6	24.5	16.2	9.7	14.5	17.6	19.6
1929	204.7	113.6	47.1	35.8	25.0	9.6	17.5	22.0	20.4
1933	157.1	88.3	31.5	30.7	21.2	7.7	19.5	24.0	24.4
1939	180.7	109.2	32.2	29.7	21.0	6.6	16.4	19.2	20.5
1941	205.1	127.2	37.3	31.7	23.2	6.4	15.5	18.2	17.2
1945	245.1	165.8	59.8	30.8	23.3	4.8	12.5	14.1	8.0
1956	607.2	404.4	108.4	134.7	112.1	9.9	22.2	27.7	9.1

NOTES BY COLUMN:

(1), (2), and (3). All years except 1945 and 1956, from Raymond W. Goldsmith, *A Study of Saving in the United States*, Princeton, 1955, Vol. III, Table W-1, pp. 14–15. For 1945 and 1956, data are from the National Bureau's Postwar Capital Market Study, mimeographed Table W-1. Data include estimates for land as well as structures.

(4 and 5). For 1900, 1914, and 1918, Goldsmith, *A Study of Saving*, Vol. I, Table R-34, p. 627. These figures are not strictly comparable with those for later years which have been revised since Goldsmith's estimates were published. The degree of noncomparability is not great enough, however, to influence the analysis of trends. For other years through 1941 data are based on J. E. Morton, *Urban Mortgage Lending, Comparative Markets and Experience*, Table 2, p. 18, adjusted to reflect revised estimates of multifamily mortgage debt made in Saul B. Klaman, *The Volume of Mortgage Debt in the Postwar Decade*, Technical Paper 13, New York, National Bureau of Economic Research, 1958, Table 6. Data for 1945 and 1956 are from Tables 3 and 4 of that study.

(6) Department of Agriculture, *Agricultural Finance Review*, various issues. Data for 1945 and 1956 are the same as shown in *Volume of Mortgage Debt*, Table 9.

(7, 8, and 9) Calculated from cols. 1 through 6, by dividing Col. 4 by Col. 1, Col. 5 by Col. 2, and Col. 6 by Col. 3.

national wealth during the war. While the value of the nation's real estate increased substantially in the postwar decade, nonfarm mortgage debt grew at a much faster rate from its low 1945 level, bringing debt-to-value ratios to record high levels by the end of 1956. Farm mortgage debt, on the other hand, increased at about the same rate as asset values, and the ratio between them was little higher in 1956 than in 1945.

Our last measure of the relatively low level of mortgage debt in the nation's economic and financial structure at the end of World War II is presented in Table 2, which relates nonfarm mortgage holdings of major types of financial institutions to their total assets in selected years

TABLE 2

Nonfarm Mortgage Loans and Total Assets Held by Main Types of Financial
Institutions, Selected Years, 1900–1956

				Share of Nonfarm Mortgage Loans in Total Assets			
End of Year	*Total Assets*	*Nonfarm Mortgage Loans*	*Ratio, (2) to (1)*	Savings and Loan Associations	Life Insurance Companies	Commercial Banks	Mutual Savings Banks
	(1)	(2)	(3)	(4)	(5)	(6)	(7)
	(billions of dollars)				(per cent)		
1900	14.7	1.9	13.2	75.7	20.5	3.8	34.5
1914	33.4	5.1	15.2	89.2	21.0	5.4	42.3
1918	54.0	6.1	11.3	87.0	17.4	3.8	41.3
1925	81.7	15.4	18.8	90.8	23.7	7.6	50.2
1929	100.4	22.4	22.3	87.8	29.9	8.0	54.4
1933	78.2	18.5	23.7	75.3	24.3	8.7	50.7
1939	111.5	17.1	15.4	72.2	16.4	5.8	40.3
1941	128.4	19.2	14.9	79.0	16.9	5.6	40.3
1945	230.7	19.7	8.6	62.5	13.1	2.7	24.6
1956	389.7	107.3	27.5	83.2	31.8	8.5	59.1

NOTES BY COLUMN:

(1) Totals of assets of institutions shown in Cols. 4–7, which for the years 1900–1933 were obtained from Goldsmith, *A Study of Saving,* Vol. I, Tables J-2, I-5, L-24, L-30, pp. 436, 455, 409, and 417, respectively. For other years, data are from the *Federal Reserve Bulletin,* May 1958, pp. 565 and 575.

(2) Totals of nonfarm mortgage loans held by institutions shown in cols. 4–7.
1900–1933: Same Source as col. 1.
1939, 1941: Based on data shown in *Federal Reserve Bulletin,* March 1953, pp. 273–274.
1945, 1956: Klaman, *Volume of Mortgage Debt,* Table 3, p. 44.

(3) Based on cols. 1 and 2.

(4 to 7) Based on sources cited above for cols. 1 and 2.

of prosperity and depression, war and peace, from 1900 to 1956. For each of the major mortgage lenders, mortgage portfolios in 1945 were much lower relative to total assets than in any preceding benchmark year. It reflected chiefly the record holdings of federal obligations acquired by institutions during the war. It reflected, also, limited opportunities for mortgage investment, and accelerated repayment of mortgage debt by both consumers and businesses. Heavy sales of government securities and rapid acquisition of readily available and higher yield mortgage loans in the postwar years raised the ratio of mortgages to total assets for each of the four major types of financial institutions to record or near-record levels by the end of 1956. An analysis of the liquidity position of financial institutions at war's end and its influence on mortgage markets is included in Chapter 3.

Mortgage Debt before and after Two World Wars

Within the framework of longer-range developments, we can examine more closely at the relative position of mortgage debt in the economy before and after World Wars I and II. Such a comparison, pictured in Chart 3, reveals basically similar movements within comparable periods around each war but with important differences in relative positions. The divergence between movements of farm and nonfarm mortgage debt is also strikingly revealed by the chart.

Clearly, the significance in the nation's economy of nonfarm mortgage debt declined sharply during both wars but in most relationships more than recovered its prewar position a decade after the conclusion of hostilities in each case. In view of the different nature, length, and extent of United States participation in each war and the changes that occurred in the structure of the economy over four decades, the relationships and movements of nonfarm mortgage debt within the economy during the periods shown were more similar than might have been expected. Some significant differences are worth noting, however.

Relative to gross national product, for example, nonfarm mortgage debt was at the same level at the end of each world war, but the decline from the beginning of World War II was much greater and the rise in the decade after it was smaller than in comparable World War I periods. As a consequence, the apparent burden of nonfarm mortgage debt in the national economy was no greater ten years after World War II than at the beginning of that war, but was much greater ten years after World War I than at its beginning. Similarly, the decline in nonfarm mortgage debt relative to total debt during the second war was much greater than during the first. The relative rise in the post-World War II decade was, however, considerably greater than in the post-World War I decade, and at the end of each period nonfarm mortgage debt was in the same position relative to total debt.

Like nonfarm mortgage debt, farm mortgage debt declined substantially relative to other economic magnitudes during both world wars, without however, regaining its prewar position, but rather remaining in the same low position to which it had declined at the end of each war. Moreover, the relative levels in the post-World War II period were much lower than those of the post-World War I period (Chart 3).

Structure of Mortgage Debt at Beginning of Post-World War II Decade

That, however measured, mortgage debt, at the end of World War II was exceptionally low compared with earlier periods and its relative

CHART 3

Mortgage Debt in the United States Economy—Before and After Two World Wars

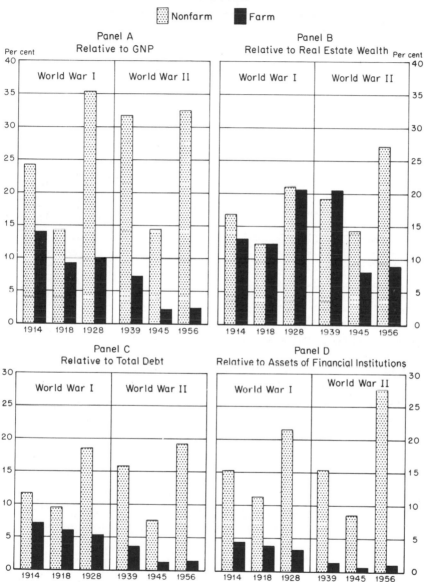

SOURCE: Data before 1945 are based on Goldsmith, *A Study of Saving*, Vols. I and III; after 1945, data are from *Survey of Current Business*; Klaman, *Volume of Mortgage Debt in the Postwar Decade*; and *Federal Reserve Bulletin*, various issues. See also Table A-3 below.

importance not much different than at the end of World War I must be borne in mind in considering the unusually large flow of funds into mortgages beginning with 1946. The interplay of economic and social forces in operation during the postwar decade, moreover, tended on balance to stimulate that flow in far greater volume than into other sectors of the capital market. The influence of these factors, including liquidity of lenders, yield differentials, federal policies, and demand for housing

TABLE 3

Structure of Mortgage Debt and Net Mortgage Flows, by
Type of Property Mortgaged, 1946–1956
(amounts in billions of dollars)

Type of Property Mortgaged	Outstanding at End of 1945		Net Flows, 1946–1956		Outstanding at End of 1956		
	Amount	Per Cent Distribution	Amount	Per Cent Distribution	Amount	Per Cent Distribution	Per Cent Increase from 1945
All properties	35.5	100	109.1	100	144.6	100	307
Nonfarm	30.8	87	104.0	95	134.7	93	338
Residential	23.3	66	88.8	81	112.1	78	381
1- to 4-family	18.6	52	80.4	73	99.0	68	432
Multifamily	4.7	13	8.4	8	13.1	9	179
Commercial	7.5	21	15.2	14	22.7	16	203
Farm	4.8	13	5.1	5	9.9	7	106

SOURCE: Klaman, *Volume of Mortgage Debt*, Tables 1 and 22.

are described in some detail in Chapter 3. Of immediate concern here is a summary appraisal of the structure of mortgage debt at the war's end —the starting point for this study—and the structural changes which occurred as a result of little more than a decade of sharp but uneven growth in the various mortgage debt sectors.

Neither the level nor the character of mortgage debt had changed much between the beginning and end of World War II—years of war restricted real estate and construction activity. Nonfarm mortgage debt had become relatively more important than farm mortgage debt by 1945 than in 1939, continuing a trend of several decades. Within the nonfarm sector, mortgage debt secured by residential properties continued as a much greater proportion than that secured by nonresidential properties, reflecting chiefly the greater aggregate value of nonfarm residential real estate and the more widespread use of the mortgage instrument to finance construction and sale of residential than of nonresidential properties. Of the $35.5 billion mortgage debt outstanding at the end of 1945, two-thirds was on residential land and structures and one-half on one- to four-family dwellings, about the same proportions as in 1939 (Table 3). Nonresidential mortgage debt amounted to one-fifth of the total amount outstanding at the end of the war, somewhat more than before the war.[1]

In the market for residential mortgages, the conventional type of loan[2] was clearly predominant at the end of World War II, comprising four-fifths of the total residential mortgage debt outstanding (Table 4).

TABLE 4

Structure of Residential Mortgage Debt and
Net Residential Mortgage Flows, 1946–1956
(amounts in billions of dollars)

Type of Residential Mortgage	Outstanding at End of 1945		Net Flows, 1946–1956		Outstanding at End of 1956		
	Amount	Per Cent Distri- bution	Amount	Per Cent Distri- bution	Amount	Per Cent Distri- bution	Per Cent Increase from 1945
Total residential	23.3	100	88.8	100	112.1	100	381
FHA	4.3	18	15.1	17	19.4	17	351
VA	0.2	1	28.2	32	28.4	25	14,100
Conventional	18.8	80	45.4	51	64.2	57	241
1- to 4-family	18.6	100	80.4	100	99.0	100	432
FHA	4.1	22	11.4	14	15.5	16	278
VA	0.2	1	28.2	35	28.4	29	14,100
Conventional	14.3	77	40.8	51	55.1	56	285
Multifamily	4.7	100	8.4	100	13.1	100	179
FHA	0.2	4	3.7	44	3.9	30	1,850
Conventional	4.5	95	4.7	56	9.2	70	104

SOURCE: Same as Table 3.

Legislation[3] authorizing the Veterans Administration to guarantee mortgages on homes purchased by veterans for owner occupancy was enacted little more than one year before the end of hostilities, and in any event only a few veterans could take advantage of it before the end of 1945. VA-guaranteed mortgages thus comprised less than 1 per cent of residential mortgage debt at the beginning of the postwar decade. One year later the proportion had increased sharply to nearly 9 per cent.

The Federal Housing Administration (FHA) mortgage insurance program, created as an antidepression measure, had been in operation for

[1] The terms nonresidential and commercial mortgage debt are used interchangeably throughout. In mortgage credit statistics, "commercial mortgage debt," is commonly used to represent "nonresidential mortgage debt" on the assumption that the bulk of all nonresidential mortgage debt is secured by commercial properties.

[2] These are loans not insured or guaranteed by the federal government.

[3] Public Law 346, 78th Congress, June 22, 1944.

over eleven years by the end of 1945. Gradually finding favor with lenders during the late thirties, FHA-insured mortgages increased steadily in importance and were given further impetus during the war as a result of special programs of mortgage insurance for defense and military housing construction. By the end of 1945, FHA-insured loans were nearly one-fifth of residential mortgage debt—a proportion about as large as any reached before by that type of mortgage.

Mortgage debt at the war's end was owned chiefly by financial intermediaries, the four main types—life insurance companies, savings and loan associations, commercial banks, and mutual savings banks—holding three-fifths of the total, a somewhat larger proportion than before the war. Among these institutions, the importance of life insurance companies —the leading mortgage investors in 1945—and commercial banks had increased sharply over that of preceding years, largely owing to the introduction of federal mortgage insurance.[4] Financial institutions other than the four main types played minor roles as mortgage investors in 1945, most of the remainder of the mortgage debt being held by individuals and other miscellaneous nonfinancial investors (Table 5).

Because of widely varying needs and preferences of investors, significant differences are found in ownership of the various types of mortgages and in the composition of portfolios of mortgage holders. Differences exist at any point in time, though the pattern of differences tends to change with changing market conditions and investor decisions. For the beginning and end of the postwar decade, differences in the participation of financial institutions[5] in mortgage markets are summarized in Tables 6 and 7. At the end of 1945, for example, financial institutions owned almost two-thirds of the nonfarm mortgage debt but little more than one-fourth of the farm mortgage debt. The farm mortgages were owned largely by federal land banks and by individuals, who often acquired them as personal investments when selling their farms. As for the nonfarm mortgage market, the participation of financial institutions as a group was much greater in residential than in nonresidential mortgages in 1945. This was so partly because of the availability of federally underwritten

---

[4] For a discussion of long-term movements in the distribution of mortgage debt by type of holder see Leo Grebler, David M. Blank, and Louis Winnick, *Captial Formation in Residential Real Estate: Trends and Prospects*, Princeton University Press for the National Bureau of Economic Research, 1956, Chapter 13; and J. E. Morton, *Urban Mortgage Lending*, Princeton University Press for NBER, 1956, Chapter 2.

[5] In the interest of brevity, and because of the relative unimportance of other types of financial institutions as mortgage investors, the term financial institutions is used here to signify only the four major types (savings and loan associations, life insurance companies, commercial banks, and mutual savings banks).

TABLE 5

Structure of Mortgage Debt and Net Mortgage Flows, by Type of Holder, 1946–1956

(amounts in billions of dollars)

Type of Mortgage Holder	Outstanding at End of 1945		Net Flows, 1945–1956		Outstanding at End of 1956		
	Amount	Per Cent Distribution	Amount	Per Cent Distribution	Amount	Per Cent Distribution	Per Cent Increase from 1945
All mortgage holders	35.5	100	109.1	100	144.6	100	307
Main financial institutions	21.0	59	90.2	83	111.2	77	430
Savings and loan associations	5.4	15	30.3	28	35.7	25	561
Life insurance companies	6.6	19	26.4	24	33.0	23	400
Commercial banks	4.8	13	17.9	16	22.7	16	373
Mutual savings banks	4.2	12	15.5	14	19.7	14	369
Federal agencies	2.4	7	3.4	3	5.8	4	142
All other holders	12.1	34	15.5	14	27.6	19	128
Mortgage companies	0.1	a	1.3	1	1.4b	1	1,832
Non-life insurance companies	0.1	a	0.1	a	0.2	a	164
Fraternal orders	0.2	a	0.3	a	0.4b	a	160
Face amount investment companies	0.1	a	0.2	a	0.3	a	232
Credit unions	a	a	0.3	a	0.3	a	708
Self-administered pension funds	a	a	0.3	a	0.3	a	1,860
Personal trust funds	1.4	4	0.1	a	1.5b	1	7
Individuals and other holders	10.3	29	12.8	12	23.2b	16	124

SOURCE: Klaman, *Volume of Mortgage Debt*, Table 2.

a Less than $50 million or less than 0.5 per cent.

b Data are for end of 1955. Estimates for 1956 holdings were not available at the time of writing but are probably close to 1955 figures.

TABLE 6

Percentage Distribution: Ownership of Mortgage Debt, by Type of Property and Mortgage, 1945-1956

Type of Property and Mortgage	All Types	Financial Institutions					All Other Holders		
		Total	Savings and Loan Associations	Life Insurance Companies	Commercial Banks	Mutual Savings Banks	Total	Federal Agencies	Other Holders
1945									
Total	100.0	59.1	15.2	18.7	13.4	11.8	40.9	6.8	34.1
Nonfarm	100.0	63.9	17.5	19.0	13.8	13.6	36.1	3.0	33.1
Residential	100.0	67.7	22.6	16.0	14.6	14.5	32.3	3.9	28.4
1- to 4-family	100.0	65.8	27.7	12.4	15.5	10.2	34.2	2.8	29.4
FHA	100.0	85.7	11.3	31.0	35.7	7.7	14.3	0.8	13.5
VA	100.0	78.0	41.0	—	30.0	7.0	22.0	—	22.0
Conventional	100.0	59.9	32.2	7.3	9.5	10.9	40.1	6.0	34.1
Multifamily	100.0	75.3	2.4	29.9	11.1	31.9	24.7	0.2	24.5
FHA	100.0	79.0	2.6	54.4	12.7	9.3	21.0	—	21.0
Conventional	100.0	75.1	2.4	28.6	11.0	33.1	24.9	0.2	24.7
Commercial	100.0	52.2	1.5	28.7	11.4	10.6	47.8	0.2	47.6
Farm	100.0	27.8	—	16.3	10.9	0.5	72.2	31.6	40.6
1956									
Total	100.0	76.9	24.7	22.8	15.7	13.6	23.2	4.0	19.1
Nonfarm	100.0	79.7	26.5	22.6	15.9	14.6	20.3	2.8	17.5
Residential	100.0	83.4	31.2	21.1	15.2	15.8	16.6	3.4	13.2
1- to 4-family	100.0	84.2	34.3	20.3	16.4	13.1	15.8	3.5	12.2
FHA	100.0	92.3	9.7	34.8	29.0	18.7	7.7	5.2	2.6
VA	100.0	88.0	23.6	25.7	13.7	25.0	12.0	7.4	4.6
Conventional	100.0	80.2	47.0	13.4	14.2	5.4	19.8	1.1	18.7
Multifamily	100.0	77.1	7.6	27.5	6.1	35.9	22.9	2.3	20.6
FHA	100.0	77.7	0.4	31.6	7.3	38.5	23.0	5.1	17.9
Conventional	100.0	76.5	10.5	25.9	5.1	35.0	23.9	2.2	21.7
Commercial	100.0	61.0	3.2	29.8	19.3	8.7	38.8	—	38.8
Farm	100.0	39.4	—	25.3	14.1	0.6	60.6	20.2	40.4

SOURCE: Klaman, *Volume of Mortgage Debt*, Tables 2 to 8, 10 to 12, 14, and 15.

TABLE 7

Percentage Distribution: Composition of Mortgage Portfolios of Main Types of Financial Institutions, 1945–1956

Type of Property and Mortgage	Selected Financial Institutions		Savings and Loan Associations		Life Insurance Companies		Commercial Banks		Mutual Savings Banks	
	1945	1956	1945	1956	1945	1956	1945	1956	1945	1956
Total	100.0	100.0	100.0	100.0	100.0	100.0	100.0	100.0	100.0	100.0
Nonfarm	93.7	96.5	100.0	100.0	88.3	92.5	89.1	94.1	99.4	99.7
Residential	75.1	84.1	98.0	93.0	55.8	72.0	71.1	74.8	80.5	89.7
1- to 4-family	58.3	75.0	95.9	95.3	34.7	61.0	60.2	71.5	45.0	65.8
FHA	16.7	12.8	8.6	4.1	19.0	16.3	30.4	19.9	7.4	14.7
VA	0.7	22.5	1.5	13.6	—	22.1	1.3	17.2	0.3	36.2
Conventional	40.9	39.7	85.8	72.6	15.7	22.6	28.5	34.5	37.3	15.0
Multifamily	16.8	9.0	2.1	2.7	21.1	11.0	10.9	3.3	35.5	23.9
FHA	0.9	2.8	0.1	a	1.9	3.8	0.6	1.3	0.5	7.7
Conventional	15.9	6.3	2.0	2.7	19.2	7.2	10.3	2.1	35.0	16.2
Commercial	18.6	12.4	2.0	2.0	32.5	20.5	18.0	19.3	18.9	10.0
Farm	6.3	3.5	—	—	11.7	7.5	10.9	5.9	0.6	0.3

SOURCE: Klaman, *Volume of Mortgage Debt*, Tables 16 to 19.

a Less than 0.5 per cent.

mortgages not eligible or suitable for investments by individuals, and partly because one of the major savings institutions—savings and loan associations—is legally and traditionally limited almost exclusively to home mortgages.

Aggregating the degrees of participation of financial institutions in the various mortgage markets obscures the wide differences that persist among them, seen in Table 6. The leading position of life insurance companies in 1945 reflected mainly their dominance in the market for nonresidential mortgages, both nonfarm and farm, and their activity in the market for multifamily residential mortgages, particularly those insured by FHA. Savings and loan associations confined their activity almost exclusively to the home mortgage market, in which they were by far the leading investor. Mutual savings banks, on the other hand, were most active as investors in multifamily mortgages, which reflected their location mainly in the East where multifamily structures are situated. In 1945, commercial banks were participating about equally in mortgages secured by all types of property but most heavily in markets for federally underwritten home mortgages.

Differences in mortgage market participation of major investors at the beginning of the decade under review are reflected in their varying portfolio composition, shown in Table 7. The specialization of savings and loan associations as conventional home mortgage lenders is clearly indicated. Commercial banks tended also to invest the bulk of their mortgage funds in one- to four-family houses, but unlike savings and loan associations divided their holdings between FHA-insured and conventional mortgages. The FHA mortgage insurance program was, as suggested earlier, a major element in the growing importance of commercial banks as mortgage lenders. Savings and loan associations, on the other hand, opposed the FHA program from the beginning, and as a group they continue to invest only a small proportion of funds in FHA-insured mortgages.[6] Life insurance companies and mutual savings banks divided their holdings more evenly than the others among mortgages secured by all major types of nonfarm properties, the former tending to favor mortgages on one- to four-family and commercial properties and the latter on one- to four-family and multifamily dwellings.

Analysis of the structure of mortgage debt by type of borrower, and hence of the demand side of the market, is hampered by the inadequacy of data on the subject. The only data available are from the Board of

---

[6] For a discussion of lending policies of savings and loan associations as well as of other financial institutions, see Chapter 6.

Governors of the Federal Reserve System on broad sectors of borrower groups. According to these admittedly rough estimates, at the end of World War II nonfarm businesses owed the largest proportion of mortgage

TABLE 8

Structure of Mortgage Debt and Net Mortgage Flows, by
Type of Borrower, 1945–1956
(amounts in billions of dollars)

Type of Borrower	Outstanding at End of 1945		Net Flows, 1946–1956		Outstanding at End of 1956		
	Amount	Per Cent Distri- bution	Amount	Per Cent Distri- bution	Amount	Per Cent Distri- bution	Per Cent Increase from 1945
All borrowers	35.5	100	109.1	100	144.6	100	307
Consumers	14.4	41	78.2	72	92.6	64	543
Nonfarm business	16.1	45	25.3	23	41.4	29	158
Corporate	7.8	22	17.0	16	24.8	17	218
Noncorporate	8.3	23	8.2	8	16.6	12	101
Farm business	4.8	14	5.1	5	9.9	7	106
Nonprofit organizations	0.2	a	0.5	a	0.7	a	250

SOURCE: Based on estimates of Board of Governors of the Federal Reserve System, *Flow of Funds in the United States, 1939–1953*, December 1955, and on internal data available at the Federal Reserve.

a Less than 0.5 per cent.

debt then outstanding, followed closely by consumers (Table 8). Farm businesses and nonprofit organizations owed only $5 billion on mortgages, or one-seventh of the total outstanding at the end of 1945.

Net Flow of Mortgage Funds in Postwar Decade

From the end of World War II through 1956, the net flow of funds into nonfarm mortgages amounted to a record $104 billion, substantially larger than the flow into any other single type of debt instrument during that period (Chart 4). The net increase in long-term corporate debt during that period, for example, was little more than half the net nonfarm mortgage flow, though both types of debt were at equally low levels at the war's end. In terms of rate of expansion, only the remarkable growth of short-term consumer credit—over 600 per cent from an exceptionally low postwar base—exceeded that of nonfarm mortgage debt.

The unusually large net nonfarm mortgage flow during the 1946–1956 period reflected in the main strong demands from consumers to finance one- to four-family houses and, during most of the period, ready availability of funds from financial intermediaries together with active market

CHART 4

Net Flow of Funds into Main Capital and Money Market Sectors, 1946–1956

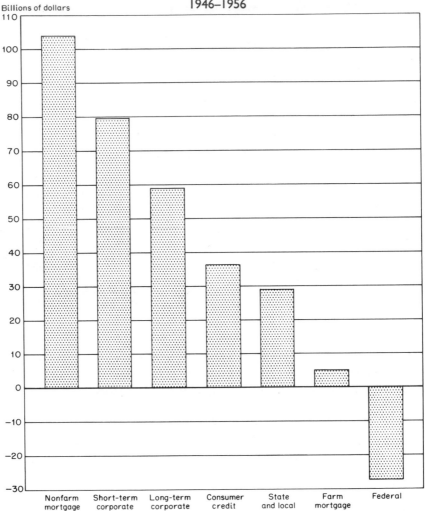

SOURCE: Data from *Survey of Current Business*, May 1957 and May 1958.

stimuli or support from federal mortgage programs and policies (see Chapter 3). Summary statistical evidence is assembled in the net flows portion of Tables 3 and 4 and in Chart 5. The $80 billion of net funds that flowed into home mortgages during 1946–1956 was ten times the net flow into multifamily mortgages and more than five times that into non-residential mortgages (Table 3). It represented nearly three-fourths of

CHART 5
Net Flow of Mortgage Funds, 1946–1956

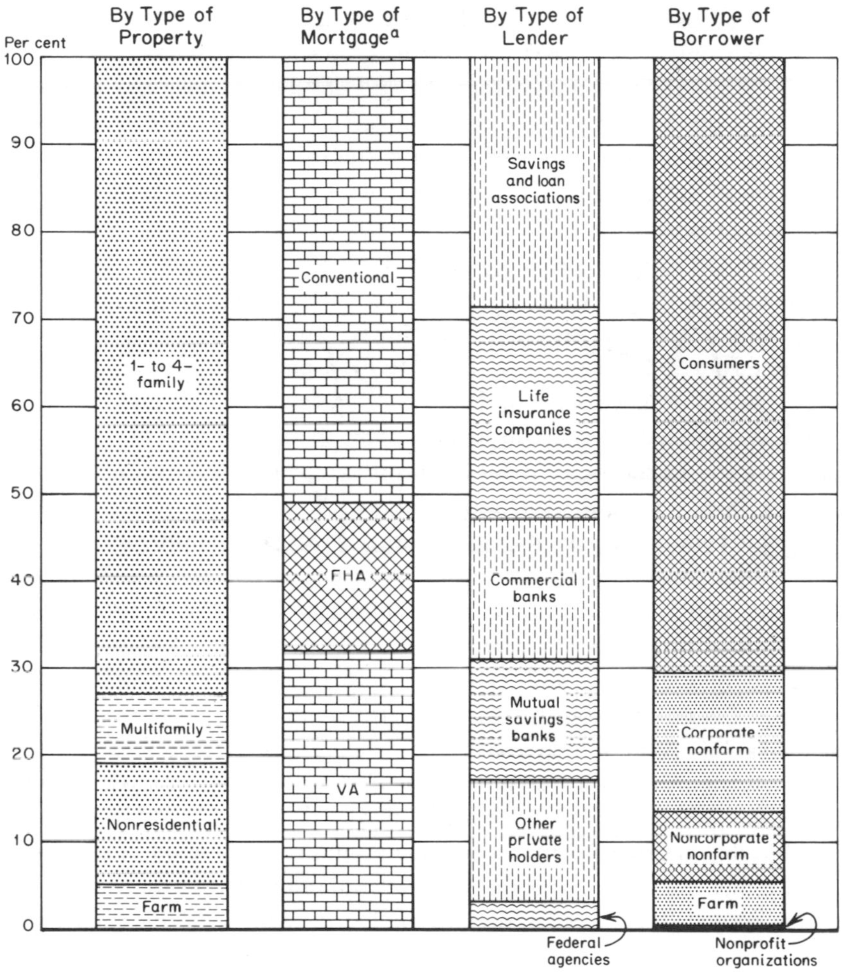

SOURCE: Data in first three bars from Klaman, *Volume of Mortgage Debt*, Tables 1 and 2. Data in last bar from Board of Governors of the Federal Reserve System, *Flow of Funds in the United States, 1939–1953*, December 1955; and internal data available at the Federal Reserve.

ᵃ Residential mortgages only.

the entire net mortgage flow in the decade and an increase of 375 per cent, more than double that for other nonfarm properties.

The record net flow of funds into home mortgages was almost equally divided between conventional and federally underwritten loans. The largest absolute net flow—over $40 billion—into any single mortgage sector went into conventional home mortgage loans, followed by $28 billion into VA-guaranteed mortgages. In terms of rate of expansion during the postwar decade, the highest by far was in VA-guaranteed loans, reflecting in large part the extremely low level at the end of 1945. Even so, the rate of increase from the end of 1946, following a ten-fold rise during the year, was still considerably greater than the entire decade's rate of growth for all but one of the other mortgage debt sectors.[7]

In view of the increased channeling of savings into financial institutions, it is not surprising that the bulk of postwar net mortgage flows—$90 billion or five-sixths—was supplied by the four main types of financial intermediaries (Chart 5 and Table 5). By far in the lead were savings and loan associations and life insurance companies, which together accounted for more than one-half of the total net mortgage flow. None of the sources of funds listed in Table 5, other than the four main types of financial intermediaries, accounted for more than 1 per cent of net mortgage lending in the years 1946–1956, although some showed a marked increase in mortgage market participation. This was true especially for mortgage companies and pension funds. Mortgage companies are, of course, fundamentally originators and servicers of mortgages rather than investors, and loans held in their portfolios represent chiefly unsold but largely committed inventory not yet taken up by final investors. The increasingly important and changing role of mortgage companies, as revealed by newly developed data, is the subject of Chapter 8 of this monograph.[8] As an ultimate investor in mortgages, pension funds were a relatively new and still insignificant source during the postwar decade. However, judging by their sharply increased mortgage activity, it is possible that pension funds will become an increasingly important lender, a possibility discussed further in the last section of Chapter 6.

Important differences in sources of funds within specific mortgage sectors were a characteristic of the postwar decade, to be observed in Table 9. Savings and loan associations, continuing in the postwar years their traditional specialized role as conventional home mortgage lenders, supplied more than half of the total funds for this type of mortgage, by far the largest proportion by any one lender in any one sector of the market. These institutions were also the most active of the participants in the market for VA-guaranteed mortgages, supplying a slightly larger proportion

[7] The exception is that of FHA-insured multifamily residential mortgages, which began its postwar rise from a 1945 level as low as that of VA-guaranteed mortgages.

[8] For a more detailed report of that study, see Saul B. Klaman, *The Postwar Rise of Mortgage Companies*, Occasional Paper 60, New York, National Bureau of Economic Research, 1959.

TABLE 9

Percentage Distribution: Net Flow of Mortgage Funds from Lenders, by Type of Property and Mortgage, 1946–1956

Type of Property and Mortgage	All Types	Financial Institutions					All Other Lenders		
		Total	Savings and Loan Associations	Life Insurance Companies	Commercial Banks	Mutual Savings Banks	Total	Federal Agencies	Other Lenders
Total	100.0	83.1	27.8	24.2	17.2	14.0	16.9	2.8	14.2
Nonfarm	100.0	84.6	29.1	23.6	17.2	14.7	15.4	2.7	12.8
Residential	100.0	87.7	33.2	22.6	16.1	15.8	12.3	3.1	9.2
1- to 4-family	100.0	88.5	35.8	22.1	17.5	13.2	11.5	3.0	8.5
FHA	100.0	94.1	8.8	35.3	27.5	22.5	5.9	6.9	-1.0
VA	100.0	87.7	27.1	25.0	15.2	23.8	12.3	7.0	5.3
Conventional	100.0	87.5	52.0	16.2	16.2	3.1	12.5	-0.9	13.4
Multifamily	100.0	78.9	7.9	27.7	3.9	39.5	21.1	3.9	17.1
FHA	100.0	78.9	a	31.6	5.3	42.1	21.1	5.3	15.8
Conventional	100.0	79.5	15.4	23.1	2.6	38.5	20.5	2.6	17.9
Commercial	100.0	65.4	3.9	29.9	23.6	7.9	34.6	a	34.6
Farm	100.0	53.5	—	34.9	18.6	a	46.5	4.7	41.9

Source: Klaman, *Volume of Mortgage Debt*, Tables 23 to 29, 31 to 33, 35, and 36.
a Less than 0.05 per cent.

than life insurance companies and savings banks of such mortgage funds.

Closest to savings and loan associations as a predominant source of funds in one sector of the mortgage market were mutual savings banks, which supplied two-fifths of the net flow of mortgage funds into multi-family residential mortgages, both FHA-insured and conventional. The active participation of savings banks as investors in VA-guaranteed mortgages reflected chiefly lending after 1949–1950, when savings banks in most states were permitted to invest in out-of-state insured and guaranteed mortgages. In the last five years of the postwar decade, mutual savings banks were the largest net investor in VA-guaranteed loans.[9]

Life insurance companies and commercial banks, financial intermediaries with entirely different purposes and functions, were the only important institutional sources of funds for nonresidential and farm mortgages. They were also the most important ultimate sources for FHA-insured home mortgages. Not only are the characteristics of the two institutions dissimilar, but so are their roles (in the aggregate) in the mortgage market. The role of commercial banks has shifted in emphasis during the postwar years from a permanent source of mortgage funds to a temporary or interim one.[10] In this respect, the role of commercial banks in the mortgage market differs not only from that of life insurance companies but also from the roles of all other savings institutions.

Investors other than the four main types of financial institutions were a major source of funds, as noted earlier, for only mortgages on farm and commercial properties. Individuals provided the bulk of the farm mortgage funds and nonfinancial corporations a large share of the nonresidential mortgage funds.

The bulk of mortgage funds supplied by financial intermediaries and others during the 1946–1956 period were borrowed by consumers to finance home purchases, a net of $78 billion. This amount was close to three-fourths of that borrowed by all economic groups in the decade and was three times the amount borrowed on mortgages by all nonfarm business. Stated differently, the net flow of mortgage funds to consumers was more than 500 per cent of their total mortgage indebtedness at the end of 1945, compared with a little over 200 per cent for nonfarm corporate business and 100 per cent for nonfarm noncorporate business. Relatively small amounts of mortgage funds were borrowed by other economic groups (Table 8 and Chart 5).

---

[9] The increased importance of mutual savings banks in mortgage markets following changes in out-of-state lending regulations is discussed more fully in Chapters 5 and 6.

[10] See Chapter 6 for a discussion of the mortgage lending policies and techniques of life insurance companies and commercial banks.

Structure of Mortgage Debt at End of Postwar Decade

More than a decade of sharp but uneven growth in the various mortgage debt sectors necessarily wrought changes in the structural organization of mortgage markets. By the end of 1956 differences had become marked in the relative importance of properties underlying mortgage indebtedness, of types of mortgages, of market participants, and of the portfolio composition of major lenders. Summary changes shown in Chart 6 outline the detailed changes given in Tables 3 through 9.

Following the much larger flow of mortgage funds for financing home construction and transfer than for other types of construction and real estate activities, one- to four-family mortgage debt increased from just over one-half to well over two-thirds of the total mortgage debt outstanding between end of 1945 and end of 1956. Such an increase in relative importance was naturally accompanied by relative declines in debt secured by all other major types of property, the sharpest decline occurring in farm mortgage debt (Table 3).

Within the one- to four-family sector, shifts in the positions of FHA-insured, VA-guaranteed, and conventional mortgages reflected in large part the attraction of VA mortgage guarantees—scarcely a market factor at the end of 1945. Little over a decade later, the amount of such home mortgage indebtedness was not far from twice that of FHA-insured home mortgage debt and more than one-half that of conventional debt. The increase in VA-guaranteed loans from less than 1 to 29 per cent of total home mortgage debt in the postwar decade compares with declines in FHA-insured one- to four-family loans from 22 to 16 per cent, and in conventional one- to four-family mortgage loans from 77 to 56 per cent (Table 4). In the financing of multifamily properties, a sharp relative increase in the use of FHA-insured loans was associated with a consonant relative decline in conventional mortgages.

Ownership of mortgage debt had become more concentrated by the end of the postwar decade, $111 billion or over three-fourths being held by the four main types of financial intermediaries compared with their holdings of $21 billion or less than three-fifths at the beginning of the period (Table 5). Each of the four types of financial institutions had increased their relative participation in mortgage markets by the end of the decade, savings and loan associations considerably more than the others. Among other market participants whose mortgage holdings can be identified, only mortgage companies had reached a position of significance by the end of the decade, owing in part to their larger than usual

CHART 6
Comparison of the Structure of Postwar Mortgage Debt,
December 31, 1945, and December 31, 1956

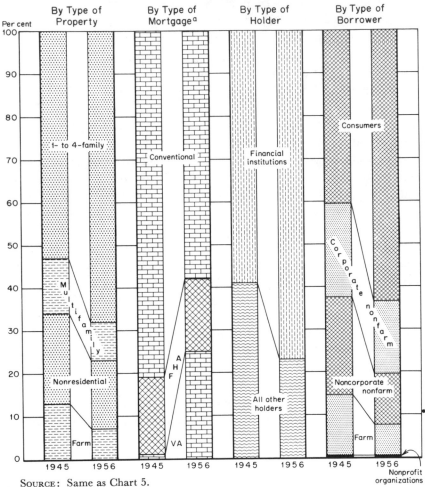

SOURCE: Same as Chart 5.

a Residential Mortgages only.

mortgage inventories relative to mortgage originations during 1955.[11]

Leading mortgage participants within the major property categories in 1945 generally maintained their positions in 1956, though there were inevitable changes in the relative degree of participation (Table 6). The more important shifts between 1945 and 1956 occurred in FHA, VA, and

[11] This situation resulted from conditions in the mortgage market in 1954 and 1955, described in Klaman, *Postwar Rise of Mortgage Companies*, pp. 55–57.

conventional residential mortgage markets and may be summarized as follows:

Sharp relative declines in

VA-guaranteed loans by savings and loan associations and commercial banks

FHA-insured multifamily loans by life insurance companies, and all FHA-insured loans by commercial banks

Conventional one- to four-family loans by savings banks, and multifamily loans by commercial banks

Sharp relative increases in

VA-guaranteed loans by savings banks and life insurance companies

FHA-insured loans by savings banks

Conventional one- to four-family loans by savings and loan associations and commercial banks

For most major types of financial institutions, postwar changes in demands made upon them for funds and in the structural organization of capital and mortgage markets led to significant changes in the composition of their portfolios during the period under study. The mounting importance of mortgage holdings relative to other assets of financial institutions, noted previously, resulted by the end of 1956 in a higher proportion of mortgages to total assets than in most preceding years for all major lenders, except savings and loan associations. Savings and loan associations also, alone among the major types of financial institutions, maintained the composition of their mortgage portfolios essentially the same in 1956 as in 1945—all but 5 per cent in one- to four-family mortgages (Table 7). The introduction of the VA mortgage guarantee program, however, reduced to some extent the concentration of their portfolios in conventional mortgage loans and cut further into the small proportion of funds invested in FHA-insured mortgages.

The most marked changes in mortgage portfolio composition occurred among life insurance companies and mutual savings banks, both shifting heavily towards one- to four-family mortgage loans. Declines in other types of mortgage holdings of the two intermediaries were distinct; the proportions of life insurance company portfolios devoted to nonresidential mortgage loans and of savings bank portfolios devoted to multifamily mortgage loans were considerably larger than those proportions for other types of financial institutions. The unusually strong attraction of VA-guaranteed loans to savings banks during the latter half of the postwar decade is manifest in their much larger proportionate investment in such loans in 1956 compared with other types of financial institutions.

Following the record flow of mortgage funds to consumers during the postwar decade, this group of borrowers owed nearly two-thirds of the total mortgage debt outstanding at the end of 1956—well over twice the amount owed by nonfarm businesses (Table 8). A decade earlier, both groups were carrying close to the same amount of mortgage debt. Other types of mortgage borrowers were indebted for an even smaller share of the total at the end than at the beginning of the postwar decade.

CHAPTER 3

Elements in the Changing Postwar
Mortgage Market

THE changed structure of mortgage debt and markets, surveyed in Chapter 2, resulted from the interplay of numerous economic, financial, and sociopolitical forces. The purpose of this chapter is to select and describe the main elements of these forces at work during the post-World War II decade. Their dynamic nature is reflected in the record of annual and quarterly changes in the flow of funds into the various sectors of the mortgage market. That record is analyzed in Chapter 5 after the basic subject of mortgage yields is explored in Chapter 4.

During most of the 1946–1956 period, the major elements, both private and federal, influencing residential mortgage market developments tended to be expansionary. During a part of the decade, however, restraining influences, also both private and public in character, acted to limit the flow of funds into mortgage markets.

In an appraisal of the major influential elements at work, the decade breaks down roughly into two equal time periods. The major turning point in the mortgage market as in other sectors of the capital market occurred in March 1951, when the Federal Reserve and Treasury reached an "accord" resulting in the withdrawal in principle of Federal Reserve support of the market for federal obligations. Several months earlier, with the outbreak of hostilities in Korea, steps had been taken by the government to limit the volume of new construction and the flow of mortgage funds, culminating in the issuance of Regulation X on real estate credit under the Defense Production Act of 1950.[1] The restraints placed by federal action on both the supply of mortgage credit and the demand for it brought to an end a unique five-year period during which, with limited exceptions, unrestrained expansionary forces had resulted in the availability of an ample supply of funds to meet large and rising demands for mortgages. While the flow of mortgage funds in the second half of the decade was substantially greater than in the first half, there was not again such an extended period of high tide in mortgage funds.

Expansionary Influences at Work, 1946–1950

With the end of World War II the stage was set for a rapid expansion in mortgage market activity, which continued almost without abatement

[1] Public Law 774, 81st Congress, approved September 8, 1950.

through 1950. Demands for mortgage credit to finance construction and real estate transactions were great; financial institutions were actively seeking new investment outlets; federal actions with respect to general fiscal and credit policies, as well as specific mortgage and housing programs, were expansionary; and mortgage yields were relatively attractive to both lenders and borrowers.

DEMAND FOR MORTGAGE CREDIT

At the war's end, the nation's needs for additional real estate facilities were acute following wartime restrictions superimposed upon the sharply reduced activity during the depressed 1930's. Families separated or dislocated during the war and requiring new accommodations, rapid demobilization of the armed forces, sharply rising marriage and birth rates, and heavy migration of population placed mounting pressure on limited housing facilities. Of the 33.5 million married couples in the United States shortly after the war's end, 3 million or nearly 9 per cent were sharing living quarters, many more in number and proportion than before the war. Uncounted other families were living in temporary, makeshift accommodations. Demands for new and improved living quarters were backed by high and rising incomes and a growing accumulation of liquid assets.

Demands for mortgage funds to finance construction and acquisition of nonresidential properties were also large, but the needs were not so pressing as those for residential facilities. A large part of nonresidential construction and transfer activity was financed from internal sources and through other sectors of the capital market, particularly the corporate bond market. Moreover, in efforts to conserve scarce materials and manpower for construction of housing, especially for veterans, federal restrictions were placed on the construction of nonresidential facilities. The restrictions remained in effect for little more than a year during the short-lived Veterans Emergency Housing Program (see the discussion of federal mortgage programs and policies, below).

LIQUIDITY OF FINANCIAL INSTITUTIONS

The flow of mortgage funds to finance production of new structures and acquisition of existing real estate in the immediate postwar years was limited more by the lack of available or newly constructed accommodations than by the supply of mortgage credit. Financial institutions found themselves in an unusually liquid position with investment portfolios heavily weighted with large holdings of U.S. government obligations.

They amounted at the end of 1945 to well over one-half of all assets held by the four main groups of financial institutions, compared with less than one-tenth for mortgages.[2] In volume of government securities held, commercial banks ranked first, followed by life insurance companies and mutual savings banks; savings and loan associations, specialized mortgage lenders, ranked last in absolute amount and also in ratio to total assets.

TABLE 10

Net Sale of Federal Government Securities and Net Acquisition of Mortgages by Four Main Types of Financial Institutions, 1946–1956
(dollars in billions)

	1946–1950			1951–1956		
	Net Sale Govern-ment Securities (1)	Net Acquisi-tion of Mortgages (2)	Ratio (1) to (2) (3)	Net Sale Govern-ment Securities (1)	Net Acquisi-tion of Mortgages (2)	Ratio (1) to (2) (3)
Selected financial institutions	36.4	30.8	118.2	12.6	59.3	21.2
Savings and loan associations	0.9	8.2	12.2	1.3	22.0	−5.9
Life insurance companies	7.1	9.5	75.8	5.9	16.9	34.9
Commercial banks	28.6	8.9	321.3	5.4	9.0	60.0
Mutual savings banks	−0.1	4.1	−2.4	2.6	11.4	22.8

SOURCE: Data from various issues of the *Federal Reserve Bulletin*.

These financial institutions were anxious to convert their large holdings of riskless but low-yielding assets into investments yielding higher returns. Moreover, outlets for the flow of new savings were needed to replace the purchase of government securities that had dominated the wartime capital markets. The Federal Reserve policy of supporting government bond prices at par made possible the sale of such securities readily and without penalty. As a result, sales of Treasury obligations proceeded rapidly during the period of support, providing a large reservoir of funds to meet private capital demands.

The $36 billion acquired from sale of government securities by financial institutions during the first five postwar years exceeded their total net acquisition of mortgages (Table 10). The large volume of funds was supplemented by an almost equally large net savings inflow of $33 billion. For commercial banks and life insurance companies the sale of

[2] Based on data from various issues of the *Federal Reserve Bulletin*.

governments provided the major source of investment funds; for mutual savings banks and savings and loan associations savings inflows were the major source. Variations in the pattern of investment behavior among the four types of financial institutions (Table 10) were the outcome of a number of important factors, legal and organizational as well as financial (discussed later in Chapter 5, the section on mortgage flows relative to other capital market flows). Briefly, while only commercial banks showed net acquisition of mortgages less than net sale of government securities through 1950, a large but unmeasurable amount of commercial bank funds flowed into construction and interim financing loans. Thus, the unusual liquidity of commercial banks permitted a larger volume of permanent financing by other institutions than might otherwise have been possible.

FEDERAL MORTGAGE PROGRAMS AND POLICIES

In a setting of ready availability of investment funds from financial institutions, the federal government took a series of steps successively liberalizing both its VA and FHA mortgage guaranty and insurance programs. In addition, several bold new housing and mortgage under-writing programs were inaugurated, and expanded secondary mortgage market facilities were provided. These actions, in conjunction with the federal policy of supporting government bond prices at par, created a financial climate in which mortgage loans were especially inviting to financial institutions in comparison with other capital market investments.

That the federal government has come to play a unique and strategic role in housing and mortgage markets is widely recognized. In no other sector of the private capital market—or of the entire nonfarm economy, for that matter—is there such broad federal participation as there is in mortgage markets. A study of postwar mortgage finance would be incomplete, therefore, without an analysis of major federal actions taken in the area since the end of the war. Legislative or administrative details, however, that are adequately provided in several cited sources, are not given here.

The guns of World War II had scarcely been silenced when the federal government took the first of several direct actions to stimulate the flow of funds into the mortgage sector of the capital market. At the end of 1945, the Servicemen's Readjustment Act of 1944[3] was amended to make VA-guaranteed loans more acceptable to both lenders and borrowers, as well as builders. Principally, the amendments provided for (1) an increase in

---

[3] P.L. 346, 78th Congress, approved June 22, 1944.

the maximum amount of government guarantee from $2,000 to $4,000, (2) an extension of maximum maturities from twenty to twenty-five years, and (3) a change in the basis of property appraisal from "reasonable normal value" to simply "reasonable value." In addition, the act authorized supervised lenders to extend VA-guaranteed loans to eligible veterans without prior approval by the Veterans Administration.[4]

In efforts to further stimulate production of housing and extension of mortgage credit for veterans, the Veterans Emergency Housing Program was put into effect in May 1946, restoring wartime construction controls and renewing liberal wartime FHA mortgage insurance provisions under Title VI of the National Housing Act.[5] Under the reactivated FHA mortgage program, property appraisals were based on the concept of "necessary current cost" rather than "value," and maximum insurable loan amounts were raised on both owner occupied and rental properties. Twice extended beyond its original expiration date, the program was finally allowed to expire on April 30, 1948. Four months later, however, with the enactment of the Housing Act of 1948, the FHA "emergency" program was reactivated until March 31, 1949, for new rental housing only (section 608 of the National Housing Act). That program was further liberalized by authorization of higher maximum insurable mortgage amounts.[6]

The Housing Act of 1948 was based on the theory that production of housing could be increased by stimulating both the demand for mortgage funds and their supply. The act, therefore, in addition to reactivating part of the FHA Title VI program, liberalized prewar terms of the permanent FHA mortgage insurance program under Title II by authorizing increases in maximum insurable loan amounts, loan-to-value ratios, and maturities. It provided, further, for special new programs of mortgage insurance and, perhaps most important in stimulating the flow of FHA and VA mortgage funds, it increased the ability of the Federal National Mortgage Association (FNMA) to purchase federally underwritten mortgages.[7]

Activities of FNMA, and government actions taken to influence them, have played a key role in the postwar mortgage market, almost entirely

[4] P.L. 268, 79th Congress, approved December 28, 1944.

[5] See Miles L. Colean, *The Impact of Government on Real Estate Finance in the United States*, New York, National Bureau of Economic Research, 1950, p. 106, for a discussion of the Veterans' Emergency Housing Program.

[6] The Veterans Emergency Housing Act proved a dismal failure and most of its provisions were discontinued by mid-1947.

[7] A more detailed description of the provisions of this act pertaining to FHA mortgage insurance may be found in the Federal Housing Administration's *Fifteenth Annual Report*, December 31, 1948, pp. 1–4. A summary of all major provisions of the act is given by Colean, *op. cit.*, pp. 124–125.

an expansive one during the first half of the decade. The first major action in that direction was taken on July 1, 1948 (one month before passage of the Housing Act of 1948) when this federally sponsored secondary mortgage market facility was completely reorganized under a new charter. The result was a greatly enlarged capacity to purchase mortgages, authority to purchase VA as well as FHA loans and to issue advance commitments to purchase them.[8] The new charter was intended to stimulate the flow of VA loans, which had been declining from its high 1947 level, partly as a result of the widening spread between rising interest rates on U.S. government and other securities and the fixed 4 per cent rate on VA loans (see Chart 6 and Chap. 5, pp. 113–114). The intended stimulus was largely nullified, however, by the restrictive provision permitting the Association to purchase only one-fourth of the dollar amount of FHA and VA loans originated by a lender. The provision was liberalized one month later in the Housing Act of 1948 to permit purchase up to one-half of the eligible mortgages originated by a lender. Little more than one year later, liberalization reached its peak with statutory authority to purchase all eligible VA loans originated by a lender.

The steady extension of FNMA's purchasing authority, the continuation of its authority to make advance commitments to purchase mortgages, and its administrative policy of purchasing all mortgages at par brought the Association a steadily increasing mortgage portfolio and placed the statutory limit on its holdings under constant pressure. The willingness of Congress to increase the limit steadily, however, maintained FNMA as an effective support to the mortgage market throughout the first half of the postwar decade. In a period of little more than nine months, through April 1950, maximum permitted mortgage holdings were increased three times—to $1.5 billion, to $2.5 billion, and to $2.75 billion. About two years later, in July 1952, a final increase to $3.75 billion was authorized.

The last increase came well after Congress had recognized that FNMA had become a prime generator of mortgage funds and had attempted to limit the drain on the Treasury in the Housing Act of 1950 by rescinding the Association's authority to make advance commitments.[9] The need to increase further FNMA's purchasing authority two years later arose from

[8] P.L. 864, 80th Congress, enacted July 1, 1948. Under its original charter granted in February 1938, FNMA was authorized to purchase only FHA loans and had a maximum borrowing authority of $220 million (increased to $840 million by the July 1 Act). For a time the Reconstruction Finance Corporation (RFC) Mortgage Company was authorized to purchase VA loans (August, 1946–June, 1947) but little use was made of this facility. From June 30, 1947, when RFC was terminated, until July 1, 1948, no federally sponsored secondary market facility existed for VA loans.

[9] P.L. 475, 81st Congress, enacted April 20, 1950.

the continued large volume of mortgage purchases made under earlier outstanding commitments (see the section of Chapter 7 dealing with the Federal National Mortgage Association).

The Housing act of 1950 was the final major piece of federal legislation to influence mortgage markets in the first half of the postwar decade. On balance, the act tended to stimulate further mortgage market activity by making VA and FHA mortgages more attractive to both lenders and borrowers.[10] VA guarantees were increased from '50 per cent and a ceiling of $4,000 to 60 per cent and a ceiling of $7,500, with the maximum maturity extended from twenty-five to thirty years. The Veterans Administration, furthermore, was given new authority to make direct mortgage loans on terms equal to those on its guaranteed loans in areas where the latter were not available from private lenders.

The authority of the Federal Housing Administration was also expanded by the Housing Act of 1950 to include two new mortgage insurance programs with liberal terms, one for small houses in rural communities and outlying areas and another for cooperative housing projects.[11]

Mortgage Markets in a Changing Setting, 1951–1956

The economic, financial, and sociopolitical setting in which mortgage markets functioned changed abruptly following the outbreak of war in Korea. While it underwent further change in later years of the post-World War II decade, the pre-Korea scene was already history. Federal programs and policies were no longer directed towards unqualified stimulation of activity. The almost unlimited liquidity enjoyed by financial institutions through the earlier price support of government securities —which for the individual lending institution made them almost interchangeable with cash—was sharply reduced by changes in federal monetary and fiscal policies. Demands for residential building and real estate, though less urgent than in earlier postwar years, continued generally strong through the second half of the decade and for a time were under

[10] The only nonliberalizing provision included in this act, in addition to the rescinding of FNMA's advance commitment authority, was the withdrawal of authority for the VA to guarantee small second mortgage loans in conjunction with FHA-insured first mortgage loans.

[11] Less than one year before passage of the Housing Act of 1950, another special purpose program was born when FHA was authorized to insure mortgages on very liberal terms for rental housing built on or near military installations (under a new Title VIII added to the National Housing Act by P.L. 211, 81st Congress, approved August 8, 1949). In 1949, also, the authority of FHA to insure mortgages on new rental housing (under the liberal section 608 program), due to expire on March 31, 1949, was extended on four different occasions and finally allowed to expire on March 1, 1950. FHA was actually authorized to continue issuing commitments under that program on applications for insurance submitted on or before March 1, 1950.

direct restraint by federal actions. Demands for industrial facilities, for consumer goods, and for municipal improvements were also large during much of the period after 1950.

In that framework, total demands on private capital and credit markets at times exceeded the available supply of funds, including commercial bank credit. As a consequence, during periods when interest rates and yields were rising because of competition for limited funds, the attractiveness to investors of federally underwritten mortgages having inflexible interest rates waned in favor of conventional mortgages and other capital market securities with completely flexible rates (see Chapter 4 for discussion of mortgage yields and Chapter 5 for analysis of shifting mortgage flows).

MORTGAGE MARKETS UNDER RESTRAINT, 1951–1953

For approximately three years after the beginning of Korean hostilities, mortgage markets were under some federal restraint, either directly by restrictive policies or indirectly by credit and monetary actions. Later, with the lifting of direct federal government restrictions, mortgage markets operated in an atmosphere alternating between credit ease and restraint, influenced by general credit and monetary policies, private capital market conditions, and the re-establishment of most of the pre-Korean federal mortgage terms and practices. In that new environment, further structural changes in mortgage markets occurred as lender reactions varied; borrowers adjusted to or withdrew from the market, and mortgage underwriting terms were alternately tightened and relaxed.

Early Post-Korean Restrictions

The Korean war started at a time when rising economic and financial activity in the United States had already reached unusually high levels. Demands for real estate and construction had expanded to the point where they were straining the nation's productive capacity and resulting in rapid increases in prices, wages, and costs. By mid-1950, even though production of building materials and construction employment were at record levels, shortages of materials and labor and consequent disorganization of markets were common. In this setting, broad restrictive actions were taken by the federal government to dampen inflationary pressures and to conserve resources necessary to the successful prosecution of the war. In construction and real estate markets, terms on which mortgage credit could be made available were restricted and nonessential construction and the use of materials were limited.

Within one month after the start of Korean hostilities, in response to direct requests of the President, the Federal Housing and Veterans Administrations took restricted terms on which they would insure and guarantee mortgage credit, and the Federal Home Loan Bank system adopted restrictive measures for member savings and loan associations. Though fairly mild, they were the first restrictive actions taken by those agencies in nearly twenty years of federal intervention in real estate and mortgage markets. The most important were increase by 5 percentage points of downpayments required on FHA and VA loans, setting construction costs prevailing on July 11, 1950 as the maximum for appraisal purposes, and reduction from $16,000 to $14,000 of the maximum FHA insurable loan on one-family houses.[12]

Measures directly limiting nonessential construction, use of materials, and limiting price increases followed in a short time. Administered by newly created or reconstituted defense agencies—National Production Authority, Office of Price Stabilization, and Wage Stabilization Board—the measures were carried out through direct prohibition of certain types of construction, requirement of authorization for other types, priorities on basic and scarce materials for nondefense uses, and regulation of prices and wages in the construction industry. The techniques of operation, frequently changed, became stabilized by mid-1951 under the Controlled Materials Plan which allocated to users the three basic metals—steel, copper, and aluminum. Supplementary "M" or limitation orders were also directed towards the reduction of nonessential production.[13]

Selective Regulation of Real Estate Credit

Federal actions restricting nonessential construction use of materials were authorized by the Defense Production Act of 1950. For mortgage markets, an added—perhaps heightened—significance of the Act lay in presidential authority to regulate nonguaranteed or noninsured real estate credit. Under Executive Order No. 10161, that authority was

[12] Other actions included requirements for higher downpayments in FHA Title I modernization and repair loans, for narrowing of allowable uses of VA direct loan funds, and for application of VA gratuity payments to the reduction of mortgage loan principal. Formerly the gratuity payment to veterans of 4 per cent of the guaranteed portion of a loan up to $160 could be used for any payments due on a purchased house. Its original purpose was to provide one year's interest on the guaranteed portion of a veteran's mortgage loan. The gratuity was discontinued as of September 1, 1953, by P.L. 149, enacted July 27, 1953.

[13] For a review of post-Korean restrictions on real estate credit and construction see two articles in the *Federal Reserve Bulletin:* "Construction Activity and Mortgage Credit," August 1950, pp. 936–937; and "Residential Real Estate Under Controls," August 1951, pp. 908–912.

delegated to the Board of Governors of the Federal Reserve System, with the stipulation that the Board "obtain the concurrence of the Housing and Home Finance Administrator with respect to provisions relating to real estate construction credit involving residential property before prescribing, changing or suspending any real estate construction credit regulation pursuant to the authority of the Defense Production Act of 1950."

Accordingly, Regulation X, the first selective control ever applied to real estate credit, was issued by the Board of Governors (effective October 12, 1950) with the concurrence of the Housing and Home Finance Administrator. Simultaneously, restrictions conforming to Regulation X were placed on FHA-insured and VA-guaranteed mortgage credit on new one- and two-family dwellings. On January 12, 1951, Regulation X was broadened to include new multifamily units and nonresidential commercial structures (office buildings, warehouses, stores, banks, hotels, motels, garages, restaurants).[14] The regulation did not restrict credit granted on existing properties, except FHA and VA loans, where it applied to both existing and new properties.

Regulation X and accompanying FHA and VA regulations were designed to reduce the demand for real estate credit, and thereby the volume of new construction and real estate transactions, by restricting the terms on which mortgage loans could be made (see Table 11). Minimum downpayments and rates of amortization together with maximum maturities were prescribed. The underlying formula allowed for a schedule of downpayments according to prices of houses. Longer maximum maturities, though not on a graduated basis, were permitted on loans secured by lower-priced houses, but no maximum maturities were specified on multifamily properties. All loans on nonresidential construction subject to Regulation X conformed to existing lending practices and administrative practicability—a maximum of 50 per cent of the value o f the property and a maturity up to twenty-five years.[15]

Successive modifications of terms prescribed by Regulation X followed, either by administrative or legislative authority.[16] In each case, changes

---

[14] *Real Estate Credit, Regulation X,* as amended effective February 15, 1951, Board of Governors of the Federal Reserve System, p. 6.

[15] Board of Governors of the Federal Reserve System, *The Regulation of Real Estate Credit Under the Defense Production Act of 1950,* prepared at the request of the Office of Defense History, Bureau of the Budget, Executive Office of the President (mimeographed), February 24, 1953, p. 11.

[16] Amendments No. 1, No. 6, and No. 11 to Regulation X described in *Federal Reserve Bulletin,* March 1951, p. 271, September 1951, p. 1132, and June 1952, pp. 650–651. See also the Defense Housing and Community Facilities and Services Act of 1951.

TABLE 11

Terms of Mortgage Lending Under Regulation X
(conventional and FHA-insured mortgages)

| | 1- TO 4-FAMILY PROPERTIES | | | | | | MULTIFAMILY PROPERTIES | | | |
| | Oct. 12, 1950 to Sept. 1, 1951 | | Sept. 1, 1951 to June 11, 1952 | | June 11, 1952 to Sept. 16, 1952 | | Jan. 12, 1951 to June 11, 1952 | | June 11, 1952 to Sept. 16, 1952 | |
TRANSACTION PRICE PER FAMILY UNIT	Maximum Loan Amount	Loan-to-Value Ratio	Maximum Loan Amount	Loan-to-Value Ratio	Maximum Loan Amount	Loan-to-Value Ratio	Maximum Loan Amount	Loan-to-Value Ratio	Maximum Loan Amount	Loan-to-Value Ratio
$5,000	$4,500	90.0	$4,500	90.0	$4,750	95.0	$4,150	83.0	$4,500	90.0
8,000	6,450	80.6	6,800	85.0	7,050	88.1	6,340	79.2	6,850	85.6
10,000	7,700	77.0	8,500	85.0	8,550	85.5	7,400	74.0	7,950	79.5
12,000	8,900	74.2	9,600	80.0	9,650	80.4	8,460	70.5	9,030	75.2
14,000	10,100	72.1	10,400	74.3	10,750	76.8	9,520	68.0	10,110	72.2
16,000	10,900	68.1	11,000	68.8	11,750	73.4	10,250	64.1	11,150	69.7
18,000	11,300	62.8	11,400	63.3	12,650	70.3	10,650	59.2	12,150	67.5
20,000	11,700	58.5	11,800	59.0	13,550	67.8	11,050	55.2	13,150	65.8
22,000	11,900	54.1	12,000	54.5	14,250	64.8	11,450	52.0	13,890	63.1
25,000	12,500	50.0	12,500	50.0	15,000	60.0	12,500	50.0	15,000	60.0
Over 25,000	—	50.0	—	50.0	—	60.0	—	50.0	—	60.0

SOURCE: *The Regulation of Real Estate Credit Under the Defense Production Act of 1950*, prepared at the request of the Office of Defense History, Bureau of the Budget, Executive Office of the President, February 24, 1953, Table 1, p. 119.

Maximum loan maturities permitted on one- to four-family properties from October 12, 1950 to September 1, 1951 were twenty-five years up to $7,000 value and twenty years for all other properties. Liberalization of terms on September 1, 1951 provided for twenty-five year maturities up to $11,000 value and twenty years for higher-priced properties. No maximum maturities were specified for loans on multifamily properties.

On loans for new construction of nonresidential properties, terms under Regulation X for all dates were a maximum loan of 50 per cent of value and maximum maturity of twenty-five years.

Terms on VA-guaranteed mortgages generally provided for loan-to-value ratios 5 percentage points higher in the lower and upper price ranges, and 10 percentage points higher in the middle price range. Maximum maturities permitted were the same as for FHA and conventional loans. Terms for VA loans were in accord with the general authorization in the Defense Production Act for preferential treatment of veterans' loan applications.

relaxed terms because of special needs associated with housing in defense areas or because of recognized inequities in various price and income groups. Finally, on September 16, 1952, just short of two years after they were first imposed, came suspension of credit restrictions under Regulation X and most of those under FHA and VA regulations in accordance with provisions of the Defense Production Amendments of 1952. The act of June 30, 1952 (the expiration date of Regulation X) extended for one year the Regulation's authority and provided further for a "period of residential credit control relaxation," during which downpayment requirements could not exceed 5 per cent of the transaction price. The period was to begin after three consecutive months with housing starts below a seasonally adjusted annual rate of 1.2 million. Production of housing having remained below that number during June, July, and August, 1952, the Board of Governors of the Federal Reserve System suspended Regulation X as of September 16, 1952.

Accompanying the suspension of Regulation X, restrictions on terms of FHA and VA loans were removed except for the requirements of a minimum downpayment of 5 per cent, a maximum maturity of twenty-five years, and a maximum FHA loan amount of $14,000 on one-family houses.[17] By April 1953, with the further abatement of inflationary pressures, all remaining credit restrictions were revoked, and statutory terms of mortgage lending were restored to the levels before October 12, 1950.

Program of Voluntary Credit Restraint

During most of the Regulation X period, a general voluntary credit restraint program, encompassing extension of real estate credit, was also in effect. General authority "to encourage financing institutions to enter into voluntary agreements and programs to restrain credit" was included in the Defense Production Act of 1950 and delegated by the President to the Board of Governors of the Federal Reserve System. In announcing the new program, the Board requested all institutions to extend credit in ways that would "help maintain and increase the strength of the domestic economy through the restraint of inflationary tendencies and at the same time to help finance the defense program and the essential needs of agriculture, industry and commerce."[18]

[17] The restrictions applied chiefly to VA loans, which before the credit regulations could be made with no downpayment and for as long as thirty years. Now for VA-guaranteed loans on houses priced between $7,000 to $8,400, a 4 per cent downpayment was required. On houses priced below $7,000, no downpayment on loans was required but closing costs up to 4 per cent of the price had to be paid in cash.

[18] "Program for Voluntary Credit Restraint," *Federal Reserve Bulletin*, March 1951, p. 263.

One standard proposed by the Board to cooperating institutions was to screen loan applications not only for credit-worthiness but also by criteria of purpose and uses of loans. As a general criterion for sound lending, the Board's view was that each loan should "commensurately increase or maintain production, processing and distribution of essential goods and services."[19]

The program was implemented by the National Voluntary Credit Restraint Committee, including representatives of commercial banks, life insurance companies, mutual savings banks, savings and loan associations, and investment banking firms. The national committee coordinated the work of a system of committees, among them, regional committees composed of representatives of participating financing institutions in divergent geographic areas. For the guidance of the regional committees in dealing with inquiries of financial institutions about particular applications for credit, the national committee issued a statement of principles and various bulletins on recommendations developed for specific types of credit.[20]

For real estate credit, recommendations were limited to transactions outside the scope of Regulation X—chiefly loans on existing properties and sale-leaseback arrangements on commercial and industrial properties. Recommendations followed a general principle of the national committee, that the function of the program was not "to make the transfer of real estate impossible or impracticable, but rather to reduce inflationary pressures by limiting the amount of additional credit created in the process of real estate transfer."[21] Financial institutions were urged to limit real estate loans to keep total mortgage debt outstanding on any property within the larger of two amounts, two-thirds of its value or the limits imposed by Regulation X on such new construction.[22] Application of the principles of the program was strongly recommended also to certain kinds of property leasing. The committee urged recognition of the fact that leasing arrangements, when used in connection with existing construction of all types and with new construction of commercial or industrial buildings, were sometimes used as substitutes for mortgage financing. Some examples of such leasing arrangements cited by the committee were

[19] *Ibid.*, p. 264.
[20] *Monetary Policy and the Management of the Public Debt, Their Role in Achieving Price Stability and High-Level Employment,* replies to questions and other material for the use of the subcommittee on general credit control and debt management, Joint Committee on the Economic Report, 82nd Congress, Part I, p. 433.
[21] Bulletin No. 4 of the Voluntary Credit Restraint Committee, "Loans on Real Estate," *Federal Reserve Bulletin,* July 1951, pp. 752–753.
[22] *Monetary Policy and the Management of the Public Debt,* p. 436.

"sale-leaseback arrangements, long-term leases which may be renewed for a nominal rental, and leases in which the lessee has the right to have rental payments applied to the purchase price in a subsequent exercise of an option to buy the leased property."[23]

The voluntary credit restraint program was suspended May 12, 1952 (four months before the suspension of Regulation X) by the Board of Governors in accordance with a recommendation of the national committee.[24] Legal authority for the program was repealed June 30 with the enactment of the Defense Production Act Amendments of 1952, which provided "that no voluntary program or agreement for the control of credit shall be approved or carried out. . . ."[25]

Some indication of the impact of selective real estate credit regulations on the flow of funds into various mortgage sectors is given in Chapter 5, pp. 126–128. The delayed decline in mortgage flows into new construction indicate the time lags in effectuating the post-Korean restrictions. They resulted partly from the unusually large volume of mortgage commitments outstanding and were in part the usual lags associated with real estate activity (see Chapter 7, pp. 175–176). The subsequent decline in mortgage lending, moreover, must be attributed largely to the concurrent operation of a restrictive monetary policy and only in part to selective credit regulations. Though the direct impact of real estate credit controls is not measurable, there can probably be little doubt that, among those in operation, the voluntary credit restraint program was the least effective. The real estate credit area covered by the program—conventional mortgage loans on existing houses—expanded steadily during the period of voluntary credit restraint, while other types of real estate credit declined. In part this may have reflected the voluntary nature of the program and in part the fact that, with all other areas of residential real estate credit under legal restraint, the one nonlegally regulated area was stimulated.

While the voluntary credit restraint program appears to have been ineffective in real estate markets, there is no way to determine whether the extension of conventional mortgage credit on existing houses would have been even greater in its absence. The question remains also whether general monetary restraints would have been so effective in the absence of the selective regulation of real estate credit through Regulation X and associated FHA and VA regulations.

[23] Bulletin No. 4, *Federal Reserve Bulletin*, January 1952, p. 24.
[24] "Suspension of Program for Voluntary Credit Restraint," *Federal Reserve Bulletin*, May 1952, p. 501.
[25] *Federal Reserve Bulletin*, July 1952, p. 772.

Monetary and Debt Management Policies and Liquidity of Financial Institutions

A turning point in postwar capital market developments was the change in federal monetary and debt-management policies, set forth in the joint announcement (March 4, 1951) by the Secretary of the Treasury and the Chairman of the Board of Governors of the Federal Reserve System. Both authorities had "reached full accord with respect to debt-management and monetary policies to be pursued in furthering their common purpose to assure the successful financing of the Government's requirements and, at the same time, to minimize monetization of the public debt."[26] The agreement resulted in the withdrawal of inflexible Federal Reserve support of the government securities market, and thus for the first time in the postwar period permitted market forces to determine prices and yields of those securities.

Concurrently, the Treasury announced a new offering of long-term nonmarketable bonds bearing a $2\frac{3}{4}$ per cent coupon in exchange for outstanding $2\frac{1}{2}$ per cent Treasury bonds of 1967–1972. One intention of the action was to discourage long-term investors from liquidating their holdings of government securities. In that new market framework, mortgage lenders could no longer look to their government securities portfolio as a ready source of funds for acquisition of mortgages. Indeed, for some months after the announcements of the accord and new Treasury offering, lenders were unwilling to sell their government securities at the reduced prices then prevailing. Hence funds available for new mortgage financing shrank as the large volume of mortgage commitments made earlier absorbed such funds available from other sources.

As demands for credit and capital continued to press upon the supply of savings during the two years following the accord, monetary and debt-management policies were directed towards the restraint of bank credit expansion and minimizing of debt monetization. By early 1953, the Federal Reserve had raised the discount rate to 2 per cent from the early 1951 low of $1\frac{3}{4}$ per cent, and the Treasury had issued a new long-term bond bearing a $3\frac{1}{4}$ per cent rate. In the face of generally rising interest rates and yields, federally underwritten mortgages with less flexible rates became unattractive to investors with alternative uses of funds. In May 1953, maximum interest rates on FHA and VA loans were increased to $4\frac{1}{2}$ per cent, a level more in line with returns on competitive investments.

Some indication of the reduced liquidity of financial institutions in

---

[26] *Federal Reserve Bulletin*, March 1951, p. 267.

the years following the "accord" is given in Table 10. Though the main types of financial institutions still owned a large volume of U.S. government bonds at the time of the accord—some $87 billion—they disposed of less than $13 billion between 1951 and 1956. This was only about one-third of the net amount sold in the first half of the postwar decade. It was, moreover, only about one-fifth of the net acquisition of mortgages in the second half, 1951–1956. In that period, therefore, in contrast to the preceding five years, it was the net inflow of savings for all types of financial intermediaries that provided the major source of funds for mortgage investment. Among the major types of financial institutions, there were marked differences in liquidity and investment behavior, just as there were in the first half of the postwar decade. The analysis of these differences will be taken up in Chapter 5.

Reduction in FNMA Support of the Mortgage Market

Reinforcing the limitations of mortgage market activity through direct and indirect credit restraints, so far noted, were a series of administrative and statutory actions reducing the broad support of the Federal National Mortgage Association. The advance commitment authority of the Association had already been repealed in April 1950, and contracts to purchase new mortgages were being made on an "over-the-counter" basis only. Further actions circumscribing FNMA support during the next three years included: (1) the requirement that mortgages, to be eligible for purchase, must be insured or guaranteed by FHA and VA and held by the originator, all within specified time limits; (2) reduction in the proportion of its loans that could be sold to FNMA by a lender; (3) allocation of funds for purchase of mortgages under emergency housing programs, reducing the amount available for general market support; and (4) suspension of purchases of mortgages not covered by those special programs.[27]

The first action, involving time limitations, was taken June 29, 1951, when FNMA announced that it would confine its purchases to mortgages insured or guaranteed on or after March 1, 1951, and held by the originator for not less than two months or more than one year. The motive underlying it was to prevent possible large-scale disposal of mortgages by lenders in order to fulfill earlier mortgage commitments or to purchase securities, following the Federal Reserve-Treasury accord and subsequent capital market changes. The second, allocation of funds for special housing, occurred during the next six months. FNMA set

---

[27] "FNMA in the Postwar Mortgage Market," *Monthly Review of Credit and Business Conditions*, Federal Reserve Bank of New York, December 1955, p. 160.

aside a total of $600 million of its uncommitted funds for the purchase of mortgages on emergency types of housing programmed by the Housing and Home Finance Administrator in critical defense areas, for military use under Title VIII of the National Housing Act, and for victims of major disasters.[28] In addition, the Association was authorized to issue advance commitments to purchase such mortgages in an amount not to exceed $200 million outstanding by the end of 1951.[29] By the end of March 1952, less than $50 million was available for the purchase of mortgages not on defense, military, or disaster housing.

In early April, with the complete exhaustion of uncommitted funds, FNMA took its third action, suspending purchase of mortgages not covered by special federal programs.[30] Purchases were resumed in early September of that year, following passage of the Housing Act of 1952. Its authorization of $900 million for advance FNMA commitments to purchase mortgages on defense, military, and disaster housing freed the remaining $362 million reserved for such purchases to be spent for other types of mortgages. Resumption of purchases outside the special federal programs by FNMA, however, restricted lenders to sale of not more than half their eligible FHA and VA mortgage loans made after March 1, 1952.[31] Previously lenders could sell to FNMA all of the VA loans they had originated during a specified period.

The additional relatively small amount of funds made available to FNMA for purchase of mortgages on nondefense and nondisaster housing was soon exhausted, and in early April 1953, the Association again suspended those purchases until the reorganization of FNMA under a new charter on November 1, 1954. Nondefense and nondisaster mortgages, however, again became eligible for purchase in July 1953, under a new "one-for-one" program authorized by the Housing Amendments of 1953.[32] The inauguration of that program brought to an end a period of about two years during which FNMA had provided little or no support to the mortgage market.

[28] Funds were set aside by administrative action for housing on three separate occasions: July 16, 1951, $350 million (FNMA Bulletin No. 185); August 31, 1951, $50 million (FNMA Bulletin No. 192); and October 2, 1951, $200 million (FNMA Bulletin No. 198).

[29] P.L. 139, 82nd Congress, approved September 1, 1951.

[30] *Background and History of the Federal National Mortgage Association*, Federal National Mortgage Association, April 30, 1955 (multilithed) p. 31.

[31] P.L. 531, 82nd Congress, approved July 14, 1952. This act also raised the advance commitment authority of FNMA to purchase defense, military, and disaster mortgages to $1,152 million. Previously the commitment authority had been increased to $252 million by Public Law 309, 82nd Congress, approved April 9, 1952.

[32] P.L. 94, 83rd Congress, approved June 31, 1953. The "one-for-one" program is discussed in the next section.

RESUMPTION OF EXPANSIONARY FORCES, 1953–1956

With the abatement of inflationary pressures, the Federal Reserve moved vigorously in the spring of 1953 to reverse its earlier policy of credit restraint. The first open-market purchases of Treasury securities in May were followed by purchases in June, August, and September to supply additional reserves to the banking system. In July, moreover, the Federal Reserve reduced bank reserve requirements on net demand deposits. In December, the Federal Open Market Committee declared its policy to be the promotion of economic growth and stability "by actively maintaining a condition of ease in the money market."[33] This policy was continued through most of 1954, implemented by reductions in the Reserve Bank discount rate in February and April, additional open market purchases in late spring, and a further lowering of member bank reserve requirements around mid-year.

Accompanying the Federal Reserve policy of "active ease," a supply of funds in excess of demand generally characterized financial markets during 1954. With the mild recession also, the net flow of savings into financial intermediaries increased at an accelerated rate and debt repayments were large. The volume of new corporate securities available to investors, on the other hand, was well below the 1952–1953 peak as plant and equipment expenditures declined. Moreover, net borrowings of the federal government were sharply reduced in 1954 and no long-term bonds were offered. Short-term credit demands by businesses and consumers were also markedly reduced in that year.

The interaction of reduced credit demands and increased availability of funds resulted in a marked general decline in interest rates and yields in financial markets. The competitive position of mortgages, therefore, especially federally underwritten mortgages, was considerably improved. Mortgages regained favor as investment media for financial intermediaries, and they made funds available through 1954 and into 1955 on far more favorable terms than in preceding years.

Coincident with the developing ease in financial markets from mid-1953 through 1954, federal actions were directed specifically towards broadening and stimulating housing and mortgage markets. In April 1953, remaining restrictions on FHA and VA loans, imposed in October 1950, were removed by administrative action, and on June 30 statutory authority to restrain such credit under the Defense Production Act of 1950 expired. Maturities up to previous statutory maxima were again permitted, for FHA loans twenty-five years (thirty years in some cases for loans on small

[33] Board of Governors of the Federal Reserve System, *Fortieth Annual Report*, 1953, Appendix, "Record of Policy Actions, Board of Governors," p. 101.

houses) and for VA loans, thirty years. Further, minimum downpayments on houses purchased with VA loans were no longer required. With the earlier suspension of Regulation X and the Voluntary Credit Restraint Program, mortgage markets thus were completely free of restrictions for the first time in nearly three years.

Moreover, to improve the competitive position of federally underwritten mortgages in the capital market, maximum interest rates of 4 per cent previously permitted on VA-guaranteed and $4\frac{1}{4}$ per cent on most FHA-insured home mortgage loans were increased in early May 1953, to $4\frac{1}{2}$ per cent. This action followed several months of reduced availability of funds for FHA and VA loans in the face of rising yields on alternative investments.[34] Under the housing amendments of 1953, maximum interest rates on other FHA home loans were increased (June 30). More important for its basic effect on mortgage markets was an amendment of earlier legislation, permitting builders and sellers to absorb discounts associated with the sale of VA-guaranteed mortgages. Thus VA loans could compete more effectively in the capital market with other loans and securities whose rates were flexible.[35] Other provisions of the Housing Amendments of 1953 made it possible for FNMA to participate more actively in mortgage markets by authorizing the Association to use, for the general purchase of mortgages, part of the $900 million reserved a year earlier for purchases of defense, military, and disaster mortgages only, and by establishing the "one-for-one" program. Under that program, FNMA was permitted to enter firm agreements with purchasers of its mortgages to buy an equal amount of eligible mortgages from such purchasers within one year. Armed with firm FNMA commitments to purchase permanent residential mortgages, builders and mortgage originators were able to obtain interim short-term financing for construction projects that probably would not be otherwise obtainable.[36]

[34] The FHA increase was authorized, effective May 2, by the Commissioner of the Federal Housing Administration, as permitted under the National Housing Act. The VA increase was authorized, effective May 5, by the Administrator of Veterans Affairs, with the approval of the Secretary of the Treasury, as provided for in the Housing Act of 1948.

[35] See Chapter 4 for a more complete discussion of mortgage interest rates and yields and the history and operation of mortgage discounts.

[36] The Federal National Mortgage Association placed the "one-for-one" program in operation on July 27, 1953, with a total purchasing authority of $500 million. It established sales prices of 96 per cent of par on VA 4 per cent loans, 97.75 on FHA $4\frac{1}{4}$ per cent loans, and par for the then recently authorized $4\frac{1}{2}$ per cent FHA and VA loans. Purchases of mortgages under that program—limited to FHA and VA loans bearing $4\frac{1}{2}$ per cent interest rates—were at par, less total charges of $1\frac{1}{2}$ per cent. The charges included 1 per cent for the FNMA advance contract to purchase plus $\frac{1}{2}$ per cent for acquisition and service costs on mortgages actually purchased. (See "Residential Real Estate Developments," *Federal Reserve Bulletin*, August 1953, p. 814.)

The use made of the one-for-one program by the mortgage and building industries appears in figures showing that sales from FNMA's mortgage portfolio increased sharply in late 1953 and advanced to a postwar peak in spring of 1954. The $500 million authorization was exhausted before the scheduled expiration of the program on July 1, 1954. At the same time, with the easing of mortgage markets, FNMA was not called upon to honor all of its commitments to purchase mortgages, and some $70 million of such commitments expired unused.[37]

The Housing Act of 1954 authorized additional federal actions to stimulate further the demand for and supply of residential mortgage credit.[38] The actions authorized included liberalization of the FHA mortgage insurance program and of the terms of loans by federal savings and loan associations as well as establishment of the Voluntary Home Mortgage Credit Program. Brief descriptions of these and other related provisions of the act will suffice here.

Liberalization of terms under which the Federal Housing Administration could insure mortgages on both new and existing properties included: raising the maximum amount of loans on one- and two-family dwellings from $16,000 to $20,000; increasing the maximum loan-to-value ratios on new properties from 90 to 95 per cent and on existing properties from 80 to 90 per cent; and lengthening maximum maturities from twenty-five to thirty years. The difference between mortgage terms on new and existing properties, formerly substantial, was nearly eliminated by the act. The FHA program was further broadened and liberalized by a new provision of far more liberal terms for insurance of mortgages on homes for servicemen than for civilians.

Federal savings and loan associations were permitted to increase the maximum amount of their home mortgage loans from $20,000 to $35,000. Supplementing this provision of the act, the Federal Home Loan Bank Board authorized, December 1954, member savings and loan associations to lengthen mortgage loan maturities from twenty to twenty-five years.

The Voluntary Home Mortgage Credit Program was designed to encourage private lenders to make funds available for federally underwritten mortgages on housing located in small and remote communities where local capital or loan facilities may be inadequate. The services are available to minority groups in any area on terms as favorable as for others. Its national committee and sixteen regional committees composed of representatives of the mortgage industry receive applications from prospective

[37] "FNMA in the Postwar Mortgage Market," p. 160.
[38] P.L. 560, 83rd Congress, enacted August 2, 1954.

mortgage borrowers, just described, and attempt to place mortgage loans with voluntary participating lenders. The primary objective of the program is to minimize or obviate the need for direct federal mortgage lending.

The same objective—ultimate substitution of private for federal ownership of mortgages—underlies another major but not liberalizing provision of the act, which authorized the reorganization of FNMA. Under its new charter, FNMA was directed to reorganize its structure into three separate and distinct operations providing for: (1) a secondary market for federally underwritten residential mortgages; (2) special assistance for financing selected types of mortgages originated under special housing programs; and (3) management and liquidation of its mortgage portfolio held or acquired pursuant to contracts entered into under its previous charter.[39]

While the Housing Act of 1954 had a significant influence on residential mortgage markets in later years, it played no part whatever in the expansion that occurred during the second half of 1954. At the time, the view was widely held that the expansion was the direct result of the liberalizing provisions of the act. It is clear, however, that the 1954 rise in mortgage and housing activity was limited almost entirely to the VA sector of the market; the 1954 Housing Act provided no change in VA mortgage terms. The act liberalized terms only of FHA loans, and the volume of such loans showed little change during 1954.[40] The increase in FHA mortgage flows a year later, mainly for financing existing houses, is traceable in large part to the liberalizing provisions of the Housing Act of 1954 (see Chapter 5, p. 129).

MORTGAGE MARKETS ONCE AGAIN UNDER RESTRAINT, 1955–1956

The pace of business activity began to quicken in late 1954 and continued strongly upward during 1955. Demands for credit by business, consumers, and governments to finance expenditures for plant and equipment, durable goods, and public projects increased to record levels. The demands strained capital and money markets and also the productive resources of the nation. A rapid upturn in interest rates, costs, and prices followed during 1955. In the construction industry cost and price advances came after nearly three years of remarkable stability. In that rapidly developing inflationary setting, federal actions were turned once

---

[39] See Chapter 7, section on Federal National Mortgage Association, for a fuller discussion of the reorganization of FNMA. See also "FNMA in the Postwar Mortgage Market," pp. 161–162.

[40] See Saul B. Klaman, "Effects of Credit and Monetary Policy on Real Estate Markets, 1952–1954," *Journal of Land Economics*, August 1956, pp. 246–247.

again toward restraining demands for mortgage credit and supply of it and toward limiting credit expansion generally.

Thus, during the closing years of the first postwar decade, activity in mortgage markets was again under restraint as in 1951–1953. There were important differences between the two periods, however, in the nature of the restraints operating. Throughout most of the earlier period, both general credit and monetary policies and specific federal mortgage programs and policies were directed towards restraint; during most of 1955 those policies were coordinated, but during 1956 they operated in opposite directions. As mortgage credit became increasingly stringent during 1955, the federal government reversed its policy of restraint in administering mortgage programs. During 1956, all major administrative and statutory actions were directed chiefly towards easing the tightness that had developed in mortgage markets. As the year and the decade ended, however, the effectiveness of the policies proved to be limited in the face of continuing strong demands for both short- and long-term loans, the effects of restrictive Federal Reserve credit and monetary policy, and the resulting rising interest rates and yields on corporate, state and local, and federal government securities.

Coordinated Actions Restraining Mortgage Activity

As the general business recovery accelerated, the Federal Reserve gradually modified its policy of "active ease" in effect through most of 1954. In its directive of December 7, 1954, the Federal Open Market Committee declared its policy to be promotion of economic growth and stability "by maintaining a condition of ease in the money market."[41] The word "actively," included in the policy directive of December 15, 1953 (see page 66) was deleted, and the new policy was designed to restrain inflationary tendencies. Between April and November 1955, four increases in the Reserve Bank rediscount rate raised it from $1\frac{1}{2}$ per cent to $2\frac{1}{2}$ per cent. Open market operations limiting bank credit expansion were initiated around early August. An increasingly restrictive monetary policy in 1956 brought the rediscount rate to 3 per cent by late summer, the highest in nearly twenty-five years.

Supplementing the monetary actions of the Federal Reserve, the federal mortgage insurance and guaranteeing agencies acted to restrain demands for mortgage credit. Effective April 28, 1955, the Federal Housing Administration and Veterans Administration required that all

[41] Board of Governors of the Federal Reserve System, *Forty-first Annual Report*, 1954, Appendix, p. 98.

closing costs for houses purchased with FHA and VA loans be paid in cash.[42] This meant that for VA mortgages the "no downpayment loan," (in total amount, with closing costs, exceeding the appraised value of the property) was eliminated. Shortly thereafter, both federal agencies increased minimum downpayments by 2 percentage points and reduced maximum loan maturities from thirty to twenty-five years.[43]

In mid-July, the Federal Home Loan Bank Board joined other federal agencies attempting to limit mortgage credit expansion by urging savings and loan associations to curb their forward commitments to make loans. This advice was followed, September 13, by requests to each Federal Home Loan Bank "to advise its member institutions to follow a loan program which will meet loan demands out of savings and loan repayments."[44] Savings and loan associations had been relying more than usually on borrowings to finance their expanded mortgage lending programs. By the end of summer advances from Federal Home Loan Banks amounted to a record $1.2 billion compared with less than $700 million a year earlier. The Federal Home Loan Banks had, in the meantime, increased interest rates to member associations in line with rates on funds borrowed in the capital market.

Reversal of Federal Mortgage Policies

Before 1955 had ended, federal mortgage policies were reversed and through 1956 were directed towards stimulation of market activity. On December 13, 1955, the Federal Home Loan Bank Board eased somewhat the restrictions imposed in September. It permitted member institutions to borrow funds for mortgage lending in amounts not to exceed 10 per cent of savings capital.[45] In January 1956, the Federal Housing Administration and Veterans Administration rescinded their previous reduction of loan maturities and restored the maximum maturities to thirty years.[46] The Federal National Mortgage Association announced an optional mortgage repurchase plan allowing, for a 1 per cent fee, repurchase within nine months of mortgages sold to FNMA at the selling price.[47] Institutions

[42] Veterans Administration, Information Service, press release, April 27, 1955; Federal Housing Administration, 1955 Annual Report of Housing and Home Finance Agency, p. 45.

[43] Veterans Administration Information Service, press release, July 30, 1955; Federal Housing Administration, press release No. 55–57, July 31, 1955.

[44] Federal Home Loan Bank Board, press release, September 13, 1955.

[45] Federal Home Loan Bank Board, press release, December 13, 1955.

[46] Veterans Administration Emergency Interim Issue (EM 4AB-128) and Federal Housing Administration letter to all approved mortgagees, January 17, 1956.

[47] FNMA press release No. 202, January 25, 1956.

could thus obtain temporary funds for new lending without permanently disposing of favorable mortgage holdings.

Administrative actions were supplemented by the Housing Act of 1956, which in the main liberalized the terms of FHA mortgage insurance and FNMA secondary market programs.[48] Loan-to-value ratios on which FHA would insure mortgages on existing one- to four-family houses were made equal to those on new houses. On multifamily rental housing both loan-to-value ratios and maximum loan amounts were increased. The Act authorized FNMA to reduce from 3 to 2 per cent the amount of stock to be bought by sellers of mortgages to FNMA, and to 1 per cent under certain conditions. It authorized FNMA to issue "standby" commitments for one year to purchase mortgages—a practice introduced earlier by financial institutions.[49] Further statutory action at about the same time extended the VA loan guarantee program for World War II veterans until July 1958, with provision for loan applications on hand to be covered up to July 1959. For Korean War veterans the VA loan guarantee program was extended to January 1965.

The federal government continued to attack the tight mortgage credit situation on both the demand and supply fronts in a coordinated action announced by the White House, September 1956. The FHA reduced downpayment requirements on houses appraised at $9,000 or less for mortgage insurance purposes. The Federal Home Loan Bank Board increased the amount of advances member institutions could have outstanding from Federal Home Loan Banks from 10 to 12.5 per cent of their savings capital. The Federal National Mortgage Association, in addition to reducing the amounts of stock to be purchased by those selling mortgages to the Association from 2 to 1 per cent of the value of mortgages sold, raised the purchase price of its standby commitments from 92 to 94 per cent of par. The new price was not far below the bottom of the range of FNMA purchase prices for immediate delivery. In addition, in order to maximize its support of the market for new houses, FNMA announced (November 1956) limitation of its purchases under the secondary mortgage market program to mortgages insured or guaranteed no earlier than four months before the proposed sale to the Association.[50]

[48] P.L. 1020, 84th Congress, August 7, 1956.

[49] See Chapter 7, section on Mortgage Commitment Techniques, for a discussion of the standby commitments. Essentially, they are given by a financial institution in consideration of the nonrefundable fee associated with such commitments. The commitment price is so far below the prevailing market price that the institution does not expect to be called upon to fulfill it.

[50] FNMA press release No. 227, November 23, 1956.

Notwithstanding the many Federal actions, funds for federally under-written mortgages continued to be difficult to obtain because of their competitive interest rate disadvantage. Reflecting demand pressures in all sectors of the capital market, yields on long-term corporate, municipal, and government securities had advanced rapidly to new postwar highs during 1956 (Chapter 4, Chart 7). To make insured mortgage loans more attractive to investors in this situation, the Federal Housing Administration increased their permitted maximum interest rate from $4\frac{1}{2}$ to 5 per cent, effective December 4, 1956.[51] The increase was the first since May, 1953, when interest rates on both FHA and VA loans were increased. The Veterans Administration had no administrative authority to increase further the interest rate on VA loans, however, which remained at $4\frac{1}{2}$ per cent as 1956 ended. The general subject of mortgage interest rates is dealt with in Chapter 4.

[51] Federal Housing Administration, press release No. 56–59, December 1, 1956. The permitted maximum interest rate for mortgages insured on multifamily housing (FHA Section 207 loans) and on cooperative housing (FHA Section 213 loans) was increased from $4\frac{1}{4}$ to $4\frac{1}{2}$ per cent.

The Postwar Pattern of Mortgage Interest Rates

THE course of mortgage interest rates and its relationship to the flow of mortgage funds are referred to in most chapters of this report. Separate treatment is given here to that subject, so fundamentally important to an understanding of postwar market developments. The influence of shifting market forces on mortgage flows has often been transmitted through changes in mortgage interest rates and yields and in their relationship to yields of other capital market securities.[1] Little current information on these points has been available, and obtaining data is difficult because of the complexities of interrelationships between mortgage interest rates, other mortgage terms, and the demand and supply of mortgage funds. Obviously, such gaps in our knowledge of this important area cannot be filled by what follows. We may hope that a future broad-scaled study of interest rates, as suggested by the National Bureau, will include the mortgage field. Meanwhile, a beginning is made here by presentation of new data on conventional mortgage interest rates, by examination of the effects of discounts on FHA and VA loans, and by analysis of the relationship of changes in mortgage yields to changes in the flow of mortgage funds.

Course of Conventional Mortgage Interest Rates

When this study was undertaken, neither monthly nor quarterly series on conventional residential mortgage interest rates were available on a current basis, and the few regional annual series suffered from many shortcomings.[2] Within the limited resources of the present study, new quarterly data on conventional mortgage interest rates were obtained, covering home and income properties separately. Their important limitations are due primarily to their source—the experience of but a few major

[1] The term interest rate generally refers to the rate specified in the mortgage contract; the term yield refers to the actual return to lenders based on the prices at which mortgages and securities are purchased in the market.

[2] Long-term interest rate series covering all types of real estate in Manhattan, the Bronx, Chicago, and St. Louis were included in the study, *Capital Formation in Residential Real Estate: Trends and Prospects*, by Leo Grebler, David M. Blank, and Louis Winnick, Princeton University Press for National Bureau of Economic Research, 1956. Only the data for Manhattan and St. Louis extended beyond 1940. Because the series are limited in geographic coverage and cover all types of real estate, interpretation becomes difficult. Other limitations of the series are discussed in Chapter 15 and Appendix O of that study, which also includes a general analysis of the long-term relationships between mortgage interest rates, general interest rates, and residential building.

life insurance companies. But, as noted later in the chapter, the series tie in well with broader annual series developed for earlier years by the National Bureau. Moreover, because of significant geographic differentials between mortgage interest rates (see the last section of this chapter), a hypothetical national series is represented better by a few large life insurance companies, which acquire conventional loans throughout the country, than it would be by larger numbers of other types of lenders whose mortgage lending activity is concentrated locally. The series to follow, therefore, notwithstanding significant qualifications, do provide a reasonably accurate measure of the general levels and movements of conventional mortgage interest rates which can be studied in relation to yields on other capital market securities in the postwar decade.

AMPLITUDE OF CONVENTIONAL MORTGAGE INTEREST RATE MOVEMENTS

Quarterly conventional mortgage interest rates on one- to four-family houses, as shown in Chart 7, fluctuated within a fairly narrow range of between 4.35 and 5.09 per cent, from 1946 through 1956. For major types of bonds, the amplitude of fluctuation during the period was substantially greater, not only relatively but even absolutely: for outstanding corporate bonds (2.49 to 3.68), U.S. government bonds (2.14 to 3.30), and municipal bonds (0.96 to 2.86). This finding of the relative amplitude of mortgage interest rates and bond yields in the postwar decade agrees generally with those of Grebler, Blank, and Winnick on movements during half a century.[3] The relative difference in the amplitude of fluctuation in the short postwar period was, however, much smaller than in the longer period from the turn of the century. Also in general agreement with findings of that study is the conformity of broad movements in mortgage rates and bond yields in reflecting the pervasive influence of capital market conditions. A significant additional fact revealed by the new quarterly series, however, is the consistent lag in the movements of mortgage interest rate changes behind those of changes in bond yields. Both the narrowness of fluctuations in mortgage interest rates and the lag in reaction to changes in capital market conditions reflect basic differences in mortgage market techniques and characteristics compared with those of other capital markets.

Other explanations of differences in amplitude of fluctuation have been advanced. The explanation given by Grebler, Blank, and Winnick relies in large part on the fact that the mortgage interest rate series refers to loans *made*, while the bond yield series they used refers to *outstandings*.

[3] *Ibid.*, p. 223.

CHART 7

Interest Rates and Yields on Mortgage Loans and Other Capital Market Securities, Quarterly, 1946–1956

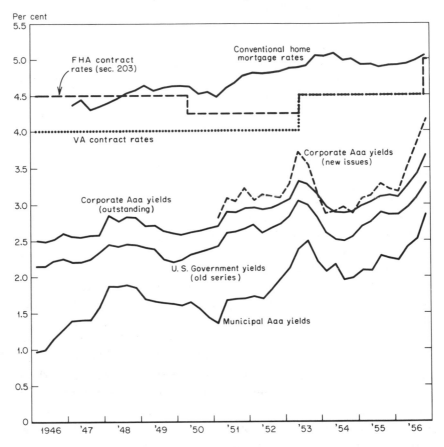

SOURCE: Data on corporate Aaa, municipal Aaa, and U.S. government securities are quarterly averages of monthly yield figures. The U.S. government bond series consists of fully taxable, marketable 2½ per cent bonds due or first callable after twelve years, through Sept. 30, 1955, and those due or callable in ten to twenty years, beginning Oct. 1, 1955. The series on outstanding corporate and municipal yields are from Moody's Investor Service; and on U.S. Governments is from the *Federal Reserve Bulletin*.

The new corporate issues series begins in 1951, from the First National City Bank of New York, and represents high grade corporate bonds adjusted to Aaa basis. Data on FHA and VA mortgage interests rates are the maximum legal rates established by statute or administrative decision. Data on conventional home mortgage interest rates are a weighted average of contract rates on loans closed by two life insurance companies from 1947 to 1951 and by two additional companies from 1951 to 1956. The series is affected little whether it is based on data from two or four companies because of close agreement in interest rate data among the reporting companies. See also Table A–4 below.

Changing market conditions can effect outstanding bonds, they conclude, only through price or yield. On new mortgage loans the effect can take the form of changes in other related factors including "loan-to-value ratios, appraisals, contract terms, noninterest costs, and the ratio of loan rejections, as well as contract interest rates. Also, since the data show contract interest rates rather than yields on mortgages, they fail to reflect changes in premiums and discounts on mortgage loans, at times important in the mortgage market."[4]

One implication of their explanation—that a yield series on new bond issues would move more narrowly than one on outstandings—is not borne out by yield data on new corporate bond offerings. The new corporate issues series shown in Chart 7, for example, fluctuated more widely during 1951–1956 than the series on outstanding corporate issues did. This observation conforms to the generally accepted view that, for most capital market securities, yields on new issues are more sensitive to market developments than are outstandings. The explanation of the narrower amplitude of mortgage interest rates compared to bond yields must lie, therefore, in the basic differences between the two types of debt instruments and between the markets in which they are negotiated and traded.

Markets characterized generally by close pricing are those in which highly standardized commodities are traded. Price is the main point of negotiation. The market for Aaa corporate issues is a good example. Most of the terms associated with public offerings—provisions for callability, sinking funds, and refundability—follow a fairly standardized pattern. In long-term bond issues, furthermore, the question of specific maturity, that is, whether repayment is to be in twenty or thirty years is of little consequence. Moreover, by definition, the credit of the borrower offering an Aaa series and usually the size of loan are not in question.

As we move away from standardized to more differentiated markets and commodities the number of variables, in addition to price, to be negotiated multiplies. In the market for direct placement of corporate securities, for example, there are more terms to negotiate than in the market for public offerings. The market for residential mortgages is an example of the most differentiated, because few markets are characterized by more one-of-a-kind deals. The credit of each borrower must be established, and "credit worthiness" becomes a function of the relative tightness of capital markets. Numerous contract terms other than price are subject to individual negotiation—downpayment requirements, amortization provisions, contract maturities, prepayment penalties, and noninterest costs. The nature

[4] *Ibid.*, p. 223.

and location of the particular residential unit securing the mortgage, moreover, are important factors in a mortgage transaction.

All these elements are more sensitive than the mortgage interest rate is to changes in financial market conditions. Downpayment and maturity provisions are particularly responsive, as reflected, for example, in the wide swings in the availability of no-downpayment thirty-year VA loans between periods of market ease and tightness. The greater responsiveness of such contract terms compared with that of interest rates stems from institutional factors also. The "stickiness" of conventional mortgage rates manifests one institutional factor, the local orientation of mortgage markets, in which a "going rate" of exactly 5 or 6 per cent, for instance, becomes accepted and changes only slowly. In mortgage markets, furthermore, there is no counterpart of the investment banker who works closely with the borrower on narrow underwriting margins, and achieves fine-drawn pricing through discounts and premiums. The mortgage lender dealing directly with borrowers rarely resorts to discounts and premiums, and seldom changes contract interest rates by less than one-fourth of a percentage point and often by not less than one-half. Moreover, the fee or premium, often paid by a lender to a mortgage broker or originator for "finding" loans, does not show up in a contract interest rate series, but is included as one of the administrative costs. For reasons growing out of market and technical peculiarities, therefore, fairly substantial and more prolonged changes in financial conditions are required to bring about changes in conventional mortgage interest rates.

The element of administrative costs, noted above, has its own place in the relative stickiness of mortgage rates. In general, the larger such costs are relative to the interest rate the more stable the interest rate is likely to be. The reason is simple: a minimum margin must be maintained between the interest rate and a lender's fixed administrative costs to assure him a reasonable return. The same reason accounts for the high and unvarying rates on consumer credit—high costs of administering a portfolio of consumer loans. Similarly on residential loans, administrative costs of acquisition, servicing, and record keeping, perhaps 75 basis points compared to 10 on corporate securities, create a relatively stable state in residential mortgage interest rates.[5]

LAG IN MORTGAGE INTEREST CHANGES

Changes in mortgage interest rates lagged consistently behind changes in bond yields throughout the postwar decade. Moreover, in each cycle

---

[5] I am indebted to Roger F. Murray for helpful discussion of the basic reasons for differences in behavior between mortgage and other long-term yields.

the timing of the lag has been generally the same—about four quarters. This timing pattern differs little whether the comparison is between mortgage interest rates and yields on outstanding or on new bond issues. Considering the imperfections in the data, the consistency of pattern is remarkable, even though some of the cyclical differences may be obscured by quarterly averages.

The timing of peaks and troughs for the various types of capital market securities, evident from Chart 7, is pinpointed in Table 12. Except for

TABLE 12

Turning Points in Interest Rates and Yields on Capital Market Securities
(quarterly averages of monthly data)

		PEAKS (quarters)			
		Corporate Bonds		U.S. Government Bonds	Municipal Bonds
Cycle	Mortgages	Outstandings	New Issues		
First	1949-I	1948-I	—	1948-I	1948-III
Second	1954-II	1953-II	1953-II	1953-II	1953-III

LAG IN MORTGAGE RATES BEHIND BOND YIELDS
(number of quarters)

First	—	4	—	4	2
Second	—	4	4	4	3

		TROUGHS (quarters)			
		Corporate Bonds		U.S. Government Bonds	Municipal Bonds
Cycle	Mortgages	Outstandings	New Issues		
First	1951-I	1950-I	—	1949-IV	1950-I
Second	1955-III	1954-III	1954-I	1954-III	1954-III

LAG IN MORTGAGE RATES BEHIND BOND YIELDS
(number of quarters)

First	—	4	—	5	4
Second	—	4	6	4	4

SOURCE: Figures are based on data shown in Chart 7.

municipals, outstanding bond yields reached their first postwar peak in the first quarter of 1948 compared with the first quarter of 1949 for mortgage interest rates. The subsequent decline in bond yields continued to a low around the first quarter of 1950 and was accompanied by little change in mortgage rates. Later the rates declined to a low in the first quarter of 1951. A new marked rise in bond yields, following the "accord" (see Chapter 3, section on monetary and debt management policies and liquidity of financial institutions), culminated in a mid-1953 peak for both new and outstanding issues (except municipals), while the advance in mortgage interest rates did not come to an end until mid-1954. The downward phase of the second cycle, for all but the new corporate issue series, ended in a third quarter 1954 trough, again four quarters before the trough in mortgage interest rates was reached.[6]

In the changed money market environment after late 1954, bond yields—on both new and outstanding issues—rose sharply through 1956 and apparently continued to rise through the third quarter of 1957. Mortgage interest rates rose much less sharply through 1956. Evidence from lenders (although actual data for 1957 are not at hand) suggests that the advance in rates gained momentum in 1957 and was still in progress as the year ended. The pattern of the first postwar decade suggests that the rise probably continued through the third quarter of 1958.

The lag of about four quarters in mortgage interest rate changes behind bond yield changes reflects the institutional structure of mortgage interest rates and the greater responsiveness to market conditions of changes in other mortgage terms, discussed earlier. Important also is the influence of the commitment technique, fundamental to the mortgage lending process. The technique, described and appraised in Chapter 7, generally involves arrangements to provide mortgage credit in the future under terms and conditions prevailing at the time the commitment is made. Interest rates on mortgage loans closed, therefore, are those in effect several months before disbursement of funds. Because life insurance companies use the commitment method more extensively than other types of lenders do in disbursing their funds, the lag of interest rate series behind bond yields, shown in Chart 7, is probably greater than that of a series based on loans closed by banks or savings and loan associations. Alternatively, an interest rate series based on current mortgage loan commitments would show a considerably shorter time lag.

COMPARISON OF INTEREST RATES ON HOME AND INCOME PROPERTY LOANS

The data obtained in this study on conventional mortgage interest rates for income properties—somewhat thinner than those for homes—may be

[6] The trough for new corporate issues is not quite clear with both the first and fourth quarters of 1954 at about the same low level, separated by a small rise in the interim quarters. In part, the movement reflects technical problems in the series.

used only as a broad guide to level and movements. The series shown in Chart 8 includes chiefly loans on large-scale apartment buildings and high-quality commercial properties (office buildings, shopping centers).

CHART 8
Conventional Mortgage Interest Rates on Home and Income Property Loans Closed, Quarterly, 1951–1956

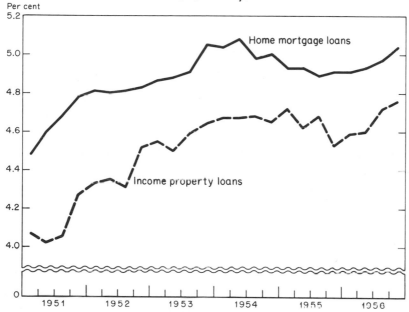

SOURCE: Data on home mortgage loans are a weighted average of contract interest rates reported by four life insurance companies. In income property loans data are a weighted average of contract interest rates from two companies, one of which reported on residential loans also. See Table A-5 below.

In accord with earlier data compiled by the National Bureau,[7] findings for the postwar decade show that interest rates on mortgage loans closed on income properties were lower than on homes. The spread has varied somewhat from a high between 50 and 60 basis points in 1951 to a low between 20 and 30 basis points through most of 1955 and 1956. The generally lower level of rates on business type property loans is due to two obvious advantages of such loans: large individual loans involve relatively low servicing costs per dollar of loan; such loans are secured by

[7] For a summary of data on conventional mortgage interest rates see R. J. Saulnier, Harold G. Halcrow, and Neil H. Jacoby, *Federal Lending and Loan Insurance*, Princeton University Press for NBER, 1958, Table 69.

properties having assured income from high-grade tenants renting space under firm long-term leases.

Evidence obtained in interviews, however, suggests that the pattern is subject to significant variations. Relatively high interest rates can often be commanded by the comparatively few mortgage lenders able and willing to make large individual loans of several million dollars. This is so particularly during periods of capital market stringency when alternative investment opportunities are plentiful. In periods such as 1953 and 1956, the spread between mortgage interest rates on home and business property loans narrows. Several life insurance companies reported informally that during 1956 and early 1957 their rates on income property loans were as high or even higher than on home loans.

The greater volatility of average interest rates on business than on home property loans is also clear from Chart 8. It is due chiefly to the greater influence of each individual loan on the business loan series than on the home loan series because the number of business-property loans is much smaller than that of home loans.

LONGER-TERM MOVEMENTS IN CONVENTIONAL
MORTGAGE INTEREST RATES

Annual data on conventional mortgage interest rates for earlier years from National Bureau studies with more recent data developed in this study permit the construction of the annual series from 1920 through 1956, shown in Chart 9. Comparability of the present series (1947–1956) with the National Bureau series (1920–1947) is made more direct by use of earlier data for life insurance companies only. The National Bureau's interest rate data for commercial banks and savings and loan associations closely parallel the life insurance company data at a somewhat higher level. The level of rates in 1947—4.2 per cent for the last year of the National Bureau series and 4.3 per cent for the first of the present series—speaks for the comparability of the series and strengthens the credibility of each.

While from 1920 to 1932 the level of mortgage interest rates remained relatively stable, around 6 per cent, the postwar rise started from a much lower level after a steep and steady drop of nearly fifteen years' duration. Thus, notwithstanding the significant increase in interest rates on both home and income property loans after World War II, levels at the end of 1956 were still well below those of the 1920's and early 1930's. It is likely, however, that further rises during 1957 carried the average level considerably closer to that of thirty years earlier.

CHART 9
Conventional Mortgage Interest Rates on Home and Income Property Loans, 1920–1956

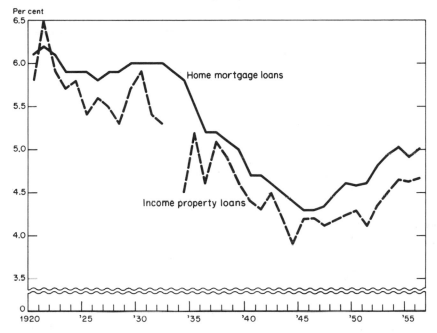

SOURCE: For 1920–1933 data are from J. E. Morton, *Urban Mortgage Lending: Comparative Markets and Experience*, Princeton for NBER, 1956, Tables C-5 and C-8. For 1934–1946 data are from unpublished tables of the National Bureau, and for 1947–1956 are from the present study. While Morton's monograph also reproduces National Bureau data for 1934–1946, these include interest rates on federally underwritten loans as well as on conventional loans, and are not completely comparable with earlier or later figures on conventional mortgage interest rates. Data for 1933 on income property loans are not available. See also Table A–6 below.

FHA and VA Mortgage Interest Rates and Prices

The overriding fact about interest rates on FHA and VA mortgage loans is their relative inflexibility. The maximum rates are established by law and regulation and tend to become going market rates. The arbitrary setting of rates outside the "free" market has been a major element influencing the allocation of funds in the capital market, tending to attract funds into mortgages and away from other types of investments during periods of market ease and to restrict the flow of mortgage funds during periods of stringency. Adjustments in FHA and VA mortgage yields made through discounts and premiums have not been wholly effective in solving the basic problems inherent in a market situation characterized by the existence of ceiling prices for one product and free prices for competitive products (see following section on discounts and premiums for discussion of reasons).

When World War II ended, the federal government was underwriting mortgages made by private lenders at fixed maximum interest rates of 4 per cent for VA loans and $4\frac{1}{2}$ per cent for FHA loans. Subsequent changes in those rates, discussed in Chapter 3, are visible in Chart 7. The early postwar rates on such government underwritten loans were markedly higher than yields on long-term government securities, while risks were little greater. The rates were also significantly higher than yields on business securities. The differential more than compensated for the higher administrative and servicing costs on FHA and VA loans compared to those on other capital market securities. Moreover, the established maximum interest rate for FHA mortgages was apparently at a higher level than conventional mortgage interest rates through mid-1948, and the rate for VA mortgages was only slightly less than conventional rates. Under these circumstances, federally underwritten mortgages were quite attractive to investors.

Except for a time during 1948 when bond yields were rising, the appeal to investors of FHA and VA loans continued strong until the Federal Reserve-Treasury "accord" of early 1951. Thereafter, while other important elements described in Chapter 3 were at work, the ebb and flow of federally underwritten mortgage funds reflected in large part the narrowing and widening differentials between fixed interest rates on FHA and VA loans and changing yields on other capital market securities. During periods of credit stringency, when yields on competitive capital market securities rose, investment in federally underwritten mortgages declined, but rose again when competitive yields fell during periods of credit ease. The relationship is shown in Chart 1 and discussed in more detail in the accompanying text. To recapitulate, inflexible interest rates on FHA and VA loans have made an important contribution to wide fluctuations in the flow of mortgage funds during alternating periods of credit ease and restraint. Moreover, existence of two types of government securities—direct obligations and loans with federal guarantees—at yield differentials determined arbitrarily outside the "free" market but obviously at variance with the market's evaluation of the differential has been an important factor in capital market instability.

DISCOUNTS AND PREMIUMS

The question to be considered here is why discounts or premiums on loans with fixed maximum interest rates have not been effective in adjusting yields to actual market conditions. Other capital market securities are traded at prices above or below par in response to changing conditions, with a resulting differential between effective yields and coupon rates. Why is such complete market flexibility not possible for federally underwritten mortgages? The answer lies in a myriad of factors—legal, moral, and psychological, as well as economic—and is associated with a background of federal statutory and administrative changes. Some knowledge of the background, briefly sketched below, is necessary to an understanding of this basic problem.[8]

Regulations limiting fees and charges made by lenders and builders against borrowers of FHA and VA loans have been in effect since the beginning of the federal mortgage underwriting programs. Until 1950, however, there were no regulations governing fees, charges, or discounts that could be imposed by lenders upon builders or sellers of houses under these programs. By legislation (Housing Act of 1950, Section 504), the Veterans Administration and Federal Housing Administration were required to limit the charges which could be made by lenders against builders. Later (September 1951) charges against a seller of existing properties were limited as well.

These Congressional actions stemmed largely from developments in preceding months during which FNMA was actively supporting the market for VA loans through the issuance of advance commitments to purchase such mortgages at par. With the private market price of VA loans at less than par, lenders were able to exact discounts from builders and turn a profit in selling mortgages at par to FNMA. "Thus, in practical effect, the lender was exacting a fee from the builder or sponsor for obtaining financing

---

[8] The discussion following to the end of this section is based largely on information included in the congressional reports and hearings given below.

81st Congress, 2nd session, Report No. 1286, Senate Committee on Banking and Currency, to accompany S. 2246, February 24, 1950. 81st Congress, 2nd session, Conference Report No. 1893 to accompany S. 2246, April 5, 1950. 83rd Congress, 1st session, Senate Banking and Currency Committee, Hearings on "Mortgage Interest Rate Problem," January 28, 1953. 83rd Congress, 1st session, House Veteran's Affairs Committee Hearings on "Proposed Sale of Guaranteed Loans at a Discount," April 29, 1953. 83rd Congress, 1st session, Conference Report No. 692 to accompany S. 2103, "Housing Amendments of 1953," June 30, 1953. 83rd Congress, 1st session, House Veterans Affairs Committee, Hearings on "Proposed Sale of Guaranteed Loans at a Discount," May 12, 1953. 83rd Congress, 1st session, House Subcommittee on Housing of Committee on Veterans Affairs, Hearings on "Fees and Charges Schedule Governing Guaranteed Housing Loans," June 18, 1953.

that actually represented the use of government funds. It is believed that this was the practice which the Congress was in the main concerned about and was desirous of curbing, although there was, in addition, concern that the cost to the purchaser would be increased."[9] The legislation enacted was considerably broader and applied to all FHA and VA loans whether or not sold to FNMA.

The 1950 legislation did not end the practice of mortgage discounting, however. Lenders and builders devised numerous practices, not covered by the law, through which discounts were considered legal or at least not patently illegal.[10] With yields on corporate and government securities rising through most of the period to mid-1953 (Chart 7), discounts were widespread, especially on VA loans. The VA interest rate (4 per cent), fixed at a lower maximum than the FHA rate (4¼ per cent), led lenders to seek to increase the effective rate by discounts and builders to obtain liberal financing on houses to be sold.

Even so, in view of the established maximum interest rate on FHA and VA loans, and the obvious legislative intent to limit discounts, many large investors—particularly life insurance companies—reduced their purchases of federally underwritten mortgages rather than resort to discounts. The Veterans Administration, in the hearings cited, expressed the view that the reluctance could not "be explained solely on economic grounds. For example, a 20-year GI 4 per cent loan purchased at a 5 per cent discount offers a yield to the investor of 4.64 per cent if . . . held to maturity and a somewhat higher yield [if] prepaid prior to maturity." Rather, the Administration believed that the reluctance stemmed "from their apprehension that the purchase of loans at very sizable discounts may subject them some day in the future to public censure, or perhaps even to criminal prosecution, although the VA solicitor has ruled that discount arrangements are legal under the act and regulations, provided they meet certain tests and conditions."[11] Such apprehension was reported more directly in later congressional testimony. "Many

---

[9] Hearings on "Mortgage Interest Rate Problem," reply of Veterans Administration to questions of Senate Banking and Currency Committee, p. 43.

[10] In particular, three practices known to be in wide general use were outlined in Hearings on "Mortgage Interest Rate Problem," p. 40: (1) Since the statute prohibited excessive charges against builders, sellers, and borrowers only, without mention of other parties to a transaction, lenders collected fees from real estate brokers or acted directly as sales brokers. (2) An agreement would be made by a lender with a builder or seller under which a purchase of loans at par and accrued interest was agreed upon if the lender was unable to sell such loans at par within a specified period. To guarantee such a purchase, a deposit subject to forfeit was posted by the builder or seller. (3) A builder would close VA loans in his own name, as a nonsupervised lender, and later sell them at a discount.

[11] *Ibid.*, p. 42.

lenders solicitous of their own good repute balk or shy away from going into the program under arrangements of that kind [see footnote 9], and they are the people that tell us, 'If you will legalize this discount so our lawyers will not tell us to be leery of whether it is or is not proper under the law, we will go into your program'.[12]"

Soon after maximum interest rates on VA and FHA loans were increased restriction of the described discount practices was undertaken by Veterans Administration directive (May 1953). Builders were required to certify that they had neither directly nor indirectly paid discounts or fees other than those explicitly allowable by statute or regulation. Strong protests by builders and lenders led to legislation (June 1953) authorizing builders and sellers to pay discounts incurred by lenders on federally underwritten loans. Such discounts, however, could not be passed on to purchasers.[13] The limitation on covering discounts in sales transactions was one important deterrent to their effective use in bringing yields on VA and FHA loans into competitive range with other capital market investments. Whereas small discounts could be covered by builders in selling price or absorbed in profit, the larger discounts required by lenders in late 1955 and 1956 made builders and sellers increasingly reluctant to reduce, by absorption of discounts, effective sales return on houses. Consequently both new house builders and sellers of existing houses turned to conventional mortgages with flexible interest rates and no need for discounts to increase effective yields.

The question whether mortgage discounts were actually being absorbed by builders or were passed on to veteran buyers has long been debated, but conclusive evidence is lacking to support either contention. Because the methods of real estate value appraisal are so inexact, one view, as expressed by a Congressman, is that the cost of discounts could readily be covered in the sale price of a house. A VA representative testified that "it was impossible to appraise houses within a 5 per cent figure. How can you come before this committee and tell us that you think the veteran will not have to absorb this [discount], when your people admit that you cannot get closer than 5 per cent to the amount of money?" The same man said that "he had checked it over and over, and said that always in some way they passed it on down to the house and to the veteran buying

[12] Testimony of T. B. King, Assistant Deputy Director of Loan Guaranty Service, Veterans Administration, in hearings on "Proposed Sale of Guaranteed Loans at a Discount," p. 1035.

[13] The legislation, included in the Housing Amendments Act of 1953 took the form of an amendment to section 504 of the Housing Act of 1950. This section was finally repealed altogether on November 1, 1954.

the house."[14] Echoing this claim, a high federal housing official stated that, however careful a valuation system may be, "I do not think anybody in the business will contend that it can be so careful that it will prevent" passing back the discount to the borrower in the price of the house.[15] In answering these contentions, the Veterans Administration claimed that the criticism was not generally valid because the VA exercised appraisal controls through refusing to recognize increases in reasonable value. "On a number of occasions VA field offices have been exhorted to exercise extreme care to avoid yielding to any upward pressure from builders to permit the reflection of the discounts through higher reasonable values. Thus . . . it is unlikely that the builder is able to recoup his discount costs through higher valuations." The VA representative pointed out the offsetting value of the "availability of GI loan credit with its very low cost and liberal terms." Giving some ground, he continued: "But we cannot deny the possibility or even the probability that in a minority of cases the builder is able to obtain higher valuations sufficient to recompense him for all—or at least part—of whatever discount he may be required to pay for his financing."[16]

The general question of the incidence of discounts need not be resolved to reach agreement that the existence of regulations prohibiting the payment of discounts by borrowers is a deterrent to the use of FHA and VA loans. This is so particularly for existing house sales with value appraisals not based on costs, of which the seller's discounts might be one. In periods of credit tightness, moreover, not only increase of discounts required by lenders, but also other factors reduced the possibility of covering them in higher selling prices and thus passing them on to borrowers. With profit margins narrowed by increased cost of building and of land acquisition and development, builders found it difficult to absorb the costs of discounts as well. Thus, they temporarily reduced or discontinued operations under federal guaranteed financing.

Most lenders, also, were reluctant to place funds in federally underwritten mortgages when yields on other capital market instruments were rising. Notwithstanding the availability of discounts on a clearly legal basis after 1953, public censure was still likely, so long as discount charges were considered at least unethical. Congressional reaction to the existence

---

[14] Statement by Representative Olin E. Teague, in questioning Mr. T. B. King, in "Proposed Sale of Guaranteed Loans at a Discount," p. 1032.

[15] Statement by Raymond Foley, then Administrator of the Housing and Home Finance Agency, in "Mortgage Interest Rate Problem," p. 12.

[16] "Mortgage Interest Rate Problem," p. 44.

of large discounts in tight capital markets contributed importantly to the shaping of public opinion on this question. A subcommittee on housing expressed stern disapproval:

"In parts of the South and West the typical price for VA-guaranteed loans seems to fall in the 95 to 97 range. Even more disturbing are the very frequent accounts of even larger discounts of from 7 to as much as 10 points . . . . The persistence of these 'horror' cases and the generally agreed upon fact of discounts as heavy as 5 to 6 per cent in some areas, even for loans to excellent credit risks in desirable projects, has caused the subcommittee grave concern.

" . . . The subcommittee is convinced that . . . the $4\frac{1}{2}$ per cent interest rate . . . is a fair rate for a virtually riskless investment. At the same time, we recognize . . . that . . . discounts in some degree are unavoidable and indeed are a necessary adjustment to changing supply and demand relationships. Large discounts, however, should not be sanctioned. A 7 per cent discount, for example, will give a gross yield for a twenty five-year loan (assuming a ten-year repayment period) of 5.53 per cent. The subcommittee regards this as an outrageous yield on a government-guaranteed obligation at a time when long-term government loans are yielding less than 3 per cent. Mortgages require a somewhat higher yield than bonds, to be sure, but no one, in our opinion, can defend a spread of such a magnitude."[17]

Such Congressional opinion has had a restraining influence upon acceptance by lenders of large discounts on federally underwritten mortgages. Large financial intermediaries, in their widely acknowledged role as public trustees, have been less willing to risk public censure than to ignore the facts of market forces. Small lenders that originate mortgage loans directly to borrowers have found it difficult to charge discount fees, and many have regarded the practice as something unsavory. These attitudes were borne out in interviews with officers of large and small institutions. Thus, from both the demand and supply side, the discount technique, because of legal requirements and equity pressures, has proved only partially effective in compensating for fixed maximum interest rates in a tightening capital market.

[17] Report No. 2 of the Subcommittee on Housing of the House Committee on Banking and Currency, "Mortgage Credit and FHA Multifamily Housing," January 31, 1956, pp. 4–5.

YIELD DIFFERENTIALS BETWEEN FHA, VA, AND
CONVENTIONAL MORTGAGES

Market evaluation of federally underwritten mortgage loans, as reflected in yields to investors, has seldom coincided with that of the federal government, as reflected in maximum statutory or administrative interest rates. During most of the first five years after World War I, FHA and VA loans commanded premiums in the market, while in the next five years they generally carried discounts. Investors' judgment of the value of federal mortgage insurance and guaranty is suggested in part by the yield spread between federally underwritten and conventional home mortgage loans. Precise measurement of that spread and also of the spread between FHA and VA loans is precluded by inadequacies of the data, and interpretation is hampered by lack of knowledge about differences in other terms of mortgage lending. Since early 1953 the Federal Housing Administration has reported average market prices of FHA loans, and similar data have been available from the Federal National Mortgage Association on both FHA and VA loans.[18] These data purportedly represent prices on secondary market transactions in mortgages available for immediate delivery. The fact that price quotations on FHA-insured loans reported independently by FNMA and FHA have been in close agreement from 1953 through 1956 increases confidence in the reliability of the data.

Comparison of FHA and VA loan prices, shown in Chart 10, indicates that both types of mortgages have remained below par since mid-1953 (close to par through most of 1954), and that FHA loan prices have been consistently higher than VA prices. The price spread has varied somewhat over the years, increasing to an average of about 0.7 of a percentage point after early 1955 compared with an average 0.4 of a point in the two preceding years. Maximum administrative interest rates on both mortgages were the same, $4\frac{1}{2}$ per cent, throughout the period shown in the chart. Investors' willingness, therefore, to purchase VA loans only at a lower price (higher yield) than FHA loans must be explained by their evaluation of other factors bearing on loan quality.

In general, contract terms—maturities, downpayments, and loan-to-value ratios—have been more liberal for VA loans than for FHA loans.

[18] Federal Housing Administration, "Average Typical Prices Offered for FHA-insured (Section 203) $4\frac{1}{2}\%$ Home Mortgage Loans—Immediate Delivery Transactions (In Market Areas of FHA Insuring Office Cities)"; and Federal National Mortgage Association, "Average Prices of Section 203 and 501 Mortgages by Agency Area on Selected Dates."

Lenders generally have regarded VA property appraisals also as tending to be more liberal than those made by FHA. The fact that the VA guaranty is for 60 per cent of a loan (not to exceed $7,500), and FHA

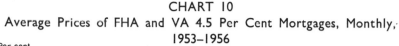

CHART 10

Average Prices of FHA and VA 4.5 Per Cent Mortgages, Monthly, 1953–1956

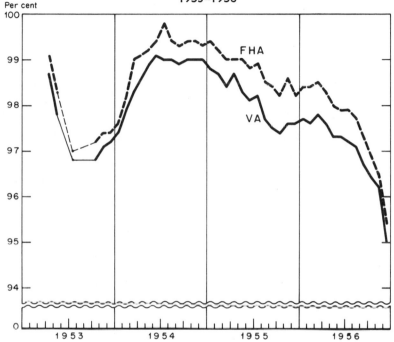

Source: Federal National Mortgage Association monthly release, "Average Prices of Section 203 and 501 mortgages by Agency Area on Selected Dates."

insurance for 100 per cent of a loan, may also have influenced investors' judgment about the quality of these mortgages.

The relative influence of each of these factors on mortgage loan prices cannot be determined. It is clear, however, that the market tends to judge the quality of FHA and VA loans to a large extent on their own merits notwithstanding the contingent liability assumed by the federal government. The criterion of quality influences not only differences between prices quoted for FHA and VA mortgages, but also differences within one type of mortgage with varying terms. For example, FNMA's purchase price schedule under its secondary market operations in late 1956 varied as much as 2½ points for both FHA and VA mortgages in the same area, depending upon loan-to-value ratios and length of maturities. Price variations by geographic area are also important, as indicated in the last section of this chapter.

CHART 11

Comparison of Average Yields on VA-Guaranteed Mortgages, FHA-Insured Home Mortgages, and Average Contract Interest Rates on Conventional Home Mortgages, Quarterly, 1953–1956

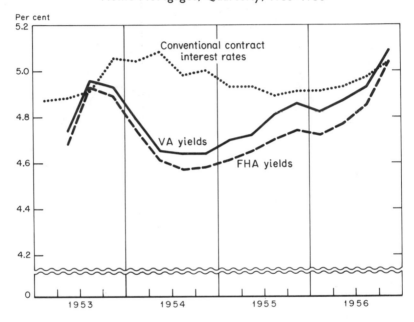

NOTE: Data on contract interest rates on conventional home mortgage loans are from the same source indicated in Chart 7. Data on FHA and VA mortgage yields are calculated from average prices shown in Chart 10 and are based on an assumed 10-year prepayment period and a 25-year average contract maturity. The difference in yields, assuming a different repayment period, would have been small. See also Table A–7.

On the basis of their market prices, average FHA and VA yields ranged between 4.6 per cent and 5.1 per cent from mid-1953 through 1956, as shown in Chart 11. Conventional mortgage interest rates during the same period ranged from around 4.9 to 5.1 per cent. Before 1953, no regularly published data on FHA and VA mortgage prices or yields are available. Scattered information suggests that, during most of the 1946–1950 period, FHA loans, carrying interest rates higher than on VA loans and for a time even higher than on conventional loans (Chart 7), commanded premium prices in the market.[19] Unpublished data on FHA mortgage prices and yields reveals that, during the period from 1948 to early 1953, their movements paralleled those of conventional mortgage interest rates very closely. With minor exceptions, quarterly conventional mortgage interest rates were consistently between 30 and 40 basis points above the market yields on FHA mortgages. Data on VA mortgage yields after mid-1953, described above, suggest a somewhat smaller spread between them and conventional rates in earlier years than that between FHA and conventional mortgage rates.

The spread between yields on mortgages underwritten by the federal government and those not so protected reflects not only the existence of the government guaranty but differences in lending terms. Federally underwritten mortgages usually bear terms more favorable to the borrower with respect to maturities, downpayments, and monthly payments. If those terms were more nearly the same, it is likely that market yields on federally underwritten mortgages would be lower and the spread between them and conventional rates greater. Such liberal terms, however, would hardly have been acceptable to lenders without the federal guaranty.

All of this implies that, even with the contingent liability of the federal government, the market does not regard FHA and VA loans as riskless assets. In judging them as investments it applies traditional standards of quality, just as in judging conventional mortgages. Thus, from the point of view of the lender, government underwritten loans with all the advantages noted, if secured by poorly located or otherwise less desirable properties, will command lower prices or higher yields than loans on more favorable or less risky properties. Most lenders interviewed in the course of this study agreed with the implications just pointed out. Among the most frequently mentioned reasons for judging government under-written loans on their own merits were: (1) the social obligation of large financial intermediaries to screen and select mortgages carefully; (2) the cost of dealing with delinquencies and defaults, which several large institutions had found to vary directly with the liberality of loan terms; (3) the unwillingness of lenders to be associated with foreclosures and bad loans; (4) the disadvantages of reinvesting foreclosed mortgage funds at unfavorable times; (5) the lack of full coverage by the Federal

---

[19] For example, in congressional hearings on the "Mortgage Interest Rate Problem," Raymond Foley, then Housing Administrator, said: ". . . some years ago when we were on a $4\frac{1}{2}$ per cent rate in the section 203 operation, the detached one- to four-family house operation in some areas of the country, the insured mortgage was commanding high premiums 103, sometimes 104."

Housing Administration of foreclosure and associated costs; (6) the greater risk exposure of VA loans, having a maximum $7,500 guarantee, in the face of the increasing size of loans. To fortify itself against that risk exposure, one large financial institution adopted a policy against accepting VA loans if the unguaranteed portion exceeded 50 per cent of the appraised value of the property.

The views just set forth about risk, yield, and terms on federally underwritten loans are, however, opposed by a minority view held by some large institutional lenders. They hold that such loans are essentially riskless and should be acquired strictly on the basis of yield comparison with direct Treasury obligations and Aaa corporate bonds without considering other characteristics. They regard most of the factors noted above as more than offset by other aspects of the government guaranty. Loans acquired at discounts and later foreclosed are repaid by the government at par. This practice often results in a profit or premium to the lender despite the costs incurred in administering the loan, attempting to forestall default, and reinvesting recaptured funds. The ultimate conclusions suggested are that the sooner a discounted mortgage goes to foreclosure the better for the investor and that the poorer the quality of a federally underwritten mortgage the higher its prices should be. The market place, however, has not yet accepted this extreme view, and prices are still directly related to quality, as they are in the conventional mortgage market.

The differential between average contract interest rates on conventional loans and yields on federally underwritten loans was considerably wider during the 1954–1955 period of capital market ease than in periods of market stringency before and after that (Chart 11). These changes in yield differentials have resulted chiefly from swings in FHA and VA yields; conventional interest rates have moved within a fairly narrow range. The pattern reflects, in part, technical inadequacies in the two series and differences between them; in part it depicts actual market influence.

Technically, the yield data are based on price quotations reported by FHA and FNMA field offices for typical transactions on immediate deliveries (Chart 10). They are simple averages not weighted by transactions and hence subject to greater fluctuation as quoted "spot" prices change. Also, the inclusion of transactions not based on prior commitments results in a series more sensitive to market changes. The conventional interest rate series, as noted previously, is a weighted average of loans closed by life insurance companies based mainly on prior commitments. It is therefore likely to be generally sluggish and less sensitive to immediate market changes than FHA and VA yields.

Among market influences bearing upon yield changes in the various series are not only changes in market conditions, but also changes in loan composition, including the quality of loans, geographic representation, loan acquisition and servicing costs, and other related factors. The influence of these factors on the various series is not measurable. Yield differentials should be considered, therefore, as only approximations of the true situation. The slight rise, shown in Chart 11, of FHA and VA yields over conventional interest rates for a time in 1953 and 1956 can be interpreted realistically to mean only that differentials narrowed markedly at those times compared with other periods of market ease. If the technical comparability of the series were better, it is likely, given the basic differences between conventional and federally under-written loans, that a truer picture of slightly higher conventional rates would have been shown.

Additional basic reasons may be suggested for the changing yield spread between conventional and federally underwritten mortgages during periods of capital market tightness and ease. In tight markets institutional lenders generally have a choice of investment outlets and are able to place funds in high-yield conventional mortgages on conservative terms for downpayments and maturities. Furthermore, they can be more stringent in selecting borrowers and properties and hence reduce their risk exposure. In this setting, lenders are reluctant to place funds in federally under-written mortgages unless yields are close to those on conventional mortgages. When markets ease and lenders find it more difficult to invest all their capital funds profitably, they are more willing to acquire federally underwritten mortgages at wider yield differentials. Demands by borrowers for such liberal-term mortgages increase faster than demands for conventional mortgages, which lenders cannot acquire in the desired quantities. Rates on conventional mortgage loans therefore decline, but only slowly because of institutional and traditional factors previously discussed. The decline in yields is probably greater than in contract interest rates because lenders are willing to pay a premium for high quality conventional loans at good rates. This is particularly characteristic of such lenders as life insurance companies, which acquire loans frequently through mortgage companies.

Geographic Variation in Mortgage Yields

Unlike corporate or government securities, which are issued and traded in national markets at nationally quoted yields, mortgages are originated and traded in numerous local markets at varying yields. Both the course of real estate values and the fortunes of mortgage borrowers are closely linked with local area developments. State laws with differing treatment of rights of mortgagors and mortgagees and the general complexity of legal arrangements tie transactions to the local rather than national level. While the interregional flow of mortgage funds has accelerated since the advent of federal mortgage insurance and guaranty, prudent lenders carefully appraise the economic, legal, and social climate of areas under consideration for lending.

The local character of mortgage markets is responsible for the geographic variation in mortgage interest rates and yields. There is no national mortgage rate; series discussed in preceding sections are only broad averages of varying geographic rates and yields. Within regional and national averages, prices and yields will, of course, vary between individual mortgages, based on the previously discussed factors of security, borrower, and terms. On mortgages of comparable quality secured by properties in different regions, however, yields vary because of a host of factors associated with local areas and because of the institutional arrangements for mortgage financing, although these differentials have declined substantially over the years.[20]

Limited current data on regional mortgage yields clearly indicate that differentials—though narrower than in earlier years—persist. Price quotations on VA $4\frac{1}{2}$ per cent mortgages, reported to FNMA by field agencies in late 1956, for example, varied from a low of 93.6 in the Los Angeles area to a high of 96.4 in the Philadelphia area (Table 13).[21] These prices represent yields of about 5.60 and 5.10, respectively, if a prepayment period of eight years is assumed on a twenty-five year mortgage. The differential of about 0.50 basis points is not much smaller than that in 1940 (footnote 20). On FHA 5 per cent mortgages, the 1956 differential between the Los Angeles and Philadelphia areas was somewhat smaller. Despite the increased interregional flow of mortgage funds and use of the process of arbitrage, regional yield variations have apparently narrowed little throughout the postwar period. Several reasons may be suggested for the persistence of variations in regional mortgage yields.

[20] "In 1890 the spread between the regions with the highest and lowest effective (residential mortgage) interest rates was 3.8 percentage points. In 1920 the spread in terms of contract rates was 2.2 points; in 1934, 1.4 points; in 1940, 0.6 point. In 1950 the median first mortgage interest rate . . . in each of the four major census regions was 5.0 per cent . . . . The tendency towards smaller regional differences . . . has resulted both from the improvement of lending facilities and the decrease in risks of mortgage lending in what were young regions in 1890 and from greater mobility of mortgage funds, through which local markets became less isolated." (Grebler, Blank, and Winnick, *op. cit.*, p. 229.)

[21] From the Federal National Mortgage Association, "Average Prices of Section 203 and 501 Mortgages by Agency Area on Selected Dates."

TABLE 13

Regional Prices for VA-Guaranteed Mortgages, by FNMA Agency Area,
January and June, 1953-1956

Region	1953		1954		1955		1956	
	Jan.	June	Jan.	June	Jan.	June	Jan.	June
Atlanta	98.5	96.5	96.9	98.2	98.0	97.6	97.2	97.2
Chicago	99.1	98.2	97.4	99.0	98.6	98.4	97.9	97.1
Dallas	98.8	98.2	97.4	99.0	98.7	97.7	97.4	97.2
Los Angeles	97.5	96.5	97.2	99.0	98.5	97.5	96.9	95.9
Philadelphia	99.4	97.7	98.0	99.4	99.8	98.9	98.3	99.2
Seattle	—	99.5	97.5	99.8	99.0	97.7	98.4	97.0

SOURCE: Federal National Mortgage Association, "Average Prices of Section 203 and 501 Mortgages by Agency Area on Selected Dates."

1. The geographic concentration of capital and the predominance of local lenders in some areas of the country have tended to make for rate differentials. Mortgage rates in eastern financial centers—Boston, New York, and Philadelphia, for example—are generally lower than in the Southwest and Far West where there is a scarcity of capital relative to demands for it.

2. Though fluidity of mortgage funds between areas has been considerably increased by the introduction of federal mortgage insurance and guaranty, it is by no means complete.

3. Costs of acquiring and servicing mortgages away from a lender's home base make for higher gross yields in capital-scarce areas.

4. Variations among state laws governing foreclosure and borrower redemption rights make recovery of funds in case of default more or less costly and difficult for lenders. Prospective difficulties naturally call for higher yield requirements by the lender. In Michigan, for example, the extended period of redemption has resulted in increased preference by lenders for the land contract over the mortgage loan.

5. Mortgage yield differentials result from variations in economic factors tending to influence area real estate and construction markets, such as industrial stability and growth, expansion in population, diversification of industry, and zoning ordinances, as well as lenders' appraisals of the long- and short-term economic potential.

6. A common desire among national lenders for geographically diversified mortgage portfolios tends to keep regional rates apart. For example, some large eastern financial institutions, in order to maintain what they consider appropriate diversification, will place funds in Pennsylvania mortgages at par, for example, even though California mortgages are available to them at 96.

97

Other broad reasons for continued geographic variation in mortgage yields lie in the imperfections still remaining in mortgage markets. Neither lenders nor borrowers have complete knowledge of transactions. Institutional arrangements for acquisition of mortgages tend to perpetuate yield differentials between areas and within the same market area. Yields in an area on mortgages of comparable quality, for example, may vary because one large financial institution intent upon increasing its mortgage investments there is willing to acquire them through its correspondent at prices above those generally prevailing. Prices of other mortgage originators in the area, however, are not affected because funds from that institution are not available to them.

CHAPTER 5
Flow of Funds into Mortgage Markets

THE impact on mortgage markets of the dynamic forces appraised in Chapter 3 and of mortgage yield factors analyzed in Chapter 4 is recorded ultimately in shifts in the flow of mortgage funds. Demonstration of precise economic cause and effect relationships throughout the period under investigation, especially during the relatively short quarterly intervals, is precluded by the nature of the data and by special institutional factors. One impediment is varying time lags between actions and results of actions in mortgage and other capital markets. Other drawbacks are general but unmeasured seasonal influences and basic differences in market practices among financial institutions. Perhaps most important is that net flow data, upon which most of the analysis in this chapter depends, obscure developments which would be apparent from figures on gross lending and repayment.[1] The statistical record developed here nevertheless illustrates and permits broad analysis of the varying impact of changes in the basic elements influencing mortgage and other capital markets upon different mortgage sectors and major types of lenders.

Net Flow of Mortgage Funds Under
Expansionary Influences, 1946–1950

The dominance of expansionary forces in the mortgage market during most of the early years of our period, described in preceding chapters, resulted in a large and generally increasing flow of funds into mortgages, culminating in a record 1950 volume not exceeded until four years later. But the picture is not one of simple growth. The flow of mortgage funds from the main types of financial institutions into the different sectors of the mortgage market fluctuated, absolutely and relatively, as lenders and borrowers adjusted to shifting capital market conditions. In total

[1] Comprehensive analysis of the gross flow of mortgage funds, upon which much of the basic groundwork was done in the course of this study, awaits future opportunity. New information developed includes annual gross lending and gross repayments data, broken down between contractual and all other types of repayments. It is at hand in considerable detail by type of mortgage for life insurance companies, mutual savings banks, and savings and loan associations. Inadequate basic data for commercial banks precluded estimation of gross flow figures for that major type of mortgage lender. Nor was it possible, in view of the primitive state of existing statistics, to develop gross flow figures for other less important types of mortgage lenders. It is hoped that preparation of refinements in the data and remaining adjustments to annual estimates of the gross flow of mortgage funds through three of the main types of financial institutions can be brought to a stage warranting publication in the near future.

figures, the flow of funds into home mortgages was markedly larger than into all other types combined, and the flow into federally underwritten mortgages exceeded that into conventional mortgages.

MORTGAGE FLOWS RELATIVE TO OTHER CAPITAL MARKET FLOWS

The total net flow of funds into mortgages during 1946–1950 was three-fourths larger than into corporate securities and three times larger than into municipal government obligations. Outstanding federal obligations declined sharply in those years (Chapter 3). In three of the first five postwar years, the annual flow of mortgage funds was substantially larger than the combined flow into other capital market instruments. The ratio of mortgage flows to total capital market flows, as shown in Chart 12, ranged from a high of over three-fourths in 1946 to a low of about two-fifths in 1949. The range was generally lower in the last five years of the decade.

The steadily declining ratio of mortgage flows to other capital market flows from the unusually high level of 1946 to the end of 1949 appears to contradict the increased attractiveness of mortgages to investors during the period, suggested in earlier chapters. The explanation lies largely in the sources of funds for investment—mortgage funds come chiefly from the four main types of financial institutions, while the bulk of funds for corporate and municipal securities come from other origins.[2] Within the total net issue of mortgages and securities, therefore, the relative attractiveness of mortgages to investors active in different sectors of the capital market may be obscured. The appeal of mortgages, relative to other capital market instruments, to the main institutional investors during 1946–1950, may be seen more clearly in Chart 13. The shifting roles of these investors within the mortgage market are indicated in Chart 14.

The unusually liquid position of financial institutions at the close of World War II (Chapter 3) led to their common goals—conversion of large holdings of government securities into higher-yield assets and development of new outlets for the inflow of savings. The speed of conversion and of new investment and the degree to which they availed themselves of opportunities in the mortgage market reflected varying financial policies and practices, legal restrictions, and organizational problems. Notwithstanding institutional differences, it is clear from Chart 13 that savings

[2] See the tables on "Summary of Flow-of-Funds Accounts" in *Flow of Funds in the United States 1939–1953*, Federal Reserve System, December 1955, pp. 24–38; and in *Federal Reserve Bulletin*, April 1957, pp. 376–381. See also Morris Mendelson, "The Flow of Funds Through the Capital Market, 1953–1955: A Progress Report," *Journal of Finance*, May 1957, pp. 164–165.

CHART 12
Net Flow of Funds into Capital Markets, 1946–1956

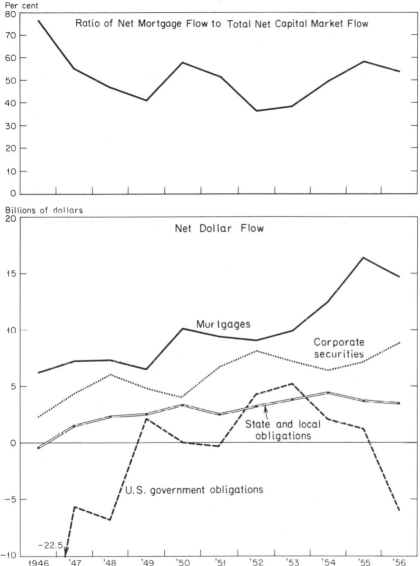

SOURCE: Data represent net annual changes in outstanding obligations. For net mort-gage flows, data for all years are from Klaman, Technical Paper 13. For other series, data for 1946–1949 are from the Board of Governors of the Federal Reserve System, *Flow of Funds in the United States , 1939–1953;* and for 1950–1955 from *Federal Reserve Bulletin, Summary Flow-of-Funds Accounts, 1950–55,* April 1957. 1956 figures are unpublished Federal Reserve estimates. See also Table A–8 below.

The ratio in the upper panel of the chart represents the relationship between the net increase in mortgages outstanding to the total net increase in corporate, state and local, and U.S. government securities. Net decreases in U.S. government securities are treated as sources rather than uses of funds.

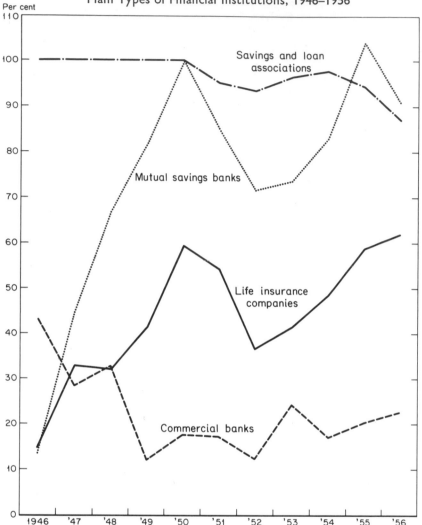

CHART 13
Ratios of Net Mortgage Flow to Total Net Capital Market Flow Through Main Types of Financial Institutions, 1946–1956

Per cent

Savings and loan associations

Mutual savings banks

Life insurance companies

Commercial banks

1946 '47 '48 '49 '50 '51 '52 '53 '54 '55 '56

Source: For each type of financial institution except commercial banks, the ratios represent the relationship of the net increase in mortgages outstanding to the total net increase in corporate, state and local, and U.S. government securities. For commercial banks the ratio is based on the same items plus bank loans. Net decreases in U.S. government securities are treated as sources rather than uses of funds.

Except for mortgage figures, taken from Klaman, Technical Paper 13, Tables 37–40, the basic net flow data upon which the ratios were taken from internal Federal Reserve Board sources. The outstandings data from which net flows figures may be calculated appear in the following *Federal Reserve Bulletin* tables: "Principal Assets and Liabilities and Number of All Banks, by Classes," "Savings Institutions: Life Insurance Companies," and "Savings and Loan Associations," *Bulletin*, April 1957, pp. 429 and 439. An additional source of information used for mutual savings banks is the National Association of Mutual Savings Banks. See also Table A–9 below.

CHART 14
Net Flow of Mortgage Funds from Main Types of Financial Institutions, 1946–1956

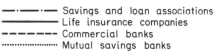

Savings and loan associations
Life insurance companies
Commercial banks
Mutual savings banks

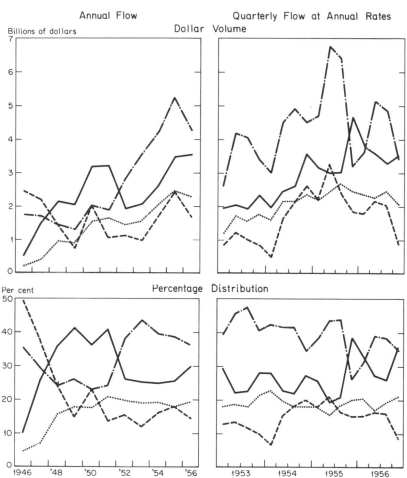

SOURCE: Klaman, *Volume of Mortgage Debt*, Table 23.

institutions regarded mortgage investments with maximum or steadily increasing favor during the five years ending in 1950.[3] Commercial banks, on the other hand, faced with a different situation at the war's end and having investment programs and objectives basically different from those of the other types of financial institutions, committed a much larger share of their net loans and investments to mortgages in the immediate postwar years than in subsequent years.[4]

Action of commercial banks in the early postwar years was unique, due largely to the unusually heavy volume of their federal government security holdings at the end of 1945. In 1946 and 1947 they reduced these holdings by more than $20 billion, representing two-thirds of their net sales during the entire period through 1956. Liquidity needs were small while the price of government bonds was supported by the Federal Reserve. With mortgage portfolios depleted and mortgage yields attractive relative to other loans and securities, banks placed an exceptionally large share of funds into mortgages during each of the years 1946–1948 compared with later postwar years. Net acquisition of mortgages by commercial banks, as shown in Chart 13, amounted to over 40 per cent of their net loans and investments in 1946 and to about 30 per cent in 1947 and 1948. The record 1946 share was about three times the proportion committed to mortgages by savings banks or life insurance companies.

The net dollar flow of mortgages originating with commercial banks in 1946 and 1947 was also appreciably larger than that of any other type of institutional investor—nearly one-half in 1946 and two-fifths in 1947 of the combined net flow from the others (Chart 14). After their swift postwar readjustment of investment portfolios, commercial banks reduced their acquisition of mortgages steadily through 1949, but sharply increased them in 1950, as construction and real estate activity accelerated. From then on, commercial banks receded as suppliers of permanent mortgage funds and advanced as suppliers of short-term construction and interim mortgage financing.[5]

[3] Savings and loan associations always try to maximize mortgage investments, in keeping with their specialized functions.

[4] See Chapter 6 for a discussion of mortgage lending policies and practices of the main types of financial institutions. Capital market activities of other types of institutional investors, which played an insignificant role as suppliers of postwar mortgage funds, are excluded here. As shown in Table 5, the net flows of mortgage funds through financial institutions other than the four main types amounted to less than 5 per cent in the full postwar decade.

[5] See Chapter 6 for a discussion of the practices and policies of commercial bank mortgage lending. See also "Commercial Banks in the Mortgage Market," *Monthly Review of Credit and Business Conditions*, Federal Reserve Bank of New York, April 1956.

Life insurance companies, like commercial banks, sold about one-third of their U.S. government obligations in the first five years after the war in order to acquire higher-yield assets. Unlike commercial banks, however, their readjustment to peacetime capital markets was less immediate, as they continued during 1946 to increase slightly their holdings of federal obligations. From a low that year of only 15 per cent of their net capital market investments in mortgages, they raised their share to nearly one-third in the following two years, about equal to the proportion for commercial banks. By 1950, their ratio of mortgage to capital market flows had risen to 60 per cent in response to the expansive forces of large borrower demands, favorable yields, Federal Reserve support of government bond prices, and liberalized federal mortgage programs. The absolute flow of mortgage funds from life insurance companies between 1948 and 1951, following two years at relatively low levels, was substantially greater than that from other types of financial intermediaries (Chart 14).

The relatively slow entrance of life insurance companies into mortgage markets after the war stemmed in part from a generally cautious attitude toward mortgage investments and in part from problems of market organization and techniques of mortgage acquisition. Some companies with acute memories of the thirties were skeptical about early postwar real estate values and sensitive about the possibility of foreclosure actions. As nationwide lenders, life insurance companies, unlike commercial banks and savings and loan associations, acquire the bulk of their residential mortgage loans through mortgage correspondent or branch office organizations.[6] Dismantled after many years of reduced mortgage activity during depression and war, their restoration was a prerequisite to effective volume operation. The time consumed delayed participation of life insurance companies in mortgage markets, particularly in the burgeoning VA mortgage loan program. The net flow of funds from financial institutions into VA-guaranteed mortgages amounted to almost one-half of their total net mortgage flow in 1946 and 1947, when insurance company mortgage lending was lagging. Multifamily and nonresidential real estate and construction markets, in which life insurance companies are leading lenders and generally place loans directly, are relatively much less important outlets for funds than home mortgages. As they gradually developed effective channels for home mortgage loan acquisition, and the favorable climate for such investment continued, life insurance companies sharply expanded their participation

[6] See Chapter 6.

in mortgage markets. By 1948, they had become the leading supplier of mortgage funds—a position held through 1951.

The investment behavior of mutual savings banks in the early postwar years was conditioned by their limited outlets for mortgage loans. They are located principally in the eastern part of the country, where real estate and construction markets were less active than in more rapidly growing areas. Moreover, until 1949 and 1950, most state statutes limited savings bank investments in mortgages to properties located within specified geographic areas, generally inside state boundaries. Thus, savings banks acquired a much smaller volume of mortgages in the immediate postwar years than their net inflow of savings and holdings of government securities would have allowed; indeed, their purchases of government securities in 1946 and 1947 amounted to $1.2 billion, almost twice the net acquisition of mortgages in those years.

When real estate and construction activity picked up generally, and banking laws of most states were amended to permit the acquisition of out-of-state FHA and VA loans, savings banks were free to expand in the field. They liquidated Treasury securities from 1948 to 1950 about as rapidly as they had acquired them in the two years before and invested an increasing share of funds in higher-yield mortgages. The share of their net capital market investments put into mortgages rose from a low of 13 per cent in 1946 to 67 per cent in 1948 and to 100 per cent in 1950. In absolute amounts, savings banks increased their net acquisition of mortgages from a little over $200 million in 1946 to over $1.5 billion in 1950, a relative gain of from 6 to 18 per cent in the total net flow of mortgage funds from the main types of financial institutions (Chart 14).

Savings and loan associations, limited by law mainly to investment in mortgages and federal government obligations, placed nearly all of their net capital market investments, 1946 to 1950, in mortgages (Chart 13). At the same time they liquidated nearly $1 billion of government bonds. Their absolute net flow of mortgage funds through 1951 was less, however, than the flow from commercial banks during the early part of the period and from life insurance companies during the latter part. While the associations did not again during that decade limit their net investment activity entirely to mortgages, after 1951 their net flow of mortgage funds exceeded those from other main types of financial institutions by a wide margin (Chart 14).

The change in relative importance of savings and loan associations as suppliers of mortgage funds was owing mainly to the amounts of their investment funds in comparison with those of other financial intermediaries. The relative attractiveness of mortgages to competing institutions may also have been a factor, however. It is possible, for example, that commercial banks and life insurance companies, having extraordinarily large reservoirs of low-yield government securities to sell in a guaranteed par market and looking favorably upon mortgage yields, reduced the opportunities for mortgage investment by savings and loan associations. Although, the associations used the bulk of their net inflow of funds from share capital and sale of governments to acquire mortgages, they could also have met larger demands for mortgage credit by increasing their borrowing from the Federal Home Loan Banks.

FLOWS INTO VARIOUS MORTGAGE MARKET SECTORS

Two basic facts stand out in even a cursory analysis of postwar mortgage market flows:[7] nearly all funds in each year were supplied by the four main types of financial institutions, and they were used to finance one- to four-family properties (Charts 15 and 16). While all other types of private lenders combined were reducing their relative mortgage market participation from over one-fourth in 1946 to less than one-tenth in 1950, the four main types of financial institutions were increasing their share of the market from four-fifths to almost nine-tenths. The 1950 proportion of the total net flow of mortgage funds provided by the main financial institutions was larger than in any other year on record through 1956. For all but commercial banks this flow represented a larger share of their net capital market investments than in any other year of the postwar decade except 1955 and 1956. Federal agencies, meanwhile, expanded their share of the market from a negative percentage in 1946 to close to one-tenth in 1949 before decreasing it again in 1950. The combined federal lending, shown in Chart 15, resulted from offsetting actions of the Home Owners Loan Corporation, which was steadily liquidating mortgages acquired during the thirties, and of the Federal National Mortgage Association, which was acquiring mortgages in support of the federally underwritten mortgage market.[8]

The absolute and relative decline in net mortgage flows from the main types of financial institutions in 1949 followed the rise in bond yields during 1948 and 1949, which attracted institutional funds. Declines in consumer demands for housing and in business demands for external

---

[7] For details of the analysis recapitulated here, see Chapter 3.

[8] The varying participation of FNMA in the market for VA and FHA mortgages is discussed in Chapter 7 and shown in Charts 19 and 20.

CHART 15

Net Flow of Mortgage Funds from Broad Lender Groups, 1946–1956

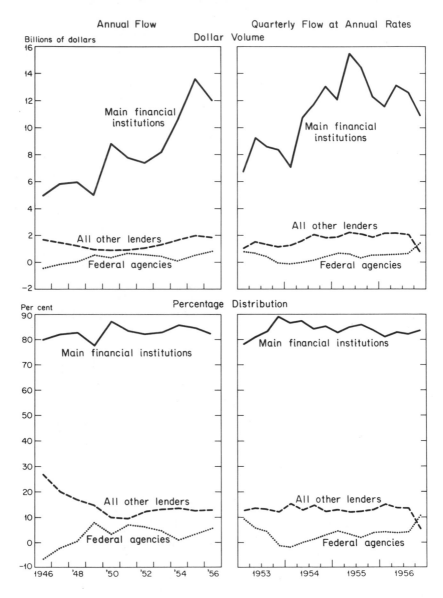

CHART 16
Net Flow of Mortgage Funds for Loans on Main Classes of Property, 1946–1956

—·—·— 1- to 4-family
———— Multifamily
– – – – – Nonresidential
················ Farm

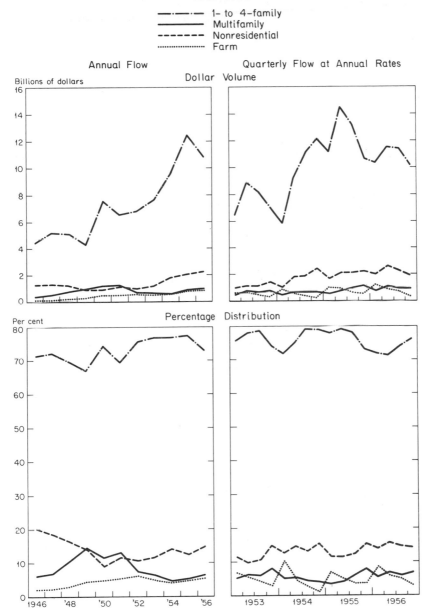

Annual Flow

Quarterly Flow at Annual Rates

Dollar Volume

Percentage Distribution

Source: Klaman, *Volume of Mortgage Debt*, Table 22.

financing accompanying the 1948–1949 business recession were also significant factors in reduction of both one- to four-family and nonresidential mortgage flows in 1949. Legislation permitting FNMA to provide increased support to the market for federally underwritten mortgages undoubtedly lessened the decline. The continued increase in the flow of mortgage funds into multifamily properties during 1949, shown in Chart 15, was due entirely to the profitable and riskless effects of the government's liberal FHA Section 608 program. Conventional mortgage financing of multifamily properties declined in 1949 following small increases in the two years before.

The short-lived 1948–1949 recession was followed by a rapidly accelerating business recovery in 1950. In real estate and mortgage markets the year 1950 stands out as one of the most expansive in the postwar decade. Even before the Korean War began in June, a combination of private market and federal government influences was at work to produce the previously mentioned record-breaking flow of mortgage funds. The production of new private housing reached a record annual rate of close to 1.5 million units in the summer of 1950, sales of existing properties were also unusually large, and nonresidential contract awards and construction were expanding rapidly. The large volume of credit readily available, however, under progressively broadened and liberalized federal mortgage underwriting programs and easier conventional lending terms, was in itself an important stimulant to the demand for housing—so dependent on credit availability and terms.

Continued unfulfilled needs for basic physical facilities, full employment, high and rising incomes, substantial liquid asset holdings, and high rates of family and household formation were, of course, basic stimulants of housing demand in that period. The large volume of credit readily available, however, under progressively broadened and liberalized federal mortgage underwriting programs and easier conventional lending terms, was in itself an important stimulant to the demand for housing—so dependent on credit availability and terms.

HOME MORTGAGE FLOWS, BY TYPE OF MORTGAGE
AND FINANCIAL INSTITUTION

While home financing dominated mortgage markets throughout the postwar decade, types of mortgages and chief sources of funds varied with shifting market forces. Among the most striking developments was the almost complete reversal of the positions of federally underwritten and conventional mortgage lending between the first and second halves of the decade. During the first half of almost uninterrupted federal expansionary policies, federally underwritten mortgage flows amounted to well over one-half to two-thirds of total net home mortgage flows. Through most of the second half-decade, conventional mortgage flows were substantially larger than federally underwritten.

The wisdom of expansionary federal residential mortgage programs and policies during the early postwar years, described in Chapter 3, when demands were pressing against limited resources of materials and labor has often been questioned. In the view of some, the result of those policies was not additional housing but rather higher prices for houses that would have been produced anyway.[9] But there can be little doubt that the demand for mortgage funds must have been increased whether to finance additional units or the same number at higher prices. Moreover, the liberal loan-to-value ratios of federally underwritten mortgage terms further spurred the volume of mortgage funds associated with a given volume of real estate and construction activity.

Type of Home Mortgage Flows

The substantially larger volume of federally underwritten home mortgage flows compared with conventional in most years through 1951 resulted from sharply shifting and nearly compensating movements between FHA and VA loans. Clearly, the two federal mortgage underwriting programs, though similar in principle and operation, have enough basic differences in their internal characteristics and the market areas served to respond differently to changing economic forces. This is evident whether loan volume is measured in terms of net mortgage flows (Chart 17), influenced by the varying pattern of repayments as well as by other independent forces, or in terms of gross flows (Chart 18), unaffected by repayment rates. On either basis, the volume of VA financing has fluctuated more widely and irregularly than either FHA or conventional mortgage financing.

The VA mortgage guarantee program, following the liberalizing amendments of late 1945 (Chapter 3), was at once attractive to both potential lenders and borrowers in the immediate postwar years. In view

---

[9] On this point, see Marriner S. Eccles, "Inflationary Aspects of Housing Finance," *Federal Reserve Bulletin*, December 1947, pp. 1,463–1,465; Leo Grebler, "Stabilizing Residential Construction," *American Economic Review*, September 1949, and *The Role of Federal Credit Aids in Residential Construction*, Occasional Paper 39, New York, National Bureau of Economic Research, 1953, pp. 64–65; Miles L. Colean and Robinson Newcomb, *Stabilizing Construction, the Record and Potential*, New York, 1952, pp. 145–147; and R. J. Saulnier, Harold G. Halcrow, and Neil H. Jacoby, *Federal Programs of Lending, Loan Insurance, and Loan Guarantees*, Princeton University Press for NBER, 1958, pp. 336–347.

CHART 17
Net Flow of Home Mortgage Funds, by Type of Mortgage, 1946–1956

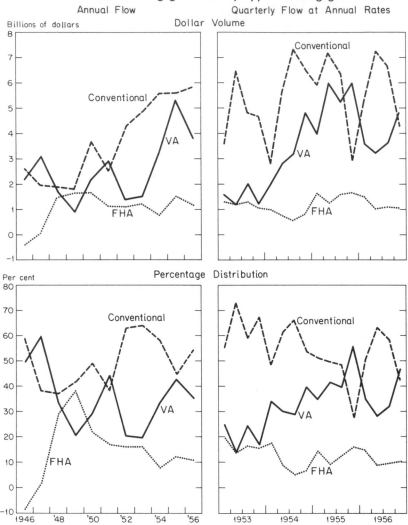

SOURCE: Klaman, *Volume of Mortgage Debt*, Table 22.

of yields available at the time on capital market securities of comparable risk, institutional investors were quite willing to lend on federally guaranteed obligations bearing a contract interest rate of 4 per cent. After the rapid demobilization of the armed forces in 1945 and 1946, veterans placed mounting pressure on the existing housing supply and, unable to find suitable rental quarters, were quite willing to borrow on

CHART 18

Gross Flow of Federally Underwritten Mortgage Loans, 1946–1956

———— VA
··············· FHA 1- to 4-family
------- FHA multifamily

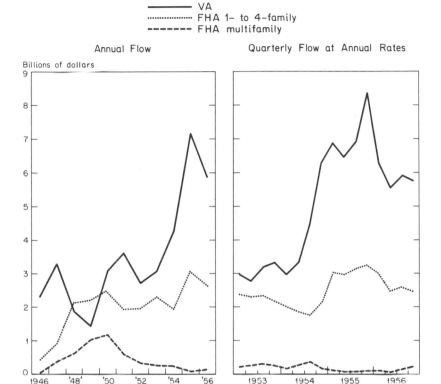

SOURCE: Data in annual reports and monthly releases of the Federal Housing Administration and Veterans Administration.

liberal VA loan terms to finance home ownership. The flow of VA-guaranteed mortgage funds increased rapidly during 1946 and 1947, its net being a larger share of the total flow of home mortgage funds than in any other postwar year. Gross VA mortgage lending amounted to $3.3 billion in 1947, nearly four times the gross volume of FHA-insured home mortgage lending, and a volume not again reached until 1951. The Veterans Administration found that "the limited supply of housing rather than a limited flow of investment money proved to be the chief restraining influence on the volume of housing loan applications."[10]

The decline in home mortgage lending during 1949, noted earlier, was almost entirely in VA loans, which had also dropped sharply in 1948.

[10] Veterans Administration, *GI Loans—the First 10 Years (1944–54)*, VA Pamphlet VA-11, June 22, 1954, pages 8–9.

Underlying the two-year decrease were a readjustment from the earlier rapid rise to unusually high levels, and the reduced attractiveness to investors of the 4 per cent VA contract interest rate in view of rising government and other bond yields (Chapter 4). Also important was the fact that, during part of the period, no secondary market facility existed to support the VA loan program.

In the general economic expansion of 1950 there was a sharp turnabout in the volume of VA mortgage lending, as borrower demands accelerated and investors once again found yields on VA loans attractive in the prevailing easy credit markets. Special factors tending to stimulate the flow of VA mortgage funds included the broadening of FNMA's authority to purchase VA loans and the liberalization of the VA program for both borrowers and lenders under the Housing Act of 1950 (Chapter 3). An indication of the easy credit markets that prevailed in 1950 was the fact that well over two-fifths of all VA loans made in that year called for no down payment, a proportion not approached again until 1955. The large volume of loan applications and commitments made in the unusual 1950 market pushed VA loan closings higher in 1951, after FHA and conventional home mortgage lending had already turned down.

The sharply fluctuating fortunes of the veterans' mortgage loan program during the first half of the postwar decade were not shared by FHA mortgage programs, as shown in Charts 17 and 18. The gross flows of funds into FHA-insured one- to four-family and multifamily housing mortgages rose steadily from a very low level in 1946 to a peak in 1950, while the flow of VA mortgage funds was going through a complete cycle. The low level of FHA-insured mortgage financing immediately after the war was brought about by reduced demands relative to those for VA and conventional loans and by discontinuance of the liberal Title VI programs under which most wartime residential construction had been financed. During 1946, in fact, the volume of FHA mortgage insurance written was markedly less than the average volume written during the war and smaller than in any year back to 1938. The reintroduction of Title VI programs on both homes and rental projects in late 1946 was followed by a sharp increase in the flow of FHA mortgage funds. On rental projects practically all FHA loans from 1947 to 1950 were made under that program. Its expiration resulted in a rapid decline after 1950 in FHA multifamily financing, and in all other multifamily housing construction. For one- to four-family houses the Title VI program was replaced by a broadly liberalized Title II program in 1948, which continued to attract an increasing amount of funds to FHA home mortgages through 1950.[11]

In addition to the stimuli provided by liberalized programs, and the unusually low level of activity in 1946–1947, there were other factors behind the increased flow of FHA mortgages in 1948–1949, years of reduced VA mortgage activity. First, the contract interest rate differential—FHA home mortgage loans at $4\frac{1}{2}$ per cent and VA loans at 4 per cent—gave FHA loans more appeal while "free market" interest rates and yields were rising. Second, the Federal National Mortgage Association provided a secondary market facility for FHA, but for VA loans during only part of the period. Third, after the gratitude-inspired rush to provide home loans for returning veterans had subsided somewhat, many institutional investors reduced their VA loan activity from the very high levels to which it had risen in favor of the tried and familiar FHA mortgage program and higher-yield conventional mortgages. Also the VA program provided only 50 per cent guarantee as against 100 per cent insurance for FHA loans.

Unlike the pattern of flows into VA and FHA mortgages, the flow into conventional home mortgages was relatively stable during 1946–1949 but increased sharply in the 1950 general expansion. The stability and rise reflected in large part the flexibility of conventional mortgage interest rates, which, after a time lag inherent in mortgage operations, rose along with rates on other capital market securities (Chart 7).[12] Investors, therefore, did not turn away from conventional mortgages as they did from VA loans when bond prices fell. It is not unlikely that the flow of funds into conventional mortgages would have been greater in the early postwar years if consumer demands for such loans had been greater. Interviews with investment officers of large financial institutions indicate that they were not able to obtain as many conventional mortgages as they wanted in this period. The same was true in most later postwar years.

Sources of Home Mortgage Funds

The shifting importance of the various types of home mortgage financing, just described, was matched by changes in market participation of

---

[11] The basic importance of the FHA Title VI program to the market for multifamily construction has been suggested in Chapter 3. For a further discussion see Leo Grebler, *The Role of Federal Credit Aids in Residential Construction*, New York, NBER, 1953, pages 26–28. Changes in FHA Title VI and Title II programs are discussed in Chapter 3, above.

[12] The nature of time lags in mortgage interest rates and in mortgage operations generally is discussed in Chapters 4 and 7.

financial institutions, including the Federal National Mortgage Association. Those changes in sources of mortgage flows are shown in Charts 19, 20, and 21. It is clear that the main shifts in ranking among lenders in both halves of the decade occurred in the market for VA mortgage loans. In the markets for FHA and conventional home mortgage loans one type of lender was dominant in most of the period through 1950—life insurance companies in FHA, and savings and loan associations in conventional. Savings and loan associations continued to be the dominant conventional mortgage lender in the second half of the decade, but life insurance companies relinquished their position of leadership in the FHA market to commercial banks and savings banks.

In the years immediately following the war, savings and loan associations and commercial banks were by far the leading participants in the rising market for VA loans. Yields were relatively favorable, their patriotic appeal was high, while life insurance companies and mutual savings banks were temporarily handicapped by underdeveloped mortgage correspondent systems and restrictive state laws, noted earlier in this chapter. In the changing capital market environment of 1948–1949, all the main types of financial institutions except mutual savings banks reduced their VA mortgage lending sharply. The savings banks increased their acquisition of VA mortgages slightly, as out-of-state lending was permitted by some states and as limited alternative investments at home offered little better yields.

During 1950 and 1951 only life insurance companies among the private lenders contributed importantly to the sharp upturn in the flow of VA mortgages. Most of the VA loan acquisitions by these institutions through 1951, after the Federal Reserve–Treasury accord, were closings based on the large volume of commitments made in the easy credit markets of 1950 and early 1951. Other private mortgage lenders showed only modest changes in their VA loan activity.

The significance of the reorganization of FNMA in 1948 (Chapter 3) with authority to purchase VA mortgages under advance commitments on an increasingly liberal basis is clearly visible in Chart 19. During 1949, when the private market for VA loans was depressed, the Association acquired more than one-third of the total net flow of VA mortgages, a larger share than any of the main types of private financial institutions. In the expanded 1950 VA loan market, only life insurance companies supplied a net volume of funds for GI loans larger than FNMA did.

FNMA played a much less significant role in the market for FHA loans during the first half-decade, being a net purchaser only during 1948

CHART 19

Net Flow of VA-Guaranteed Mortgage Funds from Main Types of Financial Institutions, 1946–1956

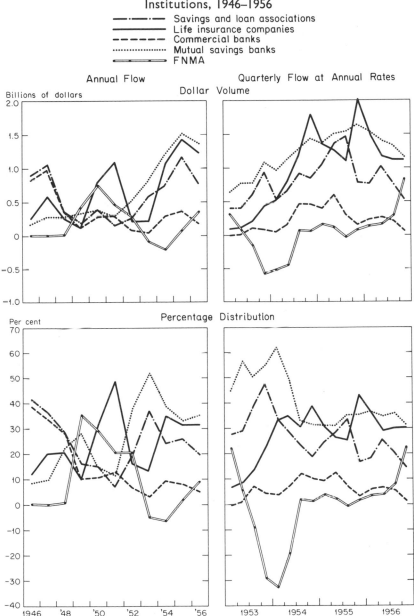

SOURCE: Klaman, *Volume of Mortgage Debt*, Tables 33 and 41.

CHART 20
Net Flow of FHA-Insured Home Mortgage Funds from Main Types of Financial Institutions, 1946–1956

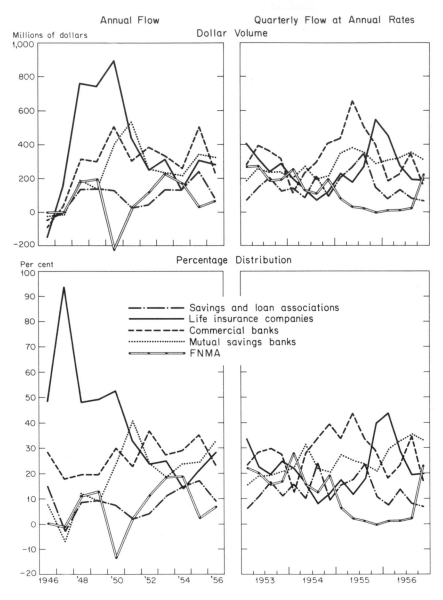

SOURCE: Klaman, *Volume of Mortgage Debt*, Tables 31 and 41.

CHART 21
Net Flow of Conventional Home Mortgage Funds from Main Types of Financial Institutions, 1946–1956

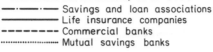

—·—·— Savings and loan associations
———— Life insurance companies
------- Commercial banks
··········· Mutual savings banks

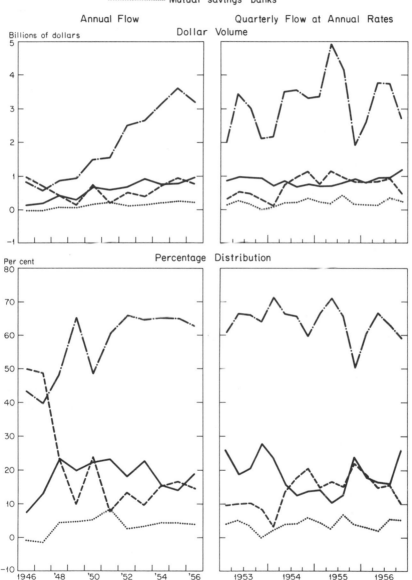

SOURCE: Klaman, *Volume of Mortgage Debt,* Table 35.

119

and 1949, when it supplied about one-eighth of the total net flow. Participation of private lenders also varied significantly from their share in the VA market, as may be seen from Chart 20. All the main types of financial institutions were slow to invest in FHA mortgages in the immediate postwar years. Responding to reactivated and liberalized FHA mortgage programs and to the resulting increase in demands, most institutional investors, led by life insurance companies, significantly increased their net FHA mortgage flows through 1950. Savings and loan associations continued their prewar aversion to the FHA mortgage program; they supplied the smallest share of FHA mortgage funds, amounting at the maximum to less than 10 per cent during 1948 and 1949.[13]

Savings and loan associations, in sharp contrast to their minor role in the market for FHA home loans, dominated the conventional home mortgage market after 1947 as few lenders have dominated any other sector of the capital market. In the first two postwar years, however, commercial banks, in an unusually liquid position, acquired conventional home mortgage loans in larger volume than that of savings and loan associations or any other type of lender. Of the total conventional home mortgage flow from financial institutions in 1946 and 1947, one-half was from commercial banks, a proportion not again approached in the postwar decade.

Net Flow of Mortgage Funds in a Changing Capital Market Framework, 1951–1956

The abrupt capital market changes following the outbreak of war in Korea and the Federal Reserve-Treasury "accord" have been described in Chapters 3 and 4. They resulted in marked shifts in the flow of mortgage funds relative to other capital market flows, and shifts also within the various mortgage market sectors. Responding to alternating forces of market restraint and expansion, the flow of funds into mortgages alternately contracted and expanded (in contrast to the almost uninterrupted expansion of the first half-decade). The tides of flows were governed largely by shifts in the supply of funds, since demands for funds continued generally strong throughout 1951–1956, though restrained for a time by Regulation X.

Financial institutions, no longer enjoying the almost unlimited liquidity of the pre- "accord" days, could not always meet all demands for funds

---

[13] See Chapter 6 for a discussion of the factors behind the aversion of savings and loan associations to FHA mortgage loans.

in the capital market. The basic importance of yield in choosing investments channeled more funds into conventional mortgages with flexible rates than into federally underwritten mortgages with their fixed maximum interest rates, except during periods of credit ease. Financial institutions with broad alternative investment outlets adjusted their total mortgage flows more frequently and widely than those with limited outlets. But all types of investors were influenced in their choice of mortgage investments by changing yields.

MORTGAGE FLOWS RELATIVE TO OTHER CAPITAL MARKET FLOWS

The net flow of funds into mortgages, while fluctuating appreciably in the second half-decade, continued to exceed the flows into other capital market securities by a wide margin in most years. The margin narrowed markedly in 1951–1953 when advancing yields on corporate and other securities (Chart 7) attracted investors. The ratio of mortgage to other capital market flows declined to a low of less than two-fifths in 1952 and 1953 from close to three-fifths in 1950 (Chart 12). Subsequently, the ratio advanced through 1955, bolstered by the lifting of direct federal mortgage lending restrictions, the shift from general credit restraint to ease, and declines in yields on competitive instruments. The moderate 1956 decline in net mortgage flows followed the return during 1955 to a Federal Reserve policy of credit restraint and restrictive federal mortgage programs, and sharp increases in corporate borrowing to finance capital expenditures (Chapter 3).

Throughout the period, changes in the flow of funds into mortgages and into corporate securities were in opposite directions in every year but 1955. It is explained partly by the behavior of life insurance companies– one important source for both types of instruments—which, generally sensitive to market yields, matched each annual increase in net acquisition of one type by a decrease in the other.[14] Not only life insurance companies but also mutual savings banks and savings and loan associations reduced their shares of net capital market investments in mortgages in 1951–1953 (Chart 13). For savings and loan associations, the relative reduction was owing to net acquisition of government securities at increasingly favorable yields following net selling in earlier years. For mutual savings banks, as for life insurance companies, the reduction was in favor of corporate and municipal securities. Commercial banks, well before 1951, reduced their share of

---

[14] This sensitivity to market yields is not so clear on a quarterly basis because of differences in timing of acquisitions, which reflect the fundamental importance of prior commitments in the mortgage field. The sensitivity of life insurance companies to changes in market yields would undoubtedly be greater than it is if acquisitions were not based on commitments made several months earlier, often under different market conditions.

investments going into mortgages as part of a rapid readjustment in investment portfolios right after the war.

Beginning around mid-1953, mortgages regained favor among financial institutions, responding to the previously described expansive forces. Life insurance companies and mutual savings banks, in particular, increased their mortgage investments strongly relative to other capital market securities through 1955. The continued high ratio for life insurance companies in 1956, after the return of restraining market forces, was due to the lengthened lag between commitments and acquisitions compared with earlier years.[15] The gradually increased ratio for savings and loan associations through 1954 was reduced later; the associations tried to improve liquidity ratios through acquisition of government bonds partly in response to requests of the Federal Home Loan Bank System that they hold mortgage commitments in line with savings inflows.

Financial institutions, in adjusting their investment activities to the new post-Korean capital market setting, showed wide variation in their patterns of net mortgage flows. Life insurance companies and commercial banks fluctuated most widely in acquisitions, going through a complete cycle between 1950 and 1956 (Chart 14). This resulted in part from their greater choice of alternative investments compared with savings and loan associations and mutual savings banks. The steep rise in annual net flow of mortgage funds from savings and loan associations after 1951 was in keeping with their specialized nature as mortgage lenders. With mortgage funds from other institutions reduced during 1952–1953, borrowers turned to savings and loan associations, which increased their share of the total net mortgage flow to well over two-fifths. That share was reduced gradually in 1954–1956 as banks and insurance companies increased their share of the total.

Quarterly movements in the flow of mortgage funds during 1953–1956, when federal monetary and housing policies were undergoing basic change, are somewhat more revealing—despite limitations of data—than annual flows are. An increase in mortgage flows from each of the main types of financial institutions through 1954, following the shift to monetary ease and removal of mortgage credit restrictions in late 1953, is apparent from Chart 14. While on an annual basis the pickup continued through 1955, quarterly data reveal important timing differences among the institutions.

Commercial banks reduced their net mortgage flows sharply after mid-1955, as the shift in Federal Reserve policy from ease to restraint quickly

---

[15] The use of the forward commitment by life insurance companies in 1954 and 1955 was fairly widespread, as noted in Chapters 7 and 8.

influenced reserve positions. Mutual savings banks, reacting somewhat more slowly to market changes, reduced their net mortgage flow—except into VA loans—after the third quarter of 1955 (Chart 19). The quarterly mortgage flow from life insurance companies and savings and loan associations is especially difficult to interpret because of seasonal operations and the technical timing pattern of mortgage acquisitions, discussed below. Allowing for these factors it seems correct that life insurance companies did not begin to reduce their net flow of mortgage funds until early in 1956 in response to restraining market influences that began almost a year earlier. The steep decline in the net flow of mortgages from savings and loan associations between the third and fourth quarters of 1955 was clearly more than seasonal. It may be traced directly to the tightening capital market at the time when the Federal Home Loan Banks found it increasingly difficult to raise funds and cautioned the associations against overextending themselves.

While the time period is too short to establish definite seasonal trends, it is unmistakeable that in the fourth quarter of each year net mortgage acquisitions of life insurance companies rose, and those of savings and loan associations declined. In the former case, the regularity of movement derives from a market technique whereby commitments or allocations of funds to originate mortgages are made early in the year to mortgage correspondents who generally complete and deliver them towards the end of the year.[16] In the latter case, it seems to result from changes brought about in part by consistent falling off at the end of each year of existing house sales, for which the associations make a considerable portion of their loans. In part the reduction of fourth-quarter savings and loan mortgage acquisitions is also to accommodate heavy seasonal withdrawals from share accounts and to pay down indebtedness to the Federal Home Loan Banks by the end of the year. No definite seasonal pattern can be discerned in movements of mortgage flows from commercial or mutual savings banks.

FLOWS INTO VARIOUS MORTGAGE MARKET SECTORS

Changes in the net flow of mortgage funds during the second half-decade, as in the first, were compounded chiefly of changes in net flows from the four main types of financial institutions on one- to four-family properties. During the 1951–1953 and 1955–1956 periods of credit stringency, the main financial institutions reduced their mortgage market participation

---

[16] See Saul B. Klaman, *Postwar Rise of Mortgage Companies*, New York, NBER, 1959, for a discussion of differences in market timing between life insurance companies and mortgage companies.

relative to that of other lenders (Chart 15). Similarly, during the 1953–1955 period of credit ease they increased their participation more than other lenders did.

This broad conclusion derived from annual data on flows may be sharpened somewhat by reference to quarterly figures. In the relative market participation of financial institutions, these data disclose a steady quarter-by-quarter increase during 1953, followed by a halting decline through 1954. Their absolute participation, however, increased sharply during 1954. A further relative decline, on balance, occurred during the quarters of 1955 and 1956. The failure of the financial institutions to increase their relative mortgage market participation steadily during most of the easy credit period from mid-1953 to early 1955 can be explained in part by technical market adjustments. Mortgage companies (accounting for a large part of the holdings of "all other lenders") were expanding their inventories with the help of commercial bank credit, while permanent investors were processing the large backlog of earlier commitments.[17] Another important market factor during 1954–1955 was the increased participation of FNMA (accounting for most of the net flow from federal agencies shown in Chart 15) following the Housing Amendments Act of 1953 containing liberalized provisions. The reduced flow of funds from private lenders in the tightened mortgage market of 1956 was accompanied by a further expansion in the activity of federal agencies.

The impact of the readjustments in mortgage markets after 1950 on the main real estate sectors varied in both timing and intensity. The reduction in net mortgage flows during 1951, following the unusual expansion of 1950, was limited entirely to the one- to four-family sector. Multifamily and nonresidential mortgage flows did not decline until 1952, during the height of general credit stringency and federal mortgage credit restrictions. The much greater decline in multifamily mortgage flows, and their continued low level through 1954 after mortgage markets had eased and the flow into other sectors had turned up, showed the effects of termination of the liberal FHA 608 mortgage program in 1950 (see Chapter 3).

The changing significance of the dominant one- to four-family sector in the total mortgage market during periods of credit expansion and contraction is strikingly shown by quarterly data in Chart 16. The unusually rapid and nearly uninterrupted expansion in the flow of home mortgage funds between the first quarter of 1954 and second quarter of 1955 increased the share of that real estate sector in total mortgage flows from less than

[17] See Klaman, *Postwar Rise of Mortgage Companies*, for a discussion of mortgage company inventories and activity relative to institutional investors in the 1953–1955 period.

three-fourths to almost four-fifths. The impact of credit restraint, greater on the home mortgage market sector than on other sectors after early 1955, is manifest in the sharp drop in one- to four-family mortgage flows, while flows into other sectors showed relatively little change. The greater volatility of the one- to four-family mortgage sector during the 1955–1956 period of credit restraint as well as the 1954–1955 period of credit ease reflected chiefly the varying flow into federally underwritten mortgages. Conventional home mortgage flows were far less volatile during periods of changing capital market yields.

Before further discussion of developments within the home mortgage market, seasonal movements in the various types of mortgage flows shown by the quarterly data in Chart 16 will be touched upon. The period under observation is, of course, too short to establish definite conclusions, but some tentative observations appear justified. In the one- to four-family sector, second and third quarter flows were invariably highest, except in 1954, and there was a second-quarter peak in each year except 1954. The disruption of a possible seasonal pattern in net home mortgage flows during 1954 may be explained by an unusual year of steady mortgage expansion following two years of contraction. The otherwise regularly higher levels during the second and third quarters of each year, compared with the first and fourth quarters, appear to follow seasonal patterns of building and real estate activity.[18] No clear pattern emerges, however, in the multi-family mortgage sector. In the nonresidential and farm sectors, there are indications of a possible seasonal pattern, with peaks at opposite ends of the year—nonresidential in the fourth quarter of each year except 1956, and farm mortgage flows in the first quarter, except in 1953.

HOME MORTGAGE FLOWS, BY TYPE OF MORTGAGE AND FINANCIAL INSTITUTION

The volatility of federally underwritten home mortgage lending (especially in the VA sector) compared with conventional home mortgage lending, which was clearly evident in the first half-decade, was strikingly apparent in the second half as well. Within the federally underwritten sector, the flow of funds into VA and FHA mortgages continued to vary markedly; fluctuations in volume and degree of change were great. Observations of changes in VA, FHA, and conventional mortgage flows during alternating periods of capital market stringency and ease suggest significantly different

---

[18] Quarterly data back to 1949, developed by the author at the Federal Reserve, indicate that in all years except 1949 the peak in one- to four-family mortgage flows was reached in the second or third quarters.

reactions of major financial institutions to investment opportunities. They suggest also changing demands of potential borrowers for different types of mortgages.

Types of Home Mortgage Flows

Analysis of the impact of shifting market forces on the major home mortgage sectors during 1951–1956 is aided by the availability of annual estimates of gross mortgage lending to finance new and existing house purchases, shown in Chart 22.[19] Two things are readily apparent: the substantially greater importance of federally underwritten mortgages in markets for new houses than for existing houses; and the almost uninterrupted expansion in conventional mortgage lending in both new and existing house markets.

During 1951, the extension of conventional mortgage credit declined on new houses and rose on existing houses; this suggests the restraining influence of Regulation X, which was limited to markets for new houses. It suggests also the ineffectiveness of the voluntary credit restraint program, aimed at the extension of real estate credit on existing houses (Chapter 3). The effect of direct real estate credit restraint imposed through associated VA and FHA regulations was delayed because of the unusually large volume of mortgage commitments obtained by builders immediately before the effective date of the regulations.[20] Because of the outstanding commitments, both gross and net flows of funds into VA mortgages continued to rise sharply in 1951. Gross lending on VA and FHA mortgages to finance existing house purchases, also under direct federal regulation, declined in 1951, however. FHA lending on new houses also declined, notwithstanding a record volume of loan applications by builders. The decline is explained in large part by a shift to the more liberal VA loans, in heavy demand by veterans anxious to purchase under pre-Regulation X terms.

The direct effects of real estate credit controls are, of course, obscured by the influence on mortgage markets of stringent monetary and fiscal policies beginning in March 1951, and of FNMA's reduced purchasing authority in early 1952 (Chapter 3). All these actions undoubtedly played a part in the drop in federally underwritten mortgage lending in 1952 and its continued low level in 1953. In addition, a major deterrent to investment in

[19] Data are not available for years before 1950.

[20] The estimated number of requests to the Veterans Administration for appraisal of new houses exceeded 90,000 in October 1950, more than in any other month of the postwar decade. October applications to the Federal Housing Administration for insurance of mortgages were also an all-time high. Both dropped sharply in the later months of 1950 and in 1951.

CHART 22
Gross Mortgage Credit Extended to Finance House Purchases, 1950–1956

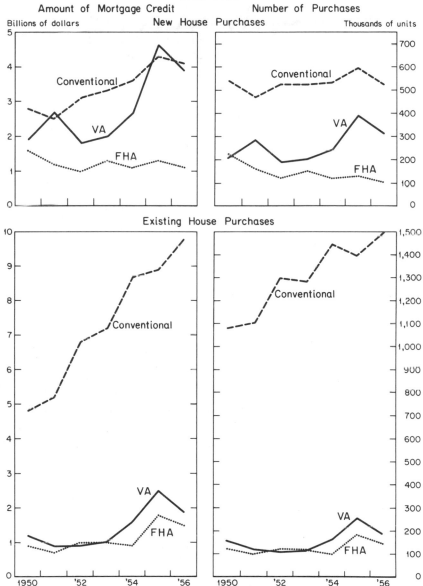

SOURCE: Data from the Federal Housing Administration and Veterans Administration and unpublished estimates made by the author while at the Federal Reserve Board. See also Table A–10 below.

guaranteed mortgages was the narrowing spread between rising yields on corporate and government securities and the fixed maximum contract interest rates on VA and FHA loans (see Charts 1 and 7). Conventional mortgages to finance both new and existing houses, meanwhile, attracted an increasing volume of funds during those years, as interest rates adjusted freely to changing capital market conditions. The share of net home mortgage flows going into conventional mortgages rose during 1952 and 1953 to well over three-fifths from around two-fifths in most preceding postwar years (Chart 17). It is, of course, not possible to say how much larger, if any, the flow of funds into conventional mortgages might have been during 1951–1953 in the absence of Regulation X. That Federal Reserve regulations and associated FHA and VA regulations may well have had a greater influence on the structure of real estate and mortgage markets— price shifts, types of houses purchased, relation between new and existing house purchases—than on the total flow of mortgage funds.[21]

The changed capital market environment after mid-1953—following reversal of monetary policy from restraint to ease, declines in bond yields and increases in FHA and VA contract interest rates, removal of mortgage credit restrictions, and renewed purchasing authority for FNMA—resulted in a relatively much greater increase in the gross flow of home mortgage funds than in the number of houses purchased with these funds. The rapid increase, 1953–1955, in VA mortgage flows on new houses (130 per cent) and on existing houses (150 per cent), for example, was larger than the increase in the number of new and existing houses purchased with such loans (91 per cent and 120 per cent respectively). The larger flow of mortgage funds per house purchase reflected in part a shift to higher-priced units and in part the ready availability of funds on unusually liberal terms. The proportion of VA loans made with no downpayment and thirty-year maturities increased from lows of about 5 per cent and 2 per cent, respectively, in early 1953 to peaks of about 45 per cent in the spring of 1955.

The increased flow of funds into VA mortgages on both a gross and a net basis was markedly greater than into FHA or conventional mortgages during that period of capital market ease. FHA mortgage flows began to

[21] See, for example, the following analyses of the effects of real estate credit controls: R. J. Saulnier, "An Appraisal of Selective Credit Controls," *American Economic Review*, Papers and Proceedings, May 1952, pp. 247–268; H. B. Schecter, "Home Financing 1949–51—Changes Under Credit Controls," *Housing Research* (Housing and Home Finance Agency), Winter 1951–1952, and "New Home Price Shifts, 1951–1952 Under Credit Controls as Amended in 1951," *Housing Research*, March 1953; and "House Purchases in the Five Months Following the Introduction of Real Estate Credit Regulation," *Federal Reserve Bulletin*, July 1951.

increase only in 1955, and then chiefly for financing existing house purchases. That increase, amounting almost to doubling, grew out of the broadly liberalized terms of FHA existing house loans authorized by the Housing Act of 1954. The difference in terms between FHA loans on new and existing houses was almost eliminated. Just as the easing of capital markets during 1953–1955 affected the flow of funds into VA mortgages more than the flow into FHA or conventional mortgages, the return to stringency in 1955–1956 bore chiefly upon the flow of VA mortgages. Both the gross volume of VA mortgage lending on new and existing houses and total net VA home mortgage flows declined appreciably in 1956. In contrast, there were but modest declines in FHA mortgage flows and little change in conventional lending.

Why were VA home mortgage flows more volatile than those of FHA after mid-1953, when contract interest rates on both types of mortgages were raised to the same level? The reader is referred to the discussion in Chapter 4 of the tendency of investors to regard the quality of VA loans as lower than that of FHA loans. In general, investors tend to pull out of VA loan markets more quickly in periods when alternative investment opportunities increase and yields rise, and to re-enter them more quickly when alternative investment opportunities are reduced and VA yields again appear attractive.

A closer analysis of the timing of home mortgage market reactions to capital market changes is permitted by quarterly data on net mortgage flows (Chart 17) and on gross FHA and VA mortgage loans closed (Chart 18). Allowing for apparent seasonal movements, the expansion in VA mortgage lending following the mid-1953 change in capital markets did not begin until early 1954; it continued upward to a peak in late 1955, after restraining forces had already returned to the fore. The reaction to the restraining forces in VA mortgage lending was not evident until early 1956, when a sharp decline in net and gross flows occurred. Prelending activity, however, indicated by appraisal requests received by VA, had begun to turn down somewhat earlier from the unprecedented volume reached in mid-1955.

Charts 17 and 18 indicate that FHA mortgage lending activity, both gross and net, also lagged behind changes in capital market conditions. In the rise, the lag was somewhat greater than in VA activity and in the decline about the same. It was not until the last quarter of 1954 that the flow into FHA home mortgages turned up and continued at a new high level through 1955. The subsequent decline began during the first quarter of 1956, as in VA markets, and leveled out at the reduced second-quarter level. Activity in FHA multifamily mortgage markets showed little re-action to basic capital market changes during 1953–1956. The principal reason for its continued low level was the termination of the FHA Section 608 program.

Sources of Home Mortgage Funds

Changes in the flow of funds into VA, FHA, and conventional home mortgages during the second half-decade, as in the first, rested upon signifi-cantly different reactions of major types of institutional investors to chang-ing capital market conditions. Those varied reactions in turn reflect the fundamental differences in purpose, policy, and function among the major financial intermediaries with respect to degree of specialization in mort-gages, methods of mortgage acquisition, types of mortgages preferred, and opportunities for alternative investments.[22] Life insurance companies and commercial banks, though basically different in their mortgage and other lending operations, have in common wide opportunities for alternative investments compared with savings and loan associations, for example; hence they reacted more sharply to changing capital market yields between 1951 and 1956.

The wide swings between contracted and expanded participation of life insurance companies, and secondarily of commercial banks, in the market for VA loans accounted in the main for the previously noted volatility of VA mortgage flows. Just as the decisive increase in VA mortgage flows during 1950 and 1951 was almost entirely from life insurance companies, so was the decline from 1951 to 1953. Net acquisition of VA loans by these institutions dropped from $1.1 billion in 1951 to little over $200 million in 1952 and 1953. Commercial banks also reduced their net VA mortgage acquisitions drastically from $290 million in 1951 to less than $50 million in 1953. In contrast, savings and loan associations and mutual savings banks continued to regard VA loans favorably during the years of credit restraint and acquired a steadily increasing amount of such loans from 1951 to 1953. Mutual savings banks, especially, having then only recently gained the right to acquire federally underwritten mortgages beyond state boundaries, forged ahead in the market.

The varied assessment by lenders of the desirability of VA loans was to bring about an incisive realignment of the four main types of financial

[22] See Chapter 6 for discussion of mortgage lending policies of the major types of financial intermediaries. See also Klaman, "Effects of Credit and Monetary Policy on Real Estate Markets, 1952–1954, "*Journal of Land Economics,* August 1956, for discussion of changes in residential mortgage lending activity of the major institutional investors during periods of credit ease and restraint.

institutions between 1951 and 1953. The positions of life insurance companies and mutual savings banks, in particular, were almost completely reversed. The former reduced their share of the net flow of VA mortgages from nearly one-half to little more than one-seventh, and the latter increased their share from one-eighth to more than one-half. The new position of leadership in VA loan markets acquired by mutual savings banks was maintained in later years of expansion and contraction, although not so dominant as in 1953.

While the savings banks and savings and loan associations continued their steady expansion of VA lending activity through 1955, life insurance companies and commercial banks reversed their 1951–1953 actions. They increased their net VA mortgage acquisitions during the period of market ease even more rapidly than they had reduced them earlier during market restraint. All four major types of private financial institutions reduced their net VA mortgage acquisitions during 1956 following the return to tightened capital market conditions in early 1955. As is evident from quarterly data, commercial banks reacted most promptly to the market change, beginning their reduction after mid-1955 (Chart 19). Mutual savings banks and life insurance companies, allowing for seasonal movements, waited to reduce their acquisitions until the first quarter of 1956. For mutual savings banks, the reduction in VA mortgage lending during 1956 was in contrast to their expansion during the earlier 1951–1953 period of general capital market stringency. It stemmed from—among other things—their built-up mortgage portfolio position and the high yields of other capital market securities. For savings and loan associations, the reduction reflected an adjustment from overcommitted positions and their reaction to pressures for restraint applied by the Federal Home Loan Banks.

The reduced availability of VA mortgage funds from private lenders during 1956 together with liberalized provisions for FNMA's purchase of mortgages led to a reversal of its policy after several years of reduced activity. Its increased participation in the VA loan market was both absolute and relative. Net purchases rose steadily from the mid-1955 low to a new record annual rate of over $800 million in the fourth quarter of 1956. FNMA's share of the VA market rose to over one-fifth to become larger than that of savings and loan associations and commercial banks.

A similar expansion occurred in FNMA's participation in the FHA home mortgage market during 1956, as private lenders withdrew from that market. Net purchases increased from an annual rate of minus $4 million in the last quarter of 1955 to a near record annual rate of plus $220 million one year later. Its one-fourth share of the net flow of FHA home mortgages in 1956 was exceeded only by the one-third share of mutual savings banks. In earlier post-1950 years of mortgage market contraction and expansion, the absolute and relative participation of FNMA in the FHA market was rising and falling in almost the reverse pattern of its participation in the VA market, to be seen by comparing Charts 19 and 20.

The varied pattern of FNMA market support is related to differences in the participation of private lenders in VA and FHA markets. The decline in net acquisition of FHA home mortgages by life insurance companies and commercial banks between 1950 and 1953 was accompanied by a decline in the net FHA mortgage flow from mutual savings banks and from savings and loan associations through 1952. In contrast, it will be recalled that in VA markets the last two types of institutions were increasing their acquisitions, while the first two were retrenching. Throughout 1954, only commercial banks increased significantly their FHA home mortgage flows (Chart 20). In the same year, the flow of institutional funds into VA mortgages, without exception, showed a big increase. Continued easing in capital markets finally brought increases in the flow of FHA funds from all types of financial institutions during 1955 to peaks almost coincidental with peaks in the flow of VA mortgages. Later declines through 1956, after the return to capital market stringency, also closely paralleled developments in VA lending activity of institutional lenders.

The differences in lender participation in VA and FHA loan markets clearly suggest differences in loan availability and in lender attitudes towards VA and FHA mortgages. Savings and loan associations have a long history of aversion towards FHA loans, as previously noted, but not carried over to VA loans. For mutual savings banks the uninterrupted rise in VA loan acquisitions from 1951 through 1955 was based on higher yields available on out-of-state lending and greater demand by borrowers for VA than for FHA loans. Similar reasons were behind the decisive increase in life insurance company acquisitions of VA loans between 1953 and 1955, while their increase in acquisitions of FHA loans was only moderate. At that time, many life insurance company mortgage loan officers, according to information in personal interviews, would have been willing to acquire more FHA loans if available through their mortgage correspondents. Commercial banks have been active in FHA loan markets since the inception of the program, both as loan originators and ultimate investors. Their activity in those markets between 1951 and 1956 and in the VA markets was similar, rising and falling in response to changes in alternative investment opportunities and to changes in reserve positions resulting from Federal Reserve credit actions.

The steady expansion in annual conventional home mortgage flows through periods of both market stringency and ease during 1951–1955 and the subsequent decline in 1956 were owing in large part to the activities of savings and loan associations (Chart 21). The regularity of the declines in the fourth quarter of each year from 1953 through 1956 also clearly reflected changes in savings and loan association activity. Reasons for such seasonal changes were suggested earlier (p. 123). The unusually sharp decline in savings and loan mortgage flows in the fourth quarter of 1955 was due in part to restraining actions taken by the Federal Home Loan Bank Board (Chapter 3).

Changes in the volume of conventional home mortgage flows among the other three main types of financial institutions in the 1951–1956 period were generally considerably smaller than those in the volume of VA and FHA home mortgage flows. Mutual savings banks, in particular, committed a consistently small amount of funds to conventional home mortgages in the period while sharply expanding their participation in newly gained out-of-state VA loan markets. Yields on conventional mortgages available to savings banks in eastern markets were often not as attractive as yields on VA loans in noneastern markets. Moreover conventional loans were not readily available in savings bank states during much of the period. Life insurance companies, however, able to make conventional mortgage loans on a nationwide basis, took advantage of flexible interest rates on them by increasing their acquisitions when yields were rising, while reducing VA and FHA loan acquisitions. Thus, the net flow from life companies into conventional mortgages increased appreciably, 1951–1953 and 1955–1956, while the net flow into federally underwritten loans declined. For both life insurance companies and mutual savings banks, the quarterly flow of conventional mortgage funds fluctuated within a narrower range than federally underwritten mortgage flows did.

Except during 1952, commercial banks tended to expand and contract their conventional home mortgage flows along with movements in federally underwritten mortgage flows. On a quarterly basis, the expansion in conventional mortgage acquisitions from the low 1954 first-quarter level culminated in a second-quarter 1955 peak and a subsequent steep decline through the fourth quarter of 1956. This cycle was similar to that traced by VA and FHA flows. The similarity of commercial bank flow patterns into the various home mortgage markets suggests that those institutions tend to adjust their home mortgage portfolios as a whole in relation to other loans and investments. They are not as concerned as life insurance companies are, for example, with internal mortgage portfolio adjustments. The difference lies in the fact that commercial banks are not as strongly committed to mortgage investments as are life insurance companies through their correspondent organizations. The broad problem of mortgage lending policies and techniques of the main financial institutions is the subject of the next chapter.

CHAPTER 6

Mortgage Lending Policies of Financial Intermediaries

Beginnings of Mortgage Lending

THE mortgage is the oldest form of debt instrument still in wide use and, hence, among the oldest forms of investment available to financial institutions. It was already well developed in the Roman era, with the rights of borrower and lender clearly defined, and evolved through English common law and German courts into the mortgage instrument of today. The Roman *hypotheca* is considered to be the direct forebear of the modern mortgage in which the borrower retains title, possession, and use of his land and property contingent upon fulfillment of his mortgage obligation. This is not to suggest that the modern mortgage is a uniform, simple document. Quite the contrary. Differences in mortgage law and practice persist throughout the United States, mortgage instruments continue to be cumbersome and costly, and foreclosure proceedings lengthy and expensive. The wide diversity of practice among states is confusing, and includes important variations regarding borrowers' rights of redemption, deficiency judgments, foreclosure costs and procedures, and lenders' rights in event of default. The several attempts that have been made over the years, since the early part of the twentieth century, to unify and simplify the variety of state mortgage laws and procedures have all met with failure.[1] The free flow of mortgage funds across state lines is, therefore, still impeded by the complexities and variations of state mortgage laws.[2] In the earliest days of American real estate finance individuals were the main source of mortgage funds, joined somewhat later by private banking houses and specialized private land banks. Despite the early and widespread failures of land banks, similar institutions were organized in the early nineteenth century to lend on farm mortgages. These also were generally unsuccessful, and throughout the eighteenth and early nineteenth centuries "individual

---

[1] See Richard U. Ratcliff, *Urban Land Economics*, New York, 1949, pp. 218ff; Miles L. Colean, *The Impact of Government on Real Estate Finance in the United States*, New York, National Bureau of Economic Research, 1950, Chap. 3; and Henry Hoagland, *Real Estate Finance*, Homewood, Ill., 1954, pp. 17ff., for discussion of attempts to develop uniform mortgage laws.

[2] See, for example, two papers in *The Mortgage Banker*: Earl B. Schwulst, "Needed Now: Uniform Laws for Out-of-State Mortgage Investing," June 1956, p. 22; and John J. Redfield, "Problems Facing Savings Banks in Out-of-State Mortgage Purchases," January 1956, pp. 36–41.

lenders remained the principal source of credit, and, in spite of Hamilton's admonitions on the incompatibility of mortgage paper with the requirements of commercial banking, state-chartered commercial banks, from the beginning of the Republic, were heavily involved in loans on both farm and town property."[3]

Beginning in the early part of the nineteenth century, other types of financial intermediaries—mutual savings banks, life insurance companies, savings and loan associations (then called building societies)—developed to broaden the sources of funds available for mortgage financing. An additional source was provided after 1863 by the formation of national banks, though they were limited in that function by severe legal restrictions. Participation by these diverse types of financial institutions in mortgage markets expanded over the decades, facilitated by previously discussed factors—increased flows of savings, gradual easing of legal restrictions, and federal programs. In the postwar decade, financial institutions have assumed an increasingly dominant role as suppliers of mortgage funds, and their operations have varied in the process. It is the purpose of this chapter to appraise the mortgage lending policies underlying operations of the main types of financial intermediaries.

Financial Intermediaries and Mortgage Markets

Among the four principal types of mortgage credit suppliers, only the savings and loan association was organized originally for the express purpose of providing long-term credit to finance real estate. The others were organized to meet community needs for commercial credit, savings, and insurance protection. They provided mortgage funds as a part of their investment activities. Among the four institutions there are differences in sources of funds and investment opportunities available to them and in operating techniques in mortgage markets. Operational differences include: orientation towards local markets or towards national markets; acquiring mortgages indirectly through correspondents or branch offices or making direct loans; emphasizing permanent loans on completed properties or short-term construction lending and interim financing; lending chiefly on individual existing properties or on large-scale new projects; making long-term advance commitments to acquire mortgages or acquiring completed mortgages in the "open market"; some concentration on federally insured or guaranteed mortgage lending or specializing in conventional mortgage lending. These operational differences reflect, among other

---

[3] Colean, *op. cit.*, p. 59.

things, differences in the basic nature and purpose of financial institutions, in the legal framework within which each type operates, in the degree of functional specialization, and in the historical and traditional background against which each type developed. In addition to broad differences in mortgage market operations, which are largely interinstitutional, important differences exist also among institutions of the same class.

To achieve an adequate understanding of factors that influence institutions in their investment policies and guide them in their mortgage lending operations, field interviews were conducted. Information was supplied by thirty-five officers in charge of mortgage departments or over-all investment policies of twenty-seven major lending institutions (most of them located in the East). Besides the four major types of financial institutions, they included mortgage companies, mortgage brokers, and real estate firms. The purpose of that approach was to develop an adequate basis for reporting on aspects of mortgage lending policies not previously treated in the literature, yet fundamental to residential mortgage market developments in the first postwar decade. Material from interviews was distributed for review and appraisal among students of financial markets in government, universities, and research organizations, and later discussed and evaluated in the light of known market developments and available data. The material thus developed and analyzed is the basis of the following discussion of broad aspects of investment policy and of similarities and differences among lender groups. As in earlier chapters, some pertinent historical background is sketched in.[4]

Life Insurance Companies

When life insurance companies were in their infancy and their assets very small " . . . the dominant investment by all odds was mortgage loans, comprising 80 to 90 per cent of invested assets. The only other investments . . . were state and city bonds, and a few bank stocks. There were no corporate securities whatever, and there was a relatively high percentage

---

[4] The reader may wish to supplement the discussion in this chapter by reference to the following works: Leo Grebler, David M. Blank, and Louis Winnick, *Capital Formation in Residential Real Estate: Trends and Prospects*, Princeton University Press for National Bureau of Economic Research, 1956; Carl F. Behrens, *Commercial Bank Activities in Urban Mortgage Financing*, 1952; R. J. Saulnier, *Urban Mortgage Lending by Life Insurance Companies*, 1950; and Ernest M. Fisher, *Urban Real Estate Markets: Characteristics and Financing*, 1951 (all published by the National Bureau of Economic Research); W. H. Steiner, "Institutional Investments," *Law and Contemporary Problems*, Durham, N.C., 1952; John Lintner, *Mutual Savings Banks in the Savings and Mortgage Markets*, Cambridge, Mass., 1948; Erwin W. Boemler, Roland I. Robinson, Frank H. Gane, and Loring C. Farwell, *Financial Institutions*, Homewood, Ill., 1956.

of cash."[5] Investment portfolios of life insurance companies have shifted markedly during the past century in response to a changing economic environment, modification of insurance investment laws, and availability of new capital market instruments. Mortgages have never again dominated the asset structure of those companies as they did in the early history of the industry, when mortgages were preferred because they were more familiar, and because other investments, now regular components of insurance company portfolios, were prohibited by strict investment laws.[6] Since the turn of the century, the share of mortgages in total assets has varied from a high of over two-fifths in the mid-twenties to a low of about one-seventh at the end of World War II. The rapid rise in life insurance company mortgage investments during the postwar decade brought the ratio to over one-third by the end of 1956. If farm mortgages are excluded, the 1956 ratio—about 31 per cent—is the highest for nonfarm mortgages in this century.[7]

FACTORS IN MORTGAGE INVESTMENT DECISIONS

As mortgage credit suppliers, life insurance companies differ from other institutional investors in several important ways: (1) they have more alternative long-term investment opportunities; (2) they operate generally within a more liberal legal framework; (3) they acquire a larger portion of their mortgages from other mortgage originators; (4) they emphasize different types of mortgage investments; and (5) their mortgage holdings are more concentrated among a small number of companies. Important differences in investment policy and practice exist among individual life insurance companies, as well as between them and other types of investors.

With a wide choice among alternative long-term investments, how do life insurance companies determine the amount of funds they will allocate for investment in mortgages during any one period? The impact on mortgage markets of changes in life insurance company investment programs makes the answer significant. The answer is not simple nor the same for

[5] George T. Conklin, Jr., "A Century of Life Insurance Portfolio Management," Chapter XIV in David McCahan, ed., *Investment of Life Insurance Funds*, Philadelphia, 1953, p. 263.

[6] *Ibid.*, p. 207.

[7] Farm mortgages were an important part of life insurance company portfolios in earlier years, particularly in the early 1920's following the upsurge in farm production during World War I with the rising demand for farm mortgage credit. The trend away from farm mortgages began with the collapse of farm prices in the 1920's and accelerated during the widespread farm failures of the 1930's. Since then farm mortgages have comprised a very minor part of insurance company assets.

For a summary history of insurance company mortgage investments, see Conklin, pp. 266–270, and Saulnier, *op. cit.*, pp. 1–15; for a more detailed discussion, see Grebler, Blank, and Winnick, *op. cit.*, pp. 199–201.

all types of companies. One leading life insurance executive answered the question in this way: "The investment officers of life insurance companies, conditioned by the internal requirements and characteristics of their industry as well as by legal requirements, seek primarily fixed debt obligations of longer term which are protected by an adequate demonstrated earning capacity and by a sufficient equity risk cushion. They face the demands of our economy for this type of capital and *invest in those fields which, risk considered, return the highest net yield.*"[8] Without question, the best yield obtainable consistent with risk is a paramount factor in the investment decisions for all companies. For some companies it appears to be the only factor, as Conklin suggests. For others, however, maximization of yield is not always decisive. Its importance in determining the flow of mortgage funds from life insurance companies usually varies with the size of company, the nature of its mortgage portfolio, and its method of acquiring mortgage loans.

The most important single consideration besides yield influencing mortgage flow is the stability and efficiency of the organizations established for the acquisition and servicing of new mortgage business. It is fundamental, particularly to the very large companies administering substantial mortgage portfolios on a nationwide basis through extensive correspondent or branch office systems.[9] Those mortgage lending organizations or correspondents had been largely disrupted, as noted previously, by the decline in real estate and mortgage activity during the 1930's and by World War II restrictions. After the war, companies hastened to establish new field organizations, in themselves considered valuable assets. To maintain loyal, efficient, and stable field organizations, companies allocate an amount of funds for mortgages considered irreducible before committing for other investments. Regardless of yield, therefore, those companies are committed to at least minimum mortgage programs, until a radical change is made in their way of doing business.

Companies that chose to establish nationwide systems of branch offices rather than correspondents for the acquisition and servicing of mortgages (of which there are only two large ones) are perhaps even more firmly committed to basic mortgage programs by their large overhead costs of operation. One large company, for example, which shifted to a branch office system when many of its independent correspondents failed during the 1930's, had decided to maintain an active mortgage program before

[8] Conklin, *op. cit.*, p. 261.
[9] For a discussion of correspondent and branch office systems and of mortgage lending organizations of life insurance companies see Saulnier, *op. cit.*, pp. 28–36.

committing itself to the high fixed costs of branch mortgage offices. It now has well over two-fifths of its assets in mortgages (the industry average, about one-third) and intends to increase that ratio.

Beyond the minimum amounts of mortgage flows maintained by the large companies, the volume of additional funds allocated by them depends essentially upon mortgage yields relative to other investment yields. Further, within the mortgage sector, shifts in favor of mortgages yielding the highest current return are common. Market conditions, however, may not permit the full adjustment desired by the largest companies. Insofar as possible, for example, in the residential mortgage sector shifts are made from federally underwritten mortgages bearing inflexible rates to conventional mortgages when free rates rise in a tightening capital market.

The larger insurance companies are faced also with the practical problem of investing large sums of money year in, year out. It is not easy for them to maximize yields or to move into and out of mortgage markets rapidly in response to changing conditions. The cost, moreover, associated with the operation of separate mortgage, bond, and other investment departments leads to a policy of portfolio diversification not always consistent with yield.

The smaller companies, with fewer funds to be placed in capital markets, with correspondents not heavily dependent upon them for business, and with one integrated investment department, operate typically with a higher degree of investment flexibility than the large companies. They can allocate funds to different sectors of the capital market on the basis of relative yield alone. While their mortgage correspondents are usually permitted to reinvest proceeds from mortgage repayments, additional advance allocations are usually not made. Instead, funds are committed for mortgages as correspondents submit applications for approval, leaving room for flexibility as capital market yields change. The chief investment officer of a moderate-sized company probably spoke for many in stating, "The only real factor influencing my investment policy is relative yield."

Two other elements that play a role in life insurance company investment policy are the percentage ratio of mortgages to total assets, and the human factor. Several companies, for example, operate within a longer-range policy which tends to set a maximum for mortgage expansion (or minimum for reduction). Having reached their goals those companies invest only that amount of new funds which will maintain their mortgage portfolios at the desired relationship to total assets, until the goals may be changed. The human factor obviously often plays an indeterminate but important part in the allocation of investment funds. A strong-minded person with long years of experience at the head of a mortgage department may get more funds for his department than a younger, less experienced executive. One executive, forty-five years in the business and twenty years as head of the mortgage loan department, characterized himself as a "fighter" who battled for his "share of company funds even though yields turn temporarily against me." Such a man has an influence on mortgage loan policy quite apart from economic considerations.

MORTGAGE LENDING POLICIES AND PRACTICES

Among companies there is wide variation in types of mortgage activities, though nearly all devote a significant share of assets to mortgage investments. Some, usually the smaller ones, concentrate on home mortgage loans, and others on large loans secured by income-producing properties, both residential and commercial. Most companies operate between the extremes, investing broadly in both owner-occupied home mortgages—conventional and federally underwritten—and income property loans. The same holds true for operations of life insurance companies more than a decade earlier.[10] The VA-guaranteed loan has been an added feature in most life insurance company mortgage portfolios since early 1946, tending to give them greater volatility.

Most mortgage operations of companies that lend in volume on residential mortgages are in permanent financing of new large-scale housing projects. Financing individual transactions for new or existing properties is better suited to local institutions familiar with local markets and with direct handling of individual transactions than to life insurance companies operating on a nationwide basis through correspondents. Large companies often handle permanent financing of commercial and industrial properties involving large sums of money directly through their home offices. Such loans are frequently secured by both existing and new structures.

During the first postwar decade portfolios of life insurance companies as a group showed a steady trend away from mortgages on rental and commercial properties and in favor of home mortgages (Chart 23). That trend is in keeping with the proportionately greater postwar demand for funds to finance single-family home construction. Nevertheless, life insurance companies continued throughout that time to be the chief single supplier of mortgage funds on commercial properties and a major supplier of funds for multifamily properties (Chapter 2).

In view of the nature of life insurance business and investment needs, most companies extend so-called permanent long-term mortgage financing,

[10] Saulnier, *op. cit.*, p. 30.

rather than short-term funds to finance construction. They are closely associated with financing construction, however, lending mainly on new properties and usually arranging for acquisition of permanent mortgages

CHART 23
Mortgage Portfolio Composition of Life Insurance Companies, 1945–1956

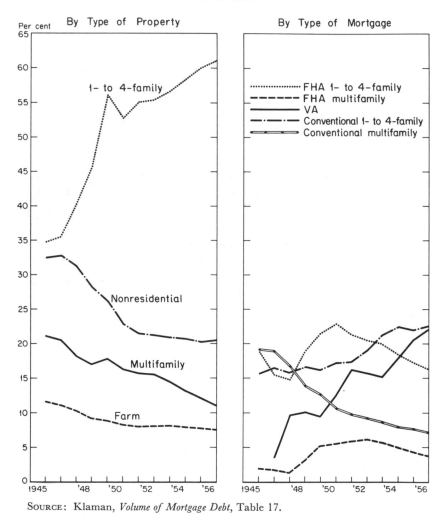

SOURCE: Klaman, *Volume of Mortgage Debt*, Table 17.

before construction begins. Company policies vary, chiefly between the long-range mortgage acquisition techniques of the larger companies, with some sacrifice of investment flexibility, and the more flexible techniques of most smaller companies that prefer to enter and withdraw from the mortgage market according to market conditions. Among the larger companies, too, there are variations within the process of long-range planning of investment programs.

Planning its mortgage program at least a year ahead, a large company interested in residential mortgages usually makes allocations of funds to mortgage companies, of which it may have nationwide connections with more than a hundred. The mortgage companies initiate loans and submit them to the life insurance company for prior approval before completion. Upon its approval, the company issues firm commitments to acquire such loans at a stated price when completed and ready for devliery.[11] A variation of this technique developed in recent years is the "forward commitment," by which the company agrees to purchase completed mortgages, not when ready for delivery, but at any time within some stated period, often eighteen months or two years after the commitment date. Some companies arrange to delay the taking up of commitments for three months or so after loans are ready for delivery. The forward commitment requires mortgage correspondents to arrange for interim financing from commercial banks beyond the time normally required to close loans and deliver them to the investing company.[12]

The process of planning mortgage investment activity for a year or two ahead and allocating and committing funds for future acquisition of mortgages necessarily reduces the companies' ability to adjust to short-term changes in market conditions. In particular, movements toward expansion are considerably more feasible than toward contraction of mortgage activity in the short run. Commitments are usually binding on the investor, and while allocations of funds may be withdrawn or reduced, most large companies are reluctant to take such action. Some flexibility in programming is maintained during the year by allocating funds on a six-month rather than on a full-year basis. Also, some unallocated funds are usually retained for investment opportunities likely to arise during the year. Reduced flexibility is partly compensated for by the advantages of operational programming inherent in the longer-range mortgage acquisition technique. Larger companies consider continuity of operations more essential than maximized yields at all times. Development of the forward commitment technique represents a further step in their efforts to smooth the flow of funds into mortgages.

[11] See Chapter 8 for a discussion of the relationship between life insurance companies and mortgage companies.

[12] See Chapter 7 for a more detailed discussion of the forward commitment and interim financing techniques.

Besides reduction in investment flexibility, the large institutional investor using the technique just described is faced with important operating problems: (1) long and uncertain time lags between decisions and commitments to invest and the actual disbursement of funds; (2) an uncertain rate of attrition in commitments; and (3) danger of overcommitment when changes in market conditions may supervene.

Time lags between the policy decision to invest a certain amount of funds in mortgages, the commitment of those funds, and the acquisition of the mortgages vary widely between companies and by type of property financed. On new residential construction the typical lag between commitment and mortgage acquisition may be between 6 and 12 months, on new commercial construction as long as 18 to 24 months, but on existing properties as short as between 3 and 6 months. The lapse of time between the initial allocation of funds (before firm commitment) and disbursement is, of course, somewhat longer. The timing of acquisitions and hence of the actual need for ready funds in the mortgage market is far less certain than in the market for corporate securities. (Arrangements for direct placements of corporate bonds between borrower and investor, for example, are quite definite as to dates so that the time of acquisition can be carefully planned.)

The significant but varying rate of attrition in mortgage commitments, and other phenomena without close parallel in long-term corporate financing, complicate planning of mortgage investments. Mortgage commitments may not be taken up because of unforeseen developments: (1) scheduled construction may be deferred; (2) mortgage loans may be smaller than commited for or entirely unnecessary; (3) funds for completed mortgages may be obtained elsewhere on more favorable terms under changing market conditions.

Experience of one of the largest American companies, for example, has been that nearly one-fifth of its mortgage commitments are not taken up. The proportion has varied widely between two-fifths and less than one-tenth, the rate being related to the relative attractiveness of terms on outstanding commitments compared with those available on new commitments. During the year beginning in the autumn of 1953, for example, when capital markets eased and interest rates declined, builders and mortgage companies were able to obtain new commitments or market their completed loans at far better prices than those already set under firm commitments. Lapse of commitments entailed the loss of only the commitment fee which was less than the spread between mortgage prices currently available and the prices arranged for under previous commitments.

During 1955–1956, on the other hand, when capital markets were tightening and new commitments were hard to come by, the attrition rate on outstanding commitments dropped sharply.

The typical rate of disbursement of mortgage funds after the date of commitment, based on the records of one large company, is shown in two panels of Chart 24. The data in panel A show that the rate of disbursement increases rapidly through the second month following commitment. Thereafter, the rate declines gradually through the twelfth month. Only a little more than 5 per cent of mortgage funds are disbursed in succeeding months. The cumulative disbursement curve in panel B indicates that typically about 85 per cent of committed mortgage funds are actually disbursed, and that over three-fifths of the committed amount is disbursed by the end of the eighth month.

During periods when funds are plentiful, financial markets easy, and competition among investors for mortgages keen, life insurance companies (as well as other types of lenders) may overcommit themselves in the mortgage market. The uncertainties of time lags and attrition associated with commitments, coupled with the need to keep large sums of money invested, have sometimes led investors to have a volume of commitments outstanding too large to be met comfortably from expected receipts. This problem of large institutional investors operating extensive nationwide mortgage programs through mortgage correspondents or branch offices was highlighted by the experience of one of the largest life insurance companies at the end of 1954. It had commitments outstanding about equal to the amount of funds anticipated for total mortgage investments during 1955, which meant that no new allocations or commitments could be made to acquire mortgages during the year. Thereupon, the company obtained short-term funds from commercial banks in a much publicized "warehousing" transaction, in which the company sold a large block of its mortgages to be repurchased within one year.[13]

Companies less in favor of the allocation and commitment process—usually the smaller ones—avoid the uncertain timing of mortgage flows associated with the regular commitment process and the short-term inflexibilities imposed by the long-range forward commitment process. They are not completely committed to a mortgage program and so take advantage of it or not according to changing capital market conditions. One moderate-sized company attempts to forecast mortgage interest rates at least six months to a year ahead, to be in a position to acquire higher-yield

---

[13] See Chapter 7 for further discussion of this type of warehousing in relation to other types.

CHART 24

Percentage Distribution: Typical Life Insurance Company Disbursement of Mortgage Funds Following Month of Commitment

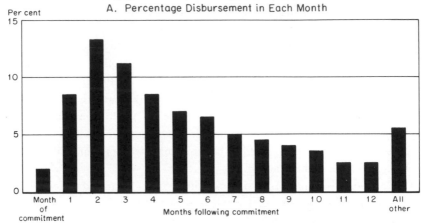

A. Percentage Disbursement in Each Month

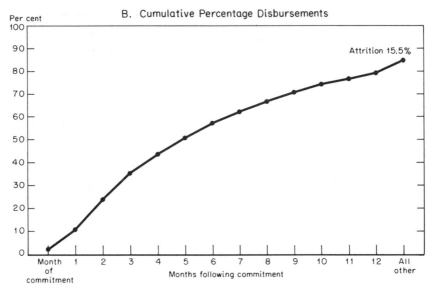

B. Cumulative Percentage Disbursements

SOURCE: The records of a large eastern life insurance company; the distribution is based on experience with loans of less than $50,000 on new and existing properties. See Table A–11 below.

mortgages and avoid having a large volume of outstanding commitments on lower-yield ones. An even greater degree of flexibility is secured by some smaller companies that acquire a substantial portion of their mortgages directly rather than through correspondents. In general, however, most smaller and moderate-sized companies acquire the bulk of their mortgages on the basis of prior commitments through mortgage correspondents and hence are subject to many of the uncertainties in timing mortgage flows that beset large companies.

Regardless of asset size or type of mortgage operation all life insurance companies alike were faced with the need for basic changes in investment policy after March 1951. Before the Federal Reserve-Treasury "accord" there was no need to allocate funds for mortgage investment. The general policy was to invest as much money in mortgages as the market would take. Maximum flexibility was permitted by unlimited access to the government securities market, supported by Federal Reserve. The change in monetary and fiscal policy required companies to allocate their funds carefully among alternative investments in accordance with their anticipated income. The large companies, therefore, adopted the allocation technique for acquiring mortgages. The day of pouring funds into markets for mortgages and corporate securities closed with the "accord." Almost without exception life insurance companies, and other institutional investors too, consider March 1951 to be the turning point of investment policy and operating techniques in postwar mortgage markets.

Mutual Savings Banks

Mutual savings banks are the oldest of American thrift institutions, dating from 1816. Organized primarily in industrial areas to encourage thrift among working class groups, these institutions spread rapidly through the eastern part of the country. They have remained geographically concentrated in the New England and Middle Atlantic States, and are relatively few in number. The little over 500 mutual savings banks in seventeen states compare with over 13,000 commercial banks, 6,000 savings and loan associations, and 1,000 life insurance companies spread over the country.

The mutual savings banks, though growing tremendously in size over the years, have continued to serve their original function of providing an outlet for the funds of small savers. Their quasi-philanthropic origins have determined and maintained their investment policies as designed principally to safeguard depositors' funds. As a result, they have achieved a record of safety over nearly a century and a half unparalleled by other types of financial institutions. It is important to understand the nature and origins of mutual savings banks in order to understand the investment policies followed by these institutions.[14]

[14] Among the best references on mutual savings banks are John Lintner, *Mutual Savings Banks in the Savings and Mortgage Markets*, Cambridge, Mass., 1948; and W. H. Steiner, "Mutual Savings Banks," *Law and Contemporary Problems*, Durham, N.C., 1952.

FACTORS IN MORTGAGE INVESTMENT DECISIONS

Mutual savings banks are more limited in their investment outlets than either life insurance companies or commercial banks, but less so than savings and loan associations. Since there are no federally chartered savings banks, each of them is limited in its investments according to the legal restrictions imposed by the state in which it operates. For the protection of depositors most savings bank states restrict investments to a "legal list" intended to insure a high degree of safety and liquidity. These lists have been modified and generally expanded in all states over the years.

Within those legal limits, savings bankers tend to choose investment policies to secure for their banks maximum net returns after due allowances for costs and risks on different types of investments.[15] While investments in corporate securities have been fairly narrowly circumscribed, mortgages have always been considered suitable investments for savings banks, subject, of course, to geographic limitations, and other bounds set, particularly on terms of lending and proportion of assets. Thus, in each year as far back as records are available until the outbreak of World War II, mortgage loans constituted the savings banks' largest single category of assets, never falling below one-third of total resources.[16]

During World War II, savings banks invested more heavily than other types of financial institutions did in U.S. government securities relative to their total assets. Their mortgage holdings declined to one-fourth of assets by the end of 1945, the lowest percentage on record. Partly because of the restricted geographic mortgage market available to savings banks, their mortgage holdings continued to decline relative to other assets in the immediate postwar years. After the 1949 and 1950 changes in investment laws governing out-of-state mortgage acquisitions (discussed below), savings banks as a group rapidly increased their mortgage holdings to nearly three-fifths of assets by the end of 1956, a larger proportion than the previous record in the 1920's.

The postwar investment policy of savings banks has, of course, varied among individual banks, particularly between larger banks that have sought out-of-state mortgage investments to employ their deposits, and small banks that have been able to keep their funds invested locally. Nearly all, however, showed a strong preference for mortgages in the first postwar decade. The generally higher yields on mortgages relative to

[15] Lintner, *op. cit.*, p. 215. His Chapter VIII provides a full discussion of investment policies and shifts in portfolio composition of savings banks.
[16] Raymond W. Goldsmith, *A Study of Saving in the United States*, Princeton University Press, 1955, Vol. I, Table L-29, page 415; Lintner, *op. cit.*, p. 299.

other investments available to them in the East attracted a steadily increasing share of savings bank funds. The consequently higher rate of interest paid on deposits has enabled savings banks to meet the increased competition for savings from other types of financial intermediaries.

In addition to the yield advantage of mortgages during most postwar years, federal mortgage underwriting and regular amortization have endowed mortgage investments with a high degree of safety and liquidity, investment criteria essential to savings banks. For many savings banks, therefore, postwar investment policy has been relatively uncomplicated— to acquire the maximum amount of mortgages consistent with deposit inflows, statutory requirements, and liquidity needs. Of the seventeen savings bank states at the end of 1956 eleven had from over two-fifths to over two-thirds of their assets in mortgages, and the banks in five of the remaining six states had over one-third in mortgages. In several states, FHA and VA loans are exempt from statutory limits on mortgage holdings, which leaves ample room for further expansion in that investment area. Self-imposed limitations and relative yield changes in later postwar years, however, could well slow down—at least temporarily—the rate of mortgage acquisitions by mutual savings banks.

MORTGAGE LENDING POLICIES AND PRACTICES

Savings bank mortgage lending policies and practices in some ways lie between those of savings and loan associations and life insurance companies. In other ways they are unique. Traditionally and by design, mutual savings banks, like savings and loan associations, have supplied funds chiefly to satisfy the needs of their own local mortgage markets. The changes in state statutes of recent postwar years, however, have opened to them the field of national mortgage lending, hitherto the domain of life insurance companies. Their formulation of mortgage programs, methods of mortgage acquisition, and types of mortgage investments, however, are in large measure peculiar to them.

Whether operating in local or out-of-state mortgage markets, or investing in new or existing, residential or commercial, properties, savings banks generally do not plan their mortgage programs as far ahead as the large life insurance companies do. The regularity of life insurance premium income permits long-range planning of investment, unique among financial intermediaries. The net movements of savings deposits to which mortgage investments must be geared, however, are rather irregular and unpredictable. For internal guidance the larger savings banks often project mortgage investment programs for a year or eighteen months ahead on the basis of the expected inflow of deposits. Allocations of funds for mortgage acquisition are made on the basis of the minimum expected inflow of deposits and of mortgage repayments and are reviewed each month in the light of actual deposits and mortgage availability. Additional funds from increased deposits or prepayments are committed to the mortgage market as they become available.

While most savings banks do not maintain as close an organizational relationship with correspondents as life insurance companies do, they frequently use the secondary market to acquire mortgages for immediate delivery (i.e., within ninety days) rather than under long-range prior commitments. Occasionally they buy from other institutional investors that wish to sell seasoned mortgages to obtain funds for new loans. The flexibility thus maintained is valuable in permitting adjustments both to changing deposit inflows and to changing capital market yields.

Without question the most significant single development influencing savings banks' postwar mortgage operations was the frequently mentioned amending of most state statutes in 1949 and 1950 on out-of-state lending. Through this legislation, limited essentially to FHA and VA mortgages, mutual savings banks, many of which had more funds to invest in mortgages than could be absorbed by local markets at prevailing interest rates, entered the national market. And the harvest was ripe. Savings banks— located chiefly in the capital surplus areas of the East—had been providing a steadily decreasing share of mortgage funds compared with other institutional investors because building and real estate activity was increasing less in New England and the Middle Atlantic states than in other sectors of the country, and their access to the widening VA loan market had been severely restricted. In their local markets competition with savings and loan associations was keen. From 1950 on savings banks accounted for a steadily growing share of total mortgage investments (Chapters 2 and 5). In the "non-savings bank" states and capital shortage areas now open to them expanding real estate and construction markets created large demands for funds and higher mortgage yields than those in the Northeast. The growth of out-of-state mortgage business was spectacular for mutual savings banks in Massachusetts and New York. At the end of 1956, banks in these two states accounted for four-fifths of the total amount of mortgage loans held by all mutual savings banks.

Of the total new mortgage loans acquired by New York State savings banks in 1955, almost one-half were on out-of-state properties, compared with a little over one-fourth in 1950, and only 3 per cent in 1946 (Table 14). The sharp increase was accounted for entirely by out-of-state purchases of VA loans, which rose from one-half of one per cent of total mortgage acquisitions of New York State savings banks in 1950 to almost two-fifths in 1955, and represented two-thirds of all VA loans acquired by those banks during the year. Out-of-state purchases of FHA loans in those years were declining.[17] Similar data on gross mortgage acquisitions are

TABLE 14

Mortgage Loans Acquired by New York State Mutual Savings
Banks Within the State and Out-of-State, 1946–1955

	AMOUNTS (MILLIONS OF DOLLARS)				PERCENTAGE RATIOS				
YEAR	Total Loans (1)	N.Y. State Loans (2)	*Out-of-State Loans*		*(3) as* % of *(1)* (6)	*(4) as* % of *(1)* (7)	*(5) as* % of *(1)* (8)	*(4) as* % of *Total FHA Loans* (9)	*(5) as* % of *Total VA Loans* (10)
			Total (3)	FHA (4)	VA (5)				
1946	424	410	14	14	—	3.3	3.3	—	77.8	—
1947	566	538	28	28	—	4.9	4.9	—	52.8	—
1948	745	621	124	124	—	16.6	16.6	—	52.5	—
1949	1,001	798	203	203	—	20.3	20.3	—	49.5	—
1950	1,734	1,241	493	484	9	28.4	27.9	0.5	50.0	4.1
1951	1,630	1,040	590	529	61	36.2	32.5	3.7	66.0	18.7
1952	1,483	955	528	365	163	35.6	24.6	11.0	64.0	40.8
1953	1,603	961	642	258	384	40.0	16.0	24.0	67.0	54.5
1954	2,022	1,138	884	217	667	43.7	10.7	33.0	61.0	62.5
1955	2,442	1,294	1,148	211	937	47.0	8.6	38.4	52.2	67.2

SOURCE: From unpublished records of New York State Banking Department.

not readily available for Massachusetts or for other states where mutual savings banks are located. Data obtained on mortgage holdings of a large Massachusetts savings bank, however, reveal a similar trend, with out-of-state mortgages accounting for well over one-third of its total mortgage holdings in 1955 compared with less than one-sixth five years earlier.

Distribution of outstanding mortgages between intrastate and out-of-state loans for all mutual savings banks is shown in Table 15. Out-of-state mortgage holdings increased from 25 to 28 per cent of total mortgage holdings from September 30, 1954 to December 31, 1955. VA loans accounted for the bulk of the increase, with such out-of-state loans

[17] Before changes in some state laws permitting out-of-state lending on VA and FHA mortgages, New York State had authorized savings banks to lend on conventional and FHA mortgages in adjoining states. Table 14, showing FHA out-of-state loans, includes, therefore, earlier loans in adjoining states which cannot be separated. Before 1949, all FHA out-of-state loans represent loans in adjoining states. The amount of conventional loans in adjoining states is very small and has been included in Table 14 with total loans in New York State.

TABLE 15

Mortgage Loans Held by Mutual Savings Banks Within Their States and Out-of-State, Selected Dates, 1954 and 1955

| | SEPTEMBER 30, 1954 | | | | | DECEMBER 31, 1955 | | | | |
| | | | Out-of-State | | | | | Out-of-State | | |
	All Holdings	Within Own State	Total	In States Without Savings Banks	In States with Savings Banks	All Holdings	Within Own State	Total	In States Without Savings Banks	In States with Savings Banks
AMOUNTS (MILLIONS OF DOLLARS)										
Total	14,288	10,712	3,576	1,942	1,633	17,396	12,492	4,904	2,974	1,930
FHA	3,704	1,501	2,203	1,106	1,097	4,142	1,793	2,349	1,258	1,091
VA	3,894	2,627	1,267	827	440	5,753	3,341	2,411	1,689	722
Conventional	6,690	6,584	106	9	97	7,501	7,359	142	26	116
PERCENTAGE DISTRIBUTION										
Total	100.0	100.0	100.0	100.0	100.0	100.0	100.0	100.0	100.0	100.0
FHA	25.9	14.0	61.6	57.0	67.2	23.8	14.4	47.9	42.3	56.5
VA	27.3	24.5	35.4	42.6	26.9	33.1	26.7	49.2	56.8	37.4
Conventional	46.8	61.5	3.0	0.5	5.9	43.1	58.9	2.9	0.9	6.0
Total	100.0	75.0	25.0	13.6	11.4	100.0	71.8	28.2	17.1	11.1
FHA	100.0	40.5	59.5	29.9	29.6	100.0	43.3	56.7	30.4	26.3
VA	100.0	67.5	32.5	21.2	11.3	100.0	58.1	41.9	29.4	12.5
Conventional	100.0	98.4	1.6	0.2	1.4	100.0	98.1	1.9	0.3	1.5

SOURCE: Special Tabulation made by National Association of Mutual Savings Banks representing 517 banks in 1954 and 523 banks in 1955. Mortgages made "within own state" in 1955 represent savings banks servicing their own mortgages within state in which savings bank is domiciled. (From unpublished report of NAMSB, "Distribution of Mortgage Investments of Mutual Savings Banks, as of December 31, 1955.")

nearly doubling. Over two-fifths of all VA loans owned by mutual savings banks at the end of 1955 were out-of-state purchases. In contrast, out-of-state FHA loans increased only slightly but at the end of 1955 represented close to three-fifths of all FHA loans owned by savings banks.

Entry into out-of-state mortgage markets, while of obvious advantage to mutual savings banks, especially the larger ones, raised a number of legal and operational problems not unlike those faced by life insurance companies in the early development of their national mortgage lending programs. The legal obstacles are, however, greater for savings banks because of the penalties and local taxes on out-of-state business to which they might be subject. It is usually necessary for savings banks to arrange to acquire out-of-state mortgage investments in a way that will not be deemed as "doing business" in a foreign state.[18] The purchase of mortgages from an out-of-state originator under an advance commitment must be done so as not to place the originator in the position of agent for the savings bank. Thus, "the commitment should be framed upon the assumption that the originator has already agreed to make the mortgage loan, and not conditionally upon the bank's commitment."[19] Such originators are generally referred to as "servicing contractors" with the banks, rather than as correspondents when associated with the life insurance industry.

Many savings banks have found it convenient to acquire mortgages from originators, not on an advance commitment basis, but after they are completed and ready for delivery—referred to as mortgages "on the shelf." Several large New York State savings banks acquire their out-of-state mortgages solely through mortgage brokers, buying seasoned or completed mortgages when ready for delivery, in accordance with inflow of deposits and mortgage repayments. In Massachusetts, on the other hand, where a large out-of-state mortgage investment program has developed, savings banks seldom acquire mortgages in this manner. A central purchasing group has been formed to act as agent for a large number of banks in the state. Operations in the Massachusetts purchasing group have been patterned closely after the life insurance company–correspondent relationship. "Servicing contractors" have been selected in various regions of the country, and association is maintained on a continuing basis.

The changing composition of postwar mortgage portfolios of mutual savings banks, shown in Chart 25, reflects the change in investment policies just described. The most striking development indicated by the chart

---

[18] For a discussion of the legal problems, see Redfield, "Problems Facing Savings Banks in Out-of-State Mortgage Purchases," pp. 36–41.

[19] *Ibid.*, p. 38.

CHART 25

Mortgage Portfolio Composition of Mutual Savings Banks, End of Year,
1945–1956

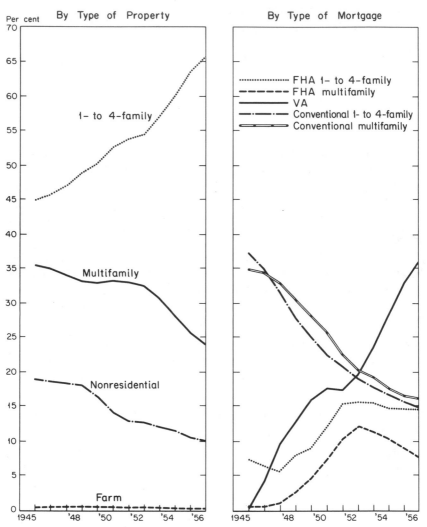

SOURCE: Klaman, *Volume of Mortgage Debt,* Table 19.

is the sharp increase in the proportion of VA loans held, from about one-sixth in 1950–1951 to well over one-third by the end of 1956, while the proportions of FHA and conventional residential loans and those on commercial properties were declining or showing little change. That rapid and marked shift was without parallel among other types of financial institutions. Also, unlike the experience of other financial institutions, acquisition of VA mortgages by mutual savings banks increased almost without interruption through periods of both credit restraint and credit ease from 1951 through 1956. As a result mutual savings banks have become the largest suppliers of funds for VA-guaranteed mortgages.[20]

While their stature as national mortgage lenders has increased in the postwar period, mutual savings banks have maintained their traditional service to local mortgage markets. Many smaller banks, and even some of the larger ones, concentrate all their mortgage lending activity in their own local territories. The others meet local mortgage demands in full before turning to out-of-state investments. All savings banks, whether placing funds locally or out-of-state, invest predominantly in permanent long-term mortgages. They originate only construction loans that will become desirable additions to their portfolios, as permanent mortgages on new properties. They lend also on mortgages secured by existing properties. As Chart 25 indicates, savings banks have a large proportion of their portfolios in mortgages secured by multifamily and commercial properties as well as by one- to four-family homes. Loans in out-of-state areas are chiefly on new residential projects. Multifamily mortgages, though declining in recent years, compose a proportion of savings banks' mortgage portfolios larger than the proportion for any other lender throughout the postwar period. That mutual savings banks are the largest single source of funds for multifamily mortgages (Chapter 2) derives largely from their concentration in the Northeast, where most multifamily real estate and construction are located.

In summary: In their mortgage lending policies and practices mutual savings banks are similar to life insurance companies in that they are important national mortgage lenders, they acquire a large part of their mortgages indirectly through originators, and in out-of-state markets invest chiefly in mortgages on new residential properties. They are similar to savings and loan associations in their concentration on mortgages as compared with other investments, in their primary attention to local mortgage markets, and in their emphasis on loans secured by individual new or existing properties in such markets. Mutual savings banks are unlike either type of institution with respect to composition of mortgage portfolios and shifts in that composition during the postwar period; in location, being chiefly in the Northeast; and in techniques developed for

---

[20] This development has been discussed in some detail and supported statistically in Chapter 5.

mortgage acquisition, including purchases in the secondary market for immediate delivery.

Savings and Loan Associations

Among institutional investors in the mortgage market, savings and loan associations are exceptional in their essentially specialized function as home mortgage lenders. The only other capital market instrument in which they invest to any extent—U.S. Government obligations—has in recent years of the postwar decade accounted for about 6 to 7 per cent of total assets. State chartered institutions in several states are permitted to invest in municipal obligations, but only a few have made such investments, and in extremely small amounts. The specialized role of savings and loan associations, moreover, is carried through even in home mortgage markets, where they deal directly with borrowers in rather limited local market areas and lend predominantly on amortized conventional home mortgages. That role has changed little since the first association was formed over a century ago by a small group cooperating for the express purpose of pooling funds regularly to enable the contributors to acquire homes.[21]

BACKGROUND AND DEVELOPMENT

During the decades of growth and adaptation to changing patterns of saving and lending, the savings and loan association has been transformed from a simple form of cooperative organization, in which nearly every shareholder was a borrower, to an institution in which saving is not necessarily associated with borrowing.[22] The change has been reflected in the change of name from building societies, or homestead societies, to savings and loan associations. Some of the earlier names, however, including building and loan associations and cooperative banks, still persist.

In the postwar years most savings and loan associations have competed effectively against mutual savings banks and commercial banks for the savings of individuals. They have been able to attract an increasingly large share of those savings mainly because of their relatively high dividend rate on share holdings, which in turn is based on high yields earned on conventional home mortgage loans. Their assets have increased at a considerably faster rate than the assets of each of the other main types of financial intermediaries.

[21] H. Morton Bodfish, *Savings and Loan Principles*, and *History of Building Societies in the United States*, New York, 1940.
[22] Colean, *op. cit.*, p. 61.

The extraordinary growth of savings and loan associations into one of the leading institutional depositories and investors of savings could hardly have been visualized by the founders. The early associations, in fact, were not intended to be permanent institutions, but rather to be disbanded after all members of the cooperatives had achieved the purpose of acquiring homes. Associations continued to be temporary until the latter part of the nineteenth century, when the permanent plan of organization took hold. The plan evolved naturally from the serial type of structure, which gave an association continuity of existence by accepting new members at frequent intervals through the issue of shares maturing serially. By the early 1890's the savings and loan movement had spread from the Atlantic seaboard to the Mississippi and Ohio valleys, the Southwest, and the Far West. The permanent plan of organization, with its separation of savers from borrowers, permitted associations to increase in number and size along with the growth of the nation.

At the same time, there was an ill-fated movement to establish "nationals," which actively solicited savings and made loans throughout the country, partly through branch offices and often by mail.[23] Many were purely promotional, fraudulent ventures. Most of the legitimate ones were poorly managed and unable to provide adequate supervision over loans made in various areas of the country. The result was widespread failures, hastened by the depression of 1893. By the end of the century, national savings and loan associations were virtually out of existence, with a loss of some $250 million to unfortunate investors.[24] The spectacular failure of the "nationals" resulted in a serious setback for the entire savings and loan movement and led ultimately to closer governmental supervision and tighter geographic limitation of activity.[25]

The recovery of the industry proceeded slowly during the beginning of the twentieth century, and received its first impetus from the housing boom of the 1920's. While the numbers of both commercial and mutual savings banks declined between World War I and the end of the 1920's, the number of savings and loan associations almost doubled from 1918 to 1929, having reached a peak of more than 12,000 in 1925. Many of the newly formed associations—small, lacking in managerial skill, and too numerous in many areas—were unable to survive the depression of the 1930's. By 1939 there were approximately one-third fewer associations than in 1929. The number was further reduced during World War II.

[23] For a discussion of the development, operation, and demise of national savings and loan associations see Bodfish, *History of Building Societies*, pp. 68–82.
[24] *Ibid.*, p. 84.
[25] Colean, *op. cit.*, p. 61.

Since the end of the war the number of associations has been relatively stable at around 6,000, with average asset size at the end of 1956 well over $5 million, compared with less than $\frac{1}{2}$ million thirty years earlier. This is still much smaller than the average asset size of the other main types of financial intermediaries.

Out of the accumulated experience of a century of success and failure, of growth and decline, savings and loan associations have evolved into the present-day modern type of financial institution. Its function remains the same—providing funds for home building and purchase. It continues to depend for its chief source of funds on the small individual saver. In every postwar year the steady growth of share capital and mortgage repayments have provided the bulk of funds invested in mortgages by savings and loan associations. Occasional additional funds have come in from sales of U.S. government obligations, chiefly in the early postwar period, and from borrowings from the Federal Home Loan Bank System, chiefly in two years of unusual mortgage lending activity, 1950 and 1955.

MORTGAGE LENDING POLICIES AND PRACTICES

Limited as they are in their investment outlets, savings and loan associations have less flexibility than other financial institutions have in adjusting their mortgage flows to changing capital market conditions. Within the mortgage market, moreover, their adjustments are limited because they are confined through law and tradition mainly to the home mortgage market. These limitations on investment policy have not handicapped the associations during most of the post-World War II decade, however, when strong demands for home mortgage loans have absorbed their large inflow of savings, and in some years have exceeded it. Through their specialization in conventional mortgage loans with flexible interest rates savings and loan associations gained a further advantage, capturing a larger share of the home mortgage market during periods of rising interest rates and yields. At such times other lenders have reduced their funds available for federally underwritten loans bearing fixed rates.[26]

Like life insurance companies and mutual savings banks, savings and loan associations invest primarily in permanent long-term mortgage loans. Like commercial banks, however, they also provide a large volume of short-term construction funds, but such loans are usually a means of obtaining long-term mortgages. Unlike life insurance companies, the

[26] See Saul B. Klaman, "Effects of Credit and Monetary Policy on Real Estate Markets, 1952–1954," *Journal of Land Economics*, August 1956, pp. 239–249; Chapter 5 of this book; and "Savings and Loan Associations in the Mortgage Market," *Monthly Review of Credit and Business Conditions*, Federal Reserve Bank of New York, 1956, pp. 96–99.

associations generally have direct contact with most of their borrowers and do not operate through correspondent or branch office organizations. The small asset size of the associations makes less necessary out-of-state outlets, which many savings banks need to keep their funds invested. In their degree of concentration on conventional home mortgage loans, savings and loan associations are unique among institutional investors.

Thus, current mortgage lending policies of the associations reflect their early history and tradition as well as the more recent changes in mortgage markets and the construction industry. Through the years, they have continued to supply the largest share of mortgage funds directly to individuals acquiring new or existing houses. More recently, they have also become important suppliers of construction funds to large-scale builders of houses for sale.

Information on the amount of loans made by savings and loan associations, classified according to loans "for construction of homes" and loans for "purchase of homes," has been available for years from the Federal Home Loan Bank Board. Unfortunately, the precise meaning of that classification has never been clear. A common interpretation has been that loans for construction of homes represent permanent mortgage loans on new houses, while loans for purchase of homes consist of mortgage loans on existing houses.[27] However, conferences with Federal Home Loan Bank Board research officials and officers of reporting associations revealed this interpretation to be incorrect. Loans classified as for construction of homes include temporary loans to builders as well as permanent loans to individuals. Loans classified as for purchase of homes include loans for the purchase of both new and existing houses. Moreover, the figures given are confused by a significant degree of duplication; loans reported once under the construction category are reported again under the purchase category.

In an effort to determine more accurately the real nature of savings and loan mortgage activity, a questionnaire was mailed to about 500 of the larger associations likely to be able to give definite information.[28] The responses received from 55 associations in 22 states—or 11 per cent of the sample—cannot be taken to represent precisely the characteristics of the entire industry. The results seem worth reporting here because they throw some light on a previously dark area, the nature of savings and loan construction lending. The amounts of loans made by reporting associations for construction of homes were 39 per cent of their total volume of mortgage

[27] See Grebler, Blank, and Winnick, *op. cit.*, p. 180, note to Table 50.
[28] The questionnaire is given as Exhibit at the end of the book.

lending in 1955; this compares with a ratio of 35 per cent for all associations in the United States. The closeness of these two figures may be taken as some indication of the representativeness of the associations reporting in the survey.

Most of the reporting associations made between one-fourth and one-half of their loans to finance home construction. There is apparently little direct relationship between size of an association's mortgage portfolio and the proportion of its new mortgage loans made for home construction, as Table 16 shows. Associations with mortgage holdings between $10 and

TABLE 16

Savings and Loan Associations Loans for Construction of Homes, by
Size of Mortgage Portfolio, Fifty-five Reporting Associations, 1955

Size of Mortgage Portfolio (\$ millions)	*Number of Associations Reporting*	*Proportion of Loans Made for Construction of Homes*				
		0–20	21–30	31–40 (per cent)	41–50	Over 50
Under 10	9	2	3	2	—	2
10–20	11	1	3	3	2	2
20–30	14	3	2	5	2	2
30–50	13	4	4	—	2	3
Over 50	8	—	—	3	3	2
Total	55	10	12	13	9	11

SOURCE: Questionnaire survey conducted in this study (Exhibit).

$50 million make a widely varying proportion of their loans for home construction. The largest associations, however, with mortgage portfolios over $50 million, reported the consistently largest proportion of loans for home construction.

The survey indicated that in their loans for home construction, most associations included loans to builders to finance construction operations as well as loans to individuals to finance new home acquisition. Among them, loans to builders generally constitute either a small or a very large proportion of total home construction loans. Associations appear to be either heavily or hardly at all engaged in providing builder financing. The frequency distribution curve describing these data, therefore, is bimodal. The relationship between size of mortgage portfolio and loans made to builders, shown in Table 17, appears to be only a little more direct than the relationship between size and total construction loans, shown in Table 16. There is some evidence, however, from Table 17 that the largest

TABLE 17

Proportion of Savings and Loan Association Home Construction Loans
Made to Builders, by Size of Mortgage Portfolio,
Fifty-five Reporting Associations, 1955

Size of Mortgage Portfolio ($ millions)	Number of Associations Reporting	Proportion of Home Construction Loans Made to Builders					
		0–20	21–40	41–60	61–80 (per cent)	Over 80	Not Reported
Under 10	9	5	1	—	—	2	1
10–20	11	3	1	1	3	3	—
20–30	14	5	—	1	3	5	—
30–50	13	1	—	5	2	3	2
Over 50	8	—	—	2	2	3	1
Total	55	14	2	9	10	16	4

SOURCE: Same as Table 16.

associations tend to make a greater proportion of their construction loans to builders than the smallest associations do.

When the proportion of construction loans to builders is related to the proportion of total home construction loans (Table 18), a closer relationship may be observed. Most of the associations originating over 40 per cent of their loans for home construction extend well over 60 per cent of such loans to builders. Conversely, those making less than 20 per cent of their loans for home construction provide less than 20 per cent to builders.

The survey results throw light also upon a time-honored assumption that savings and loan associations engage in financing builders' operations

TABLE 18

Relationship between Proportion of Savings and Loan Association Loans Made
to Builders and Proportion of Their Loans Made for Home Construction,
Fifty-five Reporting Associations, 1955

Proportion of Loans Made for Home Construction	Number of Associations Reporting	Proportion of Home Construction Loans Made to Builders					
		0–20	21–40	41–60	61–80 (per cent)	Over 80	Not Reported
0–20	10	6	—	1	1	—	2
21–30	12	4	2	3	1	1	1
31–40	13	4	—	3	1	5	—
41–50	9	1	—	1	4	3	—
Over 50	11	—	—	1	3	6	1
Total	55	15	2	9	10	15	4

SOURCE: Same as Table 16.

only as a means of acquiring permanent mortgage loans, short-term financing of such operations being not in keeping with their fundamental purposes. Answers from the 55 associations indicate that this assumption is true only with qualifications. A significant proportion of loans made by savings and loan associations to builders do not lead to permanent mortgage loans for their portfolios.

Table 19 shows clearly that only about 45 per cent of the associations reported that nearly all of their loans to builders—90 to 100 per cent—resulted in permanent mortgage loans after the new buildings had been completed and sold. An additional one-fourth of the associations reported the same result for from 75 to 89 per cent of their loans to builders. Thus,

TABLE 19

Percentage of Savings and Loan Association Loans
to Builders Resulting in Permanent Mortgage
Loans, Fifty-five Reporting Associations, 1955

Percentage of Loans to Builders	Percentage of Reporting Savings and Loan Associations
0–24	4
25–49	6
50–74	21
75–89	24
90–100	45

SOURCE: Same as Table 16.

about 7 out of 10 reporting institutions indicated that at least three-fourths of their builder loans became permanent loans for their mortgage portfolios. From another view of the data, not shown in the table, more than two-fifths of the reporting associations indicated that over 25 per cent of their loans to builders were refinanced upon completion of construction by other institutions, or otherwise did not lead to permanent loans for their portfolios.

The reasons for the outcome just described in the minority of construction loans to builders were not determined. While an association may have expected to obtain the permanent loan, the ultimate purchaser may have arranged for more favorable financing terms elsewhere, or may have purchased without a mortgage. In other cases, the builder may have obtained a take-out commitment from another institution before arranging with the savings and loan association for construction financing. In any event, the survey results as a whole suggest that, whether by intention, or circumstance, a significant number of savings and loan associations have been a source of short-term construction financing for builders as well as of long-term financing for house buyers.

It is important to know how associations make the transition from builder loans to permanent home purchase loans for understanding savings and loan lending practice and proper interpretation of national statistics. Do they make a new loan to a new owner-borrower upon completion of construction, receiving payment in full from the builder? Or do they simply arrange for the purchaser to assume the original loan made to the builder? While the questions deal almost entirely with technique, they have direct bearing upon interpretation of gross mortgage lending figures for savings and loan associations. If the first technique is used, two loans would be reported for financing one property—construction and purchase. If the second, only one loan would appear in the statistics.

From the point of view of lender practice the survey findings indicate wide differences among associations. About one-third reported that less than 20 per cent (for the majority, less than 10 per cent) of their loans to builders that led to permanent loans were replaced by new loans. More than one-half reported that over 80 per cent (for the majority, over 90 per cent) of such builder loans were paid off and replaced by new permanent loans. Thus, associations refinance either the bulk of their builder loans or a very small proportion of them with new permanent loans. Few fall into middle ground. The two extremes also characterize the distribution of the proportion of builder loans made by savings and loan associations (Table 17). In any case the reporting of two separate loans for financing one property inevitably leads to overstatement of the volume of mortgage lending reported for the nation's savings and loan associations.

The specialization by savings and loan associations in conventional mortgage lending on one- to four-family houses and the stability of their mortgage portfolio composition through most of the post-World War II decade can be seen in Chart 26. The picture contrasts with those of the portfolios of most other institutional investors, which showed important shifts during the period (see Charts 23, 25, and 27). VA-guaranteed loans played a role in the postwar portfolios of savings and loan associations about as significant as in those of other types of institutions, except for savings banks. This finding reveals as only half true the common generalization that savings and loan associations prefer conventional to federally underwritten loans. More accurately, they prefer conventional and VA loans to FHA loans. The latter accounted for little more than 5 per cent of total mortgage holdings in each of the postwar years.

What are the reasons for the unusually small volume of FHA-insured

CHART 26

Mortgage Portfolio Composition of Savings and Loan Associations,
End of Year, 1945–1956

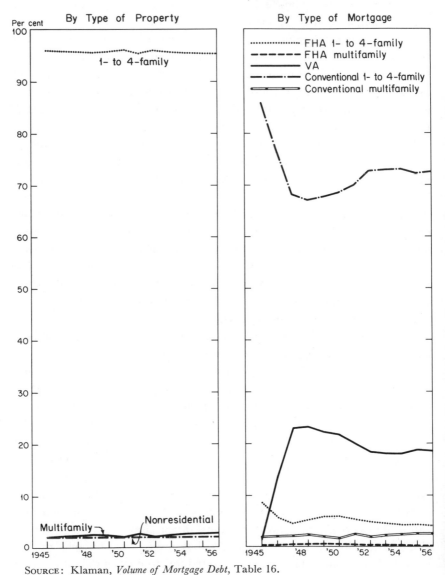

SOURCE: Klaman, *Volume of Mortgage Debt*, Table 16.

loans in savings and loan portfolios? One explanation may be that, while the incentive to serve returning veterans has overcome the drawbacks in handling VA-guaranteed loans, those drawbacks remain for FHA loans. The small size of the associations and their lack of trained investment personnel create difficulties in dealing with the technical complexities of loan origination and administration. The processing delays, too, are particularly inconvenient for savings and loan associations in their direct, face-to-face dealings with borrowers. Perhaps more basic is the fact that the savings and loan industry has been opposed to the FHA mortgage insurance program from its beginning in 1934. Its opposition was founded originally on the belief that a program of mortgage insurance embodied a philosophy fundamentally at odds with that of the reserve home loan banking institutions, established two years earlier, in the form of the Federal Home Loan Bank System. Further, it felt that federal mortgage insurance would attract more financial institutions to the mortgage lending field (as it did) and thus increase competition for the industry.

Both the savings and loan industry and the FHA mortgage insurance program have thrived over the past two decades or so, but the two have never really joined hands. Most savings and loan managers continue to avoid FHA mortgages. Some of the larger associations—the exceptions— have broken through tradition to invest a large share of their funds in FHA mortgages. So long as associations can continue to invest the bulk of their funds in higher-yielding conventional mortgages, they may be expected to invest a minimum in FHA loans.

Commercial Banks

SIGNIFICANCE OF REAL ESTATE LOANS

Commercial banks, as noted earlier, have been lending on real estate as security almost from the beginning of their development more than two centuries ago. Since the turn of the twentieth century, however, real estate loans have constituted only a small proportion of total commercial bank assets, partly because of legal restrictions on mortgage lending and partly because of the basic orientation of commercial banks towards short-term credits. That proportion has increased for national banks since the steady liberalization of national banking laws following the passage of the Federal Reserve Act in 1913. Before that, participation of national banks in real estate lending was much more restricted than that of state banks. Since 1934, development of the federally underwritten mortgage, exempt from most lending restrictions and readily marketable, has resulted in increased activity of all commercial banks in the nonfarm mortgage market.[29]

Since the end of World War II, national banks have accounted for more than one-half of the real estate loans held by all commercial banks, compared with less than one-twentieth in 1913, and about one-third in 1935. In percentage of assets, total commercial bank real estate loans have increased from about 7 per cent in 1939 and 3 per cent in 1945 to over 10 per cent in 1956. The postwar increase, while substantial, has left the mortgage-to-assets ratio for commercial banks still well below that for savings-type institutions. In addition to making long-term real estate loans, commercial banks play a unique and important role in real estate markets by providing short-term credits either for construction or for interim financing. Much of this activity is not directly measurable, and a large portion is not included statistically among commercial bank real estate loans at all.[30]

MORTGAGE LENDING POLICIES AND PRACTICES

Among the four principal types of mortgage investors, commercial banks play the most varied role in the mortgage market. Furthermore, there is a wider variation of mortgage lending policies and practices among commercial banks than among members of the other three main groups of lending institutions. Commercial banks provide three types of credit to the real estate mortgage market: long-term permanent mortgage loans; short-term construction credits; and interim financing to other real estate mortgage lenders. In addition, some commercial banks carry on a mortgage company type of operation, originating loans for sale to other investors and servicing the mortgages originated and sold.

Among the country's 13,600 commercial banks, many refrain from any type of real estate finance, many specialize in one type only, and still others operate a broad financing program including all types of long- and short-term real estate credit. In general, long-term financing of real estate is a more extensive activity of the smaller country banks than of the large city banks. Naturally, there are important exceptions. One of the main reasons for the dominant position of commercial banks in the West Coast

---

[29] For description of the liberalization of legal restrictions on commercial bank mortgage lending and other factors influencing their expansion in the field, see Grebler, Blank, and Winnick, *op. cit.*, pp. 201–203; Behrens, *op. cit.*, Chapter 1; and "Commercial Banks in the Mortgage Market," *Monthly Review of Credit and Business Conditions*, Federal Reserve Bank of New York, April 1956, pp. 47–48.

[30] "Unsecured construction loans and loans to real estate lenders which are either unsecured or secured by the pledge of mortgages owned by the borrower are not classified as real estate loans in bank condition statements." (Behrens, *op. cit.*, footnote 1, p. 47.)

mortgage market, for example, is the fact that the largest bank in the country, located there, is heavily engaged in mortgage lending activity through its many branches.[31] Another of the leading banks, located in the East, carries a large real estate mortgage portfolio in addition to supplying a heavy volume of short-term real estate credits. With few exceptions, the large New York money market banks limit their real estate credit operations almost entirely to short-term financing of construction operations and of real estate mortgage lenders, or both. Large banks in the East most extensively engaged in those two types of real estate financing were chosen as subjects for field interviews in investigating mortgage lending policies and practices of commercial banks. The choice was appropriate because of the dominant and uniquely important role of commercial banks as short-term real estate mortgage lenders, because of the increasing use of such credits in the postwar years, and because of the limited literature on the nature of such activities.

Short-term financing of construction operations is a highly specialized banking activity and, unlike long-term real estate financing, is concentrated among relatively few large banks. In the early post-World War II years many commercial banks, anxious to build up their real estate loan portfolios, made construction loans in order to obtain permanent mortgages on the completed properties.[32] This practice became much less common as long-term mortgage debt held by banks increased to desired levels. The more widespread practice of commercial banks is to supply short-term credits for construction, while permanent financing is furnished by another institution. The concentration of construction financing among a few banks is indicated in part by reference to 1950 data. They reveal that, of the $840 million in construction loans outstanding as of June 30, more than two-fifths was held by banks in the New York Federal Reserve District. Those banks accounted for only about one-sixth of all commercial bank real estate loans.[33] Evidence from interviews suggests that the situation has changed little since then.

In the booming postwar construction market, construction lending has been a lucrative field of investment for commercial banks. Even so,

---

[31] See, for example, Paul F. Wendt and Daniel B. Rathbun, *The San Francisco Bay Area Residential Mortgage Market*, Housing and Home Finance Agency, Housing Research Paper No. 20, May 1952, Chapter III, especially p. 31, footnote 54.

[32] *Ibid.*, p. 28.

[33] Data on construction loans of commercial banks were obtained from a special supplement to the June 30, 1950 commercial bank call report. Summary results of that report were published in the FDIC Report No. 33, *Operating Insured Commercial and Mutual Savings Banks, June 30, 1950*, pp. 5–7. No later data on the subject were available at the time of writing.

because it is considered a highly complex, specialized, and risky kind of operation, many of the large eastern banks have never made a construction loan or have made only a few to accommodate correspondent banks. Others have only recently established construction and mortgage loan departments.[34] Banks that have been successful construction lenders for many years have acquired the skilled management and developed the operating techniques to meet the special needs and complexities of the construction loan market and to minimize risks associated with short-term construction financing. The major risks are those of unavailability of permanent mortgage financing, unsold completed properties, and uncompleted construction.

With few exceptions, commercial banks make construction loans only after builders applying have obtained commitments elsewhere for permanent financing of proposed construction. These firm "take-out" commitments assure the bank of availability of permanent mortgage financing and of repayment of its construction loan upon satisfactory sale of the completed property. In some instances, depending on the state of the capital market, the construction lender may insist on "dual take-out commitments," under which the permanent lender agrees to purchase the builder's loans on completed but unsold properties, as well as to provide financing for those sold to acceptable purchasers.[35] This type of commitment, which is not very common, relieves the bank of any risk associated with failure to sell. Frequently, a local correspondent bank through which loans are made (see below) will commit itself to take over loans on unsold properties.

Where "dual take-outs" or local bank commitments are not available, banks may reduce the risk of unsold properties in the case of residential construction projects by requiring the builder to show executed sales contracts for a large percentage of his proposed houses. He may then proceed to build only at a specified rate in advance of sales. On commercial construction, contracts for leases are often required before funds are advanced.

In contending with the risk of uncompleted construction, banks may require performance or completion bonds. The chief reliance is judicious selection of builders, close supervision of progress at the site, and payment

---

[34] One of the largest New York banks which established a real estate and mortgage loan department in 1955 gave three reasons for its action: (1) to share in what was apparently a lucrative type of loan business, judging from operations of competitive banks; (2) to fulfill requests of correspondent banks to participate in construction financing; and (3) to meet the needs of local bank customers for mortgage loans.

[35] James F. Schneider, "Construction Loans For Your Short-Term Portfolio," unpublished doctoral thesis, Graduate School of Banking, Rutgers University, June 1952.

of construction funds at predetermined selected stages of work. Naturally, the risk of noncompletion is least on large-scale commercial projects involving established, financially responsible real estate and construction firms. In the case of construction loans on multifamily properties approved by the Federal Housing Administration, FHA insures the construction loan as well as the permanent loan and so relieves the commercial banks of most of the risk.

Most of the large eastern banks make short-term construction loans on residential projects in participation with correspondent banks situated throughout the country. (Loans on large-scale nonresidential projects, in which some banks specialize, are often handled directly.) By most arrangements the large money market bank takes 80 to 90 per cent of a given loan and the local bank the remaining percentage. The smaller banks, limited by law in the size of loan to one borrower and by their own assets, are precluded from assuming a larger per cent of construction loans. Only the participation arrangements with larger banks make it possible for them to engage in many construction financing projects.

From the standpoint of earnings those arrangements are particularly attractive to correspondent banks. The interest rate on construction loans has rarely been less than 5 per cent in the postwar period, and in periods when money markets have been tight it has risen to $5\frac{1}{2}$ and 6 per cent. Usually the local correspondent bank earns a considerably higher gross rate of return. It is generally increased by an over-ride of $\frac{1}{2}$ of 1 per cent on the large bank's share, to $9\frac{1}{2}$ per cent (on a 90 to 10 participation basis), or to 7 per cent (on an 80 to 20 basis). Another addition is the origination fee (1 to $1\frac{1}{2}$ per cent) paid by the builder, usually retained by the local bank in consideration of its work—placing the loan on the books, servicing it, and seeing it through to completion. The resulting increases in gross rate of return are from 10 to 11 per cent (on a 90 to 10 basis) and from 8 to $8\frac{1}{2}$ per cent (80 to 20). Even after costs of loan handling and administration, the net return for local correspondent banks exceeds that on other types of bank loans, with the possible exception of consumer loans. Consequently, banks that have developed the know-how for construction lending generally maintain the maximum amount permitted by statute.

There is apparently little relationship between a commercial bank's willingness to engage in short-term construction financing and its willingness to provide short-term credits to real estate mortgage lenders. Some active construction lenders engage in little or no financing of other mortgage originators, while others carry on extensive operations in both types of short-term financing as well as in long-term permanent mortgage financing.

Apart from site and location, the extent of a bank's operations in these areas of financing depends heavily on the predilections and experience of its officers. There is variation among them also in administration, some banks coordinating all real estate finance activities in one department, others maintaining separate units.

For many years, commercial banks have been in the business of extending short-term credits to mortgage loan originators, chiefly mortgage companies, to enable them to carry mortgages in inventory for the interval between origination and lodgment with institutions providing permanent financing. Several variations of this type of financing, under the general term of "warehousing," have been introduced in the postwar period. A detailed discussion of postwar variations—which have often made for complexity and confusion—is reserved for the following chapter. Interim financing of mortgage lenders by commercial banks increased sharply towards the end of the post-World War II decade in response to changes in market conditions and operating techniques. Near the end of 1956, commercial bank loans outstanding to real estate mortgage lenders amounted to $1.5 billion, compared with $0.6 billion in the summer of 1954 and $0.4 billion in mid-1950.[36] The bulk of these loans was extended by large banks in New York, Boston, Chicago, and other metropolitan centers.

Compared with the increase in interim financing loans, the expansion in commercial bank mortgage loans held in bank portfolios has been far less, but their volume has remained much larger. Unfortunately, data on the volume of short-term construction financing by commercial banks are available only for June 1950, when it was twice as large as interim loans to mortgage lenders, but equal only to about 7 per cent of permanent mortgage loans held in portfolio. In any event, "the strategic role of construction loans (and of interim loans to mortgage lenders) is far greater than is indicated merely by their outstanding amounts at any one date." Important reasons are, "construction loans and those extended to intermediate financing institutions have a relatively rapid turnover; consequently, even their quantitative importance relative to the volume of credit extended on a long-term mortgage basis is not properly reflected by an outstandings figure . . . . Furthermore, construction loans are of crucial importance in the real estate financing process in the sense that they are commonly essential to the undertaking of building projects, especially those of large scope."[37]

[36] See Table 20 in Chapter 7.
[37] R. J. Saulnier, Introduction to Behrens, *op. cit.*, p. 2.

CHART 27
Mortgage Portfolio Composition of Commercial Banks, End of Year, 1945–1956

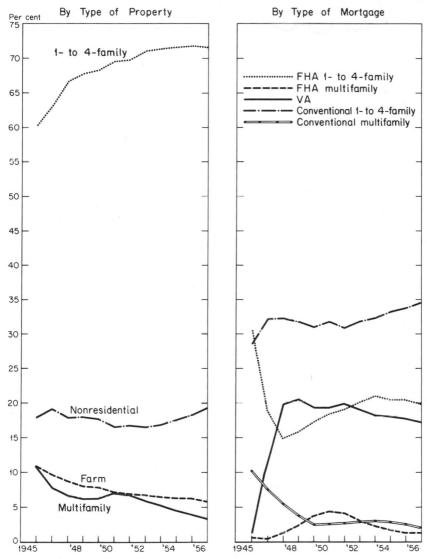

SOURCE: Klaman, *Volume of Mortgage Debt*, Table 18.

The composition of commercial bank mortgage portfolios, which consists largely of permanent long-term mortgages, has changed little during the post-World War II decade (Chart 27). Shifts among types of mortgages have been smaller than in accounts of other financial institutions, except savings and loan associations. In contrast to portfolios of mutual savings banks and life insurance companies, conventional home mortgage loans have continued to form a substantially larger part of commercial bank portfolios than either VA or FHA loans have throughout the period of sharp postwar expansion in residential mortgage lending. This difference reflects partly the lending policies of smaller country banks throughout the nation that maintain close personal contact with customers, and whose mortgage operations are similar in this respect to those of savings and loan associations. Whether lending on federally underwritten or conventional mortgages, however, commercial banks—large or small—make loans directly to borrowers in local areas (sometimes through branch offices) rather than on a nationwide basis through correspondents. The latter method is often used in their short-term construction lending operations.

Throughout the postwar decade, the mortgage portfolios of commercial banks have contained a considerably smaller amount and proportion of loans on multifamily properties than those of mutual savings banks (the leading lender) and life insurance companies. They have also included a rather steady and consistently smaller volume of loans on nonresidential properties compared with the volume held by life insurance companies. In markets for both of these income type properties, however, commercial banks have assumed an important role as construction lenders.

Other Financial Institutions in the Mortgage Market

Among other types of private financial institutions, only the mortgage company has played a significant role in the postwar mortgage market. Its role is, in fact, so unique and has assumed such increasing importance since the end of World War II that efforts were made to bring together existing data and to obtain primary information not previously available to describe and appraise its place in the nation's mortgage activities. The results of this effort were published in a separate report which is summarized in Chapter 8 of this book, to both of which the reader may turn for discussion of the postwar mortgage company.[38]

As for other types of private institutions, those that can be separately identified as mortgage investors—nonlife insurance companies, credit unions, investment companies, fraternal orders, personal trust funds, and pension funds—held a combined volume of mortgage loans amounting to little more than $3 billion at the end of 1956, or only about 2 per cent of the total mortgage debt outstanding. Because of the insignificance of

---

[38] Klaman, *The Postwar Rise of Mortgage Companies*, Occasional Paper 60, New York, NBER, 1959.

these miscellaneous institutions in the mortgage market, and the limitations on time and resources, no effort was made to appraise their mortgage lending policies. For many of them, barriers to increased mortgage investment exist in the form of legal restrictions and complexities, cumbersomeness of the mortgage instrument compared with other capital market instruments, inadequate organization for mortgage acquisition, and general prejudices and lack of knowledge about mortgage markets. At the end of 1956 little more than 2 per cent of the $120 billion in assets owned by noninsured pension funds, personal trust funds, fraternal orders, credit unions, and nonlife insurance companies was invested in mortgages.[39]

Perhaps the liveliest expectations for expanded mortgage market participation among these institutions have been expressed for pension funds. Those funds, in some views, will, in exploring outlets for ever-increasing treasuries, become attracted to the investment advantages of federally underwritten mortgages both from the standpoint of risk and of yield. The Mortgage Bankers Association of America not long ago established a committee to study pension fund characteristics. Several mortgage companies have acted to sponsor an organization established specifically to meet mortgage origination and servicing problems for pension funds and similar potential investors. Evidence of increased interest in mortgages on the part of pension funds can be found. Between the end of 1954 and 1956 those funds doubled their mortgage investments from $140 to $285 million—a much more rapid absolute and relative increase than other types of miscellaneous institutions undertook.

Even so, most pension fund administrators and students of pension fund operations foresee no great growth in mortgage investment. They argue that the relatively risk-free status of FHA and VA loans is not a controlling consideration. High-grade corporate bonds are just as likely to be paid at maturity. Moreover, the increased liquidity of federally underwritten mortgages through regular amortization is of no interest to the pension fund manager. He has no need for liquidity; rather, with the rapid growth of pension funds, the return flow of investment funds often creates new problems of selecting investment outlets.

The question of yield is of course basic, but yield is subject to many modifications. Administrative and servicing costs associated with a mortgage portfolio, higher in comparison with those for a corporate securities portfolio, narrow any market yield differential in favor of mortgages. The demonstrated present and potential future capital gains of a common

---

[39] Estimates of the Board of Governors of the Federal Reserve System, Flow-of-Funds Unit; and National Bureau of Economic Research, Postwar Capital Market Study.

stock portfolio have attracted an increasingly large share of pension fund investments into equities. Because of long-term orientation, interim price fluctuations are of small concern to administrators. Finally, just as life insurance companies and other large financial institutions are, pension funds are reluctant to be involved in real estate foreclosure action, even though capital losses in the case of FHA and VA loans are limited.[40]

[40] The discussion of why pension funds are not likely to become an important source of mortgage investment leans heavily upon the views of Roger F. Murray. See, for example, his "Pension Funds as a Market for Mortgages," *Savings and Mortgage Supply*, Proceedings of the Eighth Annual Conference of the Mortgage Bankers Association of America, 1953.

The National Bureau of Economic Research began in 1958, under Murray's direction, a research program on the impact of public and private pension systems on saving and investment. Plans for the study are outlined in the National Bureau's *Thirty-ninth Annual Report*, May 1959, pp. 63–68.

CHAPTER 7

Mortgage Market Techniques and Characteristics

THE techniques, characteristics, and institutional arrangements that have distinguished the postwar mortgage market from other sectors of the capital market are described and appraised in this chapter. Emphasis is placed on innovations in mortgage market techniques and arrangements and modifications of older ones that have been particularly characteristic of postwar years. As in the preceding chapter, a large part of what follows is based on information obtained in interviews with executives of financial institutions.

Changes in mortgage markets, it will be recalled, are a part of fundamental changes in postwar financial and economic conditions. The increasing institutionalization of saving and investment—a trend initiated decades earlier—has resulted in new techniques for efficiently channeling funds into mortgage markets and, in some instances, for assuring the continuous investment of funds for months (and sometimes years) ahead. Federal monetary and fiscal policies and the consequent alternate periods of capital market ease and tightness have also contributed to the development of those techniques to support the flow of funds into mortgage markets. The continuing trend towards a nationwide mortgage market, accelerated by federally underwritten mortgage programs, has led to increasing secondary market transactions and to a unique relationship between primary and secondary market activities. The growth of the construction industry and the increasing importance of the large-scale builder have created new needs for large-scale short-term financing. Meeting those needs by financial institutions has led to a closer relationship between interim, construction, and permanent mortgage financing. Finally, the accelerated rate of real estate turnover at increasingly high prices in the postwar period has brought about a renewal of activity in junior mortgages—the "purchase-money" variety rather than the newly originated variety.

Time Lags in Mortgage Lending

A basic and inherent characteristic of mortgage and construction markets is the time lag between a firm decision to invest in mortgages and in their acquisition. Lags are generally greater and timing much more uncertain than in other segments of the capital market.[1] They are longest and most

---

[1] One indication of this was given in Chapter 4 where the lagging movement of mortgage interest rates was shown. The problems of investment planning faced by mortgage lenders because of the uncertainty of time lags were discussed in Chapter 6.

uncertain in financing new construction, but transactions in existing real estate are also subject to significant delays between firm commitment and closing. Financing of both new and existing properties under VA and FHA mortgage guarantee and insurance takes longer to complete (paper work necessary to meet federal requirements) than comparable financing through conventional mortgages. Because of the uncertain time lags encountered in acquiring uncompleted mortgages through advance commitments, some nationwide lenders unable to judge their cash flows accurately have found it more satisfactory to acquire completed mortgages in secondary markets for immediate delivery.

As the share of postwar mortgage flows accounted for by new construction activity, federally-aided financing, and advance commitments has grown, the time lags between decisions to invest and actual flows of mortgage funds have lengthened. This means that a large share of current mortgage flows at any time stems from investment decisions made several months earlier. The flow of funds into the mortgage market, therefore, may be large and rising at a time when new commitments and funds available for financing proposed construction and real estate transactions are scarce. Conversely, new commitments may be plentiful while the flow of funds into the market is reduced. Which situation arises depends on the capital market environment. This basic characteristic of postwar mortgage finance has important implications alike for general monetary policy, for specific financial policy of institutional investors, and for accurate appraisal of mortgage statistics. The consequences of time lags add a further problem to the prevailing complexities of market analysis.

Relationship between Construction, Interim, and Permanent Mortgage Financing

Short-term as well as long-term credits are an integral part of mortgage market operations. The role of each type of credit and the relationships between them, unique in this sector of the capital market, is one of the more interesting aspects of mortgage market organization and technique.

Short-term credits in real estate finance are extended for two general purposes, to provide funds for the construction process and to meet the interim financing needs of mortgage loan originators.[2] Funds for construction financing are supplied chiefly by commercial banks and savings and loan associations. The banks make principally temporary loans pending completion and sale of the property. The associations make their

---

[2] Other purposes and types of interim financing, generally called warehousing, are discussed in detail in a later section on interim financing techniques.

loans as a basis for acquiring permanent mortgages.[3] Loans for interim real estate financing are made to mortgage lenders almost exclusively by commercial banks.

Before the rapid postwar growth of large scale residential developers and mortgage companies, construction and interim financing were fairly simple, uncomplicated operations. Construction was undertaken largely on contract for home owners and the financing was arranged either directly by the owner or by the builder for the owner. There was no doubt about the identity of the ultimate owner or mortgagee. Financing of both construction and sale of the property was generally handled by one lender in one transaction with one instrument.

After the war, the increasing importance of large-scale housing developments calling for large amounts of construction funds, and the concurrent growth of mortgage companies, often requiring continuing lines of commercial bank credit to finance mortgages carried for ultimate investors, brought important changes. The processes of construction, interim, and permanent mortgage financing, and relationships between them gave a new facet to the mortgage market. Construction financing became a specialized, separate lending operation with techniques of its own, heavily dependent upon short-term lenders. Its flow to builders is closely related to the availability of permanent mortgage financing and often to interim financing.

It is the unique characteristic of the process that before short-term funds can be obtained for construction, long-term permanent mortgage financing must usually be arranged for the ultimate sale of the completed construction. This is almost invariably true in residential construction for sale. Producers of residential property for sale, therefore, unlike producers of other durable goods, are concerned directly with arrangements for the permanent mortgage financing of their completed properties. If such financing is assured, it smoothes the way not only for obtaining construction funds but also for selling completed houses. Thus, prospective buyers of newly completed houses often find that financing has already been arranged for them. In the secondhand house market where the seller is not the producer this is less often true, although it is not uncommon for prearranged favorable financing terms to be offered as an inducement to buyers.

Despite the interdependent relationship between construction and permanent financing, the suppliers of each type of credit operate in financial

---

[3] In an important proportion of cases, however, as shown in Chapter 6, construction financing by savings and loan associations has not led to permanent loans.

markets with different characteristics. The disparity can lead to lack of short-term construction financing even when permanent take-out commitments have been negotiated. Such a situation usually occurs during periods of heavy demands for short-term commercial bank credit. During the spring of 1956, for example, when business loans were high and rising and bank reserves low, commercial banks were turning down construction loans, not because permanent financing was not available, but because of inadequate funds. During such periods, customer relations become a paramount factor, and builders having long-established banking relationships are the first to be served.

Because of the basic variations that developed in the nature and purposes of interim financing ("warehousing") in the latter part of the first postwar decade, and because of the widespread attention given to it, a later section is devoted to the subject. At this point it is pertinent only to indicate the general relationship of interim financing to construction and permanent financing. The relationship is, in fact, quite simple.

Interim financing serves generally to bridge the gap from the time construction is completed and the property sold, and the construction loan has to be repaid, to the time when the permanent mortgage papers are completed and ready for delivery to the ultimate investor. As indicated, interim financing has become more integrated into the mortgage financing process with the increasingly important role played by mortgage companies in the postwar decade as originators of mortgages for ultimate long-term investors. These companies rely heavily on short-term commercial bank credit to finance their operations, especially the holding of inventories for the interval described (see Chapter 8). Interim financing has become more important, also, as the needs of large-scale permanent mortgage investors have changed, and mortgage commitment techniques have acquired new aspects. Mortgage commitments were discussed in Chapter 6 in connection with the policies and problems of life insurance companies and mutual savings banks. The basic importance of the mortgage commitment process, however, from the standpoint of market technique and operation makes its discussion in somewhat more detail here both instructive and essential.

Mortgage Commitment Techniques

The mortgage commitment represents, in effect, a promise to provide mortgage credit in the future under specified terms and conditions. In principle it is not unlike any other financial commitment given by a lender to a prospective borrower. In actual practice, commitments have become an integral part of most mortgage transactions and one of the distinguishing characteristics of mortgage market operations. The only other segment of the capital market in which commitments play a significant role is that characterized by direct placement of corporate securities. In the markets for government obligations and for a part of the market for corporate securities (particularly that of railroad and public utility issues), characterized in the main by open market offerings and competitive bidding rather than direct negotiation, commitments have no part in market transactions.

One interesting difference between commitments in the corporate securities market and in the mortgage market is worth noting. In the former market, negotiations involve two parties—the financial institution and the corporate borrower. In the latter, where commitments to finance the permanent mortgage on new construction are under negotiation, three parties are involved—the financial institution, the builder, and the ultimate mortgage borrower, upon whose acceptance by the financial institution depends the ultimate disbursement of funds. Commitments to supply mortgage funds to finance purchase of existing properties also often involve three parties—the financial institution, the seller, and the purchaser.

Postwar innovations in mortgage commitment techniques, it will be recalled, have been developed in response to the needs of large-scale investors and to changes in capital market conditions. Two such innovations stand out, both used in connection with the financing of new residential construction. The "forward commitment," in which arrangements are made as far in advance as two years for investment of funds in mortgages to be created, was discussed in connection with lending policies and problems of financial institutions (Chapter 6). This commitment variation was developed by—and so far has been limited largely to—a few large life insurance companies that have found it well suited to the fundamental nature of their business and their long-range investment needs. The likelihood is that the forward commitment will continue in limited use by investors able to guage future income flows accurately and finding it expedient to acquire mortgages on a regular basis through a well-established permanent investing organization.

The second postwar innovation of an altogether different sort is the so-called standby commitment. It reflects both the indispensability to the construction process of an arrangement for permanent financing, and the ingenuity of the mortgage industry in adapting to market conditions at times when the supply of long-term mortgage funds becomes severely limited. As the name suggests, a standby commitment is one given by an institutional investor to a mortgage originator or a builder in which the investor pledges to purchase mortgages at a price below the prevailing market price and below the price expected to prevail when the construction is completed and the mortgage is ready for delivery. The investor, therefore, does not expect to be called upon to fulfill this type of commitment, which he gives principally in consideration of the nonrefundable fee received. The builder or mortgage originator is willing to pay the fee because the standby makes possible arrangements for construction financing upon which commencing the building operation depends.

The standby commitment is usually given for a period of from six to twelve months at a fee that varies directly with the mortgage price. The more the standby commitment underquotes the prevailing market price, the lower the fee charged. Thus, in the spring of 1956, commitments to purchase FHA or VA mortgages at 90 per cent of par were obtainable at a cost of $\frac{1}{2}$ of 1 per cent, while at 93 per cent of par commitments carried a fee of 1 per cent. Mortgage prices associated with fees vary with changes in the current market price for completed mortgages.

The origin of the standby commitment is not completely clear, but at least one claim for its invention has been made by a large New York mortgage brokerage house. It is said that the first standby was given in the summer of 1950 when permanent take-out commitments were difficult to arrange in the booming construction market of that year.[4] However, it was not until the periods of extreme mortgage tightness in 1952–1953 and 1955–1956 that the standby device came into wide use with variations depending upon the institutional investor involved. Large commercial banks, one important source of standbys, have made them often in conjunction with short-term credits extended for construction or interim financing. Thus, a bank may make a construction loan backed by its own standby commitment to purchase the completed mortgage, and accompanied by an agreement to provide interim financing (warehousing) for a short period. This is a convenient arrangement for the mortgage originator, who has a given length of time to locate a more favorable market for the completed permanent mortgage. For each of these separate services (construction financing, standby commitment, interim financing), the bank earns separate fees as well as interest.

To a lesser extent than commercial banks, long-term institutional investors also provide standby commitments. Their reason is not only to earn the fees, but also the hope of obtaining mortgages for their portfolios at

[4] Pringle–Hurd and Company, Inc., *Mortgage Market News and Comment*, September 20, 1954, p. 8.

bargain prices. Savings and loan associations, savings banks, and life insurance companies each sometimes combine standby commitments with options to purchase the mortgages under the commitment at more realistic market prices (i.e., prices higher than stipulated in the commitments) when ready for delivery. If their operations permit and the mortgages are satisfactory, these institutions have thus created an additional source of mortgages for their portfolios.

Without doubt, the standby commitment technique has proved advantageous to each of the participants, when, as anticipated, markets ease at the end of the standby period and completed mortgages are sold to permanent investors. The builder has been enabled to proceed with construction, the mortgage originator has maintained or increased his volume of business, and the institutional investor has earned a profitable fee for a promise to lend in case of need. If, however, the mortgage market tightens further during the standby period and mortgage prices decline, the standby price may become the market price, with the result that the institutional investor is pledged to unintended mortgage acquisition and the builder has paid substantially higher financing costs than he intended. While the standby committer prepared for such an eventuality may not be unhappy to have acquired mortgages at very favorable prices, the unprepared institution may be embarrassed by a lack of ready funds to honor such commitments. Many small savings and loan associations found themselves in a difficult situation in late 1955, for example, when they were unexpectedly called upon to honor standbys at a time when the Federal Home Loan Bank Board had restricted borrowings from the Federal Home Loan Banks. Some of them resorted to commercial bank credit to meet their commitments. Some large commercial banks, on the other hand, that had acquired mortgages unexpectedly when the market price fell below the standby price, were able to absorb these mortgages and sell them later at more favorable prices.

The effects of the standby commitment technique on market processes, as on individual participants, are also mixed. One favorable effect is felt during periods of temporary credit stringency in the capital market when standbys may serve the useful function of moderating declines in the availability of mortgage funds and, hence, in the volume of residential construction. Moreover, the standby technique permits the creation of a pool of completed mortgages ready for immediate delivery, an advantage to some types of institutional investors unable or unwilling to commit themselves months in advance to acquire mortgages.

An unfavorable effect lies in the destabilizing potential of the standby commitment to the mortgage market. Use of this technique makes possible an expansion in construction activity to a level that may not be sustainable, and a volume of mortgages that cannot be readily absorbed by long-term investors. Such a situation can readily result from pressure of builders for construction financing and from misjudgment on the part of standby committers of the time span of the credit stringency. There is evidence that, during part of 1955 and 1956, a volume of residential construction was undertaken larger than financial intermediaries could comfortably finance through the capital market, considering the strong demands for credit from business, consumers, and governments. Mortgage offerings exceeded takings, prices were depressed, and increasing use was made of short-term commercial bank credit to finance temporarily the excess volume of mortgages.

Interim Financing Developments

The use of short-term commercial bank credit by mortgage originators to finance their interim needs between the payment of loan proceeds to borrowers and the delivery of completed mortgages to ultimate investors has long been an integral part of the real estate financing process. Increased demands for this type of credit during the postwar decade are traceable to the standardization of mortgage contracts, resulting from the introduction of federal mortgage insurance and guarantee, and the lowering of legal barriers to out-of-state mortgage investments. The increased ability and willingness of institutional investors, with large aggregations of savings, to purchase mortgages on a nationwide basis has been accompanied by the rapid establishment and growth of mortgage companies originating and servicing loans for such mortgagees. These companies, characterized by limited capital in comparison with the volume of their operations, depend heavily on commercial bank credit.[5] Moreover, changing needs of institutional investors and periodic stringency in the market for long-term financing have further increased the use of commercial bank credits and led to numerous variations in techniques and arrangements, collectively called "mortgage warehousing."

VARIATIONS IN TECHNIQUE

Some of the arrangements for interim mortgage financing apply to mortgages already in existence, others to mortgages not yet made. Some variations concern mortgages on uncompleted houses, others, mortgages on existing properties. Some have two parties at interest, and others three

[5] See Chapter 8.

or more. Some arrangements include the pledge of specific mortgages as collateral, others general credit lines, and still others the purchase of mortgages under specified repurchase agreements. Some call for the use of bank credit for very short periods, others for considerably longer periods. Some are backed by commitments of permanent investors, others not. Most transactions deal with federally underwritten mortgages, but some with conventional mortgages. Some borrowers are builders, others mortgage originators, and still others mortgage investors. In all of these variations, the division of rights, interests, and obligations of the parties to the transaction are finely drawn and often legally complex. The one characteristic and purpose that is common to virtually all warehousing transactions is the use of commercial bank credit for an interim period pending the availability of long-term funds or the fulfillment of prearranged conditions.

The use of the term "warehousing" to describe fundamentally different types of interim financing transactions designed to achieve different purposes has led to considerable confusion and misunderstanding. Equally confusing have been the numerous terms that have sprung up in the trade to describe essentially the same kinds of transactions. It is difficult to distinguish favorite terms for identical transactions from bona fide terms to describe variations in technique. Among the more commonly used terms encountered in market interviews are the following: "committed" or "closed-end" warehousing; "uncommitted" or "open-end" warehousing; "warehouse with a standby"; "institutional" or "repurchase" warehousing; "clearing" loans, "inventory" loans, and "ordinary collateral" loans. The list could undoubtedly be lengthened. Among all the technical variations of interim financing, four types could be distinguished, each having meaningful characteristics with respect to participants, rights and obligations, fees and charges, risk, and purpose of borrowing. They are: (1) committed short-term loans; (2) committed long-term loans; (3) uncommitted loans (possibly including those under standby); and (4) institutional committed loans, or repurchase agreements.[6]

[6] The classification suggested here differs somewhat from those in the sources below, but the differences are readily detectable and should not be confusing. The only published classifications found were in *Mortgage Credit and FHA Multifamily Housing*, Report No. 2 of the Subcommittee on Housing of the Committee on Banking and Currency, House of Representatives, January 31, 1956, pp. 8–13; and in data reported by the Board of Governors of the Federal Reserve System in tables on "Credit Extended to Real Estate Mortgage Lenders by Weekly Reporting Member Banks in Leading Cities," published in various issues of the *Bulletin*, for example, September 1956, p. 1,347. The two classifications differ chiefly in that the former does not distinguish between loans secured and unsecured by mortgages, and the latter does not distinguish between loans backed or not backed by take-out commitments. Further, in *Mortgage Credit* the description of

The first and still most common type of interim financing, basic to mortgage company operations for years, involves the use of short-term commercial bank credits for periods of from 60 to 180 days. These credits are secured by permanent mortgages awaiting final processing and legal documentation, or by temporary loans on construction awaiting completion —both backed by firm take-out commitments of institutional investors. In many long-standing relationships between mortgage companies and commercial banks, a revolving line of credit is provided rather than individual credits for each transaction. When the documents are completed by the mortgage company and delivered to the permanent investor, the company uses the proceeds received to discharge its obligation to the bank. This type of loan is considered by most commercial bankers as an ordinary collateral loan made to finance a customer's sold inventory. The volume of such loans has multiplied in the postwar decade, as mortgage company operations have expanded.

The development of the long-term forward commitment by institutional investors gave rise to the need for longer-term financing of mortgage correspondents by commercial banks—a second form of warehousing. In the newer arrangement—as in the older one—loans are secured by mortgages and by firm take-out commitments of ultimate investors. On the surface, the only difference between the short-term and long-term interim financing techniques is the loan maturity. There is, however, a fundamental difference in purpose and in the obligations and rights of participants. In the short-term type the bank is performing a typical financing service for a borrower short of funds pending technical readying of an inventory of goods that will be taken and paid for immediately by the purchaser that ordered it. In the longer-term type, the inventory of loans is ready for delivery but the investor is not ready to accept it according to his planned investment schedule. In this instance, warehousing seems an apt term for a credit operation that supports storage of completed mortgages in a convenient reservoir for later tapping by an ultimate investor as funds become available. Some commercial banks regard this type of arrangement as a credit to finance a deferred purchase.

Another distinct characteristic of the second type of interim financing is

"uncommitted-line warehousing" encompasses standby commitments discussed separately here. The Federal Reserve classification, finally, does not include all the basic market variations discussed here, primarily because of problems of data collection.

The classification distinguishes between committed and uncommitted warehousing, but does not use the latter as synonymous with standby commitments. Discussions with participants in the market seemed to justify that separation, although a few institutional investors were found to regard the standby commitment as a form of uncommitted warehousing, and some used both together.

the usually unconditional commitment of the ultimate investor to purchase mortgages. Before the warehousing transaction is negotiated, the completed mortgages are subject to inspection by the investor and must have approval with respect to legal documentation, property specifications, and mortgagor qualifications. The investor agrees to purchase the mortgages at the appointed date, whether or not they go into default or delinquency during the warehousing period. In some instances, the agreement even requires the investor to take out of warehouse mortgages that have been in default for at least 90 days. During the warehousing period, amortization payments on pledged mortgages are remitted to the interim lender. The mortgages are generally recorded in the name of the ultimate investor, who may also hold the mortgages in his possession. If so, the interim lender holds a trust receipt. Technical arrangements vary in numerous ways.[7]

A third type of warehousing is similar to the first in purpose and duration except that it is not backed by a firm take-out commitment of an institutional investor. These uncommitted or open-end loans (distinguished from committed or closed-end loans of the second type) are often made to the larger, more heavily capitalized mortgage originators in a position to extend mortgage credit without prior commitments from an ultimate investor. These originators rely on their knowledge of the mortgage market and contacts within it to sell completed loans for immediate delivery. Often, in making uncommitted warehousing loans, the commercial bank also gives a standby commitment to the mortgage company or builder—a transaction known in the trade as a "warehouse with a standby." Through it, the originator unable to find a permanent investor at the end of the warehousing period may, as a last resort, fall back on the bank's standby commitment to buy the mortgage. Some observers have regarded the uncommitted warehousing loan as synonymous with the standby commitment.[8] Sufficient evidence (uncommitted warehousing loans made by commercial banks without standbys or backed by standby commitments of other lenders) was found in this study, however, to justify regarding the two techniques as separate and distinct, albeit closely related.

Commercial bank interim financing loans backed by standby commitments of other financial institutions are regarded as more risky than loans backed by regular take-out commitments. Most commercial banks regard

---

[7] I am grateful to William F. Keesler and King Upton, vice presidents of the First National Bank of Boston, and to Raymond T. O'Keefe, vice president of the Chase Manhattan Bank of New York, for providing much of the technical information underlying the discussion of the second type of interim financing.

[8] See Report No. 2 of the Subcommittee on Housing of the House Committee on Banking and Currency, pp. 8–10.

standbys as not so firm as regular commitments. Usually the regular take-out lender is interested in acquiring the loan, but the main purpose of the standby lender is often to earn a fee for a promise to lend. When unexpected market declines have occurred, standby committers have often been caught short. At best, they have requested delays in delivery of closed loans, and at worst, have tried to back out of the commitment through technical loopholes. Many commercial bankers have, therefore, classified interim loans backed by standbys in the same category as uncommitted short-term loans.

An officer of a large commercial bank, active in interim mortgage financing, has indicated the following criteria as in general use by commercial banks for granting uncommitted lines of credit to mortgage originators:

1. Ability of mortgage company to sell mortgages under adverse market circumstances

2. Diversification of borrower's sales outlets and reputation as servicer of mortgages

3. Ratio of borrower's unsold mortgages to total capital; to its service account, excluding FNMA account; and to anticipated annual sales

4. Quality of unsold loans, possible market for them, and how well they meet usual requirements of borrower's previous investors

5. Lender's appraisal of the availability of long-term funds for mortgage investment[9]

A fourth—and last in the present classification—variation in interim mortgage financing is the "repurchase" or "institutional warehousing" arrangement. The transaction is between a commercial bank and a permanent mortgage investor; the bank extends regular short-term credits secured by mortgage loans or purchases the mortgage loans under a repurchase agreement. This arrangement, which first appeared early in 1955, received wide publicity, partly because of the large size of single transactions, and partly because of implications for public policy.

Because of the large sums usually involved in such loans, many banks ordinarily participate in one transaction under the management of the bank negotiating the loan.[10] This type of loan has been used by

[9] King Upton (vice president, First National Bank of Boston), unpublished address, "Interim Financing of Closed Loans and Long-term Forward Commitments," at meeting of the Mortgage Bankers Association of America, February 23, 1956.

[10] In the warehousing transaction between Prudential Life Insurance Company and Irving Trust Company in 1955—perhaps the largest of that type—a loan under repurchase agreement of some $350 million was arranged in which 150 banks participated. In the arrangement between Institutional Securities Corporation, acting for several New York mutual savings banks, and Chase Manhattan Bank a loan for $250 million was negotiated divided among several commercial banks. Apparently less than 10 per cent of the large reservoir of funds was actually used by the borrowers.

institutional investors to serve one of two purposes: relief for an overcommitted position, or establishment of a reservoir of mortgage funds. In the first instance, an institution overly zealous in committing itself to acquire mortgages during a period of easy money may be left with insufficient funds to continue both a current mortgage investment program and to acquire mortgages committed for during an earlier period. Rather than sell government securities—perhaps in an unfavorable market—or reduce heavily its current mortgage investment program, the financial institution may prefer a warehousing arrangement. In the second, an institution temporarily lacking funds to acquire a feasible and desirable number of mortgages in a current period seeks to establish credit for that purpose until its own situation is eased. The longer-term aspects of this type of financing as well as the major purpose of establishing a pool of mortgages make it similar to interim financing under long-term forward commitments, discussed earlier.

Whether or not institutional warehousing arrangements provide for repurchase within a specified time or for repayment of a regular mortgage collateral loan has little real economic significance. It is generally a matter of legal technicality or convenience. Because of legal limitations on the amount a bank may lend to one customer, large transactions usually are made in the form of repurchase arrangements. For example, in the transaction between Chase Manhattan Bank and Institutional Securities Corporation (footnote 10) the bank agreed to make a straight collateral loan for $50 million and to purchase under repurchase agreement $200 million of mortgages. On the borrower side, a large insurance company, for example, may not care to have its financial statement show heavy bank borrowings and hence may prefer the repurchase form of agreement. Thus, the transaction between Prudential Insurance Company and Irving Trust Company (footnote 10) was entirely under repurchase arrangement, but it is unlikely that the mortgages were ever physically removed to the bank's vaults.

While the distinction between a loan and a repurchase arrangement may have little economic meaning, there is an important statistical distinction in the classification of commercial bank loans. Mortgage loans acquired by a bank under repurchase agreement are properly classified as real estate loans in reports of condition. Mortgages taken as collateral for a loan, however, must be classified as commercial loans. Undoubtedly, the large increase in the volume of warehousing transactions under repurchase agreement in 1955 resulted in a reported increase in the volume of commercial bank real estate credit loans outstanding.

Each of the four types of interim financing discussed above is an individually negotiated transaction between lender and borrower.[11] Each is, therefore, subject to variations in interest rate charges and other fees which are difficult to determine.

There is less semblance of an organized market for interim financing than for other areas of mortgage finance, and thus there is little standardization of terms. For loans in which there is little risk to commercial banks (types 1, 2, and 4), the interest rate seems generally to be 0.5 per cent above the prime loan rate with no additional loan fees or charges. Through most of 1955 the best interim loans were made at $3\frac{1}{2}$ per cent. In early 1956, the rate had risen to 4 per cent and, as the prime loan rate advanced, continued upward to $4\frac{3}{4}$ per cent by the autumn of 1956. On institutional loans that are managed by one bank for a syndicate, the managing bank usually receives a small fee for its services.[12] On smaller warehousing loans to mortgage companies, even though backed by firm take-out commitments, the interest rate may run slightly higher than on large warehousing loans to institutions.[13]

Many commercial banks will not make an uncommitted warehousing loan without making a standby commitment as well. In such cases the interest charge on the loan may be no higher than on a committed loan, but for the standby commitment a fee of from $\frac{1}{2}$ of 1 per cent to 1 per cent, in addition to the interest, may be charged, the fee depending on the standby price. Total charges on such loans, which generally run for less than one year, are thus considerably higher than on committed warehousing loans. Some banks provide uncommitted interim financing without a standby, often as special accommodation to favored customers carrying large balances with them, and at the interest rate on committed loans. Other banks will provide such financing, however, only at interest charges of from $\frac{1}{2}$ to $\frac{3}{4}$ of 1 per cent above the rate on firmly committed loans, the rate depending on the mortgage company and the standby committer, if any.

[11] A possible fifth type not discussed here is the loan not secured, or secured by collateral other than mortgages. Such a loan is ordinarily backed by a firm take-out commitment by an institutional investor and is otherwise backed by the credit status of a strong mortgage originator. In any event, as shown in Table 20, the amount of such loans has accounted only for a very small part of interim credit extended to real estate mortgage lenders.

[12] In the arrangement between Chase Manhattan Bank and Institutional Securities Corporation, the interest rate was $3\frac{1}{2}$ per cent on the first $50 million plus a service fee of $\frac{1}{16}$ of 1 per cent to Chase Manhattan on the additional $200 million for managing the arrangements with other participating banks (based on "Banks Set to Use Mortgage Funds," *The New York Times*, October 7, 1955).

[13] Report No. 2 of the House Subcommittee on Housing, p. 10, note.

From the standpoint of market participants, the advantages of the various types of warehousing arrangements are clear and seem to outweigh possible disadvantages to them. The interim lender earns a good rate of return for a loan secured generally by federally underwritten mortgages and backed often by a firm take-out commitment of a large institutional investor. The mortgage originator increases or maintains his volume of business and shares in the spread (when there is one) between the interest rate on mortgages held and interim financing charges. The institutional investor is able to compensate for an overcommitted position or have a reservoir of mortgages established for immediate investment of funds as they are received from new savings, life insurance premiums, and mortgage repayments. There may also be an additional fee earned for outstanding commitments during the interim financing period. Disadvantages may arise for the commercial bank if it has to extend a loan or acquire mortgages unwillingly when a commitment has proved less firm than expected. The mortgage originator or investor may also be at a disadvantage if mortgages are acquired at less favorable prices than expected, taking account of warehouse fees and charges.

From the standpoint of broader effects on market processes, warehousing arrangements may be either salutary or detrimental depending on the type of transaction and on market conditions. There is little question that the regular short-term interim financing loan, an integral part of the real estate financing process for years, serves a useful purpose in bridging the gap between loan closing and ultimate sale or delivery of the mortgage to a permanent investor. The question is whether the distinctive postwar innovations discussed above have constituted an appropriate use of bank credit. In this connection, the discussion on standby commitments in the preceding section is appropriate, since both techniques were developed largely to provide a flow or reservoir of mortgage credit during periods of capital stringency.

In brief, the advantages of the new warehousing techniques are that they may permit mortgage originators to operate with flexibility and may enable institutional investors to plan and carry out long-range mortgage investment programs. Used to excess, however, or during periods of extended capital market tightness, warehousing may tend to stimulate investment in construction and real estate beyond available flows of savings, with consequent later destabilizing effects on real estate markets. Warehousing not backed by firm take-out commitments, moreover, may lead to an excess of mortgages over funds available from permanent investors, with a consequent depressing result on market prices. Finally, to the extent that warehousing is an essential part of long-term forward commitment arrangements, it may contribute to market excesses. Such imbalance may result from miscalculations of investing institutions about future availability of capital funds. Their unwise attempts to build, on those miscalculations, too large mortgage inventories would add to already large mortgage flows in one period and reduce available mortgage funds in a future period.[14]

DATA ON INTERIM FINANCING

Only recently has information become available on the volume and types of interim financing credit extended by commercial banks to mortgage lenders. These data, shown in Tables 20 and 21, confirm two earlier impressions: that mortgage companies are the dominant user of such credits; and that most interim financing is carried out through direct loans secured by mortgages rather than through purchase of mortgages under resale agreement. Data are not available, however, for a classification in the detail given in the preceding section.

The volume of interim financing credit outstanding more than doubled between the summers of 1954 and 1955, following a 50 per cent increase in the four preceding years (Table 20). This sharp expansion resulted in significant changes in the characteristics of interim financing credits. Commercial bank credit extended to insurance companies increased most markedly—from less than 2 per cent of the total outstanding in August 1954 to nearly 18 per cent a year later. Most of the increase occurred in purchases of mortgages under resale agreement (type 4 discussed above), which advanced from 9 to 24 per cent of the total. At the same time interim credits extended to mortgage companies, though doubling, declined as a proportion of the total from 89 to 73 per cent, and loans secured by mortgages dropped from 85 to 70 per cent.

The shifts in the types of warehousing credits outstanding largely grew out of the single transaction of $350 million between the Prudential Insurance Company and the Irving Trust Company syndicate. As the Prudential repurchased their warehoused mortgages during 1956, interim credits to insurance companies declined sharply from the 1955 level of about 18 per cent to only 9 per cent of the total outstanding in August 1956. Total credits under repurchase agreement also declined but not so sharply. The volume of such credit arrangements with mortgage companies remained

---

[14] Some further discussion of market effects of warehousing may be found in Report No. 2 of the Subcommittee on Housing, pp. 11–13. A private investor's point of view is expressed by R. B. Patrick (financial vice president, Bankers Life Insurance Company), "There's Enough Money in Sight for Mortgage Loan Needs," *The Mortgage Banker*, May 1956, pp. 25–26.

unchanged, while it increased significantly for other types of borrowers. All types of interim financing credits extended to other types of borrowers, in fact, increased during 1956, while those to mortgage and insurance companies showed little change. The proportion of the "other" group rose to the highest on record. Borrowers in that group included savings and loan associations, mutual savings banks, builders, and other organizations. Use of interim bank credits by the financial institutions in the group may have reflected their need for such credits to finance mortgage purchases under earlier commitments, including standbys, when the net flow of long-term savings was slowing down.

Tables 20 and 21 also indicate the association of particular types of borrowers with particular types of warehousing credit arrangements. Mortgage companies typically borrow from commercial banks on the security of mortgages, although their unsecured borrowing also increased proportionately. Insurance companies typically use the repurchase arrangement, although to only a small extent before 1955, when the Prudential loan was closed. Other types of borrowers make use of all arrangements, of which the repurchase type of transaction increased most sharply since 1954.

The distribution of the unused portion of commercial bank commitments to purchase mortgage loans from mortgage companies, insurance companies, and other borrowers—or make loans to them—is quite similar to the distribution of warehousing credits outstanding among these borrowers. Included in these unused commitments, which declined from $1.3 to $1.1 billion between the summers of 1955 and 1956, are standbys. There is no way of determining what proportion they constitute of the total unused bank commitments. Some students have interpreted these data as consisting entirely of standby commitments, but that cannot be correct because the figures cover unused warehousing credits (including regular bank lines of credit) as well. It cannot be correct even if standbys are regarded as the same thing as "uncommitted warehousing," because the category includes all types of unused warehousing credits.

The relative importance of interim credits in total real estate finance varies with conditions in the financial markets. That importance is difficult to measure because suitable data are lacking. The most meaningful comparison probably is between the gross volume of interim financing and the gross volume of mortgage lending for home building and purchase. Estimates may serve to indicate approximate orders of importance. During 1955, for example, the average amount of the various types of warehousing credits outstanding was about $1.5 billion. The maturities of those credits

TABLE 20

Outstanding Interim Financing Credits Extended by Commercial Banks to Mortgage Lenders, by Type of Borrower and Type of Loan, Selected Periods, 1950–1956

(millions of dollars)

	1956				1955		1954	1950
	Nov. 14 (1)	Aug. 8 (2)	May 16 (3)	Feb. 15 (4)	Nov. 16 (5)	Aug. 10 (6)	Aug. 11 (7)	June 30 (8)
Total loans to mortgage lenders	1,525	1,465	1,354	1,425	1,623	1,408	608	404
Type of borrower								
Mortgage companies	1,182	1,137	1,051	1,148	1,182	1,025	541	—
Insurance companies	114	121	127	130	287	250	11	—
Other borrowers	229	208	175	145	152	131	55	—
Type of loan								
Secured by mortgages	1,092	1,051	968	1,066	1,110	982	516	—
Purchased under resale agreement	303	276	276	266	404	338	55	—
Unsecured or secured by other than mortgages	130	137	110	93	107	88	37	—
Type of borrower and loan								
Mortgage companies	1,182	1,137	1,051	1,148	1,182	1,025	541	—
Secured by mortgages	1,012	974	899	1,001	1,035	911	487	—
Purchased under resale agreement	113	103	107	107	109	90	44	—
Unsecured or secured by other than mortgages	57	60	45	40	38	24	10	—
Insurance companies	114	121	127	130	287	250	11	—
Secured by mortgages	7	9	10	11	20	11	2	—
Purchased under resale agreement	102	104	113	116	265	235	7	—
Unsecured or secured by other than mortgages	5	8	4	3	2	4	2	—

(continued on facing page)

TABLE 20 (continued)

	1956				1955		1954	1950
	Nov. 14 (1)	Aug. 8 (2)	May 16 (3)	Feb. 15 (4)	Nov. 16 (5)	Aug. 10 (6)	Aug. 11 (7)	June 30 (8)
Other borrowers	229	208	175	145	152	131	55	—
Secured by mortgages	73	68	59	54	54	59	26	—
Purchased under resale agreement	88	70	56	42	30	12	4	—
Unsecured or secured by other than mortgages	68	70	60	49	68	60	25	—
Unused portion of firm commitments[a]	794	1,064	1,131	1,131	1,225	1,295	—	—
Mortgage companies	536	791	851	837	889	894	—	—
Insurance companies	97	110	106	118	151	183	—	—
Other borrowers	162	163	173	176	185	219	—	—

SOURCE BY COLUMN: (1 to 7) Based on surveys of weekly reporting member banks, by the Board of Governors of the Federal Reserve System, *Federal Reserve Bulletin*, various issues, e.g., December 1956, p. 1,300. With respect to coverage the Board has stated: "Most of the loans and commitments to real estate lenders are financed at the large banks included in the weekly reporting series; banks in this series held about two-thirds of total loans of all member banks."

(8) Based on a special supplement to the June 30, 1950 commercial bank call report, and represents loans of all insured commercial banks shown in Report No. 33 of the Federal Deposit Insurance Corporation, "Assets and Liabilities of all Operating Insured Commercial and Mutual Savings Banks," June 30, 1950, p. 5.

[a] Commitments to purchase mortgage loans from, or make loans to, mortgage lenders.

TABLE 21

Percentage Distribution of Outstanding Interim Financing Credits Extended by Commercial Banks to Mortgage Lenders, by Type of Borrower and Type of Loan, Selected Periods, 1954–1956

	1956				1955		1954
	Nov. 14 (1)	Aug. 8 (2)	May 16 (3)	Feb. 15 (4)	Nov. 16 (5)	Aug. 10 (6)	Aug. 11 (7)
Total loans to mortgage lenders	100.0	100.0	100.0	100.0	100.0	100.0	100.0
Type of borrower							
Mortgage companies	77.5	77.3	77.7	80.6	72.8	72.8	89.0
Insurance companies	7.5	8.2	9.4	9.1	17.7	17.8	1.8
Other borrowers	15.0	14.5	12.9	10.3	9.5	9.4	9.2
Type of loan							
Secured by mortgages	71.6	71.6	71.7	74.8	68.4	69.7	84.9
Purchased under resale agreement	19.9	19.1	20.5	18.7	24.9	24.0	9.0
Unsecured or secured by other than mortgages	8.5	9.3	7.8	6.5	6.6	6.3	6.1
Type of borrower and loan							
Mortgage companies	100.0	100.0	100.0	100.0	100.0	100.0	100.0
Secured by mortgages	85.6	85.5	85.5	87.2	87.6	88.9	90.0
Purchased under resale agreement	9.6	9.3	10.2	9.3	9.2	8.8	8.1
Unsecured or secured by other than mortgages	4.8	5.2	4.3	3.5	3.2	2.3	1.8
Insurance companies	100.0	100.0	100.0	100.0	100.0	100.0	100.0
Secured by mortgages	6.1	7.4	7.9	8.5	7.0	4.4	18.2
Purchased under resale agreement	89.5	86.0	89.0	89.2	92.3	94.0	63.6
Unsecured or secured by other than mortgages	4.4	6.6	3.1	2.3	0.7	1.6	18.2
Other borrowers	100.0	100.0	100.0	100.0	100.0	100.0	100.0
Secured by mortgages	31.9	33.5	33.7	37.2	35.5	45.0	47.3
Purchased under resale agreement	38.4	33.5	32.0	29.0	19.7	9.2	7.3
Unsecured or secured by other than mortgages	29.7	33.0	34.3	33.8	44.7	45.8	45.5
Unused portions of firm commitments.[a]	100.0	100.0	100.0	100.0	100.0	100.0	100.0
Mortgage companies	67.5	74.1	75.2	74.0	72.6	69.0	—
Insurance companies	12.2	10.3	9.4	10.4	12.3	14.1	—
Other borrowers	20.4	15.5	15.3	15.6	15.1	16.9	—

SOURCE: Table 20.

[a] Commitments to purchase mortgage loans from or make loans to, mortgage lenders.

probably varied within a wide range of from two months to two years, the largest portion for six months or less. Assuming an average annual turnover ratio of 2.0, therefore, total interim financing extended during 1955 would have been on the order of $3 billion.

Total mortgage credit extended for the purchase of new and existing houses in 1955, according to estimates of the Board of Governors of the

Federal Reserve System, amounted to $23.5 billion, some $10.2 billion for new houses and the remainder for old houses.[15] Relating our estimate of $3 billion for gross interim financing to the estimate of $23.5 billion for mortgage loans made for new and existing house purchases suggests a quantitative importance of about one-seventh for interim lending in total home real estate finance. On the other hand, if, as observations in the market suggest, warehousing is associated chiefly with financing of new house building and purchase, the order of importance is increased to well over one-fourth.

The significance of interim mortgage financing in 1955 becomes even greater when comparison is made between the volume of new warehousing and of FHA and VA financing, since conventional mortgage loans are seldom warehoused. In 1955, the total volume of federally underwritten mortgage lending was $10.3 billion, $5.9 billion of it for new house purchases. If the whole volume of warehousing is assumed to be used for FHA and VA financing of new houses, warehousing accounted for approximately one-half of that volume in 1955. This is probably too high a ratio, for not all warehousing was used to finance VA or FHA mortgages on new housing; but it is some indication of the importance of that technique in the federally underwritten mortgage market. Compared to the total of all FHA and VA financing, warehousing accounted for about 30 per cent— still an impressive proportion. Finally, one may consider that the $1.2 billion of unused warehousing commitments outstanding during 1955 was supporting at least that amount of new construction credit.

While the quantitative significance of interim financing cannot be measured exactly, it is clear that such commercial bank credit had become of signal importance in mortgage markets by the end of the postwar decade. In 1956, the relative significance of warehousing remained about the same as that just described for 1955. To mortgage companies, in particular, interim financing from commercial banks was an essential factor in their rapid postwar growth (see Chapter 8).

Primary and Secondary Mortgage Market Characteristics and Relationships

The complexities of special institutional arrangements and techniques associated with marketing mortgages have clouded somewhat the distinction between primary and secondary mortgage markets. The lack of clarity particularly impedes attempts to separate these markets quantitatively in terms of volume, nature of transactions, prices, and costs.

[15] *Federal Reserve Bulletin*, May 1957, p. 369.

What does seem clear is that distinctions made in the mortgage market—as evidenced by general terminology and common understanding of participants—and in the scant statistics that exist are based on somewhat different interpretations of the terms "primary" and "secondary" than those generally given by economists or by participants in other sectors of the capital market.

CONCEPTS AND DEFINITIONS

While there are undoubtedly several different acceptable definitions of a primary capital market, a widely accepted one is a market in which debt or equity instruments are created in transactions between borrowers or sellers and initial lenders or buyers. A secondary market, in contrast, is one in which previously created securities are traded between investors, with or without the aid of intermediaries. The economic function of a primary capital market is to bring together seekers of funds and investors at mutually acceptable prices or interest rates. A secondary market provides a means for holders of securities in need of funds or for other purposes to dispose of holdings before maturity and for buyers to acquire financial instruments. Many investors consider the original acceptability of investments in terms of their marketability. Even though committed to long-term loans or investments, investors may find that unforeseen events or changing programs and policies often make it expedient to obtain funds through secondary markets.

In terms of that definition and of other characteristics of the mortgage market discussed below, a secondary market for mortgages scarcely existed before the advent of federal mortgage insurance in 1934 and guarantee in 1944. Before that the mortgage market consisted in the main of thousands of local primary markets in which individual borrowers obtained new loans or renewals directly from lenders on the security of individual properties. Each loan was tailored to the specific needs and requirements of borrowers and lenders. With little or no uniformity or standardization in loan contracts, shifting ownership of mortgages among investors was quite limited and expensive. It was based necessarily upon detailed examination and appraisal of property, neighborhood, borrower, and loan terms, and confined to places where the underlying property was located and local investors familiar with economic conditions.

A major exception to this pattern of market activity is that of the real estate bond market of the 1920's. In the apartment house and commercial property real estate boom of that period, investment in real estate securities became quite fashionable and widespread. To permit and encourage the participation of many individual investors in one or more mortgages, those debt instruments were broken down into real estate bonds of readily marketable face amounts, usually $1,000. The bonds, many with the collateral signature of a so-called mortgage guarantee company, were widely traded in over-the-counter markets, predominantly in New York and Chicago. Investors paid too little attention to the underlying properties or the borrowers, partly because of the so-called guarantee of the bonds and partly because of their marketability. The subsequent collapse of real estate values together with the questionable financial practices of many real estate bond houses and "guarantors" resulted in widespread losses by real estate bond-holders. The real estate bond disappeared as a widespread financial instrument.[16] The acceptability and marketability of mortgage loans among investors, therefore, was at a low ebb in the 1930's.

Introduction of federal mortgage insurance through the Federal Housing Administration in 1934 and of guarantee through the Veterans Administration in 1944 imparted to the mortgage instrument a degree of acceptability, uniformity of quality, and standardization of terms unknown before. The need of the investor for close scrutiny of property and borrower was lessened by the federal government's acceptance of contingent liability for fulfillment of the mortgage contract. Federally underwritten mortgages became broadly shiftable among investors, geographic barriers were sharply reduced, and a national secondary mortgage market began to take form.

Considerable changes also took place in basic techniques in primary mortgage markets associated with financing of new houses. The changes accompanied those taking place in the house building industry generally. Postwar changes in production and marketing of houses —especially the large-scale type of operation—and their effects on mortgage markets have been discussed in several connections. Separate and distinct transactions between each individual mortgagor and lender, typical of prewar mortgage markets, were being replaced by mass mortgage transactions between builders and lenders on behalf of numerous unknown ultimate mortgagors.

---

[16] Statistics on real estate mortgage bonds may be found in Raymond W. Goldsmith, *A Study of Saving*, Princeton, 1955, Vol. I, Tables R-41 through R-43, pp. 635–637. Among the many references on the general subject of real estate bonds the following are examples: Securities and Exchange Commission, *Report on the Study and Investigation of the Work, Activities, Personnel, and Functions of Protective and Reorganization Committee*, Part III, June 3, 1936; Louis S. Posner, "The Lesson of Guaranteed Mortgage Certificates," *Harvard Business Review*, September 1948, pp. 560–571; Ernest A. Johnson, "Long-term Real Estate Securities," *Journal of Land and Public Utility Economics*, February 1936, pp. 44–47 (includes figures on issues from *Commercial and Financial Chronicle*); *Commercial and Financial Chronicle*, 128 (1929), pp. 316–317; 138 (1934), p. 211; 140 (1935), p. 22; Genevieve Koester, "Chicago Real Estate Bonds, 1919–1938: Corporate History," *Journal of Land Economics*, 1939, pp. 49–58.

These observations are not to suggest that widespread trading exists in all types of mortgages on all types of properties or that the primary mortgage market is characterized essentially by mass transactions. On the contrary, there is still only limited secondary trading in conventional mortgages, which account for the largest share of all those originated or outstanding. In the primary mortgage market, furthermore, individual negotiations between borrowers and lenders are predominant for conventional mortgages on all types of properties, residential and nonresidential. Federally underwritten mortgages on existing houses are also usually arranged individually. Mortgage markets by their nature are basically local, and mortgage contracts still vary widely according to the individual needs of borrowers, characteristics of underlying properties, and requirements of lenders.

Introduction and ultimate broad acceptance of FHA mortgage insurance and VA mortgage guarantee largely eliminated earlier investor problems of acquiring mortgages outside local areas. Instead, new problems of market organization and mortgage acquisition for nonlocal investors arose, as previously described. As large-scale institutional investors established branch offices or worked through institutions located in other cities and states (such as real estate and mortgage companies or commercial banks) market processes and techniques of mortgage origination and ultimate investment, already discussed, became more distinctly separate than ever before. It is from that clear separation of processes that the distinction between primary and secondary marketing of mortgages has emerged. Upon understanding of the special trade meaning of the terms "origination" and "purchase" in the mortgage market hinges our understanding of the meaning of primary and secondary mortgage markets, of relationships between them, and of such statistics that exist on those market transactions.

A mortgage origination is considered in the market as a transaction in which a mortgage loan is made and closed in the name of the originator, whether or not the action is taken for another investor and regardless of the ultimate source of funds. An acquisition or purchase, then, is a transaction in which a mortgage is acquired from an originator, whether or not the mortgage was originated under a prior agreement for such purchase. In this framework, three types of transactions may be identified which would be classified by mortgage market participants as belonging to the secondary mortgage market:

1. Transactions in which mortgages are purchased by investors from originators on the basis of prior allocations of funds or firm commitments

2. Transactions in which mortgages are purchased by investors from originators without prior allocations or commitments, but with the clear intent in origination to sell rather than to hold the completed mortgage

3. Transactions between permanent investors in seasoned mortgages acquired originally by the seller as long-term investments

Of the three types of transactions considered from the standpoint of the economic concept and functions of primary and secondary markets, only the third type might properly be classified as a true secondary market transaction. The first type seems clearly to belong in the primary market classification as a special technique of mortgage acquisition which reflects the organization of mortgage markets and operations of out-of-state mortgage investors.

For the second type of transaction, appropriate classification is less clear. The "open" market in which purchases of this type are made at quoted prices, in contrast to the first type in which purchases are made in a "closed" market on the basis of prior arrangements, may be thought of as a secondary market. On the other hand, mortgages so purchased are originated for the express purpose of sale to a permanent investor, and such transactions are not unlike those in the corporate securities market where new issues are underwritten by investment bankers and offered for sale in the open market to final investors. The techniques, timing, and services performed by respective "originators" in the mortgage and corporate securities markets are, to be sure, vastly different, but the ultimate transactions seem parallel in nature. In transactions defined in 1 and 2 above, the mortgage originator may retain ownership of a mortgage for several months after completion under warehousing arrangements before "selling" to a permanent investor. Where the intent to sell is clear from the beginning, however, especially under prior commitment, extended ownership before sale does not necessarily change the basic nature of the transaction from a primary to a secondary one.

The suggestion here is that a basic criterion for distinguishing between "true" and "pseudo-secondary" and "quasi-secondary" market transactions is the intent and purpose of the seller (indicated partly by the nature of his business) in originating the loan in the first instance. By that criterion, the type 1 transaction may be thought of as a pseudo-secondary market transaction; type 2 as a quasi-secondary market transaction; and type 3 as a true secondary market transaction.

Perhaps a more colorful distinction between types of secondary market transactions is that derived from discussion with an officer of a large mortgage brokerage firm. He described the secondary mortgage market as consisting of two basic types of transactions: "nepotism loans" controlled by the large life insurance companies and savings banks on the basis of prior allocations of funds and commitments (type 1 above); and loans purchased in the "open wholesale market" created by originators without prior allocation (types 2 and 3 above). A few others representing large mortgage firms regarded the basic type of secondary mortgage market transaction as consisting of loans acquired in the open market without prior allocation or commitment. Those intermediary mortgage dealers were thus in agreement that a mortgage purchase or sale without arrangement before origination was a true secondary market transaction. They did not make the distinction suggested in this study between transaction types 2 and 3.

Just as only one type of transaction clearly fits our definition of a true secondary market, so there is only one equivocal primary market type of mortgage loan transaction. It is the loan made directly by a permanent lender to a borrower for his own portfolio. The bulk of savings and loan association mortgage activity, for example, falls into this category. Most life insurance company mortgage investment activity, in contrast, is conducted through other originators. It is this distinction between methods of loan acquisition, suggested earlier, that is used in this study to classify the few data on primary and secondary market activity. In what follows, secondary market activity encompasses all three types distinguished here.

STATISTICS ON SECONDARY MARKET ACTIVITY

While no direct data on the volume and characteristics of true secondary market transfers, as distinct from the pseudo and quasi types, could be found, some implication may be drawn from the data on transfers of FHA-insured mortgages. Other data on secondary market activity presented here are based on information obtained in the *Census of Housing, 1950*, on estimates prepared in this study from annual reports of life insurance companies, and from a special survey of savings and loan associations. None of the data provide an adequate measure of the volume and character of secondary market activity but are of interest as indicators of market organization and techniques of loan acquisition.

Tables 22 and 23 summarize data from the *Census of Housing, 1950* on originations and purchases of mortgages on owner-occupied and rental residential properties. Of the total amount of owner-occupied mortgages outstanding around mid-1950, about one-fifth was acquired by portfolio holders through purchase, compared with one-fourth for rental property

TABLE 22

First Mortgages Originated and Purchased on Owner-Occupied Properties,
by Type of Holder, 1950

	All Holders (1)	Com-mercial Banks (2)	Mutual Savings Banks (3)	Savings and Loan Asso-ciations (4)	Life Insur-ance Com-panies (5)	Mort-gage Com-panies (6)	FNMA (7)	Indi-viduals (8)	Other (9)
				AMOUNTS (millions of dollars)					
›tal	32,691	6,848	3,200	8,797	5,957	421	968	5,475	1,025
Originated	25,994	6,003	2,466	8,375	3,274	323	—	4,743	815
Purchased	6,697	845	734	422	2,683	98	968	732	210
Conventional	18,939	2,826	1,657	6,097	1,980	115	—	5,470	792
Originated	16,875	2,684	1,396	5,826	1,440	93	—	4,740	696
Purchased	2,064	142	261	271	540	22	—	730	96
FHA-insured	6,603	1,986	683	601	2,854	194	152	—	133
Originated	3,933	1,476	341	555	1,367	135	—	—	63
Purchased	2,670	510	342	46	1,487	59	152	—	70
VA-guaranteed	7,149	2,036	859	2,099	1,124	113	816	4	98
Originated	5,186	1,843	728	1,995	467	96	—	3	55
Purchased	1,963	193	131	104	657	17	816	1	43
				PERCENTAGE DISTRIBUTION					
›tal	100.0	100.0	100.0	100.0	100.0	100.0	100.0	100.0	100.0
Originated	79.5	87.7	77.0	95.2	55.0	76.7	0.0	86.6	79.5
Purchased	20.5	12.3	23.0	4.8	45.0	23.3	100.0	13.4	20.5
Conventional	100.0	100.0	100.0	100.0	100.0	100.0	—	100.0	100.0
Originated	89.1	95.0	84.2	95.6	72.7	80.9	—	86.7	87.9
Purchased	10.9	5.0	15.8	4.4	27.3	19.1	—	13.3	12.1
FHA-insured	100.0	100.0	100.0	100.0	100.0	100.0	100.0	—	100.0
Originated	59.6	74.3	49.9	92.3	48.0	69.6	0.0	—	47.4
Purchased	40.4	25.7	50.1	7.7	52.0	30.4	100.0	—	52.6
VA-guaranteed	100.0	100.0	100.0	100.0	100.0	100.0	100.0	100.0	100.0
Originated	72.5	90.5	84.7	95.0	41.5	85.0	0.0	75.0	56.1
Purchased	27.5	9.5	15.3	5.0	58.5	15.0	100.0	25.0	43.9

SOURCE: Data from *Census of Housing, 1950*, Vol. 4, *Residential Financing*, Part 1, United States, Chapter 2, Table 2, p. 40; Table 4, p. 76; Table 4.a, p. 79; Table 4.b, p. 87, and Table 4.c, p. 89.

mortgages.[17] Wide differences were reported among types of holders and types of mortgages, however. Among owner-occupied mortgages, two-fifths of those insured by FHA and over one-fourth of those guaranteed by VA were acquired by purchase compared with only a little over one-tenth of conventional loans. Of all portfolio holders, life insurance companies acquired the largest proportion of their mortgages, including over one-half

[17] For the sake of brevity, the terms owner-occupied mortgages and rental property mortgages will be used here to denote mortgages secured by owner-occupied houses and by all kinds of rental properties, respectively.

TABLE 23

First Mortgages Originated and Purchased on Rental Properties,
by Type of Holder, 1950

	All Holders (1)	Com-mercial Banks (2)	Mutual Savings Banks (3)	Savings and Loan Asso-ciations (4)	Life Insur-ance Com-panies (5)	Mort-gage Com-panies (6)	FNMA (7)	Indi-viduals (8)	Other (9)
				AMOUNTS (millions of dollars)					
Total	10,251	1,340	2,592	1,178	2,832	145	70	1,510	583
Originated	7,684	1,191	1,658	1,111	1,992	98	—	1,212	422
Purchased	2,567	149	934	67	840	47	70	298	161
Conventional	7,970	896	2,209	1,016	1,793	95	—	1,510	452
Originated	6,364	836	1,474	964	1,435	73	—	1,212	370
Purchased	1,606	60	735	52	358	22	—	298	82
FHA-insured	1,930	331	338	67	987	45	42	—	119
Originated	1,064	252	143	60	543	20	—	—	46
Purchased	866	79	195	7	444	25	42	—	73
VA-guaranteed	352	113	45	96	53	4	28	—	11
Originated	256	103	41	87	14	4	—	—	5
Purchased	96	10	4	9	39	—	28	—	6
				PERCENTAGE DISTRIBUTION					
Total	100.0	100.0	100.0	100.0	100.0	100.0	100.0	100.0	100.0
Originated	75.0	89.0	64.0	94.3	70.3	67.6	—	80.3	72.4
Purchased	25.0	11.0	36.0	5.7	29.7	32.4	100.0	19.7	27.6
Conventional	100.0	100.0	100.0	100.0	100.0	100.0	—	100.0	100.0
Originated	79.8	93.3	66.7	94.9	80.0	77.0	—	80.3	81.9
Purchased	20.2	6.7	33.3	5.1	20.0	23.0	—	19.7	18.1
FHA-insured	100.0	100.0	100.0	100.0	100.0	100.0	100.0	—	100.0
Originated	55.1	76.1	42.3	89.6	55.0	44.4	—	—	38.7
Purchased	44.9	23.9	57.7	10.4	45.0	55.6	100.0	—	61.3
VA-guaranteed	100.0	100.0	100.0	100.0	100.0	100.0	100.0	—	100.0
Originated	72.7	91.2	91.1	90.6	26.4	100.0	—	—	45.5
Purchased	27.3	8.8	8.9	9.4	73.6	—	100.0	—	54.5

SOURCE: Same basic source as Table 22; Chapter 5, Table 2, p. 348; Table 4, p. 389; Table 4. p. 393; Table 4.b, p. 395; Table 4.c, p. 397.

of their FHA and VA loans, by purchase rather than origination. Savings and loan associations acquired only a very small proportion of all mortgage holdings through purchase. Except for FHA loans, savings banks and commercial banks also acquired a modest amount of their holdings by purchase rather than origination.

Somewhat different figures, but a similar pattern, characterized activity in rental mortgages outstanding as of mid-1950. One difference worth noting in the savings banks data is the much larger proportion of con-ventional mortgage loans on rental properties than on owner-occupied properties acquired through purchase—one-third compared with less than one-sixth. While there are no data on the subject, market discussion suggests that this large proportion of rental property mortgage purchases consists chiefly of pseudo and quasi purchases from originators scattered throughout large states where the banks are located or in adjoining states.[18]

The large proportion of mortgages reported as purchased by mortgage companies (Tables 22 and 23)—surprising in view of the basic nature of mortgage company operations—is owing in large part to the activities of Institutional Securities Corporation (ISC), an organization wholly owned by New York State savings banks. The Corporation has been classified as a mortgage company by FHA for purposes of statistical reporting, and apparently also by the Bureau of the Census. ISC purchased a large volume of FHA-insured mortgages for savings banks accounts before 1950, when state statutes were amended to permit savings banks to purchase out-of-state mortgages on their own. Since 1950 purchases by the Corporation have declined sharply, as indicated by FHA data on mortgage company purchases (Table 24) and by personal interviews with ISC officials.

Ordinary mortgage companies on occasion purchase mortgages from individuals and from other originators to meet demands for mortgages. Such purchase activity was not uncommon before 1951, when demands for mortgages by investors were generally larger than the available supply. While no other except FHA data are available, it seems clear that purchases by mortgage companies have been an insignificant part of their activities in recent years.

Comprehensive data for the postwar decade on primary and secondary mortgage market activity are available only for FHA-insured mortgages in the reports on "originations" and "transfers," which the Federal Housing Administration receives directly from mortgage lenders. The institution in whose name the mortgage loan is closed and insured is considered to be the originator even though the loan is to be transferred immediately to a permanent investor. Thus, a loan made by a mortgage company for ultimate sale to a life insurance company is reported as both an origination and sale for the mortgage company and as a purchase for the life insurance company. Clearly, transfer activity as reported by FHA, summarized in Tables 24 and 25, includes pseudo and quasi transfers as well as true transfers. Some inferences about the volume of true secondary market

---

[18] Laws of some savings bank states permit acquisition of conventional mortgage loans in adjoining states.

TABLE 24

Primary and Secondary Market Activity of Main Types of Finanical Institutions
in FHA-Insured Home Mortgages, 1947–1956

(millions of dollars)

| | All Lenders | | | FINANCIAL INSTITUTIONS | | | | | | | | | | | |
| | | | | Commerical Banks | | | Mutual Savings Banks | | | Insurance Companies | | | Savings and Loan Associations | | |
YEAR	Holdings (1)	Origi-nations (2)	Trans-fers (3)	Origi-nations (4)	Pur-chases (5)	Sales (6)	Origi-nations (7)	Pur-chases (8)	Sales (9)	Origi-nations (10)	Pur-chases (11)	Sales (12)	Origi-nations (13)	Pur-chases (14)	Sales (15)
1947	4,146	895	278	276	98	86	21	30	1	185	133	25	98	3	21
1948	5,564	2,087	887	657	157	253	64	90	3	468	487	60	221	3	48
1949	7,438	2,206	1,100	672	86	281	110	145	7	507	569	80	238	4	73
1950	9,228	2,469	1,421	730	230	320	189	268	11	514	757	74	266	17	64
1951	10,647	1,929	1,313	669	194	350	126	351	11	329	666	63	174	8	71
1952	11,786	1,914	988	707	190	272	85	237	30	267	397	54	170	17	40
1953	13,319	2,262	1,375	822	131	324	107	310	8	277	566	69	233	30	51
1954	14,491	1,938	1,340	669	176	325	114	311	4	228	461	48	209	37	43
1955	16,245	3,077	1,345	1,078	244	389	222	325	20	343	574	66	378	36	46
1956	17,838	2,639	1,506	1,029	166	375	238	389	16	220	735	65	251	37	45

SOURCE: Data in Annual Reports of the Federal Housing Administration. Data on total volume of insured home mortgages originated by type of institution for years prior to 1947 are not available. Data for mortgage companies, federal agencies, and all other institutions are not shown separately, but the relative importance of purchases and sales by those institutions is given in Table 25.

TABLE 25

Purchases and Sales of FHA-Insured Home Mortgages as Per Cent of Total Transfer Activity,
by Type of Institution, 1945–1956

Year	Total Purchases or Sales (millions)	Commercial Banks		Savings Banks		Insurance Companies		Savings and Loan Assns.		Mortgage Companies		Federal Agencies		All Other	
		Pur-chases	Sales	Pur-chases	Sales	Pur-chases	Sales	Pur-chases	Sales	Pur-chases	Sales	Pur-chases	Sales	Pur-chases	Sales
1945	$478	36	26	10	1	40	5	3	4	4	35	4	22	3	7
1946	266	45	26	8	1	37	8	2	5	4	44	a	9	5	8
1947	278	35	31	11	a	48	9	1	8	3	43	a	1	2	9
1948	887	18	29	10	a	55	7	a	5	3	52	12	a	2	7
1949	1,100	8	26	13	1	52	7	a	7	2	51	24	a	1	9
1950	1,421	16	23	19	1	53	5	1	5	2	46	6	15	3	6
1951	1,313	15	27	27	1	51	5	1	5	2	51	3	6	2	6
1952	988	19	28	24	3	40	6	2	4	3	52	10	3	2	6
1953	1,375	10	24	23	1	41	5	2	4	2	61	20	2	3	4
1954	1,340	13	24	23	3	34	4	3	3	2	61	21	5	3	4
1955	1,345	18	29	24	1	43	5	3	3	2	57	8	1	2	3
1956	1,506	11	25	26	1	49	4	2	3	1	64	7	1	3	2

SOURCE: Data in Annual Reports of the Federal Housing Administration.
a Less than 0.5 of 1 per cent.

activity may be drawn from the tables, which are limited to activity in home mortgages and show face amounts of mortgages.

The total volume of FHA-insured mortgage originations has exceeded transfers by a substantial margin in each postwar year (Table 24). In most years, the ratio of transfers to originations has ranged between one-half and two-thirds, with no steady pattern of growth or decline. Compared with the face amount of home mortgage loan holdings of all lenders, transfers have varied between 8 and 16 per cent, the lower percentages prevailing in more recent years.

Among financial institutions, the pattern of activity is similar to that suggested by 1950 Census data: insurance companies and savings banks having a volume of purchases well in excess of originations; savings and loan associations and commercial banks having a volume of originations far greater than purchases. Sales of FHA-insured home mortgages by savings banks, insurance companies, and savings and loan associations were very small throughout the first postwar decade; indeed, in the case of savings banks and insurance companies markedly smaller than purchases. Commercial banks, on the other hand, showed a substantial volume of sales that in most years was much greater than purchases. As indicated in Table 25, mortgage companies and commercial banks account for the bulk of all sales activity, insurance companies and savings banks for the bulk of all purchases.

In these data on originations, purchases, and sales can we distinguish between true secondary market activity and pseudo- or quasi-secondary market activity? An approximation may be attempted on the basis of our knowledge of the nature of financial institutions' operations in the mortgage market. If we assume that sales by mortgage companies (Table 25) are entirely of the pseudo or quasi type, then the maximum amount of true FHA mortgage sales would, in most postwar years, amount to less than one-half of total reported FHA transfers, and in some years to little more than one-third. A minimum estimate of true mortgage transfer activity might be approximated also by excluding sales by commercial banks, on the assumption that those institutions originate FHA-insured mortgages chiefly for resale to other institutions. Of sales by only the principal types of savings institutions—savings banks, savings and loan associations, and insurance companies—by the Federal National Mortgage Association, and by miscellaneous lenders, the minimum volume of true sales of FHA-insured mortgages would amount to between 12 and 30 per cent of total sales of those mortgages in the postwar years.

This must be considered the minimum range, of course, because some proportion of commercial bank sales represent seasoned mortgages from portfolios, just as do sales from savings institutions—primarily in the business of holding mortgages. Thus, somewhere between the minimum and maximum figures cited lies an approximation of true secondary market activity in FHA-insured home mortgages. If we arbitrarily assume one-half of commercial bank sales to be of seasoned mortgages, then in 1956, for instance, the volume of true transfers would amount to $352 million, or about 2 per cent of the face amount of mortgages outstanding at the end of 1956. Even at maximum, the proportion of true transfers to outstandings would be less than 5 per cent.

On this basis (eliminating all mortgage company sales and one-half of commercial bank sales), the volume of true secondary market activity in FHA-insured home mortgages may have amounted to between 12 and 13 per cent of primary market activity (originations) in 1955 and 1956. It may have been somewhat more in 1953 and 1954 (averaging around one-sixth), when originations were considerably smaller and transfers almost the same as in the later years. In postwar years before 1953 the ratio of secondary to primary market activity ranged between 13 and 18 per cent, except in 1950 and 1951 when the ratio reached almost one-fourth, because of the large proportion of sales by FNMA under the "one-for-one program."[19]

Without comprehensive data comparing primary and secondary market activity in VA and conventional home mortgages, an idea of the proportion of secondary market activity can be gleaned from general knowledge of market techniques and from a few data on purchases by savings banks (Table 15), and life insurance companies (Table 26). It is clear that VA secondary market activity of all types, quasi and pseudo as well as true transfers, is at least as large a proportion of primary activity as the proportion of secondary activity in FHA home mortgage markets. It seems logical to conclude, therefore, considering the similar nature of the instruments, that true secondary market activity in both VA mortgages and FHA home mortgages is about the same proportion of total market activity.

Nothing is known about the volume of trading in conventional mortgages except that, for obvious reasons, it is considerably smaller than the trading in federally underwritten mortgages. Data from the *Census of Housing, 1950* (Table 22) indicate that the percentage of conventional home mortgages outstanding in mid-1950 acquired by purchase was between one-third and one-fourth of the percentage of federally underwritten mortgages so acquired. A comparable ratio of true secondary

---

[19] See Chapter 3 for an explanation of this program.

market transfers in conventional mortgages to transfers in federally under-written mortgages suggests that the former account for about 5 per cent, more or less, of total primary activity in conventional home mortgages. Primary lending on conventional mortgages accounts for the largest part of home mortgage lending—between two-thirds and three-fourths in recent years, on the basis of mortgage recordings. If our estimated percentages are weighted by these proportions, it would appear that true secondary market activity in home mortgages of all types represents somewhere between 7 and 10 per cent of total primary activity, and approximately 2 to 4 per cent of the amount of total home mortgage debt outstanding.

Data on market activity in FHA multifamily mortgages are available in the same detail as for FHA home mortgages. By application of a similar estimating technique, the ratio of true secondary to primary market activity for FHA multifamily mortgages seems to be somewhat higher and more erratic than the ratio for FHA home mortgages. One difference to be taken into account is that the bulk of originations and sales of FHA multifamily mortgages is made by commercial banks, not by mortgage companies. One explanation is that commercial banks make most of the construction loans on FHA multifamily properties. Such loans are insured by the Federal Housing Administration (unlike most one- to four-family construction loans insured by FHA only after the permanent mortgage is closed) and reported in the statistics as originations. When construction is completed and the permanent mortgage taken over by the ultimate inves-tor, the transaction is recorded by FHA as a sale and purchase. In esti-mating the volume of true secondary market activity in FHA multifamily mortgages, therefore, it is probably appropriate to eliminate all sales by commercial banks as well as by mortgage companies. Conventional mort-gages on multifamily properties are traded about as infrequently as conventional mortgages on one- to four-family properties.

Concerning some other aspects of secondary market activities of major types of financial institutions, for an indication of the importance of out-of-state purchases of mortgages by mutual savings banks, see Chapter 6. Data on the significance of mortgage purchases (quasi and pseudo, and true) in the activities of life insurance companies and of savings and loan associations are presented in Tables 26 through 28. Data shown are sub-ject to an unknown amount of error, but the general order of magnitude and the comparisons among types of mortgages are undoubtedly accurate enough to warrant a few broad conclusions.

Total purchases of mortgages by life insurance companies have consti-tuted something over one-third of their total mortgage acquisitions since

TABLE 26

Mortgage Loans Purchased by Life Insurance Companies, 1946–1955

Year	Total (1)	1- to 4-Family				Multi-family (6)	Commercial (7)	Farm (8)
		Total (2)	FHA (3)	VA (4)	Conventional (5)			
		AMOUNTS (millions of dollars)						
1946	415	310	88	192	30	39	57	9
1947	808	637	120	426	91	56	91	24
1948	1,022	837	445	227	165	111	59	15
1949	894	670	530	65	75	148	66	10
1950	1,713	1,436	620	716	100	175	80	22
1951	1,900	1,557	547	800	210	187	135	21
1952	1,233	987	366	274	347	120	107	19
1953	1,438	1,208	483	359	366	80	128	22
1954	2,003	1,737	395	1,122	220	92	153	21
1955	n.a.	n.a.	612	1,474	n.a.	n.a.	n.a.	n.a.
		PERCENTAGE DISTRIBUTION OF TOTAL MORTGAGE ACQUISITIONS						
1946	25	40	63	74	8	18	10	5
1947	29	41	59	71	14	22	11	9
1948	30	42	52	62	21	24	10	5
1949	26	37	54	50	11	24	8	3
1950	35	45	51	74	10	30	11	6
1951	37	47	64	62	18	32	13	5
1952	31	42	60	64	26	25	14	5
1953	33	45	65	79	24	23	15	5
1954	37	50	65	81	15	24	14	5
1955	n.a.	n.a.	65		n.a.	n.a.	n.a.	n.a.

SOURCE BY COLUMN:

(1, 2, 6, 7, 8) For years 1946–1953, unpublished data obtained by the Federal Home Loan Bank Board (FHLBB) in annual surveys of mortgage lending activities of life insurance companies. Ratios of loans purchased to total acquisitions indicated by these data were applied to revised figures on acquisitions (FHLBB, *Nonfarm Mortgage Investments of Life Insurance Companies*, 1955, p. 3) to derive adjusted figures for loans purchased. The relationship between purchases and acquisitions shown by the FHLBB data were checked for recent years and found to agree closely with information contained in annual statements of ten leading life insurance companies accounting for about one-half of total life insurance company assets in 1954. The 1954 annual statements were, therefore, used as the basis for deriving data in 1954, since FHLBB discontinued receiving purchase and origination figures after 1953.

(3) Derived from unpublished FHA data on face amount of originations and purchases of life insurance companies (published figures are for all insurance companies). Acquisitions, upon which percentages shown in this table are based, were derived by applying to total FHA mortgage acquisitions, as reported by the Institute of Life Insurance, the ratio of FHA one- to four-family acquisitions to total, as indicated by FHA data.

(4) Calculated by subtracting figures on originations reported by VA from figures on acquisitions reported by the Institute of Life Insurance.

(5) Col. 2 minus sum of Cols. 3 and 4.

n.a. = not available.

1950, compared with an average of a little over one-fourth in preceding postwar years (Table 26). The bulk of these purchases has been of one- to four-family mortgages, mostly insured or guaranteed by the federal government. Throughout the postwar decade purchases accounted for the largest proportion of FHA and VA mortgage acquisitions—a proportion showing, however, erratic fluctuations through the years. The proportion of conventional home mortgage loans obtained through purchase has been fairly modest throughout, and larger in the later than earlier years.

TABLE 27

Primary and Secondary Mortgage Market Activity of
Savings and Loan Associations, 1952–1955
(millions of dollars)

	Outstanding (end of year)	Originations	Purchases (during year)	Sales
1952	18,396	6,617	151	201
1953	21,962	7,767	289	161
1954	26,193	8,969	463	279
1955	31,584	11,432	508	399

SOURCE: Based on data for all associations insured by the Federal Savings and Loan Insurance Corporation and shown in FHLBB release, "Mortgage Lending Activity of Savings and Loan Associations," September 1955. Loans originated by insured associations accounted for from 88 to 92 per cent of loans originated by all associations in 1952–1955, and ratios of transfer activity were assumed to be about the same.

While quantitative evidence is lacking, market observation and discussion lead one to conclude that these data on mortgage purchases of life insurance companies reflect chiefly pseudo- and quasi-secondary methods of loan acquisition, and only in minor part true secondary market trading in seasoned mortgages. Thus the data reinforce the general impression that most mortgages on commercial and farm properties in portfolios of life insurance companies are originated directly by them, rather than being acquired indirectly through originators, as home mortgages are. The latter are obtained mainly through mortgage loan correspondents, usually on the basis of prior commitments. Purchases of seasoned mortgages from portfolio holders are only occasional, when available funds exceed earlier expectations and planning. Life insurance companies rarely sell mortgages from their portfolios.

Data on secondary market activities (defined in the broadest sense) of savings and loan associations, made available for the first time in 1955, confirm general knowledge of the insignificance of such activity with respect to their own mortgage operations. These data, shown in Table 27, are somewhat surprising, however, in that the absolute volume of mortgage purchases by savings and loan associations is quite significant in comparison with the volume purchased by life insurance companies and by savings banks—both considered to be active participants in secondary markets.

Between 1952 and 1955 mortgage purchases and sales by savings and loan associations increased significantly but remained a small part of their total mortgage activity, never exceeding 2 per cent of outstandings or 5 per cent of acquisitions. The total volume of savings and loan mortgage purchases in those years was nevertheless substantial, about one-fourth of that of life insurance company purchases and about one-half of that of savings banks.

Additional evidence on the nature and characteristics of savings and loan secondary market activity was obtained as part of a survey made in this study and noted in Chapter 6. The primary purpose of the survey was to clarify problems associated with gross mortgage lending activity of savings and loan associations. Supplementary questions on mortgage purchases and sales, a little known aspect of savings and loan activity, were included also. Returns from the survey were too small to justify firm conclusions in quantitative form, but not too small to be used as guides to characteristics of purchases and of sales activity—also practically unknown before that. In view of limitations in the data, calculations were made from survey results in the form of percentage distributions, presented in Table 28. The figures should be considered primarily as approximate magnitudes. Some encouragement about the validity of the data, however, may be drawn from a comparison with similar data for all insured associations. For the latter group, mortgage purchases, as reported by the Federal Home Loan Bank Board (Table 27), accounted for 3.7 per cent of mortgage originations in 1953, 5.2 per cent in 1954, and 4.4 per cent in 1955. In the survey made for this study, mortgage purchases in those years represented 3.8, 8.5, and 3.9 per cent, respectively. The difference is significant only for 1954 and the direction of change between years is identical.

Of the 58 savings and loan associations responding to the questionnaire, 33 or nearly three-fifths indicated that they had engaged in some purchasing or selling of mortgages during the three years from 1953 through 1955. Among states, California accounted for both the largest number of associations and largest amount of transfer activity. Of the 11 California associations reporting in the survey, 9 indicated that they had bought or sold mortgages. Most other associations reporting secondary market activity were located in the Midwest and Southwest.

Moi tgage purchases of savings and loan associations are made more often than not on the basis of prior commitments. They consist principally of VA loans, and are obtained most frequently from mortgage companies (Table 28). The conclusion seems fair, therefore, that a large part of savings

TABLE 28

Percentage Distribution of Amounts of Mortgage Purchases and Sales by Savings and Loan Associations, 1953–1955

	Purchase			Sale		
Type of Purchase or Sale	1953	1954	1955	1953	1954	1955
Total	100	100	100	100	100	100
Prior commitment						
With	52	58	60	3	3	2
Without	48	42	40	97	97	98
Type of mortgage						
VA	73	85	73	63	76	66
FHA	16	8	15	7	3	2
Conventional	11	6	13	30	21	32
Type of purchaser or seller						
Life insurance company	—	—	—	16	17	30
Savings bank	—	—	—	57	57	56
Commercial bank	—	—	3	—	8	10
Savings and loan						
association	4	12	28	3	11	1
Mortgage company	73	56	56	15	1	2
FNMA	11	24	7	—	6	—
Other[a]	13	7	7	9	—	1

SOURCE: Replies of 58 savings and loan associations in survey made in this study.
[a] Individuals and the Veterans Administration.

and loan purchase activity is of the pseudo- or quasi-secondary type. The only private financial institutions, except mortgage companies, from which a significant proportion of mortgages is purchased are other savings and loan associations. In 1955, especially, such purchases rose sharply, perhaps because of the tight position experienced by some as a result of borrowing restrictions imposed by Federal Home Loan Banks. For those associations, sale of mortgages from portfolio became necessary in order to honor outstanding commitments. Purchases from FNMA were especially important in 1954, when savings and loan associations had more funds available than investment in private mortgage markets could absorb. The data indicate that, on occasion, savings and loan associations have purchased mortgages from private individuals and from the Veterans Administration. The latter purchases consisted chiefly of direct loans made by VA to veterans unable to obtain financing from private lenders.

Mortgage sales made by savings and loan associations, in contrast to purchases, were almost entirely without prior commitment. While consisting largely of VA loans, they included a significant proportion of conventional mortgages. Such activity is fundamentally of the true secondary market variety. Most sales were made to savings banks and life insurance companies, although most other types of institutions were represented among the purchasers. The reader is reminded (Chapter 6) that the high percentage of sales to savings banks shown in the table reflects in the main the activity of one large California savings and loan association. Perhaps most surprising in the data on sales is the large proportion of conventional mortgages. That they were sold to all types of financial institutions is the only information we have on the characteristics of such mortgages. Undoubtedly both newly originated and seasoned mortgages were included, the latter probably increasing proportionately towards the end of 1955 when some savings and loan associations were pressed for funds.

With respect to secondary mortgage market activities, we may recall that general brokerage business is prohibited for federal savings and loan associations. The law allows them to sell any type of mortgage loan at any time so long as total sales in a calendar year do not exceed 20 per cent of the dollar amount of mortgage loans held at the beginning of the year. Federal associations may purchase any type of mortgage loan originated by them. They may purchase federally insured and guaranteed loans (up to a maximum amount of $35,000) on property located outside of their regular lending area—usually within a radius of fifty miles from an associations' home office.[20]

MARKETING ORGANIZATION, COSTS, AND PRICES

The institutional framework of primary and secondary mortgage markets, defined however broadly or narrowly, overlaps both ways. Some institutions participate more extensively in one market than the other; some perform more specialized functions than others; but most participate in both markets to some degree.[21] Briefly, the structural organization of mortgage markets consists of mortgage originators, construction lenders, interim lenders, brokers, and ultimate investors. Of the functions implied by these terms only mortgage origination and brokerage are performed by specialized organizations—mortgage companies and mortgage brokers—created for those purposes and performing few other functions. Other

[20] For more details on these regulations see *Rules and Regulations of the Federal Savings and Loan System*, as amended, Federal Home Loan Bank Board, Secs. 145.6–5, 145.6–6, and 145.11.

[21] The functions and operating techniques of major market participants were discussed in Chapter 6 and some aspects of market organization have been touched upon above.

major types of market participants perform at least two or more functions in the market.

Savings and loan associations, for example, primarily originate mortgages directly for ultimate investment, but engage in construction lending as well. Commercial banks provide construction and interim financing, originate mortgages for resale to others, and also hold large mortgage portfolios for investment. Savings banks acquire mortgages for ultimate investment by direct origination or acquisition through other originators. They occasionally make construction loans. Life insurance companies are engaged in permanent mortgage lending either through direct origination or indirect acquisition.

All participate to some extent in the buying and selling of mortgages, as indicated in the preceding section. There are no specialized institutions, organized markets, or established exchanges through which trading in mortgages takes place, except the federally organized and sponsored Federal National Mortgage Association (see the next section). Purchases and sales of mortgages in the "open market"[22] are arranged either directly by the participants themselves or through mortgage brokerage houses, which operate also in primary markets. No data on the relative proportions of direct trading and trading through intermediaries are available. Information from interviews suggests that the largest proportion is carried on through direct negotiation, on the basis of general knowledge of the market and contacts in it. While many individuals and small organizations are engaged locally in mortgage brokerage business, only a handful of large-scale brokers, with principal offices in New York, arrange transactions on a national scale.

In the secondary mortgage market, marketing costs are difficult to separate from prices. When funds available for investment exceed the supply of mortgages, lenders may be willing to pay fees or premiums to obtain them. When the reverse situation obtains, fees decline or disappear. The fee is essentially a cost of marketing or a part of the mortgage price. Marketing costs, in the sense of direct charges for mortgage purchase or sale, are incurred only when brokers have arranged a transaction. When transactions are directly negotiated between participants, no marketing costs are involved. In brokerage transactions, marketing costs to clients generally range from $\frac{1}{4}$ to $\frac{1}{2}$ of 1 per cent of the mortgage loan. The smaller the transaction, the higher the percentage rate and cost.

---

[22] The "open market" concept includes quasi- and true secondary transactions as defined earlier. Pseudo-secondary transactions are excluded because they are based on prior arrangements and may be considered as occurring in a "closed" market.

In primary mortgage market transactions, the basis of marketing costs charged by brokers is the same as in the secondary market. In the primary market, however, several other charges or fees, which vary with market conditions and types of services, are levied directly by lenders against borrowers or builders. A 1 per cent fee is common for the origination of a permanent mortgage, for a construction loan, or for a firm take-out commitment. The charges may all be levied and earned by the one lender involved (for example, a savings and loan association may provide the construction loan, take-out commitment, and permanent mortgage financing in a package transaction). Or they may be charged by several lenders, when each provides a specialized service (for example, a commercial bank may charge the construction loan fee, a mortgage company the mortgage origination fee, and an insurance company the commitment fee). The charges, if considered part of marketing costs, raise the cost of primary mortgage marketing substantially above that of secondary mortgage marketing.

Perhaps the nearest approach to a specialized institution or organized trading place in the private secondary mortgage market is provided by the large-scale mortgage brokerage house (distinct from the mortgage company, the subject of Chapter 8). One outgrowth of the increasing volume of secondary market transactions during the postwar decade is the rapid growth in business of the few national brokerage houses, rather than in any significant increase in their number. Mortgage brokers have arranged transactions for most major types of institutions and between them— savings banks, commercial banks, savings and loan associations, pension funds, and mortgage companies. Insurance companies, however, have seldom made use of brokerage services.

While no statistical evidence is at hand, interviews suggest that the largest part of secondary market transactions arranged by brokers is the quasi rather than true secondary type. One reason is that the over-all volume of true secondary trading transactions is still relatively small. Another is that the development and use of the standby commitment technique in periods of credit stringency has increased the proportion of mortgages originated without firm take-out commitments and offered upon completion for sale in the open market. Mortgage originators having such mortgages available and offering them at standby prices often seek the services of mortgage brokers to find buyers. Mortgage investors, on the other hand, unwilling or unable to commit for mortgages months in advance, may approach brokers to obtain through them mortgages for immediate delivery. The broker maintains his market for mortgages through trade journal and direct mail advertising of mortgage offerings and investors' specifications.

Lack of data and confusing market terminology make comparison of primary and secondary mortgage market prices extremely difficult. There is no way to compare directly the price of an originated mortgage with its price when sold in the secondary market. Unlike the situation in corporate or government securities markets, information about specific mortgage instruments according to borrower or underlying property is not generally available. Nor is distinction between a new issues market and a secondary market so clear as it is in those others. A definite distinction is made, however, between pricing mortgages available for immediate or for future delivery. Further ambiguity about mortgage prices arises because FHA and VA loans, with fixed interest rates, are originated and also traded in terms of discounts or premiums, while conventional loans, with flexible interest rates, are originated at par on the basis of changing interest rates but are traded, like FHA and VA mortgages, in terms of discounts or premiums from par.

For the purpose of price comparison, pseudo- and quasi-secondary market transactions may be considered equivalent to primary market transactions because they involve newly originated mortgages. Mortgages of comparable quality (judged so by the market on the basis of underlying property and location, mortgage terms, type of borrower) will generally command the same price. This is true whether they are originated directly by the investor; obtained indirectly through an originator on the basis of a prior commitment (pseudo-purchase); or obtained for immediate delivery from an originator without prior commitment (quasi-purchase). The mortgage with prior commitment will, of course, bear the price agreed upon at the time the commitment was made. It may be higher or lower than the market price by the time the mortgage is delivered. Price differentials, which may exist between pseudo- and quasi-type transactions, reflect differences in timing rather than in nature of transactions. True secondary market trading in mortgages, on the other hand, may command a premium over otherwise comparable mortgages because of "seasoning." Evidence on this point is thin, however, because of the limited number of transactions and transactors in that market.

Some originators have testified that they have been able to get higher prices from investors—as much as 1 per cent higher—on mortgages held for a year or so after completion than on those sold immediately upon completion. This is attributed to the greater assurance that can be given the investor about the credit worthiness of the mortgagor, the promptness of his payments, the soundness of the underlying property and its location. Discussion with FNMA officials has also revealed that investors often prefer to purchase somewhat seasoned mortgages from FNMA's portfolio. Mortgages that are too old in the sense that outstanding balances have been reduced to low levels are undesirable because the return is small compared with the cost of servicing—the same for small and large mortgages. But because there is no organized or continuous market for trading in older mortgages, each transaction is subject to individual negotiation, the price being influenced by the relative bargaining position of the participants, among other special considerations. Chief of those determining the level of mortgage prices in the true secondary market are the general financial situation and the prevailing prices in the primary mortgage market.

THE FEDERAL NATIONAL MORTGAGE ASSOCIATION

In the American capital markets the existence of a single federally sponsored and organized secondary market facility is unique. An analysis of the nature and characteristics of primary and secondary mortgage markets, therefore, requires a description and appraisal of the role of the Federal National Mortgage Association (FNMA). An appraisal of the impact on postwar mortgage markets of major statutory and administrative changes in FNMA operations was given in Chapter 3. In this section we are concerned with the developing history and operations of FNMA from its pre-World War II background and early charters to its latest reorganization in November 1954.

Background and Development

During its lifetime beginning in 1938, FNMA has been organized under three separate charters, reflecting changing needs in the mortgage market and changing philosophies about the nature and scope of federal intervention in this market. The original formation of the Association occurred against a background of federal efforts to stimulate housing construction, building materials production, and mortgage investments following the unprecedented decline during the Great Depression. The basic program of federal mortgage insurance was to be supplemented in part by a program to achieve greater liquidity and marketability of institutional mortgage investments, especially FHA-insured mortgages. To this end, federal chartering of private national mortgage associations to buy and sell first mortgages on residential real estate was authorized in 1934 under the supervision of the Federal Housing Administrator.[23]

[23] National Housing Act, Title III, enacted June 27, 1934.

Initially, to obtain charters, mortgage associations were required to have paid-in capital of $5 million in cash or government securities. Supplementary capital to finance operations was to be obtained through issue of notes, bonds, debentures, or other obligations to the general public. Amounts allowed were up to ten times the par value of capital stock but not in excess of the face value of insured mortgages, cash, and government obligations owned by an association. The organizations authorized were thus similar to mortgage banks long popular in Europe.

When no private national mortgage associations were formed under the original act, a series of liberalizing amendments was enacted over a period of about three and one-half years, successively reducing capital stock requirements and increasing borrowing capacity, authorizing direct lending on some types of FHA-insured mortgages, and exempting associations from all federal, state, and local taxes. Still not a single private national mortgage association was organized. Finally, perhaps to demonstrate the feasibility of such associations, the Reconstruction Finance Corporation was asked by the President, under authority granted earlier, to organize and manage a national mortgage association in Washington.

On February 10, 1938, the National Mortgage Association of Washington was chartered by the Federal Housing Administrator with an initial paid-in capital and surplus of $11 million and borrowing capacity limited to twenty times that. Further, the RFC was prepared if necessary to contribute an additional $40 million to the capital of this and other national mortgage associations, if formed. The functions of national mortgage associations were at that time defined as "maintaining an active market for insured mortgages and a steady flow of mortgage money at relatively favorable interest rates, and of providing an avenue of investment for individuals and institutions heretofore unable to benefit directly from the insured mortgage program."[24]

On April 5, 1938, the National Mortgage Association of Washington was named Federal National Mortgage Association, better known subsequently as "Fanny May." While authority for chartering private national mortgage associations still existed, none were formed. The act of July 1, 1948, providing for the reorganization of FNMA under a new charter rescinded authorization for them.

The failure to establish a privately owned secondary mortgage market facility in the 1930's was probably the result of a combination of circumstances. For some time following the enactment of the FHA mortgage

[24] "Opening the Mortgage Association Field," *Insured Mortgage Portfolio*, Federal Housing Administration, p. 3, March 1938.

insurance program, FHA-insured loans were not readily acceptable to mortgage lenders. Their provisions for long-term amortization, relatively high ratios of loan-to-value, and relatively low interest rates were radical departures from mortgage lending practices then in effect. In 1934 and 1935, home mortgage loans of less than $100 million were insured by FHA, less than 5 per cent of the two-year total volume of home mortgage loans made. In 1936 the volume of FHA mortgage insurance increased substantially but, by 1938, when the last federal attempt was made to encourage formation of private national mortgage associations, the rate of expansion had slowed considerably. During the three years 1936–1938, only about one-sixth of home mortgage lending was insured by FHA compared with three-tenths in the postwar decade.

Mortgage bankers and investors were reluctant to invest in the capital stock of untried associations dealing in untried mortgages when real estate and building activities were depressed. Even if FHA mortgages should become widely accepted on the market, the outlook for profitable operation of national mortgage associations seemed doubtful. The prospective net return on invested capital seemed low, judging from likely costs of operation and borrowing. Then, after establishment of a federally owned corporation to buy and sell federally underwritten mortgages, there was little chance that a private mortgage corporation would be organized.[25]

FNMA, during the first phase of its operations from February 1938 to July 1948, was limited to the purchase of FHA-insured mortgages and to a maximum lending capacity of $220 million. Under those limitations and the impact of World War II, the Association's activities were on a fairly modest scale. Total purchases during the decade amounted to $318 million and sales to $166 million. Mortgage repayments and other receipts reduced FNMA's portfolio to only $4 million by the end of 1947. Practically all

[25] Three years before the National Mortgage Association of Washington (later FNMA) was established, the RFC Mortgage Company, on March 14, 1935, under authority granted three months earlier (P.L.1, 74th Congress, Jan. 31, 1935), became a subsidiary of the Reconstruction Finance Corporation "to assist in the reestablishment of a normal mortgage market." Originally, rather than acting as a secondary market facility, the company provided direct loans for new construction or refinancing of income properties, as HOLC was doing in the residential housing area. By 1936, in the absence of national mortgage associations, the RFC Mortgage Company was authorized to purchase from original mortgagees certain kinds of FHA-insured mortgages. Similar authority was given in 1946 to purchase VA-guaranteed mortgages, not yet eligible for purchase by FNMA. As FNMA became more firmly established and real estate markets strengthened, the RFC Mortgage Company, no longer needed, dissolved in June 1949.

During its operation the company had purchased over 63,000 FHA-insured loans ($252 million), 24,000 VA-guaranteed loans ($141 million), and had made direct mortgage loans ($102 million) almost entirely on commercial properties. The company's portfolio was transferred to RFC in mid-1947. With the dissolution of RFC in mid-1954, remaining holdings of $64 million were absorbed by FNMA.

purchases were made during the prewar years when real estate activity and institutional originations of FHA-insured mortgages were increasing. Most sales were made after 1942, when war restrictions sharply limited building activity and the supply of funds to be invested was far greater than mortgages available in the private market.

First Reorganization, July 1, 1948

Increased capitalization ($21 million), lending capacity (40 times capital and earned surplus), and broadened authority to purchase and make commitments to purchase mortgages were given FNMA in its 1948 reorganization. Rapid increase in activity followed. Four later changes increased maximum lending capacity to a high of $3,650 million. Several other statutory and administrative changes over a six-year period alternately expanded and restrained FNMA's activities under its 1948 Charter.[26]

Developments during that period showed clearly that FNMA was not serving as a secondary market facility, as that term is ordinarily understood. Rather, it had become a special support for government sponsored housing and mortgage programs, which were not acceptable in private financial markets. The Association's policy of purchasing FHA and VA mortgages at par, regardless of market price, built up rather steadily its holdings—chiefly mortgages least acceptable to private investors. From July 1, 1948 to November 1, 1954 (the date of its latest reorganization) FNMA purchases of mortgages were $4.3 billion and sales only $1.4 billion. Its holdings increased from $50 million at the beginning of the period to $2.4 billion. Most of FNMA's activity was in VA mortgages.

Second Reorganization, November 1, 1954

After 1948, as FNMA was transformed into a primary source of mortgage funds, support—both private and government—developed for establishment of an organization which would operate as a true secondary mortgage facility and with limited dependence on federal funds. Under the Housing Act of 1954, FNMA was again rechartered and was directed to reorganize its structure into three separate operations providing for: (1) a secondary market for federally underwritten residential mortgages; (2) assistance for financing selected types of mortgages originated under special housing programs; and (3) management and liquidation of mortgages held or acquired by contracts under its previous charter. For each of these operations the Association was separately accountable.

---

[26] See Chapter 3 for more detail.

New Secondary Market Facility

The 1954 mandate from Congress required FNMA to prevent excessive use of its secondary market facilities, which were to be self supporting. Accordingly, mortgages were purchased over-the-counter only, at market prices not exceeding par. A mortgage price schedule was established. Prices varied according to location and type of property, mortgage terms, and market conditions. A "purchase and marketing fee" was introduced —$\frac{1}{2}$ of 1 per cent of the outstanding loan balance of "readily marketable" mortgages, 1 per cent for others. The maximum amount of mortgage per dwelling unit eligible for purchase was increased from $10,000 to $15,000. Restrictive requirements eliminated were: that mortgages be held for a minimum period by originators before sale; that purchases be made only from original mortgagees; and that purchases be limited to no more than one-half of VA mortgage originations by these mortgagees, and to one-fourth of FHA.

New financing provisions were aimed essentially at ultimate substitution of private for federal ownership. Initial capital consisted of $21 million of capital and surplus from the former Association (paid in by the U.S. Treasury) plus accumulated surplus, reserves, and undistributed earnings of $72 million. Preferred stock—total of the above, $93 million—was issued to the Treasury by FNMA.[27] Sellers of mortgages to FNMA were required to subscribe to common stock—not less than 3 per cent of the unpaid principal of mortgages sold. In addition, FNMA could issue (subject to Treasury approval) debentures up to ten times its capital and surplus, but not in excess of mortgage holdings, cash, and government or government-guaranteed securities.

Some objections were raised to the restrictive nature of FNMA's new secondary market facility. But so long as funds for mortgage investment were readily available in private and secondary mortgage markets investors made little use of FNMA's facilities and protesting voices were not loud. As increasing tightness took hold in private credit markets during late 1955 and 1956, however, the policies and operating techniques adopted to prevent excessive use of FNMA's secondary market facilities came under increasing pressure. As a result, liberalizing actions were taken in the late summer and autumn of 1956.

Requirements for subscription to stock by sellers of mortgages to FNMA were reduced twice from the original 3 per cent to 1 per cent of outstanding mortgage balances. The Association adopted a private market technique

[27] This Treasury-owned stock is to be gradually retired from the proceeds of the sale of common stock and debentures, and from retained earnings.

of combating credit stringency—issuing standby commitments for a period of one year. As FNMA raised the offering price on standbys to near its own purchasing price for mortgages, it approached its old policy of supporting primary mortgage markets. By this time, however, FNMA had achieved greater flexibility in determining mortgage prices under the Housing Act of 1956, which authorized establishment of prices "within the range of market prices rather than at the market price."

FNMA's activity under the new secondary market program remained small for several months. Mortgage funds from private investors were ample in late 1954 and early 1955, and requirements of the new program were not yet familiar to the market. As private credit became progressively tighter in late 1955 and 1956, and investors became better acquainted with the new operation, purchases of mortgages by FNMA increased rapidly, as shown in Chart 28. Just as before the 1954 reorganization, the bulk of FNMA purchases under the secondary market program was of VA mortgages.

The sharp increase in mortgage purchases during 1956 was due in part to adoption by FNMA in late January of a "mortgage purchase option plan," allowing sellers to FNMA to repurchase the same mortgages at the same prices within nine months. Adoption of that form of warehousing, already in use in the private market, and, a little later, adoption of the previously noted standby commitment technique indicated the Association's willingness to embrace approved private market techniques to help ease mortgage credit stringency.

To finance its secondary market operations, FNMA had sold, by November 1956, $300 million of short-term obligations to the public. Through June 1956, sales of common stock in connection with its mortgage purchases amounted to a little over $7 million, and net income from operations to $1 million (after federal income tax). Clearly, there was still a long way to go before the $93 million Treasury-owned stock would be retired and the secondary market facility be operated under private ownership.

Programs for Special Assistance, Management, and Liquidation

As previously noted, FNMA's new charter provided for two other separate functions: special assistance for mortgages originated under certain housing programs; and management and liquidation of the existing mortgage portfolio.

Under the special assistance program, FNMA is authorized to purchase or make commitments to purchase such home mortgages as the President shall decide to be in the public interest. His decision is contingent upon

"(1) the conditions in the building industry and the national economy and (2) conditions affecting the home mortgage investment market, generally, or affecting various types of home mortgages." Mortgages purchased under the program, at prices to be determined by FNMA, are limited to

CHART 28

Mortgage Purchases of FNMA Under Reorganized Secondary Market Program, November 1, 1954–1956

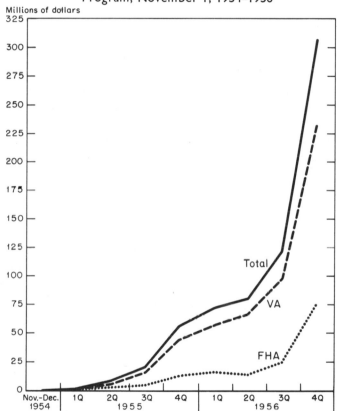

Source: Federal National Mortgage Association.

what (while perhaps not at the time acceptable to private institutional investors) would meet those standards under usual circumstances. Sellers of such mortgages are required, instead of purchasing FNMA stock, to pay fees—$\frac{1}{2}$ of 1 per cent of the mortgage amount, and 1 per cent for commitments to purchase. The special assistance program is supported entirely by loans from the Treasury. Mortgages designated eligible for special assistance include those on housing in Alaska and Guam, on housing in defense or military programs and for victims of major disasters, on co-operative housing projects, and on housing built under urban renewal programs. By the end of 1956, only about $20 million in commitments to purchase mortgages was outstanding, and less than $1 million in mortgages had been purchased.

FNMA's function of managing and liquidating its portfolio of mortgages purchased or committed for before November 1, 1954 ("with a minimum of adverse affect upon the home mortgage market and a minimum loss to the Federal Government") is financed by borrowing from the Treasury and by sale of unguaranteed debentures to private investors. The first public offering (January 1955) was $570 million of three-year debentures. These and subsequent obligations are distinct from those issued under the secondary market program, and proceeds from their sale are for the reduction of the Association's indebtedness to the Treasury.

FNMA Mortgage Purchases and Sales, by Type of Investor and by Geographic Area

Comparable data are not available on FNMA sales and purchases of mortgages by type of financial institution, by geographic area, or separately for the periods before and since the Association's 1954 reorganization. The data at hand, however, indicate clearly the dominance of mortgage companies among FNMA's customers. As shown in Table 29, for example, from 1949 through 1956, mortgage companies comprised three-fourths of all sellers of mortgages to FNMA.

TABLE 29

Percentage Distribution of Sellers of Mortgages
to FNMA, 1949–1956

Type of Seller	Per cent
Mortgage companies	75
Savings and loan associations	12
Banks and trust companies	11
Insurance companies	2

SOURCE: Federal National Mortgage Association.

Mortgage companies were also the largest purchasers of mortgages from FNMA, as shown in Table 30, but not so dominant as in sales. The dominant position of mortgage companies as sellers to FNMA is, of course, consistent with the character of their activities, but the large volume of purchases from FNMA needs explanation. Most of those purchases were

TABLE 30

Number of Purchasers and Amount of Purchases of Mortgages from FNMA,
and Percentage Distribution of Each, August 1949–June 1955

TYPE OF PURCHASER	Number of Purchasers	Amount of Purchases			PERCENTAGE DISTRIBUTION OF:			
		Total	FHA (millions)	VA	Purchasers	Amounts Purchased		
						Total	FHA	VA
Mortgage companies	228	$506	$104	$403	38	36	21	44
Life insurance companies	54	355	135	220	9	25	27	24
Savings and loan associations	111	149	28	120	19	10	6	13
Mutual savings banks	63	186	109	99	11	13	22	8
Commercial banks	104	156	83	73	17	11	16	8
Casualty insurance companies	6	21	17	4	1	2	3	a
Others	27	50	30	20	5	4	6	2
Total	593	1,423	506	917	100	100	100	100

NOTE: Includes only institutions purchasing $200,000 or more mortgages during the specified period.

SOURCE: Information in FNMA booklet "Investors Purchasing $200,000 or more of FHA-insured and VA-guaranteed mortgages from the Association during the period August 1949 through June 1955."

a Less than 0.5 of 1 per cent.

for resale to ultimate investors, and were made between mid-1953 and mid-1954 under the "one-for-one program" (see Chapter 2) in exchange for FNMA take-out commitments. The assurance of firm take-out commitments from FNMA enabled mortgage companies to carry on a mortgage originating business when such commitments were not readily available from private investors.

Among the main types of financial intermediaries, those purchasing the largest volume of mortgages from FNMA were also the most active purchasers in private secondary markets—life insurance companies and savings banks. Savings and loan associations and commercial banks, however, also accounted for a significant proportion of purchases. Life insurance companies were the dominant purchaser of both VA and FHA mortgages, but among other types of institutions there was considerable variation by type of mortgage.

Relative to their total numbers, only a small proportion of the main financial intermediaries were users of FNMA's secondary market facilities. Only 54 life insurance companies (of an approximate 1,000) and only 63 savings banks (of more than 500) bought mortgages from FNMA between 1949 and 1956; in sharp contrast, relatively large numbers of mortgage companies used the Association's facilities. To be expected in view of marked differences in characteristics and asset sizes among types of financial intermediaries, the group accounting for the largest number of purchasers did not always account for the largest volume of mortgages purchased (Table 30).

The geographic distribution of FNMA's secondary market activities is indicated in Table 31. The data on purchases and sales are not strictly

TABLE 31

Geographic Distribution of FNMA Mortgages Purchases, 1954,
and Sales, 1945–1955
(amounts in millions of dollars)

	Purchases			Sales	
State	Mortgage Portfolio Nov. 1, 1954	Percentage Distribution	*State*	Sales during Aug. 1949– June 1955	Percentage Distribution
California	453	19	New York	318	22
Texas	280	12	California	111	8
Michigan	249	11	Texas	109	8
Florida[a]	140	6	Michigan	107	8
Oklahoma[b]	137	6	Massachusetts	87	6
Total	1,259	53	Total[c]	732	51
All other states	1,109	47	All other states	691	49
Total	2,368	100	Total	1,423	100

Source: Data from Federal National Mortgage Association.

[a] Accounted for 3 per cent of sales.

[b] Accounted for 2 per cent of sales.

[c] These states together accounted for less than 0.5 of 1 per cent of purchases.

comparable. Purchase data refer to the location of properties securing mortgages in the Association's portfolio on the date of its last reorganization. Sales data refer to the location of purchasers of FNMA-held mortgages during the six-year period ending June 1955. Since practically all of FNMA's mortgage acquisitions were from sellers located in the same states as the property securing the mortgages, the figures may be considered conceptually close enough for valid comparison. And differences in dates and timing should not invalidate broad comparison.

The concentration of mortgage purchases among five states in the West, Southwest, and South reflects the postwar real estate building boom and the shortage of private capital in those rapidly growing regions. Conversely, the large volume of sales in the East (New York and Massachusetts), chiefly to savings banks and life insurance companies, is a reflection of excess capital in need of investment outlets. At that time, FNMA was serving the useful secondary market function of channeling funds from capital excess to capital short areas. The appearance of three states— California, Texas, and Michigan—among the most important in sales as well as in purchases is due mainly to the large volume of sales made to mortgage companies in those states under the "one-for-one program." It is likely that without FNMA sales under the program those states would not have ranked so high in FNMA sales activity. Even including "one-for-one" sales, however, it is clear that the significance of those three states as purchasers from FNMA is far less than it is as sellers. The reverse is true of New York and Massachusetts investors in FNMA-held mortgages. Because of the nature of their business, and as indicated by their limited volume of sales to the Association (less than $\frac{1}{2}$ of 1 per cent of the total), those institutions were buying for permanent portfolio investment rather than to assure FNMA's commitment for later mortgage originations.

Junior Mortgage Financing

An appraisal of the institutional framework of the postwar mortgage market would not be well rounded without reference to the nature and character of the market for junior or second mortgage financing. Limited data and market observation indicate substantially increased use of junior mortgages since World War II.[28] Yet, there is little organized knowledge and no regularly reported information on the volume, nature, and character of the junior mortgage market.

Within the scope of this study, it has been possible to determine only in broad outline the salient features of that market—participants, pricing and operating techniques, types of mortgages and properties, and relationship of primary and secondary markets. Our limited knowledge of markets for junior mortgage financing needs to be expanded and techniques for keeping abreast of current developments in that field need to be developed. In the meantime an analysis is offered here based primarily on market interviews with professional participants located in a few large eastern cities.

SIZE OF THE MARKET

Comprehensive data on the postwar volume of junior mortgage debt secured by residential—but not other—properties are available only for

[28] *Census of Housing, 1950*, Vol. IV, *Residential Financing*, Part 1, United States; *National Housing Inventory, 1956*, Vol. II, *Financing of Owner-Occupied Residential Properties, United States;* Fred E. Case, "The Uses of Junior Mortgages in Real Estate Financing," *Journal of Finance*, March 1955; William N. Kinnard Jr., "Junior Mortgages in Real Estate Finance: A Case Study," *Journal of Finance*, March 1956.

1950 and 1956 from the Bureau of the Census. Even for the residential sector, since data for those two years do not cover the same categories, estimates are necessary. Estimates, shown in Table 32, indicate that the total volume of outstanding junior residential mortgage debt nearly tripled between 1950 and 1956—from $1.5 billion to $4.2 billion. The increase

TABLE 32

First and Junior Mortgages on Residential Properties, 1950 and 1956

Type of Property and Mortgage	1956			1950		
	First Mortgage (1)	Junior Mortgage (2)	Percentage Ratio (2) ÷ (1) (3)	First Mortgage (4)	Junior Mortgage (5)	Percentage Ratio (5) ÷ (4) (6)
	AMOUNT (billions of dollars)					
Total	112.1	4.2	3.7	42.9	1.5	3.6
1- to 4-family	99.0	3.2	3.2	35.9	1.2	3.3
Conventional	55.1	3.0	5.5	21.2	0.76	3.6
Federally underwritten[a]	43.9	0.2	0.4	14.7	0.43	2.9
Multifamily	13.1	1.0	7.6	7.0	0.35	5.0
	NUMBER (thousands of units)					
Total				9,443	824	8.7
1- to 4-family				9,172	785	8.6
Conventional				6,588	459	7.0
Federally underwritten[a]				2,584	326	12.6
Multifamily				271	39	14.4

SOURCE: For 1950, data were derived from *Census of Housing, 1950*, Vol. IV, *Residential Financing*, Table 2, and pp. 157, 159, 317, 319, 348, 349, 467, 469, 549, 551, 589, 591, 601, 602.

For 1956, data in col. 1 are from Technical Paper 13, Table 1, p. 38. Col. 2 figures are estimates derived on the assumption that the percentage increase between 1950 and 1956 in junior mortgages on the various types of properties bore about the same relationship to the increase in first mortgages as was the case for owner-occupied one-family properties shown in Table 33.

[a] For junior mortgages, refers to VA only.

was about the same as that for outstanding first mortgage debt. The 824,000 junior mortgages in 1950 had probably expanded to well over 1 million by the end of 1956.

A more meaningful indication of the postwar growth in junior mortgage financing is seen in developments in the conventional, as distinct from the federally underwritten, sector. In 1950, a substantial part of the outstanding volume of residential junior mortgages were VA-guaranteed—nearly

TABLE 33

First and Junior Mortgages on Owner-Occupied One-Family Unit Properties,
1950 and 1956

Type of Property and Mortgage	1956			1950		
	First Mortgage (1)	Junior Mortgage (2)	Percentage Ratio (2) ÷ (1) (3)	First Mortgage (4)	Junior Mortgage (5)	Percentage Ratio (5) ÷ (4) (6)
	AMOUNT (billions of dollars)					
Total	82.8	2.1	2.5	27.7	0.9	3.2
Conventional	37.5	1.9	5.1	15.2	0.5	3.3
Federally underwritten[a]	45.3	0.2	0.4	12.5	0.4	3.2
	NUMBER (thousands of units)					
Total	12,713	867	6.8	7,052	622	8.8
Conventional	6,900	714	10.3	4,840	322	6.7
Federally underwritten[a]	5,813	513	2.6	2,212	300	13.6

SOURCE: *National Housing Inventory, 1956,* Volume II, *Financing of Owner-Occupied Residential Properties, 1958,* and U.S. Department of Commerce release, "Mortgage Debt on Owner-Occupied, One Dwelling Unit Properties, United States, 1950 and 1956," July 12, 1958.
The total amounts of first and junior mortgages outstanding at the end of 1956 (cols. 1 and 2) were taken from *National Housing Inventory,* Volume II, p. 3, fn. 1. The breakdown of these totals between conventional and federally underwritten mortgages was derived by multiplying the average amounts of loans outstanding by the number of loans outstanding.
[a] For junior mortgages, refer to VA only.

one-half those on owner-occupied one family properties (Table 33), and over one-third of those on all one- to four-family properties (Table 32). The VA-guaranteed second mortgages were made in combination with an FHA-insured first mortgage under a special federal program that was discontinued May, 1950. The 50 per cent decline in VA-guaranteed second mortgages between 1950 and 1956—from $400 million to $200 million—has obscured somewhat the real nature of the postwar expansion in basic junior mortgage financing.

The Census Bureau, reporting on financing of owner-occupied one-family properties in the 1956 national housing inventory, announced that junior mortgage debt increased more slowly than first mortgage debt between 1950 and 1956.[29] Actually, quite the reverse was true in conventional mortgage markets—the only meaningful sector for junior mortgage finance. While the number of conventional first mortgages on owner-occupied one-family properties increased by little more than 40 per cent

[29] Bureau of the Census, press release, July 12, 1958.

between 1950 and 1956, the number of second mortgages more than doubled. The much faster growth of second mortgages increased their proportion of the number of outstanding first mortgages from 6.7 to 10.3 per cent (Table 33). Similarly, the amount of second mortgage debt outstanding on owner-occupied one-family properties nearly quadrupled between 1950 and 1956—$0.5 billion to $1.9 billion—while the amount of first mortgages only slightly more than doubled.

The growth of junior mortgages on total one- to four-family properties was estimated to have paralleled that on owner-occupied one-family properties. The $3 billion junior mortgage debt outstanding at the end of 1956 was 5.5 per cent of the amount of first mortgage debt compared with 3.6 per cent in 1950 (Table 32). Junior mortgages on large-scale residential properties were a greater proportion of both number and amount of first mortgages in 1950 and 1956 than was the case for smaller residential units.

A comparative look at pre-World War I proportions of first and second mortgage debt may be instructive. In early 1934 outstanding junior mortgage debt was 8.7 per cent of the number and 4.4 per cent of the amount of first mortgages outstanding on owner-occupied properties.[30] Those percentages were larger than in 1950, on either owner-occupied one-family or all one- to four-family properties. But by the end of 1956, following a rapid expansion, conventional junior mortgages were more important relative to first mortgages than in 1934. The 1956 proportions of second to first mortgages could hardly have been so high as they were during the height of the real estate boom in the 1920's, however, when FHA and VA programs were unknown and low loan-to-value ratio first mortgages were the general rule.

Without comprehensive data on the volume of junior mortgages outstanding on nonresidential properties, fragmentary market evidence suggests that such financing is at least as important as it is in residential markets. Study of one small local mortgage market (Middletown, Connecticut), for instance, suggests that for most years back to 1920 the volume and relative importance of junior mortgages on nonresidential properties were substantially greater than on residential properties.[31]

NATURE AND PURPOSE OF JUNIOR MORTGAGE FINANCING

Findings on the nature and purpose of second mortgages in different parts of the country suggest a number of different explanations. In a study of

---

[30] David L. Wilkens, *Residential Real Estate*, New York, NBER, 1941.
[31] Kinnard, *op. cit.*

the Los Angeles market it was found that most mortgages on owner-occupied properties were created to finance their purchase.[32] In Middletown, Connecticut, on the other hand, junior mortgage debt placed on properties already owned substantially exceeded that incurred for purchase.[33] Second mortgages used to finance property purchases in Middletown usually involved transfer of funds rather than of credit. In Los Angeles most second mortgages were "purchase-money" mortgages taken back by the seller of a property, rather than new money furnished by a lender. The findings of the present limited investigation suggest that on owner-occupied properties, at least, most postwar second mortgages were originated as deferred purchase-money mortgages in connection with real estate transfers. The Middletown pattern may represent a rather specialized case—a small local market isolated from outside sources of mortgage funds. The pattern in Los Angeles, which parallels that in eastern cities surveyed in this study, is probably more representative of the nature of second mortgage market activity as a whole.

In the booming real estate and construction market of the twenties, the extensive use of junior mortgage financing had a rather definite purpose—to supplement first mortgage loans available to buyers from lenders only at relatively low loan-to-value ratios. In the post World War II decade, the needs of buyers changed. Liberalized mortgage credit under federal mortgage programs and changed mortgage lending attitudes among private lenders combined to lessen the need for junior mortgages. As real estate values rose and equities increased, however, mortgages on existing properties were lowered relative to values. New buyers often found it necessary to refinance completely or obtain supplementary credit to finance purchases. Frequently, the existing first mortgage on a property was a long-term low-interest rate FHA or VA loan. Prospective purchasers found such mortgages desirable and sellers found they enhanced the value of their property, especially in periods of tight credit when interest rates were rising. Transfers of such properties, therefore, were frequently made subject to (or with assumption of) the existing first mortgage supplemented with a purchase-money second mortgage taken back by the seller.

With the generally more liberal financing terms for new than for existing properties, many sellers found that a favorable price for used property could be obtained only by taking a purchase-money mortgage in lieu of cash over the primary mortgage. Even for new houses, however, many builders financing construction under conventional mortgages found it

---

[32] Case, *op. cit.*
[33] Kinnard, *op. cit.*

necessary to take purchase-money second mortgages in order to sell completed houses. In Los Angeles it was found that during 1952 and 1953, for example, an increasing number of builders and contractors were listed as mortgagees in recordings of junior mortgages.[34]

Purchase-money mortgages have been commonly created, also, in the sale of multifamily rental and commercial properties. A large proportion of second mortgages created in transfers of such properties, however, represented actual transfers of funds from lender to borrower, rather than extension of credit from seller to purchaser. Limited information suggests, also, that the frequency of second mortgages on those properties initiated for loans not associated with purchase was higher than on small residential properties.

MARKET PARTICIPANTS

The chief source of credit for second mortgages, whether of the deferred purchase or money loan type, is the individual or the closely-held private corporation. The reason is that financial institutions are generally precluded by law from accepting junior liens on real property, unless they also hold the first lien. In 1950, individuals and others held about 85 per cent of the total volume of junior mortgage debt outstanding on residential properties.[35] The surveys in Los Angeles and Middletown for later years indicate the continued dominance of individuals in the market for second mortgages. If the 1950 Census finding approximated the 1956 situation as well, then individuals held an estimated $3.6 billion in second mortgages at the end of 1956. This was about one-fourth of the $14.8 billion in total mortgages held by individuals at the end of 1956.[36]

Many diverse types of individuals and firms maintain varying professional interests in junior mortgages and make a market for them. The interests may be incidental to main activities, sideline investments, or the primary or sole activity. The chief types of market participants are real estate brokers, real estate speculators, mortgage brokers, mortgage traders, mortgage investors, and investment syndicates under trust arrangements.

Real estate brokers not infrequently have to find a market for purchase-money mortgages in order to negotiate property sales successfully. Real estate speculators typically operate by acquiring properties as cheaply as possible in all-cash transactions, and selling quickly at the highest possible prices by accepting minimum down payments and purchase-money

---

[34] Case, *op. cit.*, p. 48.

[35] *Census of Housing, 1950, Residential Financing.*

[36] Saul B. Klaman, *The Volume of Mortgage Debt in the Postwar Decade,* Technical Paper 13, New York, NBER, 1958, Table 1.

mortgages over a new first mortgage. Usually the speculator sells his purchase-money mortgages quickly to get cash for continued operations.

Some mortgage brokers and traders limit their activities essentially to transactions in the market for junior mortgages. While the number of such operators is unknown, in the markets investigated there seemed to be few relative to the volume of transactions. Brokers in second mortgages perform the same function as brokers in other services or commodities do by bringing buyers and sellers together for a price. Traders, on the other hand, operate by actually acquiring second mortgages with their own funds and reselling generally to individual investors for a profit. Operating techniques of brokers and traders vary as indicated in the next section.

Investors in second mortgages comprise several different types of individuals and firms. Professional investors acquire mortgages for their own portfolios, either by purchasing already created purchase-money mortgages or lending funds directly on the security of junior property liens. Investment-minded individuals acquire second mortgages occasionally for a supplementary income or, if retired, for major income. The investment syndicate, in which individuals pool funds to acquire second mortgages, is usually organized as a corporation by an attorney or accountant who generally acquires and manages investments under a trust arrangement.

MARKET ORGANIZATION AND TECHNIQUES

The diverse groups of participants play their roles in highly specialized, widely scattered local markets. Transactions in primary and secondary markets are closely related, and little organization exists in either market. Primary transactions are essentially of two types: execution of a purchase-money mortgage by buyers and sellers of property; actual transfer of funds to finance purchase or continued ownership of property. The professional mortgage broker, trader, or investor plays a fundamental role in both types of transactions; in execution of a purchase-money mortgage, he is part of the immediate primary transaction; in transfer of funds, he is a necessary link to secondary sources of funds.

Sources of funds for second mortgages, largely noninstitutional, are usually not known to prospective borrowers. The services of a mortgage broker are generally essential to any primary junior mortgage transaction. He typically maintains a classified file of investor clients obtained chiefly through advertisements, circular letters, and word-of-mouth.[37] The

---

[37] When second mortgage funds are available from relatives or friends, resort to the professional market is of course not necessary. Kinnard noted in his study that "a considerable number of family or 'friendship' loans" were recorded in Middletown, Connecticut.

broker's fee paid by the borrower for placing second mortgages varies with the amount of loan and between cities. In one large eastern city, typical fees are 2 per cent for the first $50,000 of loan and 1 per cent for the rest. For small loans, the percentage charge is much higher to provide a minimum fee, usually set by the broker. A major deterrent in placing "new money loans," on second mortgages in many states is restrictions on interest rates allowed under existing usury laws. Maximum interest rates under those laws vary widely between states, from 6 per cent in Washington, D.C. and New York, to 10 per cent in Florida and California, and 12 per cent in Connecticut. In some states corporations may not plead usury, and hence corporate owners of property—usually large-scale multifamily and commercial—can borrow on second mortgages more easily than individuals can.[38] In states where usury rates are low relative to yields in the open market, individuals can negotiate direct money loans only by giving to lenders large discounts through devices that circumvent the intent if not the letter of the laws.

Because of interest rate limitations that operate in primary market transactions, many brokers and traders and investors confine their activities to the secondary market. Those transactions involve chiefly purchase-money mortgages, on which—through legal discounts or bonuses—effective yields are raised substantially above contract interest rates. The active secondary market exists because purchase-money mortgages created in primary transactions are often not retained by the individual sellers of property or real estate speculators. Rather than hold such second mortgages created as part of real estate purchases, they seek to convert them into immediate cash through real estate and mortgage brokers, mortgage traders, or directly through sale to known investors. Ultimate investors are located in the way already described for the primary market.

Marketing techniques vary widely among professional operators. Brokers rely either upon circularized notices listing mortgage offerings with details on prices, outstanding balances, underlying properties, first mortgage characteristics, and rents and expenses (for income-properties) or upon attempts to make their offices into organized market places with mortgage offerings available. Some mortgage traders have adopted programs of selling second mortgages to individuals under repurchase agreements. The trader warrants to repurchase, at the request of the investor, any second mortgage in default for at least forty-five days at the original sale price

[38] New York State's 1956 legislation permitting corporations to interpose a defense of usury with respect to mortgage credit on one- and two-family houses (General Business Law 346) has made new second mortgage money loans on such properties more difficult to obtain.

minus principal payments received. Such traders interviewed in this study had capital investment equal to at least 10 per cent of their outstanding obligations.

Both brokers and traders depend for their supply of second mortgages upon realtors, builders, and speculators who find it necessary to arrange junior financing. Recently those groups have increasingly used the advance commitment technique, basic in the market for first mortgages. The second mortgage broker or trader, for example, makes an advance commitment (after the usual inspections and approval) to a real estate operator or builder to buy or find a market for purchase-money second mortgages created in a real estate transaction.

PRICES AND TERMS OF JUNIOR MORTGAGES

Commonly, a second mortgage transaction is made at a specified contract interest rate, combined with a discount or "bonus" on the face value of the note given by the seller or borrower to the investor. The discount is almost always a part of secondary market transactions. It is also frequently used in primary markets, where maximum interest rates under usury laws are low relative to secondary market yields. Occasionally, contract interest rates truly reflect yield, but evidence on this point is not readily available in public or other records. That reported rates on second mortgages are only a little higher than rates on conventional first mortgages is explained in large part by use of the technique of discounting and by the effects of usury laws.[39]

Traded prices of second mortgages vary widely between and within local markets. Many characteristics of second mortgage markets contribute to varying prices for mortgages of similar quality: their local character, the limited organized outlets and investors, and the lack of knowledge of one-time participants seeking to sell purchase-money mortgages. Varying prices are also attributable to the imperfect nature of the market and to the varying quality of the "paper." Quality of so imperfect a product is often a matter of individual judgment. Professional investors, however, generally look to the same set of criteria in establishing prices for second mortgages. The more important are: location of property; type and characteristics of property; borrower's credit worthiness; terms of first and second mortgages—regular payments to principal, length of loan, and interest rate; amount of equity in property; amount of second mortgage note; age of second mortgage—new or seasoned.

[39] Compare Tables 7 and 8 of *Census of Housing, 1950, Residential Financing.*

The location of the property securing a second mortgage is of obvious importance because of the variation in state foreclosure laws. It is especially important in judging the quality of a mortgage offered in a market in a metropolitan area including more than one state. In addition to the obvious bearing on mortgage quality of the kind and condition of the property, higher rating is usual for second mortgages on income properties. Owners are often corporations with favorable credit ratings—essential for marketing a second mortgage at almost any price. In addition, the value of such properties can be ascertained in relation to income produced.

The terms of both the first and second mortgages are important in determining the quality of junior liens. The terms of the first have an effect since inability of the borrower to carry first mortgage payments jeopardizes the security of the second. If the second mortgage is not fully amortized at maturity, the remaining balance and length of life of the first may be decisive when the second mortgage becomes due and payable. If the first mortgage may be easily refinanced to provide funds to pay off the junior lien, the quality of the second mortgage is enhanced. The terms of the second mortgage directly affect its quality in the market. The longer the maturity and the larger the proportion of the loan remaining to be paid off at maturity, the larger the discount. The higher the contract rate of interest, the lower the discount.

The amount of equity a second mortgage borrower has in his property is a major consideration. It is a measure of protection against declines in real estate values. It is also a measure of the borrower's interest in maintaining ownership, especially in bad times. The amount of the second mortgage note sometimes influences the rate of discount, because small notes at rates equal to rates on larger ones are not acceptable to investors when each involves equal quality and servicing. A seasoned mortgage that has proved its soundness will command a higher price than one recently created.

The wide range of quality factors and other market imperfections in the second mortgage market lead to wide variation in prices and yields. Yields, as noted earlier, are a function of the contract interest rate, discount, and maturity. Limited observations indicated that, in late 1956, with contract interest rates between 5 and 8 per cent, discounts on second mortgages secured by owner-occupied properties ranged from 2 to 6 per cent per year of remaining maturity and on those secured by income properties between $2\frac{1}{2}$ and 4 per cent per year. Within the range of typical maturities this means that total discounts ran from a low of 6 to 9 per cent to a high of 40 to 50 per cent, resulting in yields to investors of from 8 to 25 per cent. Yields in the 10 to 15 per cent range seemed quite common in secondary markets investigated.[40] The high yields are due, in addition to unusual risks, to conditions prevailing in the second mortgage market: imperfect knowledge of the market; limited sources of funds; borrowers' need for credit not available from financial institutions; and the willingness of sellers, able to obtain inflated prices for properties on the basis of purchase-money mortgages, to discount such mortgages heavily for cash.

Junior mortgages on most types of property carry maturities ranging between 3 and 12 years, considerably shorter than maturities of first mortgages. The 1950 Census survey figures indicate that the median term on conventional junior mortgages on owner-occupied properties acquired in 1949 and 1950 was 8 years, compared with 11 years on conventional first mortgages. Only one-eighth of conventional junior mortgages were written for maturities of 15 years or more, compared with over one-fourth on conventional first mortgages. The difference between terms on the two types of conventional mortgages was somewhat narrower on rental properties. Apparently, since 1950 maturities on junior mortgages have shown little change, while maturities on conventional first mortgages have lengthened somewhat.

Required amortization on junior mortgages increased markedly between 1950 and 1956, just as it had for first mortgages. Census data show that regular payments on principal were called for on 82 per cent of conventional second mortgages outstanding on owner-occupied one-family houses at the end of 1956, compared with 70 per cent in 1950. Comparable figures for conventional first mortgages were 91 and 78 per cent respectively.[41] A smaller proportion of rental property mortgages—firsts and seconds—are regularly amortized.

Limited evidence obtained in this study suggests that partial amortization of second mortgages on both residential and nonresidential properties is at least as common as full amortization. Some brokers and traders found that junior mortgages requiring partial amortization only, with payment in full at the end of a relatively short term (3 to 5 years), were more marketable than those requiring full amortization in a relatively long period (8 to 11 years). Investors preferred to commit funds for short-term mortgages with opportunity to renew or liquidate loans at the end of the contract period. Other professional investors, however, characterized the partially

---

[40] In the 1953 survey of Los Angeles mortgage brokers, Case reported discounts varying from 20 to 50 per cent.

[41] *National Housing Inventory, 1956*, p. 4.

amortized junior mortgage as the contract with "a happy hope" clause, and avoided it. The larger the "balloon payment" required at termination, the stronger the faith needed that the contract would be fulfilled in the stated period. These investors preferred to put their funds in the more realistic longer-term fully amortized mortgages.

CHAPTER 8

The Postwar Rise of Mortgage Companies

AMONG the most striking developments in the postwar mortgage market has been the extraordinary growth of mortgage companies. This growth has been closely associated with basic changes in the institutional framework of the market and with the development of new lending techniques and characteristics. The unique and increasingly important role of mortgage companies in the capital market has not been adequately recognized mainly because of the lack of information upon which to base a description and analysis of their activities. In an effort to fill this gap in our knowledge of financial institutions, a major segment of this study was devoted to an investigation of the operations and financial structure of mortgage companies, including the development of new data. This chapter summarizes the results of this investigation, being a shortened version of the more complete report, *The Postwar Rise of Mortgage Companies*. Most of the tables included in that publication have not been reproduced here and the reader interested in more detail may, therefore, prefer to read the Occasional Paper. The appendix of that paper includes a detailed description of sources of data, techniques of analysis, and several base tables.

Nature and Characteristics of Mortgage Companies

The modern mortgage company is typically a closely held, private corporation, whose principal activity is originating and servicing residential mortgage loans for institutional investors. It is subject to a minimum degree of federal or state supervision, has a comparatively small capital investment relative to its volume of business, and relies largely on commercial bank credit to finance its operations and mortgage inventory. Such inventory is usually held for a short interim between closing mortgage loans and their delivery to ultimate investors.

More than any other type of institution active in mortgage markets, mortgage companies owe their present structure and method of operation, as well as their extraordinarily rapid postwar growth, to the introduction and later expansion of federal mortgage insurance and guaranty. The Federal Housing Administration and Veterans Administration mortgage underwriting programs, with their standardized mortgage contracts, uniform and improved property and borrower appraisal techniques, and minimization of risk, have reduced geographic barriers to mortgage investment and enhanced negotiability of contracts. In the broadened national mortgage market that developed, accompanying the marked postwar expansion in residential building and financing, mortgage companies grew rapidly in response to the increased need by out-of-state investors for local institutions to originate and service mortgages.

In its postwar operations and growth, the mortgage company has provided a bridge between primary and secondary mortgage markets and a channel for the flow of both short- and long-term funds, often from capital surplus to capital deficit areas. The mortgage company has been a key factor in the expanded use of short-term bank credit in mortgage operations, as it has adapted its operations to new commitment and lending techniques and used such credit more intensively to supplement long-term funds in periods of capital market stringency. Today's mortgage company differs radically from its predecessors, both in organization and operations.

In its various stages of development from the early nineteenth century to the 1930's, mortgage banking was represented by four distinct types of institutions and operations:

1. Mortgage banks originating mortgages and issuing to the public their own obligations secured by these mortgages
2. Mortgage guarantee companies originating mortgages and selling them and mortgage bonds, guaranteed for principal and interest to institutions and individuals
3. Mortgage loan companies originating and selling mortgages directly to investors
4. Mortgage brokers arranging transactions between borrowers and lenders without direct ownership of the mortgages

For all types of organization, the chief investor in mortgages was the individual. In the legal sense three parties had an interest in types 1 and 2 and two in types 3 and 4. Both the mortgage bank and mortgage guarantee company had direct obligations to the general public, either through debentures or guarantees, in addition to their relation to mortgage borrowers and lenders. Neither the mortgage loan company nor the broker, on the other hand, had direct obligations outstanding to anyone as a result of the transactions each arranged.

Introduction of the FHA mortgage insurance program in the midst of the depression in 1934 set the stage for the appearance of the modern mortgage company, whose further growth was sharply stimulated by the VA mortgage guarantee program established in 1944. These federal programs, providing for the underwriting of mortgages on very liberal terms to borrowers, minimizing risk to lenders, and facilitating mortgage arrangements for builders, were basic to the accelerated postwar demand for home mortgage loans, to the flow of funds from institutional investors across state borders, and to the growth of large-scale home builders and mass merchandising programs. The profitable and specialized task of arranging for and channeling the flow of mortgage funds from investors to merchant builders and ultimately to home purchasers became the province of the mortgage company, and the process entailed marked changes in its structure and methods of operation.

Among institutional investors, life insurance companies, legally least bound to local investments, became strongly attracted to a national mortgage investment program. For most of these companies, the problem of acquiring and servicing out-of-state mortgage investments was resolved by appointment of locally owned and operated mortgage correspondents rather than by establishment of branch offices or subsidiaries of the parent company. The mortgage banking industry undoubtedly owes a large part of its growth and character to this basic decision of the life insurance companies. Later, when legal barriers to out-of-state investments in FHA and VA loans were removed for other institutions, the pattern of mortgage acquisitions established by insurance companies was followed, particularly by many mutual savings banks.

Because, at the beginning of the federal mortgage insurance program in the early thirties, there were few mortgage companies relative to the increased demand for their services, the life insurance companies selected as mortgage correspondents, real estate companies, brokers, attorneys, and others connected with the real estate industry. Thus many of today's mortgage companies have predecessors that operated for a shorter or longer period in one or another phase of the real estate business. The few pre-FHA mortgage companies shifted the focus of their activity from individuals to institutional investors because individuals are not permitted to hold FHA-insured mortgages and the long-term amortized mortgage is not well suited to their investment needs.

Thus, the FHA mortgage insurance and VA guaranty programs and the widespread adoption of the long-term amortized mortgage materially altered the organization and structure of the mortgage banking industry. At one and the same time the new type of mortgage instrument attracted large-scale institutional investors to a national mortgage market and discouraged the participation of the individual investor. Many mortgage companies, formerly engaged in initiating mortgage transactions largely on their own responsibility for sale to individuals, became the direct representatives of institutional investors in local markets. The bulk of the business of most mortgage companies shifted from conventional residential and nonresidential mortgages, in the prefederal mortgage underwriting days, to federally underwritten home mortgages. Finally, a new type of profitable activity—mortgage servicing—required by the monthly amortization of mortgages and the escrow of funds for tax and insurance payments became the source of the basic and generally largest component of net income of mortgage companies.

Essentially, then, the business of the modern mortgage company (unlike that of mortgage lenders who originate or acquire mortgage loans with the intention of holding them in their own portfolios) is to originate and service mortgage loans for the accounts of institutional investors. Most mortgage companies, so defined, engaged in one or more related activities, including real estate management, brokerage, and insurance, construction, and land development. Conversely, many real estate firms also originate and service mortgage loans for principal investors. Some financial intermediaries, moreover, notably commercial banks, carry on this type of business, originating mortgages expressly for sale to other institutions. The distinguishing characteristic of the mortgage company, as classified for purposes of this study, and following criteria of the *Standard Industrial Classification* manual of the federal government, is that its *principal* activity is the origination and servicing of mortgages.

In relation to their volume of mortgage lending and servicing, present-day mortgage companies in the main are characterized by small capital investments, just as were those in earlier decades. According to one early writer, "The first feature of mortgage banking in America which strikes the observer is that the mortgage companies are many in number, the capital of each, with a few exceptions, being small."[1] Whether mortgage companies in operation in 1955 would be considered "many in number" is a relative matter. The number is, unfortunately, not precisely known but may be estimated closely enough for comparison with the numbers of other types of financial institutions. The membership of the Mortgage Bankers Association of America includes a little over 1,000 institutions classified as mortgage companies, but their number undoubtedly includes some organizations whose principal activity is not mortgage banking. Mortgage companies that were FHA-approved mortgagees[2] in 1955 numbered some 865. The true number probably lies somewhere between the

---

[1] D. M. Frederiksen, "Mortgage Banking in America," *Journal of Political Economy*, March 1894, p. 213.

[2] These are institutions approved by the Federal Housing Administration to deal in FHA-insured mortgages. For a discussion of requirements to qualify as an FHA-approved mortgagee, see the Appendix of Saul B. Klaman, *The Postwar Rise of Mortgage Companies*, Occasional Paper 60, New York, National Bureau of Economic Research, 1959.

two. Thus the number of mortgage companies is much smaller than that of commercial banks or savings and loan associations, but considerably more than mutual savings banks, and almost equal to that of life insurance companies.

REGULATION OF ACTIVITIES

Unlike other institutions in the mortgage market, mortgage companies are subject to little direct regulation or supervision. Most of them, as private corporations, are regulated only by the general corporation laws of the states in which they are incorporated. They are not subject to the rigorous supervision and control of state or federal financial authorities, as are banks, savings and loan associations, and insurance companies. FHA-approved mortgagees, however—the bulk of all mortgage companies—are liable to periodic examination and audit by the Federal Housing Administration. Following initial approval, such examination consists principally of an audit of financial statements filed annually with FHA, and irregular sight inspection of company records by FHA auditors. Within broad limitations of financial soundness, FHA-approved mortgage companies are not restricted to certain investments or assets. The Veterans Administration makes no special requirements of mortgage companies originating VA-guaranteed mortgage loans, which include practically all FHA-approved mortgage companies. The comparatively limited supervision of mortgage companies may perhaps be explained on the grounds that they do not hold deposits or other large reservoirs of funds of the general public as do financial intermediaries.

Mortgage companies are, also, far less restricted in geographic area of activity and branch office operation than most other types of financial institutions are. Here, again, restrictions are limited to FHA-approved mortgagees and are at present based on policy decisions of the Federal Housing Administration rather than on administrative or statutory requirements. Current FHA policy allows approved mortgage companies to originate and service loans anywhere in their states of residence and to originate loans in other states where they have servicing arrangements with local FHA-approved mortgagees. In order both to originate and service out-of-state loans, FHA-approved mortgage companies must establish branch offices in the chosen localities. All independent mortgagees[3] are permitted to establish such branch offices, subject to FHA approval, within their own and contiguous states. Only the larger approved independent

[3] Loan correspondents are not permitted to establish branch offices. (See *Ibid.*, Appendix footnote 31, for distinction between independent mortgagees and loan correspondents.)

mortgagees may establish offices in noncontiguous states since the minimum net worth requirement is $250,000 compared with $100,000 to qualify as an FHA-approved independent mortgagee.

But the typical mortgage company, small in size and volume of business, operates in a single office and confines the bulk of its activity to the metropolitan area in which it is located. In recent years, however, several of the larger companies have developed intercity branch office systems covering an entire state, and a few of the largest have expanded their operations beyond state lines. Within the broad limitations established by the Federal Housing Administration for out-of-state and branch office operations of its approved mortgagees, it is conceivable that a few mortgage companies may eventually establish nationwide mortgage operations.

SOURCES OF INCOME

The chief regular sources of gross income for mortgage companies are fees derived from their principal activities, mortgage origination and servicing. In recent years, fees for servicing mortgages secured by small residential properties have become fairly standardized at $\frac{1}{2}$ of 1 per cent of the outstanding balance of the loan. For loans on large scale rental housing and commercial properties, however, servicing fees are far less standardized and considerably smaller, ranging usually from $\frac{1}{8}$ to $\frac{3}{8}$ of 1 per cent. The fee rate varies inversely with the amount of the loan because costs of servicing individual loans are similar, regardless of the amounts involved. Mortgage companies sometimes make concessions in fees in order to place large loans on their servicing accounts.

Maximum rates for origination fees on FHA and VA loans are fixed by the respective administrative agencies at between 1 and 2.5 per cent.[4] There are, of course, no established maximum fees for conventional loans. For conventional construction loans, origination fees have varied with market conditions but have seldom gone below 1 per cent or exceeded 2 per cent. For other conventional loans of good quality, origination fees have seldom been charged borrowers, but instead have been collected in the form of a premium price of around $\frac{1}{2}$ of 1 per cent above par from principal investors anxious to acquire them.

Another important source of gross income for mortgage companies is interest earned on mortgages held in inventory. Such interest income is,

---

[4] Statutory and administrative regulations have varied, but in nearly all recent years origination fees for FHA home loans have been established at $20 or 1 per cent of the amount of the loan, whichever is greater; and for loans to lot owners to build homes, at $50 or 2.5 per cent, whichever is greater. On FHA multifamily loans, the maximum origination fee is 1.5 per cent; on VA loans the maximum origination fee is 1 per cent.

however, largely offset by interest payments to commercial banks on short-term loans necessary to finance mortgage inventory. On balance, therefore, net income attributable to interest on mortgage holdings is relatively small. Companies occasionally earn income from the sale of mortgages at prices above their origination or purchase price, but few engage in such speculative activity. Typically they originate mortgages under prior arrangements with investors at agreed prices, so that for the industry as a whole such gains on a net basis are relatively small. The participation of mortgage companies in related supplementary activities is reflected in earnings from insurance commissions, real estate brokerage and management, land acquisition and development, and occasionally from building operations.

There are no industry-wide data on the relative contributions to gross revenues of the various sources of income discussed above. Income statements for each of the three years—1951, 1953, and 1955—obtained by the author from a few mortgage companies of varying size in the Washington, D.C. area, however, are suggestive of the income composition. These statements indicate that income from servicing and origination fees accounted for between two-fifths and two-thirds of gross income in each of the three years. Servicing fees alone typically contributed between one-third and two-fifths of gross income. Relative income from origination fees varied, expectably, more widely between companies and between years, from a low of one-eighth to a high of one-third. Reflecting the varying participation of companies in related activities, income from other sources fluctuated widely, from 5 to 10 per cent in insurance commissions, 3 to 26 per cent in real estate sales and management fees, and 12 to 25 per cent in interest received on mortgage holdings.

The bulk of mortgage company expenses consists of employee and officer wages and salaries, and interest paid to banks, which, according to the few statements at hand, accounted for between one-half and over two-thirds of gross expenses in the years 1951, 1953, and 1955. Other important expense items include taxes, rent, and advertising.

RELATIONSHIP TO INVESTORS AND BORROWERS

Mortgage companies act as intermediaries between borrowers (both builders and home purchasers) and institutional investors, usually located in different parts of the country. In generating and holding business, therefore, mortgage companies must maintain close and continuing contacts with both potential sources of demand for and supply of mortgage funds.[5]

[5] For administrative details of mortgage company operations, see Robert H. Pease and Homer V. Cherrington, *Mortgage Banking*, New York, 1953, especially Chapters 14 to 18.

Because of their dependence on external short-term financing to operate successfully their business, they must also maintain a close relationship with commercial banks. This dependence on commercial bank credits is one of the main distinguishing features between modern mortgage companies and earlier mortgage banks and guarantee companies, which financed their operations through the issuance of debentures or mortgage participation certificates.

Mortgage companies in the postwar decade have tended to concentrate their activities in FHA and VA home mortgage loans, often in connection with new large-scale housing projects in metropolitan areas. They negotiate and close the bulk of these and of conventional mortgage loans on the basis of prior allocations of funds and advance commitments to buy mortgages from principal investors. Few loans in recent years have been originated by mortgage companies on their own responsibility for unknown investors (see section on "Loan closings and investor commitments"). On the basis of firm commitments from institutional investors to purchase completed mortgages (subject to the satisfaction of stated conditions), the mortgage company is able to arrange construction financing from a commercial bank for his builder customers and, at a later point, interim financing for itself. The latter type of financing is necessary to enable mortgage companies to close mortgages and carry them in inventory pending the processing of papers and delivery to ultimate investors.

Clearly, then, modern mortgage companies, unlike their predecessors, look chiefly to financial institutions rather than to individuals as outlets for mortgage loans and, among the institutions, depend most heavily upon life insurance companies. The policy of most insurance companies to acquire nonlocal loans through mortgage correspondents has been basic to the development and growth of the mortgage banking industry. In recent years, mutual savings banks have become an increasingly important outlet for mortgage company loans. Commercial banks and savings and loan associations, however, rarely acquire mortgages from mortgage companies. Some mortgage companies, reflecting their early background and history, continue to sell an important proportion of their loans to individuals. Sales of mortgages to individuals, however, amounted to much less than 5 per cent of all mortgage company sales in 1955.[6]

There are wide variations and gradations of arrangements, contractual and otherwise, existing between mortgage companies and institutional investors for the acquisition of mortgage loans. One common arrangement

[6] See section on "Principal purchasers of mortgage company loans" and Table 35 for information on types of purchasers of mortgage loans originated by mortgage companies.

is the contractual correspondent-investor relationship in which a mortgage company acts as the sole representative of a financial institution in the origination and servicing of mortgage loans in a designated area. The investor generally allocates funds or otherwise commits itself to purchase mortgages on a continuing basis from the correspondent, the amount varying with conditions in capital markets, portfolio needs, and volume of repayments on loans serviced for the investor. Mortgage companies generally maintain this kind of relationship with large life insurance companies and with some large savings banks.

Typically, under this arrangement, correspondents may receive allocations of funds from principals twice a year for six-month periods. The kinds of loans desired by investors under these allocations are generally indicated or known to the mortgage company through continuously close contact. Armed with a specified fund allocation and knowledge of investors' loan preferences, the correspondent proceeds to arrange for mortgage loans through builders, land developers, realtors, architects, other regular customers, or prospective new borrowers. The mortgage company will generally not firmly commit itself to make these loans, however, until it has submitted them to the principal investor for prior approval and received firm commitments to purchase them at a stated price and under other stated particulars. The investors' commitments may be either for immediate purchase of loans when completed and ready for delivery, or with some stated period in the future regardless of when the loans may be ready. Under the latter or forward type of commitment, described earlier, it is, of course, necessary for the mortgage correspondent to arrange for appropriate commercial bank warehousing credits. Some mortgage companies originate loans entirely for one investor, usually so large that the exclusive arrangement provides an advantageous volume of business for the correspondent. Other companies, dealing with investors of various types, perhaps have the advantage of somewhat greater flexibility in being able to negotiate a wider diversity of loans, each acceptable to at least one of their principal investors.

Another type of mortgage company-investor relationship is characterized, in effect, by the absence of a continuing contractual arrangement. Such a relationship is often preferred by smaller investors who come into the mortgage market from time to time as they desire mortgage investments. Such investors seldom make allocations of funds to correspondents; they may acquire loans from one or more mortgage companies in the same general area and enter into servicing contracts on the basis of individual transactions. In dealing with these investors, mortgage originators with limited capital more commonly submit prospective loans for prior approval and commitment than originate them on their own financial responsibility.

AGE, GROWTH, AND GEOGRAPHIC DISTRIBUTION

Modern mortgage banking in this country, as it operates today, is a relatively young industry. It has had a spectacular growth in the postwar decade, far greater than that of other financial institutions active in the expanding real estate and mortgage markets. Growth in number and assets of mortgage companies has been greatest in those areas that have experienced a particularly sharp expansion in residential building and sales and are generally removed from financial centers. The greater growth of companies located in areas where other financing institutions are not numerous reflects the importance of one basic economic function the companies perform, that of channeling funds from capital surplus to capital deficit areas.

Age

The youth of the mortgage banking industry is affirmed by the fact that of 854 companies operating as FHA-approved mortgagees in 1954, 445, or more than one-half, were incorporated in the postwar decade. Nearly one-fourth of these, moreover, were incorporated in the five years beginning in 1950. The stimulus given to the mortgage banking industry by the FHA is indicated in part by the number of companies incorporated in the five-year period following that agency's organization in 1934, a larger percentage—15 per cent—than in any other five-year period before 1945; more of those now in the larger asset-size groups were incorporated from 1935 to 1939 than in any other period. The median age of FHA-approved mortgage companies in 1954 was less than nine years and less than one in five could trace their lineage from before the Great Depression.

Logically enough, there is a close relationship between asset size of company and year of incorporation, proportionately more of the smaller than larger companies having been incorporated in recent years. Of the 194 companies incorporated in the last half of the postwar decade, 156 or four-fifths still had assets of less than $1 million at the end of 1954. Further, three-fifths of these and about one-half of the $1 to $2 million asset-size companies were incorporated in the postwar decade, whereas less than one-third of the larger companies are of such recent origin. Above the $2 million assets line, the relationship between size and age is less direct suggesting that, at this point, factors more important than age—management, area of operation, and policies of principal associated investors—

influence growth. (For greater detail on age of mortgage companies by asset size, see Table 1 of *The Postwar Rise of Mortgage Companies*.)

Growth

For financial enterprises, as for other industries, increases in the number of institutions, in amount of assets, and in volume of business are common measures of growth. By any of these criteria, mortgage banking has had an extraordinarily rapid growth in the postwar decade. This period, in which federally underwritten mortgage lending expanded rapidly and large-scale institutional investors widened their mortgage horizons to areas not previously explored, was especially propitious for the establishment of many new mortgage companies, the number nearly doubling in ten years.[7] During this same period the number of commercial banks, savings banks, and savings and loan associations, each far greater than mortgage companies, was declining slightly. Although life insurance companies also doubled in number and were about as numerous as mortgage companies at the end of 1955, the newcomers in the postwar decade were much smaller in size compared with the old established companies than were the new crop of mortgage companies compared with the old.

Far more spectacular than the doubling in number of mortgage companies was the tenfold increase in assets between 1945 and 1955, from an estimated $160 million to $1.8 billion. The much faster rate of growth in assets than in number of companies was reflected in the sharp rise in the average amount of asset holdings per company, from less than $350 thousand to over $2 million. The rate of growth was faster in the first half of the postwar decade, primarily because of the low starting point; the absolute increase in both total and average assets, however, was much greater after 1950 than before.

There have been substantial differences in the growth rate of mortgage companies in various asset-size classes, as suggested by Chart 29. The few companies having over $10 million in assets as of 1954 showed by far the greatest expansion in total assets during the postwar decade. The class ranking next in rate of growth was at the other extreme, the large number of companies with less than $1 million in assets, showing a slightly higher rate than companies in the $5 to $10 million class. For all sizes, the first

[7] The number of mortgage companies in earlier postwar years is probably understated slightly so that the rate of growth may be slightly overstated. Since the number is based on companies operating as FHA-approved mortgagees in 1954 or 1955, companies that existed in earlier years and subsequently went out of business are not included. Also excluded, of course, for all years are those mortgage companies not FHA-approved by 1954 or 1955. Both those groups are undoubtedly small parts of the total, however, and their omission should have little effect on the analysis.

CHART 29
Asset Growth of Mortgage Companies, by 1954 Asset-Size Class, 1945–1955

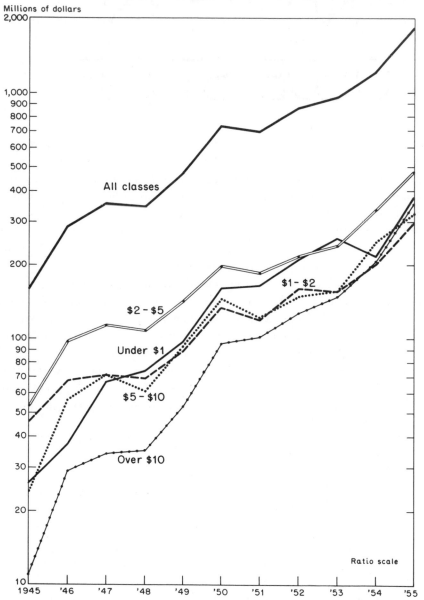

SOURCE: Klaman, *Postwar Rise of Mortgage Companies*, Tables 9 and A-1 through A–9.

half-decade's expansion rate was substantially greater than the second half-decade's, but the rates of growth were much more even among size classes in the second half of the decade than in the first. The sharp increase in total assets held by the smallest companies was, in part, the result of their more than doubling in number; but for the largest companies the great increase in total assets was due more to growth of individual companies than to the increase in their number.

TABLE 34

Mortgage Companies Classified by Asset Size in 1946 and 1954
(millions of dollars)

1946 Asset Size	1954 Asset Size											Total Companies
	Under 1	1–2	2–3	3–4	4–5	5–6	6–7	7–8	8–10	10–15	Over 15	
Under 1	302	80	24	13	7	5	2	1	1	—	—	435
1–2	—	13	8	11	3	5	4	3	—	2	—	49
2–3	—	4	5	—	6	2	4	1	1	2	1	26
3–4	—	3	—	4	1	1	—	—	1	—	3	13
4–5	—	—	—	—	1	—	1	—	1	—	—	3
5–9	—	—	—	—	—	—	—	—	—	—	1	1
Companies not in operation in 1946	254	41	15	4	4	4	—	2	—	2	1	327
Total companies	556	141	52	32	22	17	11	7	4	6	6	854

SOURCE: Records of the Federal Housing Administration. Data for companies having under $1 million in assets are based on a 10 per cent sample.

Another and perhaps more instructive way of looking at asset growth of mortgage companies in the postwar decade is by the extent of upward shift in asset holdings of individual companies. The sharp shift which occurred between 1946 and 1954 is shown graphically in Table 34. In the very small companies this upward shift in assets is much less pronounced than in the others. Of the 435 companies with less than $1 million in assets in 1946, over two-thirds were still in the same group in 1954—though, of course, the relative rate of asset growth of some must have been very high. By contrast only 23 or one-fourth of the 92 companies having assets of more than $1 million in 1946 were still in the same size class in 1954, and about half of them had at least doubled their assets.

Only a handful of companies moved counter to the trend, to higher asset-size classes in 1946 than in 1954. For example, of the 141 companies holding between $1 and $2 million in 1954, 121, or 86 per cent, either had held less than $1 million or were not in operation during 1946. Of 22 companies having between $4 and $5 million of assets in 1954, half had less than $1 million or were not operating, and another two-fifths held between $1 and $3 million in 1946. In the top of the asset-size class, only 1 of the 12 companies holding more than $10 million in 1954 had approached this amount in 1946, while the remaining 11 companies had less than $4 million or were not in operation during 1946.

The postwar growth of mortgage companies is not adequately measured by their increasing number and assets alone. Consideration must especially be given to the volume of business done, which in the mortgage banking industry is generally measured by the amount of mortgage loans serviced for investors. Data on mortgage servicing, unfortunately, are available only for a few recent postwar years and are based chiefly on estimates developed in this study. These estimates rely on the special survey of mortgage companies made for this study and on data obtained earlier in registration statements under Regulation X when this selective real estate credit regulation was in effect.

According to these sources, the estimated volume of mortgages being serviced by mortgage companies had grown to $20 billion by the end of 1955, more than half again the estimated 1953 volume of about $12 billion, and more than three times the mid-1951 volume of $6 billion. This growth in servicing was considerably faster than in total home mortgage debt, so that by the end of 1955 mortgage companies were servicing between one-fifth and one-fourth of the one- to four-family mortgage debt compared with about one-eighth in 1951[8] (see Table 5 of Klaman, *The Postwar Rise of Mortgage Companies*). The marked and increasing significance of mortgage companies in the home mortgage market reflects mainly their activity in federally underwritten mortgages. The estimated volume of FHA and VA loans being serviced by them was approaching one-half of the total outstanding by the end of 1955, compared with one-fourth in mid-1951. Finally, comparison of this volume with the home mortgage holdings of investors that are their chief servicing clients—life insurance companies, mutual savings banks, and the Federal National Mortgage Association—indicates that these institutions were having almost two-thirds of their total home mortgages and about four-fifths of those federally

[8] Comparison is made with one- to four-family mortgage debt rather than with total mortgage debt, because the bulk of all mortgage company activity is in the home mortgage market. Compared to total mortgage debt outstanding, the ratio of mortgage loans serviced by mortgage companies is, of course, smaller, but the relative growth is equally impressive, from less than 8 per cent in mid-1951 to 15 per cent dy the end of 1955.

underwritten serviced by mortgage companies, compared with one-third and two-fifths respectively in 1951.

The profitability of mortgage banking, reflected in the increasing volume of business, was undoubtedly a basic factor contributing to the attraction of new firms to the industry and the expansion of older firms, and hence to continued growth. Data on actual mortgage company earnings, either gross or net, are unfortunately not available. Some rough approximations may be suggested, however, from related information on volume of mortgage servicing and servicing fees and on income composition.

Gross income from mortgage servicing apparently increased from about $27 million in 1951 to $88 million in 1955, if we assume a weighted average servicing rate for the industry of about 0.45 per cent and apply this to estimates of servicing volume previously discussed. With the further assumption, on the basis of evidence from a few companies cited earlier, that servicing income contributed between one-third and two-fifths of total gross income of the mortgage banking business, it appears that gross income increased from between $68 and $83 million in 1951 to between $200 and $265 million in 1955, or more than threefold. During this same period the number of companies increased by only about 11 per cent so that gross income per company increased by more than $2\frac{1}{2}$ times.

Because ratios of gross expense to gross income vary widely throughout the industry, it is possible to make only the roughest sort of guess about net income. A few companies in Washington, D.C., in special reports for this study, had ratios of gross expense to gross income between just under 80 to just over 90 per cent. If these ratios were representative, net income after taxes for the mortgage banking industry in 1955 would have been around $35 million, with a range of somewhere between $25 to $50 million, compared with a range of between $8 and $17 million in 1951. When related to average reported net worth in 1955 of about $226 million, the 1955 net income range suggests a rate of return for the industry in that year of between 11 and 22 per cent. At the lower boundary, this return is a little smaller than the 13.5 and 14.1 per cent returns reported in 1955 for sales finance and consumer finance companies, respectively. At the upper boundary, it is substantially greater than in these financial enterprises, or in commercial banking with an 8.1 per cent return.[9] In either case, the mortgage banking industry appears to rank among the more profitable groups of financial enterprises.

[9] *Consumer Instalment Credit*, Board of Governors of the Federal Reserve System, Part I, Vol. 2, *Growth and Import*, Chapter 1, "Financial Characteristics of Principal Consumer Lenders," 1957, Table 16, p. 31.

Geographic Distribution

Mortgage companies may be found in most states of the Union, but in number and amount of assets held there is a high degree of concentration in a few states and regions. In 1954, the last year for which comprehensive geographic data were available, well over one-half of mortgage company assets and two-fifths of the number of mortgage companies were located in the Pacific, East North Central, and West South Central states. Concentration was even more marked in 1945, but in different regions. Only the East North Central region maintained its leading ranking in 1954 but the proportion of mortgage companies and assets in this region was well under that of 1945. Partly, this reflected the great growth in mortgage companies in the Pacific and West South Central regions between 1945 and 1954, paralleling the marked expansion in population, residential building, and economic activity generally in these areas. Equally important perhaps, are the twin facts that these areas are far from the capital market centers of the East and that the local mortgage originating institutions, primarily commercial banks and savings and loan associations, were unable to supply all the funds needed. In this situation many new mortgage companies gained a foothold and rapidly expanded, together with older companies, as they placed and serviced an increasing volume of mortgage loans for large-scale eastern institutional investors entering these growing and profitable markets. In sharp contrast, the older industrialized New England region that experienced little increase in population and relatively modest gains in residential building and general economic activity, and is noted for its concentration of local thrift institutions having ample funds for local mortgages, offered no advantages for mortgage company location. The smallest fraction of all mortgage companies were located in New England—in Connecticut and Massachusetts only—and they held less than 1 per cent of all assets in both 1945 and 1954.

The great growth in mortgage companies in the Pacific and West South Central regions reflects principally developments in two leading states, California and Texas, where growth of assets in the postwar decade exceeded that of other important states by a wide margin. By 1954 one-seventh of all mortgage companies having nearly one-fourth of all industry assets were located in these two states alone.

Many of the states and regions that lead in mortgage company location are also among the most important in federally underwritten and total home mortgage lending. For example, three of the leading mortgage company regions—the East North Central, Pacific, and South Atlantic—have

similar proportions of mortgage company assets and of federally underwritten and total home mortgage activity. On the other hand, there is a
wide divergence between the importance of mortgage companies and of
mortgage lending activity in the Middle Atlantic and New England states.
The former region is the most important in federally underwritten lending
but is pulled down to fifth in mortgage company assets by New York State
where few mortgage companies are located because of the concentration
there of local lending institutions. Partly for the same reason, only a few
mortgage companies are located in New England, although this region is
more important than several others in VA and conventional mortgage
lending especially.

Among the six leading mortgage company states, four—California,
Pennsylvania, Texas, and Michigan (in that order)—rank among the first
six in federally underwritten mortgage activity, and three—California,
Illinois, and Pennsylvania—rank among the first six in total home mortgage lending activity.[10] For both federally underwritten and total home
mortgage lending activity New York ranks second and third, respectively,
but ranks nineteenth in total mortgage company assets. (See Tables 6, 7,
A-13 and A-14 of Klaman, *The Postwar Rise of Mortgage Companies* for details
of geographic distribution of mortgage companies and mortgage lending
activity.)

Mortgage Operations

As outlined in preceding sections, the mortgage company's chief function is
to originate and service mortgage loans for institutional investors, holding
these loans in inventory for a short term in the period between mortgage
origination and sale to institutions. Little quantitative information has
been available, unfortunately, on the characteristics of mortgage company
activities; on the types of mortgage loans they handle; on the distribution
of mortgage sales among mortgage investors; or on the dependence of
mortgage companies on investors' firm commitments or fund allocations.
Some useful information on these activities, as well as quarterly balance
sheet data, for the years 1953–1955 was obtained in the special survey of
mortgage companies made for this study. In interpreting the findings of
this survey, the limitations of the data should be borne in mind. These
limitations, discussed in the appendix of Klaman, *The Postwar Rise of
Mortgage Companies*, result chiefly from the small number of reporting
companies relative to the universe, and from the disproportionate number
of large companies included among respondents. The data are generally

[10] It is likely that Texas would also be a leading state in nonfarm mortgage recordings,
but data are not available for this state.

of a lower order of dependability, therefore, than the data on financial structure obtained from FHA records which are discussed in the following section.

MORTGAGE AND CONSTRUCTION LOANS

In the postwar decade, mortgage companies typically were more active in arranging permanent financing for new than for existing properties. Arrangements for short-term financing of construction are also frequently made by mortgage companies for builder clients. Such financing is usually arranged directly through a commercial bank, but it is not uncommon for the mortgage company to advance the construction funds and to replenish its cash through a commercial bank loan. Either way, the ultimate source of construction funds is the commercial bank. The chief advantage to the mortgage company in making construction loans directly to builders is the fee (between 1 and 2 per cent of the loan amount depending on market conditions), but the many problems and risks entailed deter most companies from such direct financing. To attain and support a significant volume of activity, a highly trained staff is usually required to observe closely construction progress and minimize delays, to supervise loan payments at various stages of construction, and to guard against the establishment of prior liens.

According to survey data, only about 10 per cent of all mortgage loans closed during each of the years 1953 to 1955 were for construction purposes, while about one-fourth of mortgage holdings at the end of these years were construction loans, as shown in Chart 30. The larger proportion of construction loans held than closed by mortgage companies is a logical reflection of the fact that construction loans, involving separate advances over a period of months, generally stay on the books somewhat longer than regular loans. The latter require considerably less time for processing and closing and, except for unusually long periods of "warehousing" under some types of "standby" and "forward" commitments, pass from the closing stage to final sale to investors in from 60 to 180 days. The decline in the proportion of construction loans held at the end of 1955 while closings showed no change probably resulted from the longer period of regular mortgage loan holdings in 1955 under changing market conditions of that year.

Within the averages, wide differences in construction lending prevail among mortgage companies. Well over one-third of the 81 companies responding to this question in the survey held no construction loans at all in 1955, while one-fourth showed 40 per cent or more of their mortgage holdings to be construction loans. The median proportion of construction

CHART 30

Mortgage versus Construction Loans Held and Closed by Mortgage
Companies, 1953–1955 (percentage distribution of dollar amounts)

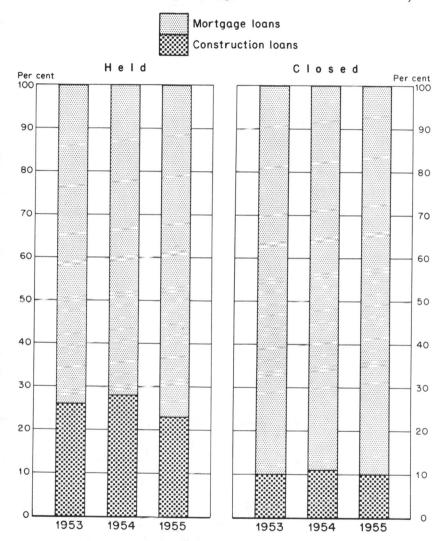

SOURCE: Special survey of mortgage companies in which respondents supplying data on
which this chart is based held one-fourth of the amount of estimated mortgage loans held
by all FHA-approved mortgage companies in years shown.

loan holdings was one-seventh compared to a mean of nearly one-fourth. The data by size of company must be interpreted with caution because of the small number reporting, although it may be broadly indicative of differences among companies. In general a higher proportion of the largest companies (over $5 million in assets) make construction loans than of the smallest companies, but among the companies with over $1 million in assets making such loans there seems to be little relationship between size of company and proportion of construction loan holdings.

TYPES OF MORTGAGE LOANS

The concentration of mortgage company operations in federally underwritten mortgage loans, especially those guaranteed by the Veterans Administration, is shown in Chart 31. In each of the years 1953, 1954, and 1955, from three-fourths to well over four-fifths of loans closed and about nine-tenths of loans held were federally underwritten. In each case, a rising percentage of loans was VA-guaranteed, reflecting the increased desirability of such loans to institutional investors in the changing capital market situation of that period. The somewhat larger proportion of federally underwritten loans held than closed by mortgage companies (and conversely, the smaller proportion of conventional loans held than closed) is due largely to two factors: (1) the longer time required for processing and documenting of both FHA and VA loans than conventional loans; and (2) the virtual limitation of warehousing and other market techniques to federally underwritten loans, which makes it possible (or necessary) for mortgage companies to hold such loans in inventory longer than conventional loans.

Among 66 responding companies holding about one-fifth of the total amount of mortgage loans held by all mortgage companies in 1955, more than two-thirds reported that less than 20 per cent of their loans closed were conventional mortgages. Almost three-fourths of the responding companies, on the other hand, reported that at least 40 per cent of their loans closed were VA-guaranteed and over 20 per cent were FHA-insured. A similar breakdown of activity characterized mortgage holdings. The largest companies, those having over $5 million in assets, showed by far a larger proportion of holdings in VA loans and a smaller proportion in conventional loans than the other companies. Most companies in each size group, however, reported that the bulk of their mortgage loans closed and held were federally underwritten.

Survey results tend to confirm the general impression that mortgage companies concentrate their activities on real estate loans secured by

CHART 31
Types of Mortgage Loans Held and Closed by Mortgage Companies, 1953–1955
(percentage distribution of dollar amounts)

Conventional
FHA
VA

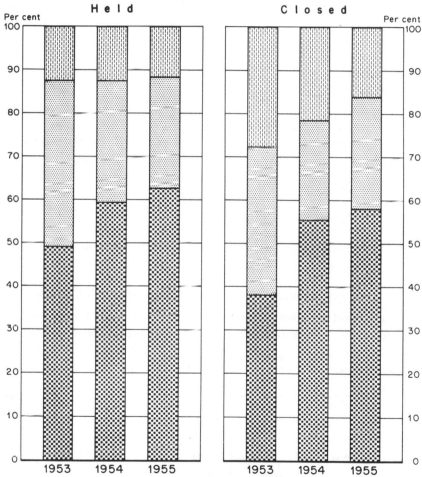

SOURCE: Special survey of mortgage companies in which respondents supplying data on which this chart is based held over one-fifth of the amount of estimated mortgage loans held by all FHA approved mortgage companies in the years shown.

one- to four-family properties. In addition to VA and FHA loans which are almost entirely on one- to four-family houses,[11] the bulk of conventional mortgage loans closed and held by mortgage companies are on such properties. But companies that reported a breakdown of their conventional loans were only about half as many as reported other data, and the resulting figures are too thin to present in detail. As a broad indication of the pattern of conventional loans handled by mortgage companies, however, over four-fifths of the conventional loans closed by 40 companies were on one- to four-family properties. One-half of the companies reporting indicated that their conventional mortgage lending activity in 1955—both loans closed and held—was limited exclusively to loans on one- to four-family properties. Most of the remaining companies showed, with little variation by size of company, well over one-half of their conventional loans to be on small homes.

The small proportion of conventional loans made on income-producing properties by mortgage companies is readily explained by the fact that many institutional investors find it expedient to originate most such loans directly. A large percentage of these loans are made on multifamily and commercial properties located in industrialized eastern cities, where life insurance companies and savings banks most active in this type of lending are. Moreover, most of these loans involve much larger sums of money than home mortgage loans, require specialized knowledge of appraisal and lending techniques, and justify the time and effort spent on direct negotiations by institutional lenders.

PRINCIPAL PURCHASERS OF MORTGAGE COMPANY LOANS

The growth of mortgage companies has been closely related to the increased participation of life insurance companies in the postwar mortgage market. Most life insurance companies acquire the bulk of their FHA and VA loans in out-of-state markets through mortgage company correspondents. Results of the special survey made in this study confirm the general impression that this type of institutional investor is the dominant purchaser of mortgage company loans, but suggest there also that this dominance has declined somewhat in recent years.

As shown in Table 35, the proportion of reporting mortgage companies that depend exclusively on life insurance companies for their sales has declined from well over one-fourth in 1953 to somewhat over one-sixth in

[11] Only a small fraction of all VA loans originated since the inception of the program are on multifamily properties, and data from the Federal Housing Administration indicate that the bulk of FHA loans closed by mortgage companies are on one- to four-family properties.

TABLE 35

Distribution of Mortgage Loans Sold by Selected Mortgage Companies
to Institutional and Other Investors, 1953–1955

(per cent of companies)

Percentage of Mortgage Loans Sold	1953			1954			1955		
	Life Insurance Companies	Mutual Savings Banks	All Others	Life Insurance Companies	Mutual Savings Banks	All Others	Life Insurance Companies	Mutual Savings Banks	All Others
0	2.5	46.7	41.8	1.2	39.5	34.8	1.1	35.1	31.9
1.0– 9.9	1.3	8.9	22.7	1.2	7.0	30.2	4.4	7.7	36.2
10.0–19.9	5.1	12.7	16.5	7.0	17.4	18.6	4.4	15.4	19.8
20.0–29.9	3.8	10.1	7.6	2.3	9.3	7.0	2.2	15.4	2.2
30.0–39.9	2.5	5.1	3.8	4.7	3.5	4.7	3.3	3.3	4.4
40.0–49.9	3.8	5.1	3.8	5.8	9.3	—	5.5	5.5	2.2
50.0–59.9	6.3	3.8	2.5	4.7	7.0	3.5	6.6	6.6	2.2
60.0–69.9	6.3	2.5	—	10.5	1.2	—	11.0	4.4	—
70.0–79.9	13.9	1.3	—	11.6	2.3	—	9.9	3.3	—
80.0–89.9	8.9	2.5	1.3	15.1	2.3	1.2	21.9	1.1	1.1
90.0–99.9	17.7	1.3	—	16.2	1.2	—	12.1	1.1	—
100.0	27.9	—	—	19.7	—	—	17.6	1.1	—
Total	100.0	100.0	100.0	100.0	100.0	100.0	100.0	100.0	100.0
Median %	85.0	3.6	3.6	80.8	12.0	5.0	80.8	14.6	5.0
Number of companies	79	79	79	86	86	86	91	91	91

SOURCE: Special survey of mortgage companies.

1955. A similarly proportionate reduction occurred in the share of companies selling over 90 per cent of their loans to life insurance companies. During these years mutual savings banks substantially increased their out-of-state mortgage activities, particularly in VA loans, providing an important supplementary outlet for mortgage company sales. Whereas in 1953 almost one-half of all reporting mortgage companies sold no mortgages at all to savings banks, by 1955 the comparable proportion was reduced to slightly over one-third. Moreover, one-sixth of the mortgage companies reported that at least 50 per cent of their sales went to savings banks in 1955, compared with one-ninth in 1953 (Table 35). More mortgage companies sold some mortgages to other investors, including savings and loan associations, commercial banks, and the Federal National Mortgage Association, in 1955 than in 1953 but the proportion of such sales to total sales continued to be very small and even decreased. The percentage of companies selling over 20 per cent of their loans to other investors declined sharply between 1953 and 1955, from almost one-fifth to one-eighth, as a reflection chiefly of decreased reliance on FNMA under changing market conditions.

The survey suggests that the larger mortgage companies depend less on life insurance companies or have more diversified sales outlets than smaller companies. A distinctly inverse relationship was reported between size of company and percentage of mortgage sales to life insurance companies, for each of the years 1953 through 1955. The largest companies, in addition, show a wide variation in the percentage of their sales to life insurance companies, with about an equal number selling over 80 per cent and less than 60 per cent to these investors. Over two-fifths of these large mortgage companies, compared with from one-eighth to one-fourth of all the others, sold less than 60 per cent of their loans to life insurance companies. It is not possible to determine from these data whether the large companies became large because of their ability to develop diversified sales outlets, or were able to attract new types of investors because they were already large. It is, of course, known that some of the country's largest mortgage companies are correspondents for only one investor, let alone one type of investor—but these are exceptional.

LOAN CLOSINGS AND INVESTOR COMMITMENTS

As noted several times, few mortgage companies undertake to close and sell loans on their own financial responsibility. They are able to originate a volume of mortgage loans much larger than their own resources permit because loan closings are typically based on firm investor commitments to purchase, and are financed by bank loans. In providing interim financing to mortgage companies, commercial banks prefer (and some insist) that mortgages offered as collateral be backed by investors' take-out commitments. In recent periods of tight credit the standby, rather than the regular take-out commitment, has frequently been the basis for mortgage company loan closings and for commercial bank interim financing.

An approximation of the degree of mortgage company dependence on investor commitments was determined from answers to a survey question which asked: "In the normal course of your business operations, about what percentage of your mortgage loans do you close only after receiving a firm commitment to purchase, or an allocation of funds, from an institutional investor, and what percentage do you close without a prior commitment or allocation of funds?" Of 90 companies responding to the question, 70 or nearly four-fifths closed 90 per cent or more of their loans only after receiving an allocation of funds or firm commitment from an institutional investor to purchase. A few of the largest companies, those having over $5 million in assets, were able and willing to close a significant proportion of loans on their own responsibility. These companies constituted one-third of all those reporting yet they accounted for seven-tenths of the number closing less than 90 per cent of their loans on the basis of firm commitments. Even these large companies, however, closed the bulk of their loans on firm commitments (see Table 17 of Klaman, *The Postwar Rise of Mortgage Companies*).

The technique of originating mortgage loans on the basis of fund allocation or firm commitments came into wide use early in 1950. Before the war, operating on a much more limited scale, mortgage companies generally closed loans on their own responsibility, and financed a large portion of the loans so acquired through commercial bank lines of credit while seeking permanent buyers for their inventories. After the war until the spring of 1950, when institutional investors were actively seeking a greater volume of loans than was available, mortgage companies had little difficulty in marketing all the loans they could originate, and hence they operated extensively without prior commitments. The change in market conditions following the Federal Reserve-Treasury "accord" and the intermittent stringency that has been a part of the capital market scene ever since have resulted in widespread adoption of the prior commitment technique. At the risk of oversimplification, the situation may be summarized as follows: the tighter the capital market, the greater the dependence of mortgage company operations on investor commitments; the easier the market, the less the dependence.

Financial Structure

Perhaps the outstanding characteristic of the financial structure of mortgage companies is its relative simplicity. In originating and servicing mortgage loans for institutional investors, mortgage companies use funds principally for closing mortgages and carrying them temporarily in inventory. The chief source of funds to finance this activity is commercial bank loans. This financial pattern is typical for mortgage companies in all asset size classes, with a somewhat greater specialization of uses and sources of funds among larger than smaller companies. Moreover, the financial structure in its broad outline remained largely unchanged over most of a postwar decade of rapid and uneven growth in total mortgage company resources. The asset-size distribution of the mortgage banking industry, however, has shown a marked upward shift as asset growth has more than offset the establishment of many small new companies since World War II.

ASSET-SIZE DISTRIBUTION

The sharp upward trend in asset size of mortgage companies can be seen clearly from Table 36, which shows that the number of companies having under $1 million in assets declined from over four-fifths of all companies

TABLE 36

Distribution of Mortgage Companies and Assets, by Asset-Size
Class in Selected Years, 1946–1954
(dollars in millions)

Asset Size Class	Number of Companies			Amount of Assets		
	1946	1950	1954	1946	1950	1954
All Classes	527	713	854	286	731	1,202
Under 1	435	506	556	95	164	217
1–2	49	105	141	65	142	201
2–5	42	79	106	118	237	333
5–10	1	15	39	8	97	248
Over 10	—	8	12	—	91	204
			PERCENTAGE DISTRIBUTION			
All classes	100	100	100	100	100	100
Under 1	83	71	65	33	23	18
1–2	9	15	17	23	20	17
2–5	8	11	12	41	32	28
5–10	a	2	5	3	13	21
Over 10	—	1	1	—	12	17

SOURCE: Same as Table 34.
a Less than 0.5 per cent.

in 1946 to under two-thirds in 1954. At the same time, while there was only one company with assets of over \$5 million in 1946, the number had risen to 51 and 6 per cent of the total by 1954.

CHART 32

Lorenz Curves of Assets of Mortgage Companies, 1946, 1950, and 1954
(cumulative percentage distribution of number of companies
and of their assets, ranked by size of assets)

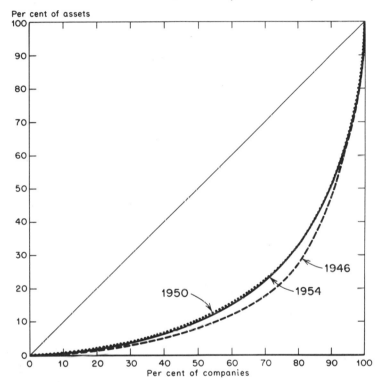

SOURCE: Individual company summary records from Federal Housing Administration.

Also indicated in Table 36 is the continuing unequal distribution of assets among mortgage companies that has accompanied the upward post-war shift in size distribution. For example, in 1946, the largest 8 per cent of the companies held 44 per cent of total assets, while in 1954 the largest 6 per cent held 38 per cent of the assets. This unequal distribution of mortgage company assets is measured graphically by Lorenz curves shown in Chart 32. The extent of inequality is measured by the size of the area between the curves and the diagonal line of equal distribution, compared to the entire triangular area traced by the diagonal line and the horizontal and vertical axes of the chart.[12]

The chart indicates that there was very little change in the degree of asset concentration among mortgage companies over the postwar decade although that decade witnessed such marked over-all asset growth and shifts within size groups. Compared with the asset-size distribution among other types of financial institutions, that of mortgage companies is far more even than that of insurance companies (both life and property), somewhat more even than that of commercial and mutual savings banks, and about the same as the asset-size distribution of savings and loan associations.[13]

USES AND SOURCES OF FUNDS

Mortgage company uses and sources of funds over the postwar decade, as reflected in assets and in liabilities and net worth, respectively, are shown in the combined balance sheets summarized in Tables 37 and 38. (Several additional combined balance sheets by asset-size class of company are given in Tables A-1 through A-10 of Klaman, *The Postwar Rise of Mortgage Companies.*)

For the decade as a whole, growth in mortgage and construction loans was markedly greater than in other components or total assets and increased as a proportion of total assets from less than one-half to over three-fourths between 1945 and 1955. This sharp growth reflects in part the unusual character of the beginning and terminal years of the decade, the first a year of transition from war to peace with little mortgage activity, the last a year of great prosperity and unusually rapid expansion in mortgage lending. Through most of the period under review, mortgage loans accounted for between two-thirds and three-fourths of mortgage company assets.

While mortgage companies are not engaged in the business of making mortgage loans as permanent investment of their own funds, their mortgage holdings rise in years of increased mortgage activity because of an increased volume of loan closings held in temporary inventory for ultimate sale. Without exception, sharp year-to-year gains in total assets have reflected even sharper relative gains in mortgage inventory, as shown in Chart 33. In the three annual periods of most rapid asset growth—1945–1946, 1949–1950, and 1954–1955—the rise in mortgage inventory accounted for

[12] For a fuller discussion of size distribution among financial intermediaries, see Raymond W. Goldsmith, Appendix C in mimeographed Supplementary Appendixes to *Financial Intermediaries in the American Economy since 1900*, New York, National Bureau of Economic Research, 1958 (available for reference in the NBER library).

[13] *Ibid.*, Appendix C, Chart C-1.

CHART 33
Total Assets, Mortgage Loans, and Notes Payable of Mortgage Companies, 1945–1955

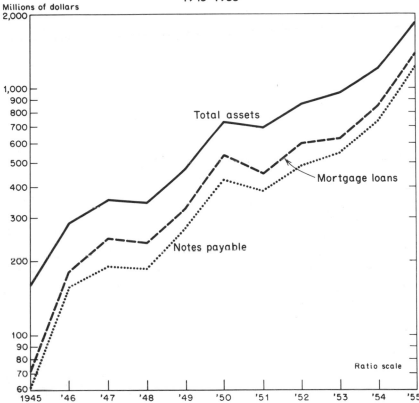

SOURCE: Table 37.

between four-fifths and nine-tenths of the increase in total assets. The relatively greater use of funds for mortgage inventory than for other purposes in these years is reflected clearly in Chart 34, which shows the rise in ratio of mortgage loans to total assets for each of these periods. Such increases have been fairly general among companies in all asset size classes.

There appears to be a direct relationship between size of company and proportion of assets in mortgage loans. In most years the very large companies (over $10 million in assets in 1954) had well over four-fifths of their assets in mortgage loans, compared to a proportion of between one-half and two-thirds for the smallest companies (under $2 million in assets). This relationship is readily explainable by the fact that both relatively

TABLE 37

Combined Balance Sheet of Mortgage Companies, 1945–1955
(millions of dollars)

	1945	1946	1947	1948	1949	1950	1951	1952	1953	1954	1955
Assets											
1. Total assets	159.9	285.8	354.7	346.5	472.2	730.8	692.6	861.1	955.9	1,202.3	1,822.3
2. Cash (inc. escrows)	30.0	35.9	42.7	46.7	58.9	82.6	113.7	127.8	151.3	170.0	225.0
3. Mortgage and construction loans	71.4	181.4	248.8	237.3	326.5	535.7	454.1	597.8	623.6	844.6	1,372.2
4. Mortgage loans	n.a.	n.a.	n.a.	n.a.	n.a.	n.a.	n.a.	490.5	501.0	643.0	1,113.8
5. Construction loans	n.a.	n.a.	n.a.	n.a.	n.a.	n.a.	n.a.	107.3	122.6	201.6	258.4
6. Notes and accounts receivable	5.7	10.6	12.2	11.9	19.2	32.1	33.8	34.6	54.8	46.8	66.2
7. Title I and other small loans	0.7	3.7	1.6	2.3	2.5	1.9	2.5	3.7	3.4	2.0	2.5
8. Other current assets	25.4	18.6	16.4	13.9	15.9	17.1	17.8	18.1	20.0	23.2	25.3
9. Noncurrent assets	26.7	35.6	33.0	34.4	49.3	61.4	70.7	79.1	102.8	115.7	131.1
Liabilities and net worth											
10. Total liabilities and net worth	159.9	285.8	354.7	346.5	472.2	730.8	692.6	861.1	955.9	1,202.3	1,822.3
11. Escrows	16.9	17.4	22.2	27.3	32.6	51.0	69.3	82.0	95.5	108.7	142.9
12. Notes payable, total	61.1	155.2	189.4	185.0	272.6	425.8	383.3	485.9	544.1	733.8	1,207.0
13. To banks	58.0	147.4	179.9	175.8	259.0	404.5	364.1	466.5	522.3	711.8	1,170.7
14. To others	3.1	7.8	9.5	9.2	13.6	21.3	19.2	19.4	21.8	22.0	36.3
15. Accounts payable	9.0	15.5	19.3	11.8	14.2	22.1	20.5	19.7	20.5	24.4	31.1
16. Undisbursed mortgage loans	5.0	14.5	29.2	21.0	25.1	66.7	25.5	53.7	52.2	61.1	115.8
17. Other current liabilities	4.9	6.8	10.8	10.2	12.4	19.1	22.8	23.0	22.2	32.1	38.1
18. Noncurrent liabilities	11.1	11.2	8.6	7.6	12.1	18.1	19.1	27.2	34.1	32.9	44.5
19. Net worth	51.9	65.2	75.1	83.6	103.3	128.0	152.1	169.5	187.3	209.4	242.9

SOURCE: All data are based on records of the FHA except the breakdown of mortgage and construction loans and notes payable (lines 4, 5, and 13, 14, respectively) which are based on relationships indicated by the special survey of mortgage companies. The breakdown of notes payable shown for years prior to 1952 is based on general knowledge that the bulk of mortgage company borrowing has always been from banks, and on the specific assumption that the ratio of bank to total borrowing was about the same as in 1952. The relationship between mortgage and construction loans, on the other hand, is subject to greater fluctuation, and in the absence of data for years prior to 1952, estimates were not attempted.

n.a. = not available.

TABLE 38

Percentage Distribution: Combined Balance Sheet of Mortgage Companies, 1945–1955

	1945	1946	1947	1948	1949	1950	1951	1952	1953	1954	1955
Assets											
1. Total assets	100.0	100.0	100.0	100.0	100.0	100.0	100.0	100.0	100.0	100.0	100.0
2. Cash (inc. escrows)	18.8	12.5	12.0	13.5	12.5	11.3	16.4	14.8	15.8	14.1	12.4
3. Mortgage and construction loans	44.7	63.5	70.2	68.5	69.1	73.3	65.5	69.5	65.2	70.3	75.3
4. Mortgage loans	n.a.	n.a.	n.a.	n.a.	n.a.	n.a.	n.a.	57.0	52.4	53.5	61.1
5. Construction loans	n.a.	n.a.	n.a.	n.a.	n.a.	n.a.	n.a.	12.5	12.8	16.8	14.2
6. Notes and accounts receivable	3.6	3.7	3.4	3.4	4.1	4.4	4.9	4.0	5.7	3.9	3.6
7. Title I and other small loans	0.4	1.3	0.5	0.7	0.5	0.3	0.4	0.4	0.4	0.2	0.1
8. Other current assets	15.8	6.5	4.6	4.0	3.4	2.3	2.6	2.1	2.1	1.9	1.4
9. Noncurrent assets	16.7	12.5	9.3	9.9	10.4	8.4	10.2	9.2	10.8	9.6	7.2
Liabilities and net worth											
10. Total liabilities and net worth	100.0	100.0	100.0	100.0	100.0	100.0	100.0	100.0	100.0	100.0	100.0
11. Escrows	10.6	6.1	6.3	7.9	6.9	7.0	10.0	9.5	10.0	9.0	7.9
12. Notes payable, total	38.2	54.3	53.4	53.4	57.8	58.3	55.3	56.4	56.9	61.0	66.2
13. To banks	36.3	51.6	50.7	50.7	54.8	55.4	52.6	54.2	54.6	59.2	64.2
14. To others	1.9	2.7	2.7	2.7	3.0	2.9	2.7	2.2	2.3	1.8	2.0
15. Accounts payable	5.6	5.4	5.4	3.4	3.0	3.0	3.0	2.3	2.1	2.0	1.7
16. Undisbursed mortgage loans	3.1	5.1	8.2	6.0	5.3	9.1	3.7	6.2	5.5	5.1	6.4
17. Other current liabilities	3.1	2.4	3.1	3.0	2.6	2.6	3.3	2.7	2.3	2.7	2.1
18. Noncurrent liabilities	6.9	3.9	2.4	2.2	2.5	2.5	2.7	3.2	3.6	2.8	2.4
19. Net worth	32.5	22.8	21.2	24.1	21.9	17.5	22.0	19.7	19.6	17.4	13.3

SOURCE: Derived from Table 37.

n.a. = not available.

CHART 34

Relationships Among Mortgage Loans, Notes Payable, and Total Assets
of Mortgage Companies, 1945–1955

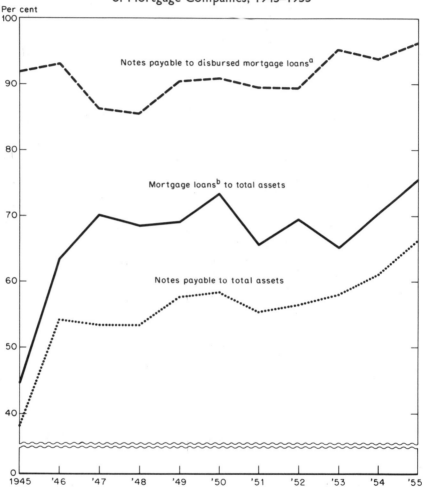

SOURCE: Table 37.

a Total mortgage and construction loans adjusted by subtracting undisbursed loans.
b Includes construction loans.

small and relatively large mortgage operations can be accommodated in minimum physical facilities. The small company consequently devotes a larger proportion of its assets to fixed plant and equipment than does the large company. Further, smaller mortgage companies may choose to engage more extensively in mortgage related activities in order to use their facilities more effectively.

Several mortgage companies, moreover, although originating and servicing a large volume of loans, show little or no mortgages in their financial statements. These companies may be either FHA loan correspondents[14] not privileged to close FHA-insured mortgages in their own names or companies using accounting procedures in which mortgage inventory is not considered an asset. Among the latter are companies, technically without mortgage inventories, that prefer their loans, originated for institutional investors, to be closed directly by commercial banks and held by them until ready for delivery to the permanent mortgagees. This procedure would, of course, eliminate mortgages and notes payable to banks from balance sheets. Companies operating in this manner are, however, in the distinct minority.

The operating procedure for the great majority of mortgage companies, as suggested earlier, is to close and hold mortgages with borrowed bank funds pending sale to investors. Thus, paralleling mortgage loans as the chief use of mortgage company funds, notes payable to banks constitute the chief source of funds. Mortgage companies borrow small amounts from nonbank sources, but these have been typically less than 5 per cent of notes payable. Total notes payable increased from $61 million in 1945 to $426 million in 1950 and to over $1.2 billion in 1955. The increase in bank borrowing accounted for over two-thirds of the total sources of mortgage company funds over the postwar decade.

That bank borrowing[15] and mortgage inventory are closely related in amount and importance in the financial structure of mortgage companies, irrespective of company size, is indicated in Charts 33 through 35. The fact that bank borrowing accounts for a somewhat smaller proportion of total assets than do mortgage loans (Chart 35) is owing to two factors: (1) significant amounts of undisbursed loans included in the mortgage total and reported separately among liabilities but not included among notes payable; and (2) to the appreciable net worth of mortgage companies.

[14] See the Appendix of Klaman, *The Postwar Rise of Mortgage Companies*, for the distinction between loan correspondents and independent mortagees.

[15] In the subsequent discussion, "bank borrowing" and "notes payable" will be used interchangeably, for, while not precisely the same, upwards of 95 per cent of notes payable are owed to banks.

CHART 35

Main Assets and Liabilities of Mortgage Companies, 1946, 1950, and 1955

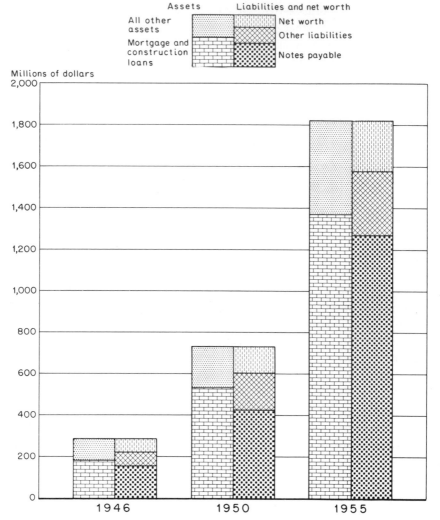

When the mortgage and construction loan total is adjusted for undisbursed loans, the ratio of notes payable to mortgage funds actually disbursed rises considerably, and for most postwar years comes to well over 90 per cent, as indicated in the top line of Chart 34. In no year does the ratio fall below 85 per cent.

Among uses and sources of mortgage company funds other than mortgage loans and notes payable, cash and net worth are most significant.

The largest part of the cash amount was, throughout the postwar decade, escrow funds as shown in Tables 37 and 38, other cash constituting a limited use of mortgage company funds. The bulk of escrow funds represents payments received from mortgagors during the year and held in trust, pending ultimate disbursement for taxes, insurance premiums, and other purposes, usually in separate bank accounts where they are not available for general mortgage company operations. Administrative regulations of FHA specifically require FHA-approved mortgagees to maintain separate accounting for escrow funds collected on FHA loans and prohibit their use in any way other than for the contracted purpose. VA regulations, however, make no similar requirements, and for conventional mortgage loan escrow funds there are no regulations on supervision and handling. Thus, while escrow accounts are a substantial item in the financial statements of mortgage companies, they are not utilized for financing the companies' activities.

Net worth of mortgage companies relative to total assets declined sharply over the postwar decade from nearly one-third in 1945 to less than one-seventh in 1955, reflecting the rapid postwar asset growth of these institutions. Year-to-year relative declines between 1945 and 1946, 1949 and 1950, and 1954 and 1955 were particularly marked, in line with the sharp increase in mortgage inventory in these periods. In absolute amount, however, net worth has increased almost fourfold in ten years from about $50 million to $240 million. Most of this increase undoubtedly reflects retained earnings rather than newly invested capital, although available data do not permit the separation of these two components of net worth changes.

Relative to their total assets, net worth of smaller companies is much greater than that of larger companies (see Tables A-6 through A-10 of Klaman, *The Postwar Rise of Mortgage Companies*). There is also a much greater variation in ratios among smaller companies than larger ones. For companies with assets of less than $1 million, for example, the proportion that had a net worth to assets of less than 25 per cent and of over 60 per cent was not much different. For companies with over $5 million in assets, on the other hand, none showed a net worth to assets ratio of over 40 per cent and for the bulk of companies the ratio was less than 10 per cent. Median ratios of net worth to assets ranged from 40 per cent for the smallest companies to 8 per cent for the largest companies.

It is difficult to compare the significance of net worth in the financial structure of mortgage companies with that of other financial institutions because of the different nature of mortgage company operations. These companies earn most of their income from mortgage servicing fees rather than from interest on mortgage holdings or other assets, the chief income source for financial intermediaries. When net worth of mortgage companies is compared with the volume of mortgages they serviced in recent years, the ratio drops sharply to between 1 and 2 per cent. Relative to earnings, therefore, it is undoubtedly true that mortgage companies have and require a much smaller net worth than do other types of financial institutions.

Short-Term Movements in Uses and Sources of Funds, 1953–1955

Quarterly data on the financial structure of selected mortgage companies were obtained in a special survey made for this study (see the second part of the Appendix to Klaman, *The Postwar Rise of Mortgage Companies*). While subject to some short-comings inevitable in a small questionnaire survey, the data are nonetheless useful as guideposts to short-run changes in uses and sources of funds during a period encompassing both stringency and ease in capital markets. The dollar volume and composition of assets and liabilities of responding mortgage companies is shown in Table 39. The substantial agreement in the composition of resources for corresponding dates between the selected mortgage companies that reported quarterly data and the much larger number reporting annual data to FHA is seen by comparing Tables 38 and 39.[16] The close relationship between mortgage loans, notes payable, and total assets for both groups of companies is apparent also from a comparison of Charts 33 and 36.

The quarterly movements shown in Chart 36 reflect both changes in capital market conditions and the basic nature of mortgage company operations. During the first two quarters of 1953, the volume of mortgage inventory changed little as capital markets were under strong pressure from Federal Reserve restrictive actions and from persistent private demands for capital. The level of holdings showed little further change in the second half of 1953, when the market eased slightly and interest rates generally declined. From the beginning of 1954 on, as investors became increasingly active in mortgage markets in a framework of continuing credit ease and declines in competitive interest rates, the growth in mortgage inventories held by companies was sharp and continued without interruption through the third quarter of 1955. The leveling off in the last quarter of 1955 reflected an earlier reduction in the rate of new investor commitments in a tightening capital market and the sale of completed mortgages from inventory.

[16] For reasons noted in the Appendix of Klaman, *The Postwar Rise of Mortgage Companies*, the most appropriate comparison is between the September 30th figures for each year in Table 39 with the corresponding annual figures shown in Table 38.

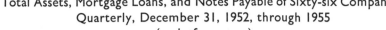

CHART 36

Total Assets, Mortgage Loans, and Notes Payable of Sixty-six Companies,
Quarterly, December 31, 1952, through 1955
(end of quarters)

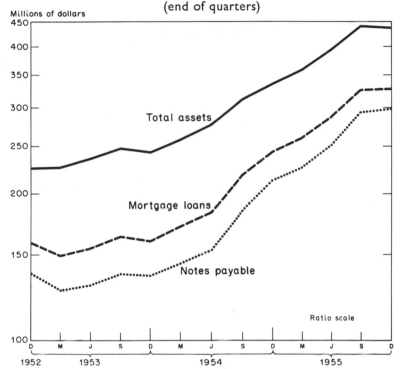

SOURCE: Special survey of mortgage companies.

These movements in mortgage holdings are suggestive of time lags in mortgage company activity following changes in capital market conditions. The most rapid rate of growth occurred after mid-1954, about a year after markets began to ease. In that period institutional investors were increasing their allocations of funds and commitments for mortgages to mortgage companies. Most of these arrangements did not result in completed mortgages until the third quarter of 1954, when mortgage inventory increased sharply together with bank borrowing to finance the loan closings. Mortgage inventories and bank loans continued to expand at a somewhat faster rate than total assets through the end of 1955. This trend can be seen from Chart 36 but is probably somewhat clearer in Table 39 which shows an increase in the ratio of mortgage loans to total assets from 66 to 70 per cent between June 30 and September 30, 1954, and to 75 per cent on December 31, 1955.

TABLE 39

Percentage Distribution: Combined Quarterly Balance Sheet of Sixty-six Selected Mortgage Companies, December 31, 1952 through 1955

	1952	1953				1954				1955				Line
	Dec. 31	Mar. 31	June 30	Sept. 30	Dec. 31	Mar. 31	June 30	Sept. 30	Dec. 31	Mar. 31	June 30	Sept. 30	Dec. 31	
Assets														
1. Total assets (*$ millions*)	225.0	225.9	235.7	247.1	242.9	257.7	276.6	310.5	334.6	356.8	392.8	439.8	437.5	1.
2. Cash (inc. escrows)	14.7	16.7	16.7	17.1	17.3	17.9	18.4	15.6	14.1	15.0	14.6	14.1	12.0	2.
3. Mortgage and construction loans, total	70.2	66.1	65.4	65.9	65.8	66.5	66.0	70.2	72.8	72.7	72.9	73.9	74.8	3.
4. Mortgage loans	57.6	53.9	53.5	53.1	52.9	54.6	51.3	54.8	55.4	54.7	56.0	58.6	60.7	4.
5. Construction loans	12.6	12.2	11.9	12.8	12.9	11.9	14.7	15.4	17.4	18.0	16.9	15.3	14.1	5.
6. Notes receivable	1.4	1.6	2.1	1.9	2.1	2.4	2.5	2.3	2.6	2.2	2.4	2.1	2.4	6.
7. Accounts receivable	2.2	2.6	2.6	2.6	2.9	2.1	2.7	2.8	2.2	1.9	2.1	1.9	1.9	7.
8. Other assets	11.5	13.0	13.4	12.5	11.9	11.1	10.4	9.1	8.3	8.2	8.0	8.0	8.5	8.
Liabilities and Net Worth														
9. Total liabilities and net worth (*$ millions*)	225.0	225.9	235.7	247.1	242.9	257.7	276.6	310.5	334.6	356.8	392.8	439.8	437.5	9.
10. Escrows	9.5	12.3	13.4	13.6	11.5	13.2	14.5	12.7	9.9	11.0	11.7	11.2	9.0	10.
11. Notes payable, total	60.7	56.2	55.0	55.2	55.9	55.8	55.2	59.3	63.5	63.3	63.9	66.6	68.1	11.
12. To banks	58.1	54.5	52.7	52.2	53.7	53.5	52.8	57.3	61.9	61.6	62.3	64.7	66.3	12.
13. To others	2.6	1.7	2.3	3.0	2.2	2.3	2.4	2.0	1.6	1.7	1.6	1.9	1.8	13.
14. Accounts payable	2.5	2.0	2.4	2.2	3.0	2.5	2.7	2.2	1.7	2.0	1.7	1.5	1.7	14.
15. Undisbursed mortgage loans	4.5	3.8	4.9	5.4	6.0	5.5	6.0	6.3	6.7	6.0	6.0	4.8	4.1	15.
16. Other liabilities	6.6	8.3	7.7	7.3	7.0	6.7	5.8	5.2	5.2	4.7	4.9	4.6	5.6	16.
17. Net worth	16.3	17.4	16.6	16.3	16.6	16.3	15.8	14.3	13.0	13.0	11.8	11.3	11.5	17.

SOURCE: Table 27 of Klaman, *The Postwar Rise of Mortgage Companies.*

While the rates of change in mortgage company assets and mortgage inventories varied considerably between quarters, a rather definite seasonal pattern of operations is suggested by the data, with the rate of growth in total assets, mortgage loans, and notes payable successively larger through the first three quarters of each year and declining in the fourth quarter (see Table 29 of Klaman, *The Postwar Rise of Mortgage Companies*). The substantially greater rate of increase in the third quarter of 1954 compared with the other years is a reflection of the abrupt change in capital markets between mid-1953 and mid-1954, noted above. Further, the continued large increase in the fourth quarter of 1954 was undoubtedly the result of the usually heavy buildup of commitments in earlier months of that year.

The peaking of growth in mortgage inventory in the third quarter of each year results from the nature of the relationship between mortgage companies and institutional investors and from the seasonal nature of building activity. Financial institutions, especially life insurance companies dealing regularly with mortgage companies, usually make their allocations and commitments for mortgages early in each calendar year. Arrangements to finance residential construction and sales are then made by mortgage companies. The houses and permanent mortgages are not completed or delivered until several months later. As mortgages are closed on houses finished and sold, the temporary mortgage inventories held by mortgage companies increase at an accelerating rate to a peak rate in the third quarter. By the fourth quarter of the year, the rate of building and of completing new mortgages slows down, while mortgages already completed and processed are taken up by permanent investors, with a resulting decline or a slowing down in the rate of increase in mortgage companies' inventories. The close relationship between quarterly rates of growth in mortgage inventory and bank borrowing to finance such inventory is evident in Table 39.

There is little reason to expect any similarity of movement during the year or a consistent relationship between total home mortgage debt and mortgage debt held by mortgage companies, and none seems to be indicated by a comparison of columns 1 and 2 of Table 40. Changes in total home mortgage debt reflect the combined actions of several different types of institutions and of individuals acquiring mortgages generally for permanent investment rather than short-term inventory. As market conditions changed, the quarterly peak rate of growth in total home mortgage debt shifted from the second quarter in 1953 to the fourth quarter in 1954, and back to the second quarter in 1955; but this did not alter the seasonal pattern of mortgage companies' inventory holdings.

There does, however, appear to be a definite complementary relationship between growth in mortgage company inventories and in mortgage holdings of life insurance companies, which predominate in purchases of mortgage loans from mortgage companies. As indicated in columns 3 and 4 of Table 40, the greatest increase in life insurance company mortgage holding occurs consistently in the fourth quarter of each year, reflecting chiefly acquisitions of VA-guaranteed mortgages. The clear implication

TABLE 40

Percentage Changes in Mortgage Inventory of Mortgage Companies and
One- to Four-Family Mortgage Debt Outstanding, 1953–1955

End of Quarter	Mortgage Holdings of Mortgage Companies (1)	1- TO 4-FAMILY MORTGAGE DEBT		
		Total (2)	*Held by Life Insurance Companies*	
			Total (3)	VA-guaranteed (4)
1953 Mar. 31	−5.4	2.7	2.9	0.7
June 30	3.1	3.7	2.9	0.9
Sept. 30	5.7	3.3	2.8	1.6
Dec. 31	−1.9	2.7	3.2	3.2
1954 Mar. 31	7.2	2.2	2.7	3.6
June 30	6.5	3.4	3.3	5.5
Sept. 30	19.5	4.0	3.5	7.8
Dec. 31	11.7	4.2	4.6	10.7
1955 Mar. 31	6.5	3.8	3.6	7.3
June 30	10.5	4.7	3.5	6.3
Sept. 30	13.5	4.1	3.5	5.2
Dec. 31	0.7	3.3	5.4	9.0

SOURCE: Col. 1: From Klaman, *The Postwar Rise of Mortgage Companies*, Table 29.
Cols. 2, 3, and 4: Derived from quarterly figures shown in various issues of the *Federal Reserve Bulletin*, for example, May 1956, pp. 490 and 491.

is that the rate of growth in mortgage company inventories declines sharply in the fourth quarter of each year as life insurance companies increase the rate of their acquisitions of mortgages, especially federally underwritten mortgages, the chief market interest of mortgage companies.[17]

Concluding Comments

The modern mortgage company is a financial institution not quite like any other on the American capital market scene. Its functions are similar, in

[17] Figures on gross mortgage acquisitions by life insurance companies are, of course, a more direct measure of market activity but were not used in Table 40 because no comparable quarterly figures exist for other institutions. Actually, examination of the gross acquisitions figures for the years 1953–1955 indicates that the largest volume of mortgages was acquired by life insurance companies in the fourth quarter of each year, bearing out the above analysis based on net acquisitions data.

a way, to those of municipal bond dealers and securities underwriters who act as intermediaries between borrowers and lenders and carry temporary inventories with the help of short-term bank credit. They are similar, in other ways, to those of sales finance companies that rely heavily on commercial bank and other external financing to extend consumer credit and carry large inventories of net receivables. The mortgage company is unlike these institutions, however, in that it operates largely on the basis of prior commitments from financial intermediaries and originates loans primarily to obtain accounts for servicing mortgages. It thus maintains a close and continuing relationship with institutional investors that has no counterpart among other types of institutions.

The study establishes that the remarkably rapid postwar growth of mortgage companies has been associated with the introduction and expansion of federal mortgage insurance and guaranty programs. Between three-fourths and nine-tenths of mortgage loans closed by mortgage companies in each of the years 1953 through 1955 were VA-guaranteed or FHA-insured. Clearly, the future pattern of mortgage company development and growth will depend heavily on the future course of these federal credit aid programs. Efforts by mortgage companies to expand their conventional loan business might be blunted by legal restrictions on out-of-state operations by financial intermediaries, by competition from local lenders traditionally engaged in this type of operation, and by numerous problems in conducting a conventional loan business for investors at a distance and in attracting investors to it.

Among major types of financial intermediaries, only life insurance companies and mutual savings banks deal extensively with mortgage companies, and the banks are subject to geographic restrictions on their conventional mortgage lending activities. The already great dependence of mortgage companies on life insurance companies, therefore, would undoubtedly increase with an increased proportion of conventional lending. It is unlikely that mortgage companies could find increased outlets for conventional loans among commercial banks and savings and loan associations, which typically compete in origination of loans, instead of purchasing them from mortgage companies. In any case, savings and loan associations are also subject to geographic lending restrictions. Even among life insurance companies, many might be reluctant to expand their out-of-state conventional mortgage investments materially because of the lack of uniformity in mortgage contracts and in state statutes, the generally greater exposure to loss in case of default or foreclosure, and the need for closer examination and supervision of properties pledged. On the other hand, the experience and techniques developed by mortgage bankers in the origination of federally underwritten mortgages may be successfully adapted to conventional mortgage lending. A few mortgage companies already carry on a large volume of conventional mortgage origination and servicing for investors. In the final analysis, any significant expansion of conventional mortgage business by mortgage companies will depend on the ability and willingness of investors to increase their activity in this area and of borrowers to adjust to the more restrictive conventional mortgage loan terms.

In any event, the likelihood that the role of the federal government in mortgage and housing markets will diminish significantly in the years ahead is not very great. Recent counter-cyclical policy has relied heavily on adjustments in federal housing and mortgage programs. Mortgage insurance under FHA is among the earliest and most basic federal aids in the field of real estate finance. It is now deeply entrenched in the American real estate scene and is likely to continue as a basic part of domestic economic policy independent of political events.

The more recently introduced VA-guaranty program for veterans of World War II has already been extended twice beyond its original expiration date of July 1957. When it may be allowed to terminate—if at all—will depend mainly upon prevailing economic and political conditions. Moreover, the Korean VA loan program is established until early 1965. Several million veterans remain eligible for loans under both programs.

While it is clear that the potential flow of mortgage funds under federally underwritten programs is large, it seems equally clear that this flow will continue to fluctuate widely so long as the federal government continues its policy of maintaining relatively inflexible interest rates on VA and FHA mortgages. The postwar record plainly indicates that alternate shifts between ease and stringency in Federal Reserve monetary policy and in capital market conditions have been accompanied by exaggerated swings in federally underwritten mortgage flows. These swings have been coincident with a widening and narrowing of the spread between relatively stringent interest rates of VA and FHA contracts and the flexible yields of corporate bonds. The flow of conventional mortgage funds, on the other hand, has fluctuated only narrowly as private lenders have been free to adjust interest rates to changing financial conditions.

So long, therefore, as mortgage companies continue to concentrate their activities in federally sponsored mortgages, they will be particularly vulnerable, compared with other types of financial institutions, to changing financial conditions and to unpredictable federal statutory and administrative changes.

APPENDIX

APPENDIX

Supplementary Tables
to Text Charts

These tables underlie charts for which data are not readily available from the text. More detailed data will be found in the tables of Saul B. Klaman, *The Volume of Mortgage Debt in the Postwar Decade,* Technical Paper 13, New York, National Bureau of Economic Research, 1958.

TABLE A-1

VA and FHA Gross Mortgage Flows, and Yield Differentials Between Contract Interest Rates on VA and FHA Mortgages and Yields on New Issues of Aaa Corporate Bonds, Quarterly, 1951–1958

(gross flows in millions of dollars)

Quarter	*VA Loans* Yield Differential[a]	Gross Flow	*FHA Loans* Yield Differential[a]	Gross Flow	Quarter	*VA Loans* Yield Differential[a]	Gross Flow	*FHA Loans* Yield Differential[a]	Gross Flow
1951					1955				
I	119	978	144	586	I	143	1,720	143	748
II	91	855	116	479	II	138	1,616	138	743
III	96	908	121	441	III	123	1,728	123	784
IV	78	873	103	423	IV	130	2,092	130	810
1952					1956				
I	95	779	120	418	I	133	1,573	133	753
II	86	643	111	411	II	97	1,383	97	619
III	89	609	114	512	III	65	1,477	65	649
IV	91	690	116	602	IV	34	1,435	34	617
1953					1957				
I	72	745	97	594	I	30	1,366	80	514
II	53	694	71	574	II	−5	912	45	476
III	95	796	95	582	III	−18	814	57	549
IV	135	829	135	539	IV	6	669	81	712
1954					1958				
I	163	741	163	500	I	76	425	151	904
II	160	828	160	464	II	98	255	161	959
III	154	1,122	154	441	III	48	472	98	1,219
IV	162	1,566	162	538	IV	33	712	83	1,468

Source to Chart 1.

[a] Basis points.

TABLE A–2
Ratios of Nonfarm Mortgage Debt to Gross National Product and to Total and Private Debt, 1900–1956

End of Year	Ratios of Nonfarm Mortgage Debt to: GNP	Total Debt	Private Debt	End of Year	Ratios of Nonfarm Mortgage Debt to: GNP	Total Debt	Private Debt	End of Year	Ratios of Nonfarm Mortgage Debt to: GNP	Total Debt	Private Debt
1900	25.1	9.3	10.2	1921	20.3	10.8	13.8				
1901	23.6			1922	22.3	11.6	14.8	1942	19.3	11.9	22.0
1902	23.4			1923	21.9	12.9	16.2	1943	15.5	9.5	20.9
1903	22.1			1924	24.8	13.9	17.3	1944	14.1	8.0	20.7
1904	23.8			1925	28.4	15.8	18.5	1945	14.4	7.6	22.9
1905	23.0			1926	28.7	16.5	19.9	1946	17.6	9.3	24.0
1906	20.3			1927	32.5	17.5	20.9	1947	18.9	10.5	24.3
1907	19.1			1928	35.3	18.5	21.8	1948	19.8	11.7	25.3
1908	22.7			1929	35.3	19.3	22.2	1949	22.2	12.7	27.0
1909	20.5			1930	41.4	19.7	23.0	1950	23.4	13.6	26.6
1910	20.4			1931	47.9	20.1	24.4	1951	23.0	14.4	26.6
1911	21.4			1932	58.8	19.7	25.0	1952	24.3	15.1	27.3
1912	20.8	8.0	8.7	1933	54.4	18.1	24.1	1953	25.6	15.6	28.4
1913	21.6			1934	45.4	17.2	24.1	1954	29.5	17.4	32.9
1914	24.2			1935	39.2	16.3	23.5	1955	30.9	18.0	30.1
1915	22.9			1936	33.9	15.5	22.9	1956	32.5	19.2	31.2
1916	19.6	11.7	12.5	1937	30.8	15.3	22.9				
1917	16.4	11.2	12.9	1938	33.1	15.7	23.7				
1918	14.3	9.5	12.1	1939	31.7	15.8	23.9				
1919	13.6	9.1	11.9	1940	29.8	15.7	23.8				
1920	14.8	10.0	12.8	1941	24.8	14.7	22.8				

Source to Chart 2.

TABLE A–3
Relative Position of Nonfarm and Farm Mortgage Debt in the United States Economy Before and After Two World Wars

Period	Ratio of Mortgage Debt to Gross National Product Nonfarm	Farm	Ratio of Mortgage Debt to Real Estate Wealth Nonfarm	Farm	Ratio of Mortgage Debt to Total Debt Nonfarm	Farm	Ratio of Mortgage Debt to Assets of Main Financial Institutions Nonfarm	Farm
World War I Comparison								
1914	24.2	14.0	16.8	13.0	11.7	7.1	15.2	4.4
1918	14.3	9.2	12.3	12.3	9.5	6.0	11.3	3.8
1928	35.7	10.0	21.5	20.6	18.5	5.3	21.5	3.2
World War II Comparison								
1939	31.7	7.2	19.2	20.5	15.8	3.6	15.4	1.3
1945	14.4	2.2	14.3	8.0	7.6	1.2	8.6	0.6
1956	32.5	2.4	27.1	8.9	19.2	1.4	27.6	1.0

Source to Chart 3.

TABLE A–4

Comparison of Interest Rates and Yield on Mortgages and Other Capital Market Securities, Quarterly Averages, 1946–1956

| Quarter | Corporate Aaa Bond Yields | | Municipal Aaa Bond Yield | U.S. Government Bond Yield | Mortgage Interest Rates | | |
	Out-standing	New Issues			FHA Contract Rates	VA Contract Rates	Conventional Mortgage Rates
1946 I	2.50	—	0.96	2.14	4.50	4.00	—
II	2.49	—	0.99	2.14	4.50	4.00	—
III	2.52	—	1.15	2.23	4.50	4.00	—
IV	2.60	—	1.28	2.25	4.50	4.00	—
1947 I	2.56	—	1.40	2.20	4.50	4.00	4.37
II	2.54	—	1.41	2.20	4.50	4.00	4.44
III	2.57	—	1.41	2.24	4.50	4.00	4.31
IV	2.58	—	1.59	2.34	4.50	4.00	4.35
1948 I	2.85	—	1.87	2.45	4.50	4.00	4.40
II	2.77	—	1.87	2.42	4.50	4.00	4.46
III	2.83	—	1.89	2.45	4.50	4.00	4.54
IV	2.82	—	1.85	2.44	4.50	4.00	4.58
1949 I	2.71	—	1.69	2.40	4.50	4.00	4.64
II	2.71	—	1.66	2.38	4.50	4.00	4.57
III	2.63	—	1.64	2.24	4.50	4.00	4.61
IV	2.60	—	1.63	2.20	4.50	4.00	4.63
1950 I	2.58	—	1.61	2.24	4.50	4.00	4.63
II	2.61	—	1.65	2.31	4.25ᵃ	4.00	4.62
III	2.63	—	1.56	2.34	4.25	4.00	4.52
IV	2.67	—	1.43	2.38	4.25	4.00	4.55
1951 I	2.70	2.81	1.35	2.42	4.25	4.00	4.48
II	2.90	3.09	1.68	2.61	4.25	4.00	4.60
III	2.89	3.04	1.69	2.62	4.25	4.00	4.68
IV	2.95	3.22	1.70	2.66	4.25	4.00	4.78
1952 I	2.96	3.05	1.73	2.72	4.25	4.00	4.81
II	2.93	3.14	1.69	2.61	4.25	4.00	4.80
III	2.95	3.11	1.82	2.67	4.25	4.00	4.81
IV	2.99	3.09	1.98	2.73	4.25	4.00	4.83
1953 I	3.07	3.28	2.13	2.84	4.25	4.00	4.87
II	3.32	3.72	2.39	3.05	4.50	4.50	4.88
III	3.27	3.55	2.51	2.99	4.50	4.50	4.91
IV	3.13	3.15	2.22	2.82	4.50	4.50	5.05
1954 I	2.96	2.87	2.07	2.60	4.50	4.50	5.04
II	2.88	2.90	2.17	2.51	4.50	4.50	5.08
III	2.87	2.96	1.94	2.49	4.50	4.50	4.98
IV	2.89	2.88	1.98	2.55	4.50	4.50	5.00
1955 I	2.98	3.07	2.09	2.69	4.50	4.50	4.93
II	3.03	3.12	2.08	2.76	4.50	4.50	4.93
III	3.10	3.27	2.29	2.89	4.50	4.50	4.89
IV	3.12	3.20	2.25	2.85	4.50	4.50	4.91
1956 I	3.10	3.17	2.23	2.86	4.50	4.50	4.91
II	3.26	3.53	2.41	2.96	4.50	4.50	4.93
III	3.42	3.85	2.52	3.10	4.50	4.50	4.97
IV	3.68	4.16	2.86	3.30	5.00ᵃ	4.50	5.04

Source to Chart 7.

ᵃ Refers to quarter in which contract rate was changed by statute or administrative action.

TABLE A–5

Comparison of Average Interest Rates on Conventional Mortgage Loans
Closed on Homes and Income Properties, Quarterly, 1951–1956

Quarter	Home Mortgage Loans	Income–property Loans	Differential in Interest Rate
1951			
I	4.48	4.07	0.41
II	4.60	4.02	0.58
III	4.68	4.05	0.63
IV	4.78	4.27	0.51
1952			
I	4.81	4.33	0.48
II	4.80	4.35	0.45
III	4.81	4.31	0.50
IV	4.83	4.52	0.31
1953			
I	4.87	4.55	0.32
II	4.88	4.50	0.38
III	4.91	4.59	0.32
IV	5.05	4.64	0.41
1954			
I	5.04	4.67	0.37
II	5.08	4.67	0.41
III	4.98	4.68	0.30
IV	5.00	4.65	0.35
1955			
I	4.93	4.72	0.21
II	4.93	4.62	0.31
III	4.89	4.68	0.21
IV	4.91	4.53	0.38
1956			
I	4.91	4.59	0.32
II	4.93	4.60	0.33
III	4.97	4.72	0.25
IV	5.04	4.76	0.28

Source to Chart 8.

TABLE A–6

Comparison of Average Interest Rates on Conventional Mortgage Loans Closed on
Homes and Income Properties, Annually, 1920–1956

Year	Home Mortgage Loans	Income Property Loans	Year	Home Mortgage Loans	Income Property Loans
1920	6.1	5.8	1940	4.7	4.4
1921	6.2	6.5	1941	4.7	4.3
1922	6.1	5.9	1942	4.6	4.5
1923	5.9	5.7	1943	4.5	4.2
1924	5.9	5.8	1944	4.4	3.9
1925	5.9	5.4	1945	4.3	4.2
1926	5.8	5.6	1946	4.3	4.2
1927	5.9	5.5	1947	4.34	4.12
1928	5.9	5.3	1948	4.49	4.18
1929	6.0	5.7	1949	4.61	4.24
1930	6.0	5.9	1950	4.58	4.29
1931	6.0	5.4	1951	4.61	4.11
1932	6.0	5.3	1952	4.82	4.35
1933	5.9	—	1953	4.94	4.50
1934	5.8	4.5	1954	5.03	4.65
1935	5.5	5.2	1955	4.91	4.62
1936	5.2	4.6	1956	5.01	4.67
1937	5.2	5.1			
1938	5.1	4.9			
1939	5.0	4.6			

Source to Chart 9.

TABLE A–7

Comparison of Calculated Yields on FHA and VA Home Loans
and Contract Interest Rates on Conventional Home Loans,
Quarterly, 1953–1956

Quarter	FHA Calculated Yields	VA Calculated Yields	Conventional Contract Interest Rates
1953			
I	—	—	4.87
II	4.68	4.74	4.88
III	4.93	4.96	4.91
IV	4.89	4.93	5.05
1954			
I	4.74	4.79	5.04
II	4.61	4.65	5.08
III	4.57	4.64	4.98
IV	4.58	4.64	5.00
1955			
I	4.61	4.70	4.93
II	4.65	4.72	4.93
III	4.70	4.81	4.89
IV	4.74	4.86	4.91
1956			
I	4.72	4.82	4.91
II	4.77	4.87	4.93
III	4.85	4.93	4.97
IV	5.04	5.09	5.04

Source to Chart 11.

TABLE A–8

Comparison of Net Mortgage Flows and Other Net Capital Market Flows,
1946–1956 (amounts in billions of dollars)

Year	Percentage Ratio Mortgage Flow to Total Capital Market Flow	*Net Flow of Funds into:*			
		U.S. Government Obligations	State and Local Government Securities	Corporate Securities	Mortgages
1946	76.5	−22.5	−0.4	2.3	6.2
1947	55.0	−5.7	1.5	4.4	7.2
1948	46.8	−6.8	2.3	6.0	7.3
1949	41.1	2.1	2.5	4.8	6.5
1950	58.0	a	3.3	4.0	10.1
1951	51.6	−0.3	2.5	6.7	9.4
1952	36.7	4.3	3.2	8.1	9.0
1953	38.4	5.2	3.8	7.2	9.9
1954	49.8	2.0	4.4	6.4	12.5
1955	58.4	1.2	3.7	7.1	16.4
1956	54.0	−5.9	3.5	8.8	14.7

Source to Chart 12.
a Less than $50 million.

TABLE A–9

Percentage Ratios of Net Mortgage Flows to Total Net Capital Market Flows through
Main Financial Institutions, 1946–1956

Year	Savings and Loan Associations	Life Insurance Companies	Mutual Savings Banks	Commercial Banks
1946	100.0	14.7	13.3	43.1
1947	100.0	32.6	44.4	28.2
1948	100.0	31.9	66.7	32.6
1949	100.0	41.2	81.8	11.9
1950	100.0	59.3	100.0	17.5
1951	95.0	54.2	85.0	17.2
1952	93.3	36.5	71.4	12.2
1953	96.4	41.3	73.5	24.2
1954	97.7	48.4	83.0	17.0
1955	94.3	58.7	104.1	20.2
1956	87.0	61.8	90.9	22.5

Source to Chart 13.

TABLE A–10

Gross Mortgage Credit Extended to Finance House Purchases, and Number of
Houses Purchased, 1950–1956

Year and Type of House	Mortgage Credit Extended (in billions of dollars)				Number of Houses Purchased (in thousands of units)			
	Total	FHA	VA	Conventional	Total	FHA	VA	Conventional
New houses								
1950	6.3	1.6	1.9	2.8	974	224	209	541
1951	6.4	1.2	2.7	2.5	917	163	286	468
1952	5.9	1.0	1.8	3.1	839	123	192	524
1953	6.6	1.3	2.0	3.3	878	152	203	523
1954	7.3	1.1	2.7	3.6	897	122	243	532
1955	10.2	1.3	4.6	4.3	1,114	131	388	596
1956	9.2	1.1	3.9	4.1	945	105	313	526
Existing houses								
1950	6.9	0.9	1.2	4.8	1,367	126	160	1,081
1951	6.9	0.7	0.9	5.2	1,326	100	123	1,103
1952	8.6	1.0	0.9	6.8	1,531	123	109	1,299
1953	9.2	1.0	1.0	7.2	1,518	120	115	1,283
1954	11.1	0.9	1.6	8.7	1,712	101	164	1,448
1955	13.3	1.8	2.5	8.9	1,838	187	256	1,395
1956	13.3	1.5	1.9	9.8	1,835	148	188	1,499

Source to Chart 22.

TABLE A–11

Typical Disbursment of Mortgage Funds
Following Date of Commitment

Month	Percentage of Funds Disbursed	Cumulative Percentage Disbursements
Month of commitment	2.0	2.0
Months following commitment		
1	8.5	10.5
2	13.3	23.8
3	11.2	35.0
4	8.5	43.5
5	7.0	50.5
6	6.5	57.0
7	5.0	62.0
8	4.5	66.5
9	4.0	70.5
10	3.5	74.0
11	2.5	76.5
12	2.5	79.0
All other	5.5	84.5
Attrition	—	15.5

Source to Chart 24.

Questionnaire on Mortgage Market Activity of Savings and Loan Associations

General Instructions and Explanatory Notes

This questionnaire, consisting of three sections, is designed to obtain information not now available on (1) gross flows of mortgage funds; (2) the nature of construction loans; and (3) secondary mortgage market activity. If you find that your records do not enable you to complete the questionnaire for each year specified or in the detail requested, please provide as much of the information as you can. Where precise figures are lacking do not hesitate to make estimates either in dollar amounts or percentages of totals, based on your experience. We are particularly anxious to get for mortgage loan repayments a breakdown between loans paid in full and other repayments, and for your lending activity a breakdown between construction loans to builders and other mortgage loans. A more detailed explanation of each section is given below.

SECTION 1

This section relates to the gross flow of funds through your mortgage portfolio, distinguishing between loans to builders and other types of mortgage loans, as defined below. It relates, also, to the composition of mortgage loan repayments as between loan repaid in full and contractual repayments (including partial prepayments). The latter are, of course, the more regular type of repayments that may be anticipated from the portfolio, while repayments in full are more volatile, reflecting conditions in real estate and mortgage markets. Distinguishing between these two types of repayment is important not only to an understanding of current market behavior, but to an appraisal of future gross flow patterns.

Some specific explanations of items in this section follow:

(1) The heading loans to builders (I-A, II-A) refers to loans made to operative builders for the purpose of financing construction for resale to others. Include all such loans closed whether or not funds have been disbursed. *Do not include* loans to individuals for construction of their own homes even though they may be included in Item 28.a, loans "for construction of homes," of the *Monthly Report* submitted to the Federal Home Loan Bank Board.

(2) In reporting loans repaid in full under Item IV-A, include all terminating balances of mortgages prepaid in full, maturing under contract, on

properties foreclosed or acquired by deed and transferred to real estate, and similar deductions from your mortgage loan account.

(3) Include under Item IV-B, "other repayments," the total amount of funds received from regular contractual repayment of principal, together with amounts received from partial repayments or curtailments of mortgages.

N.B.E.R

July 1956

SECTION 1

Changes in Mortgage Loan Portfolio
($000)

	1955	1954	1953	1952
I. Outstanding balance, beginning of year				
A. Loans to builders				
B. Other mortgage loans				
II. Loans made during year				
A. Loans to builders				
B. Other mortgage loans				
III. Loans purchased during year				
IV. Loans repaid during year				
A. Repayments in full				
B. Other repayments				
V. Loans sold during year				
VI. Outstanding balance, end of year				
A. Loans to builders				
B. Other mortgage loans				

SECTION 2

This section relates entirely to Item 28.a, loans "for construction of homes," submitted in the *Monthly Report* to the Federal Home Loan Bank Board. It is intended to identify the type of loans included under this item, distinguishing between loans similar in character to those reported under Item 28.b, loans "for purchase of homes," and short-term loans to builders for financing the construction process only. It is recognized that many of the latter type of loans result, upon completion and sale of the property, in permanent home purchase loans for your portfolio. The process of changing from construction to home purchase loans, however, often involves re-financing the property from builders to purchasers, with separate transactions recorded in your loan accounts and reported to the Federal Home Loan Bank Board. The latter agency specifically requests in its instructions for making out the *Monthly Report*: "If property securing a construction loan is sold to a new owner-borrower to whom a purchase loan is made by the association, the purchase loan should be included under Item 28.b (loans 'for purchase of homes') for the month in which the purchase loan is closed." It is hoped that the extent of this double reporting can be determined from answers to questions in this section.

N.B.E.R

July 1956

SECTION 2

General Questions on Loans for Construction of Homes

(As reported in Item 28.a of *Monthly Report* to Federal Home Loan Bank Board)

I. A. What proportion of your total mortgage loans closed was reported as loans "for construction of homes" in Item 28.a of the *Monthly Report* submitted to the Federal Home Loan Bank Board in 1955........%; 1954........%; 1953........%.

B. Of these loans made "for construction of homes" in 1955, about what proportion was made to individuals to finance construction of homes for their own occupancy ....%; and what proportion was made as loans to builders to finance construction of homes for resale to others........%.

II. A. About what proportion of construction loans made to builders is generally retained or refinanced by your association as home purchase loans when property is completed and sold........%; and what proportion is paid off or refinanced by others........%.

B. Of those construction loans to builders that lead to home purchase loans for your portfolio, about what proportion is replaced by a new loan to a new owner-borrower, and then reported again as loans "for purchase of homes" in Item 28.b of the *Monthly Report* to the Federal Home Loan Bank Board........%; and what proportion is taken over, or assumed directly by the new owner-borrower, and is thus not reported again........%.

SECTION 3

Participation in the secondary mortgage market by savings and loan associations, while still rather small, has apparently increased substantially in recent years. It is the purpose of this section to determine the extent and nature of such participation in the past three years. If this section does not apply to your association's activities, write "None" across the sheet.

Under Part II of this section, mortgage purchases or sales "with prior commitment" (or allocation of funds) refer to those transactions that were arranged before the mortgage came into existence. Transactions "without prior commitment" refer to purchases and sales negotiated after the mortgage was completed and held in portfolio.

SECTION 3
Secondary Market Activity

I. Please provide the approximate amounts of sales and purchases of mortgages in recent years.

	1955	1954	1953	1950	1947
Sales					
Purchases					

II. Please indicate the approximate percentages for the following table about the nature of your secondary market activity, types of mortgages traded in, and types of institutions with which you have been trading.

PER CENT

	1955		1954		1953	
	Purchases	Sales	Purchases	Sales	Purchases	Sales
Nature of activity						
With prior commitment						
Without prior commitment						
	100.0	100.0	100.0	100.0	100.0	100.0
Type of mortgage						
VA						
FHA						
Conventional						
	100.0	100.0	100.0	100.0	100.0	100.0
Type of institution						
Life insurance companies						
Mutual savings banks						
Commercial banks						
Savings and loan associations						
Mortgage companies						
FNMA						
Other (please specify)						
	100.0	100.0	100.0	100.0	100.0	100.0

SUBJECT INDEX

Amortization terms, xxii, xxviii, 58, 77, 237
Attrition in mortgage commitments, *see* Commitment technique, forward commitments

Brokers, 213–215, 232–235

Closed-end loans, *see* Interim financing, variations in
Commercial banks:
lending policy and portfolio composition, 7, 19–20, 29, 37–38, 104, 165–172, 214
liquidity of, *see* Liquidity of financial institutions
primary vs. secondary market activity of, 201–208
purchases and sales to FNMA, 224–225
regional differences in policy, 166–167, 169
supplier of funds, xxii, 5, 7–8, 10, 34–36, 38, 43–44, 47, 100–104, 106, 108, 116–122, 130–133, 136
See also Interim finance, commercial bank extension of
Commitment technique:
firm commitment:
and lags, 176
and mortgage company operations, 21, 143, 246–247, 263
See also "Take out" commitment
FNMA's use of advanced and standby commitments, 54–55 n., 64–65, 72, 85, 116, 222, 225
forward commitments:
attrition rate of, 17, 144–145
brokers' and traders' use of advance commitments, 235
effect on regulation of credit, 126
explained, 22, 143, 178–179
lags due to, 17, 21, 122, 126, 144, 175–176
life insurance companies' use of, xxiii, 17, 22, 71, 122, 123, 143–147, 177–179, 187, 189, 246–247
mutual savings banks' use of, 18, 153
overcommitments, 17, 23, 145–146, 187, 189
relation to interim finance, 23, 143, 145, 178, 184–190, 246–247
savings and loan associations' use of, 71, 122
"Standby" commitments, 19, 23, 215, 263
effects of, 22, 181–182

explained, 22, 179–180
relation to warehousing, 180, 183–186, 188
sources of, 180–181
"Take out" commitment, 22, 215
"dual take out" commitments, 168
and open-end loans, 185
origin of, 180
required by banks for construction and interim loans, 19, 162, 168, 177–178, 184–186, 188, 189, 263
See also Interim financing, relation to commitment technique
Construction loans, 21, 23, 136, 142, 155, 175
by commercial banks, 19–20, 104, 166–169
as per cent of mortgage lending, 159–161
risk on, 168–169
by savings and loan associations, 18, 158–163
source of, 176
See also Interim financing
Contract terms:
changes in terms of federally underwritten loans, 11, 13–14, 53, 57–60, 63, 67–68, 72, 77–78
on conventional loans, 59
effect of market conditions on, 77–78
standardization of, 77–78
VA vs. FHA terms, 90–92
See also Amortization terms, Downpayment terms, *and* Maturity terms
Corporate bond (debt), xxi, 5, 26, 39
Correspondent and branch systems, 8, 16–20, 105, 116, 123, 136, 139–141, 146–147, 150, 153, 159, 168–169, 172, 241, 246–247, 260

Defense Production Act of 1950, 49, 57, 60, 66
Demand for mortgage loans, xxiv–xxv, xxix–xxx, 6–7, 38–39, 44, 48, 50, 55–56, 107, 110–111, 114
Discounts and premiums, 77–78, 90, 93–95, 216
failure to adjust yields, 12–13, 83–89
on junior mortgages, 235–237
See also Interest rates
Downpayment terms, xxviii, 57–58, 60, 67, 72, 77–78, 90, 93, 114, 128

Federal Home Loan Banks, 18, 107, 122–123, 159
credit policy, 57, 68, 71–72, 212

Federal Housing Administration:
credit policy, 57–58, 60, 70–71
legislation authorizing, 53, 55, 85
regulation of fees on loans, 85
See also Mortgage loans, federally
underwritten
Federal National Mortgage Association:
changes in authority of, 7, 11, 53–54,
64–65, 67, 69, 110, 114, 116, 126,
217–224
geographic distribution of sales and
purchases, 226–227
"one-for-one" program, 65, 67–68, 225,
227
policy of, 54, 64–65, 67–69, 71–72, 107,
116–118, 131–132
purchases and sales by type of investor,
222–226
repurchase plan, 71–72, 222
use of commitment technique, *see*
Commitment technique, FNMA
use of
See also Secondary markets
Federal Reserve policy, 7, 10–11, 14, 49,
51, 63–64, 66, 70, 80, 84, 105, 120–
122, 128
selective controls, 13, 49, 58–62, 67, 120,
126
Fees on loans, 78, 81, 84–85, 173, 214–215
on junior mortgages, 234
as mortgage company income, 244–245
Financial institutions:
supplier of funds, xxii, xxiv, 5, 9, 34, 42,
45, 100, 104 n., 107
See also Commerical banks; life insurance companies; Mutual savings
banks; Savings and loan associations
Flow of mortgage fund, *see* Mortgage loans
Fluctuations:
interest rates, 12, 75–80
mortgage flows, 9–13, 84, 88, 111–115,
121–130
seasonal trends, *see* Seasonal trends

Geographic variations:
FNMA activity, 226–227
mortgage company distribution, 254–
255
in yields, *see* Interest rate, geographic
differences
Gross mortgage flow, 99, 163, 283, 289
advantage of gross analysis, xxviii
availability of data on, xxiv, xxviii, 91 n.
and yield differentials on, 13–15, 283

Hamilton, Alexander, 136
Home Owners Loan Corporation, 107

Housing Acts:
of 1948, 53–54
of 1950, 54–55, 114
of 1952, 65
of 1954, 68–69, 129, 220
of 1956, 72

Individuals, as supplier of funds, 6, 34,
44
Institutionalization of mortgage market,
xxii
Interest rates, 285
comparison of rates on conventional,
FHA, and VA loans, 9–10, 12, 84,
90–95, 128, 285, 288
construction loans, 169
conventional loans, 12, 15, 82–83, 128
amplitude of, 12, 75–78, rates on home
vs. income property loans, 12, 75–76
80–82, 286–287
federally underwritten loans, effect of
inflexible rates on, 9–13, 56, 63, 67,
73, 83–84, 124, 281
failure of discounts and premiums to
adjust rates on, 12–13, 83, 85–89
maximum rates on, 9, 11, 13, 67, 76,
83–84, 86–87, 90
geographic differences in yields, 15, 75,
92, 95–98
and gross flows, 13–15, 283
interim loans, 188
junior mortgages, 234–237
lags in, 12, 75, 78–80
long-term position of, 82–83
new and outstanding loans, 75, 77
sensitivity of insurance company policy
to, 121, 130, 139–140
See also Contract terms; Discounts
and premiums; Fluctuations
Interim financing:
advantages and disadvantages of, 23, 189
commercial bank extension of, 19–22, 44,
52, 104, 143, 166, 169–170, 177–
178, 180, 182–195
data on, 23, 190–195
dependence of mortgage companies on,
20–21, 23, 67, 143, 178, 182–184,
190–195, 239, 246–247
explanation of, 22–23
interest on, 188
life insurance company use of, 23, 145,
183–194
relation to commitment technique, construction loans, and permanent
financing, 23, 143, 145, 175–178,
180, 183–190, 246–247
variations in, 182–189
Internal sources of finance, 50

Junior mortgage financing, 16, 175
  market organization and techniques, 233–235
  nature and purpose of, 230–232
  "purchase money" type, 175, 231–234
  size of market, 227–239
  sources of funds for, 232–233
  terms and prices of, 235–238

Lags:
  in mortgage company activity, 277
  in mortgage flows, 11–13, 62, 129
  in mortgage interest rates, 12, 21, 75, 78–80, 115
  between decisions and mortgage acquisitions, 21, 122, 144–146, 175–176, 290
Life insurance companies:
  and commitment technique, see Commitment techniques, forward commitments
  early history of policy, 137–138
  effect of interest rate on investment decisions, 121, 130, 139–140
  importance of primary and secondary markets for, 201–210
  lending policy and portfolio composition 6–7, 16–17, 29, 37–38, 47, 105, 136–137, 141–147, 214
  liquidity of, see Liquidity of financial institutions
  purchases and sales to FNMA, 224–225
  relation to mortgage companies, see Correspondent and branch systems
  role as supplier of funds, xxii, 5–8, 10, 34–36, 38, 42–44, 47, 100–103, 105–106, 108, 116–123, 130–133, 136
  See also Interim finance, life insurance company use of
Liquidity of financial institutions, 7, 11, 50–52, 55, 63–64, 100, 104, 120, 122
Loan-to-value ratio, xxi–xxii, xxviii, 53, 59, 68, 72, 77, 90, 111, 219, 231
Local vs. national markets, 136, 148–151, 155–156

Maturity terms, xxviii, 53, 55, 58–60, 66–68, 71, 77–78, 90, 93, 128, 237
Methodology, questionnaire, 291 ff.
Mortgage Bankers Association of America, 173, 242
Mortgage companies, xxiii
  age of, 21, 248–249
  asset-size distribution, 264–266
  capital of, 242
  financial structure of, 21, 264, 266–279
  geographic distribution of, 254–255
  growth of, 20, 249–253

importance of primary and secondary markets for, 201–208, 212
  nature and operations of, 6, 20–21, 143, 172, 178, 213, 239–242, 245–248, 255–260, 262–263, 279
  number of, 242–243
  profitability of, 21, 253
  purchasers of mortgage company loans, 260–262, 280
  purchases and sales to FNMA, 224–225
  regulation of, 243–244
  relation to life insurance companies, 20–21, 143, 146–147, 178, 241, 246–247, 260–263; See also Correspondent and branch systems
  source of income, 244–245
  as supplier of funds, 6, 42, 45–46, 124
  use and sources of mortgage funds, 266–274
  See also Interim finance, dependence of mortgage companies on
Mortgage flows, see Mortgage loans; Gross mortgage flow; Fluctuations
Mortgage loans, conventional:
  amount outstanding, 5, 33, 45
  first and second liens on, 228–230
  fluctuations compared to federally underwritten loans, 9, 12, 115, 125–128
  interest rates on, 9, 12, 15, 56, 76
  primary and secondary markets for, 201–202, 207–210, 212
  size of flow, 5, 9, 33, 41, 45, 100, 110–112, 126, 128
  source and ownership of, 5, 10, 19, 36, 42–44, 116, 119–120, 133–134
Mortgage loans, farm:
  amount outstanding, size and changes in, 25–26, 28, 30, 32–33, 45, 284
  insurance companies' policy towards, 138 n.
  net flow of, 32
  primary and secondary markets in, 209–210
  source and ownership of, 6, 34, 36–38, 43–44
Mortgage loans, federally underwritten:
  amount outstanding, 6, 33–34, 45
  contract terms, see Contract terms
  effect of rigid interest rates on, 9–10, 12–15, 54, 56, 114–115, 121
  federal action concerning, 7, 52–55, 57–60, 64–73
  first and second liens on, 228–230
  fluctuations in conventional, FHA, and VA loans compared, 9–10, 11–13, 111–115, 125–130
  gross flows in, 13–15, 113–114, 126–128
  lags concerning, 11–13, 129

Mortgage loans, federally underwritten:
(*continued*)
market judgment on FHA vs. VA loans,
90–92
changes in maximum interests on, 11,
13–14, 63, 67, 73, 76, 128
relation to growth of mortgage companies, 240–241
seasonal trend in, 125
size of flow, 5–6, 9–10, 33, 41–42, 45, 100,
110–114, 126, 128
sources and ownership of, 10, 19, 36–38,
42–44, 47, 105, 116–120, 130–133,
155, 220
state laws concerning, *see* State laws
concerning mortgages
Mortgage loans, home:
amount outstanding, size and composition of, 6, 32–33, 45
composition of flow, 5, 9, 33, 42, 110–
115, 125–130
federal action concerning, *see* Mortgage
loans, federally underwritten
first and second liens on, 228–230
flow of, size and fluctuations in, 5, 9, 11,
32–33, 40–42, 100, 110–115, 124–125
source and ownership of, 5, 36, 38, 43–
44, 47, 105–106, 115–120, 130–134
Mortgage loans, income property, 12, 75–
76, 80–83, 141
Mortgage loans, multifamily:
amount outstanding, size and composition, 32–33, 45
federal action concerning, *see* Mortgage
loans, federally underwritten,
first and second liens on, 228–230
flow of, fluctuations and size, 9, 32–33,
40, 110, 114, 124
primary and secondary markets for, 208–
209
source and ownership of, 5–6, 36, 38,
43–44, 47, 105, 141, 155
Mortgage loans, nonresidential, v, viii–xxix
amount outstanding, 32–33
federal action concerning, 58–59; *see also*
Mortgage loans, federally underwritten
flow of, size and fluctuations, 9, 32, 124
junior mortgages on, 230
seasonal trends in, 125
secondary and primary markets for,
209–210
source and ownership of, 6–7, 36, 38,
43–44, 50, 105, 141
Mortgage loans, owner-occupied property:
acquisition by purchase vs. origination,
200–201
first and junior mortgages on, 229–231

Mortgage loans, residential:
amount outstanding, xxi, 28, 32–33
contract terms of, *see* Contract terms
demand for, *see* Demand for mortgage
loans
first and second liens on, 227–230
institutionalization of holdings of, *see*
Institutionalization of mortgage
market
rental, acquisition by purchase vs.
origination, 202–203
size of flow, 32–33
source and ownership of, xxii, 36–43
See also Mortgage loans, home;
Mortgage loans, multifamily
Mortgage loans, total:
amount outstanding, size, 5, 25–32, 284
composition of debt, 5–6, 9, 32–39, 45–46
composition of flow, 5, 32–45, 109, 123–
124
early history of, 135–136
first and second liens on, 228–230
fluctuations in, 9, 11, 121, 123–124
gross flows in, 99, 163
size of flow, 5, 7–9, 11, 32, 99–102, 121,
123–124
source and ownership of, 5–6, 8–10,
34–36, 46–47, 100, 103–108, 121–
123, 135–136
Mortgage-total asset ratio, 16, 140, 148–
149, 166
Mutual savings banks:
factors in investment decision, 148–149
importance of primary and secondary markets for, 18, 201–208, 211,
213
lending policy and portfolio-composition,
6–7, 17–18, 29, 37–38, 47, 106,
149–155, 214
liquidity of, *see* Liquidity of financial
institutions
out-of-state purchases, 17–18, 106, 149–
153, 208
purchases and sales to FNMA, 224–225
role as supplier of funds, xxii, 5–8, 10,
34–36, 38, 43–44, 47, 100–104, 106
108, 116–119, 121–122, 130–133,
136

National Housing Act of 1934, 53, 217 n.
National Voluntary Credit Restraint Committee, *see* Voluntary Credit Restraint Program

"One-for-one" program, *see* Federal
National Mortgage Association
Open-end loans, *see* Interim financing,
variations in

Out-of-state purchases, growth of mortgage companies, 18, 20, 241
See also Correspondent and branch systems; Mutual savings banks, out-of-state purchases

Pension funds, 42, 172–174
Performance (or completion) bonds, 168
Permanent mortgage financing, 141–143, 155, 158, 162–163, 175
relation to interim and construction financing, 166–170, 175–178
See also Commitment techniques, forward commitments; Interim financing
Premiums, *see* Discounts and premiums
Primary market, *see* Secondary market

Repurchase agreements, for secondary mortgages, 234
See also Interim financing, variations in

Risk:
construction loans, 168–169
interim loans, 185–186, 188
VA and FHA loans, 15, 89, 93–94

Sales-leaseback arrangements, xxix, 61–62
Savings and loan associations:
history of, 156–158
importance of primary and secondary markets for, 201–213
lending policy and portfolio composition, 6, 18–19, 29, 37–38, 42, 47, 158–165, 214
liquidity of, *see* Liquidity of financial institutions, purchases and sales to FNMA, 224–225
as supplier of funds, xxii, 5–6, 8, 10, 34–36, 38, 42–45, 47, 100–104, 106–108, 116–123, 130–133, 136

use of standby commitments, 181
Seasonal trends, 123, 125
mortgage company activity, 277–279
savings and loan association activity, 12
Secondary markets, 10, 16, 150
concept and definition of, 23–24, 196–200
and FNMA, 54, 69, 72, 114–115, 217–224
growth of, xxii, 24, 54
for junior mortgages, 233–234
organization of, 213–217
statistics on size, 200–213
See also Federal National Mortgage Association
Servicemen's Readjustment Act, 5 n., 52–53
"Servicing contractors," 153
Standardization of contract terms, *see* Contract terms
State laws concerning mortgages, 8, 17–18, 106, 116, 148–151

Usury laws, 234–235

Veterans Administration
credit policy of, 57–58, 60, 70–71
legislation authorizing, 33, 55, 85
regulation of charges and discounts, 85–88
See also Mortgage loans, federally underwritten
Veterans Emergency Housing Program, 50, 53
Voluntary Credit Restraint Program, 60–62, 67–69, 126
Voluntary Home Mortgage Credit Program, 68–69
See also Voluntary credit restraint program

"Warehousing," *see* Interim financing

Behrens, Carl F., xxvii n., 137 n., 166 n., 170 n.
Blank, David M., xxiii, xxvii n., 34 n., 74 n., 75 n., 96 n., 137 n., 138 n., 159 n., 166 n.
Bodfish, H. Morton, 156 n., 157 n.
Boemler, Erwin W., 137 n.
Bureau of the Census, 227–228, 232 n., 235

Case, Fred E., 227 n., 231 n., 232 n.
Cherrington, Homer V., 245 n.
Colean, Miles L., xxvii n., 53 n., 111 n., 135 n., 136 n., 156 n., 157 n.
Conklin, George T., Jr., 138 n., 139 n.

Department of Commerce, 27, 229

Eccles, Marriner S., 111 n.
Edwards, Edward E., xxvii n.

Farwell, Loring C., 137 n.
Federal Deposit Insurance Corporation, 167 n., 193
Federal Home Loan Bank Board, 71 n., 209–211, 213 n.
Federal Housing Administration, 14, 53 n., 71 n., 73 n., 127, 204–205, 209, 218, 251, 265, 268
Federal National Mortgage Association, 65, 91, 96 n., 97 n., 223–226
Federal Reserve Bank of New York, 104, 158 n., 166 n.
Federal Reserve System, 29, 31, 39, 41, 58 n., 66 n., 70, 76, 100–102, 128, 183, 193, 195, 253, 278
First National City Bank of New York, The, 14, 76
Fisher, Ernest M., xxvii n., 137 n.
Foley, Raymond, 88 n., 93
Frederiksen, D. M., 242 n.

Gane, Frank H., 137 n.
Goldsmith, Raymond W., 27–29, 31, 148 n., 197 n., 266 n.
Grebler, Leo, xxiii, xxvii n., 34 n., 74 n., 75 n., 96 n., 111 n., 115 n., 137 n., 138 n., 159 n., 166 n.

Halcrow, Harold G., xxvii n., 81 n., 111 n.
Hoagland, Henry, 135 n.
House Committee on Banking and Currency, 89 n., 183 n., 185 n., 188 n., 190 n.
House Veterans Affairs Committee, 85

Institute of Life Insurance, 209

Jacoby, Neil H., xxvii n., 81 n., 111 n.
Johnson, Ernest A., 197 n.
Joint Committee on the Economic Report, 61 n.

Keesler, William F., 185 n.
King, T. B., 87 n., 88 n.
Kinnard, William N., Jr., 227 n., 230 n., 231 n.
Klaman, Saul B., 69 n., 130 n., 158 n., *The Postwar Rise of Mortgage Companies*, xxx n., 4 n., 20, 42, 46 n., 123 n., 124 n., 172 n., 242 n., 250, 252, 255, 263, 266, 271 n., 273–274, 276–278
The Volume of Mortgage Debt in the Postwar Decade, xxviii n., 4 n., 27–29, 31–32, 35–37, 41, 43, 101–103, 112, 117–119, 154, 164, 171, 228, 232 n., 283
Koester, Genevieve, 197 n.

Lintner, John, 137 n., 147 n., 148 n.

McCahan, David, 138 n.
Mendelson, Morris, 100 n.
Moody's Investor Service, 76
Morton, J. E., xxvii n., 28, 34 n., 83
Murray, Roger F., 78 n., 174 n.

National Association of Mutual Savings Banks, 102, 152
Newcomb, Robinson, 111 n.

O'Keefe, Raymond T., 185 n.

Patrick, R. B., 190 n.
Pease Robert H., 245 n.
Posner, Louis S., 197 n.
Pringle-Hurd and Company, Inc., 180 n.

Ratcliff, Richard U., 135 n.
Rathbun, Daniel B., 167 n.
Redfield, John J., 135 n., 153 n.
Robinson, Roland I., 137 n.

Saulnier, Raymond J., xxvii n., 81 n., 111 n., 128 n., 137 n., 138 n., 139 n., 141, 170 n.
Schecter, H. B., 128 n.
Schneider, James F., 168 n.
Schwulst, Earl B., 135 n.
Securities and Exchange Commission, 197 n.

Senate Committee on Banking and Currency, 85–86
Steiner, W. H., 137 n., 147 n.

Teague, Olin E., 88 n.

Upton, King, 185 n., 186 n.

Veterans Administration, 14, 71 n., 113 n., 127

Wendt, Paul F., 167 n.
Wickens, David L., xxiii, xxvii n., 230 n.
Winnick, Louis, xxiii, xxvii n., 34 n., 74 n., 75 n., 96 n., 137 n., 138 n., 159 n., 166 n.